A Death i

Royal Asiatic Society Hong Kong Studies Series

Royal Asiatic Society Hong Kong Studies Series is designed to make widely available important contributions on the local history, culture and society of Hong Kong and the surrounding region. Generous support from the Sir Lindsay and Lady May Ride Memorial Fund makes it possible to publish a series of high-quality works that will be of lasting appeal and value to all, both scholars and informed general readers, who share a deeper interest in and enthusiasm for the area.

Other titles in RAS Hong Kong Studies Series:

Ancestral Images: A Hong Kong Collection Hugh Baker

Cantonese Society in Hong Kong and Singapore Marjorie Topley, Jean De Bernardi (ed)

Custom, Land & Livelihood in Rural South China 1750–1950 Patrick Hase

Dragon and the Crown: Hong Kong Memoirs Stanley Kwan with Nicole Kwan

Early China Coast Meteorology: The Role of HK 1882–1912 Kevin MacKeown

East River Column: Hong Kong Guerrillas in the Second World War and After Chan Sui Jeung

Escape from Hong Kong: Admiral Chan Chak's Christmas Day Dash, 1941 Tim Luard

For Gods, Ghosts and Ancestors Janet Scott

Forgotten Souls: The Social History of Hong Kong Cemetery 1845–1918 Patricia Lim

Governors, Politics and the Colonial Office Gavin Ure

Hong Kong Internment 1942–1945: Life in the Japanese Civilian Camp at Stanley Geoff Emerson

Ireland's Imperial Mandarin: Sir Robert Hart Mark O'Neill

Portugal, China and the Macau Negotiations 1986–1999 Carmen Mendes

Public Success, Private Sorrow: The Life and Times of Charles Henry Brewitt-Taylor Isidore Cyril Cannon

Reluctant Heroes: Rickshaw Pullers in Hong Kong and Canton 1874–1954 Fung Chi Ming

Resist to the End: Hong Kong 1941–1945 Charles Barman, Ray Barman (ed)

Scottish Mandarin: The Life and Times of Sir Reginald Johnston Shiona Airlie

Six Day War of 1899: Hong Kong in the Age of Imperialism Patrick Hase

Southern District Officer Reports: Islands and Villages in Rural Hong Kong John Strickland (ed)

The Lone Flag: Memoir of the British Consul in Macau during World War II John Reeves

Watching Over Hong Kong: Private Policing 1841–1941 Sheila Hamilton

A Death in Hong Kong

The MacLennan Case of 1980 and the Suppression of a Scandal

Nigel Collett

CITY UNIVERSITY OF
HONG KONG PRESS
香港城市大學出版社

Editor	Joanna PIERCE
Editorial Interns	CHENG Tsz Nok
Design	KO Po Yee

Création 城大創意製作

Photographs 1, 3, and 8 are from the Bridgewater Collection.
Photographs 2, 4, 5, 7, and 28 are from the National Archives.
Photographs 6, 9, 10, 11, 12, 13, 14, 15, 16, 17, 18, 19, 24, 25, and 27 are from the *South China Morning Post*.
Photographs 20 , 21, 23, and 26 are from the *Standard*.
Photograph 22 is by Judith Mackay.

ISBN: 978-962-937-347-4

Published by
City University of Hong Kong Press
Tat Chee Avenue
Kowloon, Hong Kong
Website: www.cityu.edu.hk/upress
E-mail: upress@cityu.edu.hk

Printed in Hong Kong

In memory of

Elsie Tu,

without whom this story would never have been revealed,

and of

Aileen Bridgewater,

without whom I would never have written it.

Contents

Introduction

In January 1980, the body of a young Scottish police officer, John MacLennan, was found in his locked police quarters along with a suicide note. He had apparently shot himself five times. It soon became known that he had been about to be charged with homosexual acts, then still illegal in Hong Kong, and that he and others had alleged that he was being victimized because he was aware of the names of homosexual police officers far senior to him. This caused a public outcry and such pressure upon the government that a Commission of Inquiry was appointed to investigate the case. In the course of the eight months in which the inquiry sat, a succession of senior figures found themselves examined and often discredited in public. The commission's report was widely seen as a whitewash but it, and the case itself, had lasting effects on Hong Kong, one of which was the eventual decriminalization of homosexual acts a decade later.

Behind the case lay something more sinister, the sexual exploitation of underage boys by prominent figures in Hong Kong's establishment. Although MacLennan had no part in this, the discovery of this scandal led directly to his death. It was, as were similar contemporary examples of the sexual exploitation of juveniles in Britain, a scandal that was kept firmly under wraps.

This book seeks to recount the story of John MacLennan's life and death, and to put it into the context of the suppressed scandal for which his case became something of a smokescreen.

It also seeks to reveal the workings of the organs of government and control in one of Britain's last colonies, as they were faced with the need to deal with crimes that endangered their status and power.

Some of what is published here is well known, but much is new. The report of the Commission of Inquiry published in 1981, and the local press reports of the time, give a good basis of fact, all of which is already in the public domain. Some accounts of various aspects of the case have been published in works dealing with other matters of the time, particularly: Elsie Elliott / Tu's 1981 *Crusade for Justice* and 1988 *Autobiography*; Aileen Bridgewater's 1985 *Talk of Hong Kong*; John Conway's 1994 *To Speak for the Dead*; and Kate Whitehead's 2001 *Hong Kong Murders*. The case has also featured in fiction, especially Ken Bridgewater's 2013 novel *Open Verdict* and on the stage in Agnes Allcock's 2013 adaptation *Behind the Curtain*.

This book, however, is the first to attempt a comprehensive account and analysis. It makes use of a large number of interviews with many who were involved in the case; these are listed in the bibliography. The records deposited by the late Elsie Tu in the library of the Hong Kong Baptist University and those held in the private Bridgewater Collection have provided much new material, as have files in the British National Archives at Kew and those records issued to the author by the British Foreign Office under a Freedom of Information Act request (and which are now housed with the Bridgewater Collection). Hong Kong sources have proved less fruitful, either because of the failure of the Hong Kong Government to retain records or make them open to the public, or through their refusal to allow access to what exists. For example, all departments of the Hong Kong Government and the

Hong Kong Police have denied the existence of transcripts of the inquiry, meaning that only those excerpts from that transcript held in the library of the University of Hong Kong are available to researchers.

Finally, it is the personal hope of the author that this book may at last do justice to a young police officer whose sexual orientation made him such a victim of persecution by his own colleagues that he was driven to kill himself. The waste of John MacLennan's life is a reminder of what all too easily can occur if law and prejudice combine to discriminate against a minority that has no defence.

Nigel Collett
Hong Kong, Malmesbury and Rostock
May 2017

Acknowledgements

I would like to thank all those who helped me with this book, including the many who have given me information that has contributed towards it, but who have expressed the wish to remain anonymous.

In particular, I would like to thank those experts who informed me about particular parts of the story I tell. Barrie Barlow gave information on the inquiry and the figures who took part in it. Justice Clare-Marie Beeson assisted with information about Howard Lindsay and Inspector Michael Fulton. Justice Kemal Bokhary helped with details of the inquiry and its principal participants. Murray Burton was expansive in his help with information about the running of the Commission of Inquiry and those involved in it. Rachel Cartland was the source of a good deal of advice on the Hong Kong civil service and government of the period, and commented to my enormous benefit on the text. Peter Crush's description of his own circumstances illuminated the corruption endemic in Hong Kong before the ICAC. Graham Elsom gave me insights into the gay community in Hong Kong and introduced me to many of his friends and contacts who were prepared to talk about it. Geoffrey Charles Emerson helped me with information about Hong Kong's gay scene before decriminalization. Iain Grant was of huge help in assisting me to get closer to John MacLennan and events at Ho Man Tin. Peter Griffiths kindly helped with information about Hong Kong's legal situation in the late 1970s early 1980s. Peter Hunt gave me information on the state of the RHKP at the time and described many of the personalities in the story. Peter Moss did me the great favour of reading the text and was of much help regarding the characters involved as well as about the gay scene in the Hong Kong of the 1970s–'80s. Justice Conrad Seagroatt assisted me with descriptions of the inquiry, the characters who took part in it and with information concerning the MacLennan family. Steve Verralls also read the text, clarified many points regarding the Royal Hong Kong Police and corrected the many errors of a layman unfamiliar with police structures and titles. Stuart Wolfendale gave me interesting and amusing information about the homosexual and gay scenes in Hong Kong. I had the great pleasure to meet author Danny Wong in London and to hear his account of the Waltzing Matilda and the gay scene of which it formed a centre. Leo Wong helped me with research and with Chinese aspects of the book in Hong Kong. I was very fortunate that Jason Wordie read my draft and gave me invaluable advice on the historical background and many of the details of the time. I was privileged that Sir Ti-Liang Yang spoke to me about aspects of the Commission of Inquiry that he chaired. I am deep in the debt of all of these I have named here and give them my warm thanks.

I acknowledge the authority of the Crown to quote from documents in the British Public Records Office and those records provided me by the Foreign and Commonwealth Office under a Freedom of Information request. I thank Ken Bridgewater for authority to publish items and extracts from the Bridgewater Collection. I am very grateful to the University of Hong Kong Libraries for their permission to quote from items in their collection and to the Hong Kong Baptist University Library for permission to quote from the Elsie Tu Collection. I thank

Chameleon Press for permission to quote from Andrew and Elsie Tu's *Shouting at the Mountain*. I would like to thank the staff of the National Archives in Kew and of the Hong Kong Public Record Office in Kwun Tong for their invaluable help and advice. My search for information in Hong Kong was conducted largely in two libraries, that of the University of Hong Kong and that of Hong Kong Baptist University. I would like here to express my warm appreciation for the hospitality and help I received from the librarians of both libraries, where I very much enjoyed working.

I have been very fortunate in my publisher, City University Press, and in particular in my editor, Joanna Pierce, whose advice, guidance and very careful editing of the text have improved this book immensely.

I owe particular thanks to the late Elsie Tu, who had reached the remarkable age of 102 when she died in 2015, sadly before this book could be published. Elsie gave me access to her records and granted me several interviews to describe her participation in the events of the time. It was a great privilege to know her and to hear her story.

Finally, I would like to thank the late Aileen Bridgewater and her husband Ken, whose suggestion that I write the story started me off on this quest, and whose provision of the extensive set of documents that they had accumulated made this book possible. It is a great sadness that Aileen did not live to see the publication of the story she had long sought to have made public. I am enormously grateful to Ken for permitting me to dedicate this book to her memory, and will always be in their debt for their friendship.

In what I now lay before the public, the mistakes are, of course, my own.

Abbreviations

ADS	Assistant Divisional Superintendent
AG	Attorney General
BBC	British Broadcasting Corporation
CAPO	Complaints Against the Police Office
CBE	Commander of the Most Excellent Order of the British Empire
CIB	Criminal Investigation Bureau
CID	Criminal Investigation Department
CJ	Chief Justice
CMG	Companion of the Order of St Michael and St George
CP	Commissioner of Police
CPG	Central People's Government
CPM	Colonial Police Medal
CS	Colonial Secretary to 1976, then Chief Secretary
DC	Detective Constable
DC (Ops.)	Deputy Commissioner (Operations)
DCI	Director of Criminal Investigation
DDI	Divisional Detective Inspector
DPP	Director of Public Prosecutions
DUS	Deputy Under Secretary
FCO	Foreign and Commonwealth Office
GCHQ	Government Communications Headquarters
HE	His Excellency
HMG	Her Majesty's Government

HMT	Ho Man Tin
HQ	Headquarters
ICAC	Independent Commission Against Corruption
ID	Identity
IPA	International Police Association
J	Justice
Kt.	Knight.
MP	Member of Parliament
OC	Officer Commanding
Pc	Police Constable
PIE	Paedophile Information Exchange
PTU	Police Tactical Unit
PWD	Public Works Department
Q & A	Question and answer
QC	Queen's Counsel
QPM	Queen's Police Medal
RAF	Royal Air Force
RHKP	Royal Hong Kong Police
RMP	Royal Military Police
RTHK	Radio Television Hong Kong
SB	Special Branch
SC	Senior Counsel
SCOPG	Standing Committee on Pressure Groups
SIU	Special Investigation Unit
SOG	Special Operations Group
SSOP	Senior Staff Officer Personnel
TVB	Television Broadcasts Ltd
UMELCO	The Office of the Unofficial Members of the Executive and Legislative Councils
USRC	United Services Recreation Club
WPC	Woman Police Constable
YE	Your Excellency

List of Characters

Alan (family name not known)	Chinese masseur introduced by Peter Sung to John MacLennan in 1979, and who refused to give witness against him.
Angell, Nicholas	RHKP Inspector, friend of John MacLennan at Kwun Tong and Ho Man Tin.
Astin, Ray	Acting Director of Public Prosecutions in 1978; Assistant to the Attorney General, 1979–1980.
Atkinson, Jock	RHKP Chief Inspector, John MacLennan's superior at Kwun Tong, 1974–1975.
Barlow, Barrie	Crown Counsel representing the Attorney General and the Legal Department at the Inquiry.
Beeson, Clare-Marie	Crown Counsel, friend of Howard Lindsay, told of Fulton set-up in 1979.
Beveridge, John	Second Counsel to the Commission of Inquiry, 1980–1981.
Blackburn, Eric	RHKP Assistant Commissioner, Director of Personnel and Training in 1978; Senior Assistant Commissioner in 1980; Deputy Commissioner (Management) in 1981.

Blaker, Peter	Lord Privy Seal and Minister of State at the Foreign and Commonwealth Office, 1979–1981.
Bokhary, Kemal	Barrister, representing the SIU at the Inquiry.
Bridgewater, Aileen	Commercial Radio talk show host.
Briggs, Sir Geoffrey	Chief Justice of Hong Kong, 1973–1978.
Brooks, Robert	RHKP Superintendent, New Territories CID to 1978; commander of the SIU, 1978–1981.
Burns, Ashley	Solicitor, Johnson, Stokes & Master, representing Inspector Michael Fulton.
Burns, Christopher	RHKP Inspector, best friend of John MacLennan, with whom he trained in 1973, then served in Kwun Tong, 1974–1975.
Burton, Murray	Solicitor at Zimmern & Co., Solicitor to the Commission of Inquiry, 1980–1981.
Carratu, Vincent	Retired British Police Officer, head of a London investigating company, investigator for the Commission of Inquiry.
Cater, Sir Jack	Commissioner of the ICAC, 1974–1978; Chief Secretary of Hong Kong, 1978–1981.
Chan, Norman	Administrative Officer, Secretary to the Commission of Inquiry, 1980–1981.

Che, Anson	ICAC Senior Regional Liaison Officer, Tuen Mun, 1978–1982, who received envelopes containing bribes given John MacLennan in Yuen Long.
Cheung, Jimmy	Prostitute introduced to John MacLennan by Bobby Po in 1979, and who gave witness against him, but warned him.
Chow, Ka Sze/ K.C.	Businessman intermediary to procurer Molo Tsui for Sir Geoffrey Briggs.
Chu, Eddie	Prostitute, pimp and false witness against John MacLennan.
Clancy, Paddy	RHKP Assistant Commissioner, Director of Criminal Investigations, 1978–1980; Senior Assistant Commissioner in 1979.
Conway, John	Retired Metropolitan Police Constable, privately investigating John MacLennan's death.
Daniell, Henry	Magistrate, Fanling.
Downey, Bernard	Barrister representing the MacLennan family at the Inquest.
Duffy, John Richard	Lawyer and businessman convicted of gross indecency.
Duffy, Joseph	Crown Counsel, liaising with the SIU
Elliott, Elsie (later Tu)	Urban Councillor, school supervisor and campaigner.

Eu, Audrey	Assistant Counsel to the Commission of Inquiry.
Ford, David	Secretary for Information to 1980; Hong Kong Commissioner in London, 1980–1981.
Fulton, Michael	RHKP Inspector and homosexual informer; Senior Inspector in 1980, dismissed in 1980.
George, "Slasher"	Lover of John MacLennan.
Graham, Gus	RHKP Inspector, member of the SIU.
Grant, Iain	RHKP Senior Inspector, OC CID Ho Man Tin, 1979–1980.
Griffiths, John	Attorney General of Hong Kong, 1979–1983.
Gurka, Tony	Head of Hong Kong Investigation & Security Company, assisting the Carratu team.
Haldane, Warwick	Solicitor, for a time representing Inspector Fulton.
Hancock, Blake	RHKP Inspector, serving at Ho Man Tin, 1979–1980.
Handley, Matt	RHKP Inspector, with John MacLennan in the Metropolitan Police in 1977 and in Fanling 1978, and living in Ho Man Tin, 1979–1980.
Henry, Roy	RHKP Deputy Commissioner (Operations) in 1973; Commissioner of Police in 1979.
Hodge, Andrew	Crown Counsel, representing the RHKP at the Inquest and the Commission of Inquiry

Huthart, Gordon	Proprietor of Disco Disco, charged by the SIU in 1979.
Illingworth, Michael	RHKP Assistant Commissioner, District Commander New Territories.
Ingham, Charles	Crown Counsel, representing Senior Superintendent Jack Trotman at the Inquiry.
Johnston, Jack	RHKP Assistant Commissioner, Director of Criminal Investigations, 1978–1979; District Commander Kowloon, 1980.
Jones, Tom	Crown Solicitor.
Kong, Billy	RHKP Chief Inspector, Sub-Divisional Inspector, Kowloon City, 1979–1980, for a short time in charge of the scene of John MacLennan's death.
Kwok, Ricky	Prostitute witness against John MacLennan.
Lam, Raymond	Boyfriend of Inspector Michael Fulton, who alleged that John MacLennan tried to pick him up at the telephone kiosk in Ho Man Tin.
Lau, David	Student, who alleged that John MacLennan made sexual advances to him in Yuen Long in 1978.
Lau Wun	Friend of David Lau, involved in the Yuen Long incident in 1978.
Leggatt, Andrew	Barrister, representing the Governor at the Commission of Inquiry.

Leonard, David	Magistrate, Coroner for the MacLennan Inquest.
Leung Sze-piu	RHKP Sergeant, member of the SIU.
Li Kwan-ha	RHKP Chief Superintendent, Chief Staff Officer Criminal Investigations New Territories in 1978; Acting Assistant Commissioner, District Commander Kowloon in 1979; Assistant Commissioner, Deputy Director Criminal Investigations, 1980–1981, author of the report into police procedures at the scene of John MacLennan's death.
Lindsay, Howard	Crown Counsel charged with gross indecency and forced to resign in 1979.
Liu Man,	RHKP Detective Constable, for a short time a member of the SIU, lover of Peter Sung, whom he betrayed in 1979.
Llewellyn, Stephen	Solicitor at Hamptons, Winter & Glynn, representing John MacLennan during the Yuen Long incident and on the day before his death.
Logan, Colin	Civil servant in the Security Branch, prosecuted by the SIU as "Colin the Whipper" in 1979.
Loughrin, Craig	RHKP Inspector, member of the SIU, 1979–1980.

Lucas, Max	Crown Counsel, representing the Legal Department at the Inquiry.
MacDougall, Neil	Director of Public Prosecutions.
MacKillop, Norrie	RHKP Chief Inspector, member of the SIU, 1979–1980, commander of the SIU, 1981–1982.
MacLehose, Sir Murray	Governor of Hong Kong, 1973–1983.
MacLennan, John	RHKP Inspector, accused of gross indecency, committed suicide in 1980.
McGovern, Patrick	Jesuit priest, member of the Legislative Council and UMELCO
McLean, Ian	Businessman link with procurer Molo Tsui, murdered in 1980.
Moor, Peter	RHKP Assistant Commissioner, District Commander Kowloon in 1974; Deputy Commissioner (Operations), 1979–1983.
Moorfoot, Barry	Senior Crown Counsel, Coroner's Officer for the MacLennan Inquest.
Muller, Felix	RHKP Inspector, friend of John MacLennan in training and at Ho Man Tin.
Neligan, Michael	First Counsel to the Commission of Inquiry in 1980.

Neoh, Anthony	Barrister, Further Counsel to the Commission of Inquiry.
Niamatullah, Abdul Majid	Barrister, representing Inspector Michael Fulton at the Inquiry.
Over, John	Ex-British Police Officer, RHKP Senior Assistant Commissioner, Director of Management and Development, 1979–1981.
Pannell, Tony	Architect, Foreman of the Jury for the MacLennan Inquest.
Pelly, Marcus	RHKP Superintendent, Assistant Divisional Superintendent Ho Man Tin, investigator of John MacLennan's death.
Po, Bobby	Prostitute, 'Big Mouth Woman', witness against John MacLennan, but warned him.
Purdon, Corran	Major-General, RHKP Deputy Commissioner for Administration, 1978–1981.
Quine, Richard	RHKP Assistant Commissioner, Director of Criminal Investigations to 1978.
Quinn, Michael (Mike/Mick)	RHKP Chief Inspector, second-in-command of the SIU.
Rattigan, Patrick	Magistrate, Fanling.
Reeder, Terry	Ex-British Chief Inspector, deputy of the Carratu team.

Rich, Norman	RHKP Chief Inspector, Interpol office, investigated John MacLennan in the Yuen Long incident in 1978.
Roberts, Sir Denys	Chief Secretary of Hong Kong to 1978; Chief Justice of Hong Kong, 1978–1988.
Ross, William	RHKP Chief Superintendent, commander of the Special Operations Group.
Rowlands, Martin	Secretary for the Civil Service.
Sanguinetti, Albert	Barrister, representing Elsie Elliott at the Inquiry.
Seagroatt, Conrad	Barrister, representing the MacLennan family at the Inquiry.
Slevin, Brian	RHKP Commissioner of Police, 1974–1979.
Stanford, Dick	Barman at the Waltzing Matilda Inn, SIU informer, boyfriend of Jeff Tso.
Stevens, Paul	Solicitor at Hampton, Winter & Glynn, representing John MacLennan on the day of his death.
Sun Kam-hung	Lula, prostitute, false witness against John MacLennan.
Sung, Peter	Prostitute, lover of DC Liu Man, police informer, who was a witness against John MacLennan.

Tin, Stephen	RHKP Inspector, member of the SIU.
Trotman, Jack	Senior Superintendent, Divisional Superintendent Ho Man Tin, John MacLennan's superior.
Tsang, Michael	Prostitute, false witness against John MacLennan.
Tsang Shin	RHKP Station Sergeant implicated in the Wan Chai corruption case in 1976, who made the allegation against John MacLennan at Yuen Long in 1978.
Tso, Jeff	Prostitute, boyfriend of Dick Stanford, false witness against John MacLennan, perpetrator of the Lee Garden Hotel set-up of the Carratu team in 1980.
Tsui, Molo	Procurer and police informer.
Tung, Ah	Prostitute, pimped by Molo Tsui, false witness against John MacLennan.
Whitely, Ian	TVB presenter.
Yang, Ti Liang	High Court Judge, Commissioner of the MacLennan Inquiry.

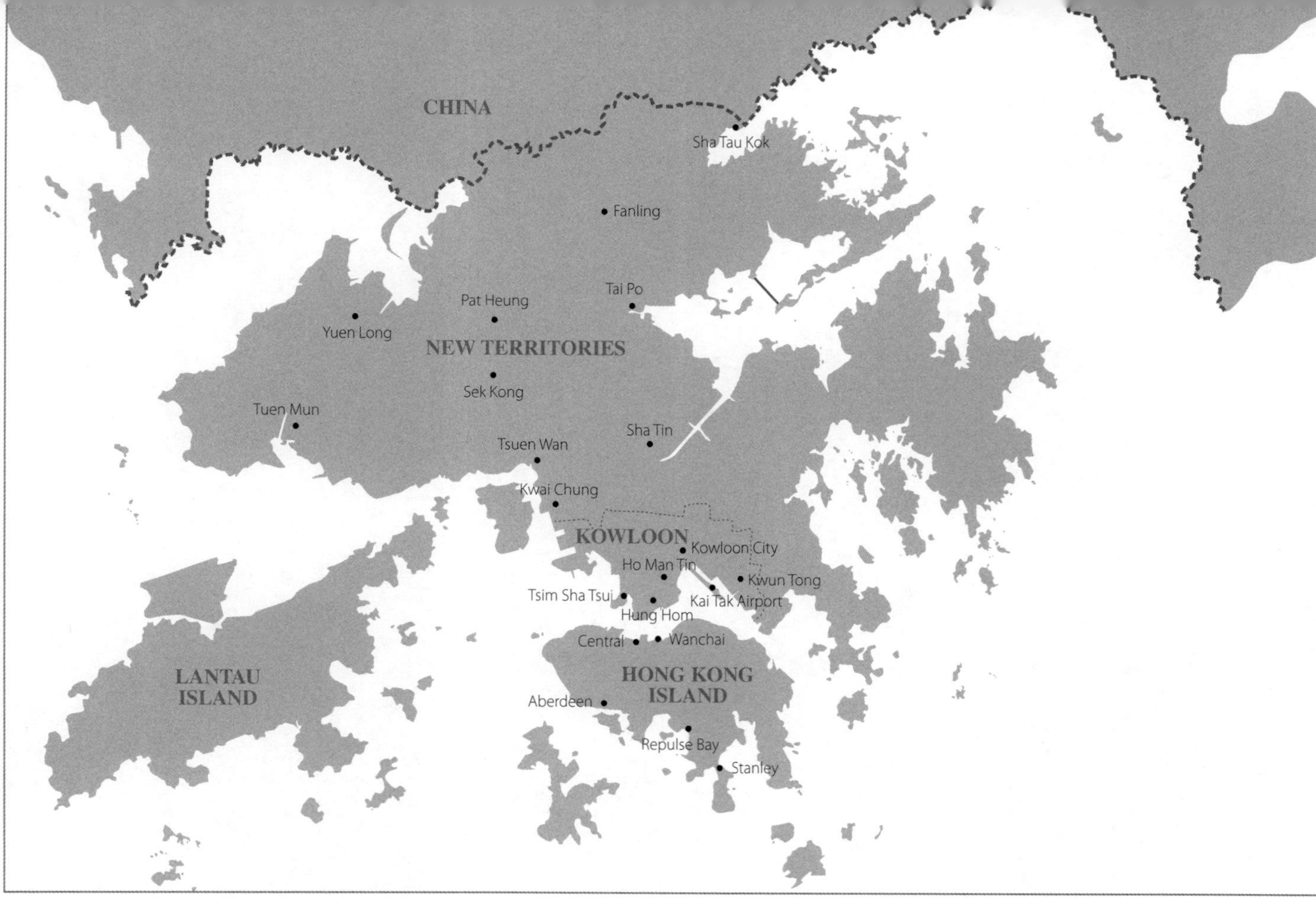
CHINA
Sha Tau Kok
Fanling
Tai Po
Pat Heung
Yuen Long
NEW TERRITORIES
Sek Kong
Tuen Mun
Sha Tin
Tsuen Wan
Kwai Chung
KOWLOON
Kowloon City
Ho Man Tin
Kwun Tong
Tsim Sha Tsui
Kai Tak Airport
Hung Hom
Central
Wanchai
HONG KONG
ISLAND
LANTAU
ISLAND
Aberdeen
Repulse Bay
Stanley

A Death in Hong Kong

The MacLennan Case of 1980 and the Suppression of a Scandal

1

Scotland

John MacLennan's birth certificate gives his time and date of birth as thirty minutes past midnight on the morning of 3 October 1950, and places the event at Wester Rarichie, Nigg, where his father worked as a grieve or farm overseer.[1] Wester Rarichie is a village in Easter Ross in the Highlands of Scotland, two-thirds of the way up Scotland's east coast. It is a settlement so small, merely a farm and a group of six single-storey cottages, that it does not appear at all on some road maps. Nigg, the district's administrative centre, sits on the Fearn Peninsula that juts out into the Cromarty Firth. It is scarcely a town, a straggle of farms and houses along one of two minor roads that reach down to the mouth of the firth. This is a big, rolling, and still empty country, where life in 1950 consisted of farming, fishing and weaving; simple, innocent even, but hard.

John's father Joseph (known in the family as Joe) had married John's mother, Katherine Mary Munro (who to everyone was simply Katie), in nearby Tarbat, Portmahomack in 1944. There were many Munros in the Fearn peninsula; Nigg was the home of Colour-Sergeant James Munro of the Sutherland Highlanders who won the Victoria Cross at Lucknow during the Indian Mutiny in 1857. The families were part of the landscape. Joe had farmed there, always for other owners, since before the birth of his first child, Ron. John was their second child. Eight years later, he was followed by a sister, Anne.[2]

To everyone who knew him, John was always just Johnny, a sweet, charming child, the favourite of a very close-knit family. Wester Rarichie was not a place to find friends easily, for there were few who lived close by, but in his last year in primary school in Pitcalnie, Johnny found a soulmate in Robin Sutherland, with whom he became so close that both their families labelled them "the two ugly sisters". They would run and cycle together, often with Robin's brothers William and John (so to avoid confusion, they called Johnny MacLennan "Wee John"), riding fifteen or twenty miles through the countryside but always getting home before nightfall. At the level crossing at Arabella or at the nearest station at Hill of Fearns, they would watch trains steaming up and down the Far North Line, and occasionally, but luckily not to any dire effect, place a few objects on the line. This and a few other minor indiscretions gave Johnny a reputation in the village as a bit of a prankster.

Johnny did quite well at school for he loved reading, a good thing in the dark, cold winter months that the Highlands usually threw at the hardy people who farmed there. In better weather, he would help his father on the farm or go fishing with him. He was close to Joe, a big man who towered over him and usually took his part in any quarrels with his elder brother, Ron. Johnny doted on his sister. When Anne was only three, he started to take her on his bicycle to Sunday school at their local kirk in Nigg, a church that boasts a memory of pagan days, an eighth-century Pictish slab, the Nigg Stone. Johnny taught Anne her alphabet and numbers.

The farm in Wester Rarichie was a marvellous place in which to grow up, with trees old and large enough for tree houses, of which Johnny always had to build the biggest and the best in the neighbourhood. There, he would spend hours watching birds, alone as his mother would never allow Anne to climb up to join him. Their farmhouse had plenty of space, and Johnny had a whole room full of the usual boy's collections of stamps and a train set, for which Katie's father spoiled him with gifts of engines, carriages, and track. Alone in the family, his grandfather liked to call him Jake.

Johnny loved to play tricks on the old man and his father. One night when both men came back from the pub in Dingwall past nine o'clock, they went to sleep in the armchairs in front of the fire. Johnny was awake as he was babysitting Anne, and he gently removed the fob watches they were both wearing and put them forward to 3 a.m. He then woke them up to complain about how tired he was because they had kept him up so late. Mortified, his father and grandfather made him promise not to tell his mother as she'd "murder them" and tiptoed off to go to bed, only to meet Katie coming out of the kitchen. Johnny loved life, his mother always said.

Later, the family moved to another farm where Joe was again employed as the overseer. Torgorm Farm was near Conon Bridge, south of Dingwall at the foot of the Black Isle peninsula, less isolated than Wester Rarichie, although still fairly remote. Their new home, a bungalow cottage rather than a large farmhouse, looked out north towards the Cromarty Firth and northwest towards the often snow-capped line of Ben Wyvis. In the winter, the land could be bleak, but in the summer the barley, grown for local whisky, spread golden as far as the eye could see. Joe grew some of this and kept beef cattle on the farm's pasture.

Johnny wore his first kilt at the age of fourteen or fifteen and was tremendously proud of it. He was by now at the Dingwall Academy, the largest secondary school in the Highlands. He lost his appendix while studying there, but he was otherwise a healthy boy. As far as the family knew, he never had any girlfriends in his teens, which was not uncommon for boys of their area, for courtship there was a serious matter, sex before marriage was anathema, and marriage was usually entered into late. In the Highlands, especially on the farms, men were often in their mid-thirties before they wed. "Mum and Anne were his girlfriends", the family later recounted.

Whatever feelings of sexual attraction he felt at puberty, Johnny kept them to himself. He remained friends with Robin Sutherland throughout his teens, and Sutherland, who was a young man known to like the lassies, later said that he "saw no sign of Johnny being gay". At the time, and certainly in that place, there was no public discussion of homosexuality, which by almost the entire country, let alone by a regular churchgoing family like the MacLennans, was not at all understood, rather regarded as a perversion, a sickness, and a sin. The only role models available to a young man growing up who felt he might be drawn to those of his own sex were drag artists like Danny La Rue and actors like Charles Hawtrey. Few could have conceived of growing up to become like Kenneth Williams and Hugh Paddick's flamboyant

"Round the Horne" characters Julian and Sandy, whom they would have heard on the radio. Nor, had they even understood that these two Polari-speaking "deviants" were gay, would many have wished to emulate them. John MacLennan's conservative character would have recoiled at the idea that he was like any of those. It was best, and all too easy, to put any unwelcome sexual thoughts to the back of the mind and to seal the door firmly upon them.

After Johnny finished local schooling, the family decided to send him to board at the gleaming Falkirk Technical College, which had opened in Stirlingshire in 1963. The college aimed to prepare boys for industrial careers and although it had over 2,500 pupils, it took only 160 boarders.[3]

Falkirk was in central Scotland, not far from the Firth of Forth, just south of Stirling and almost equidistant between Glasgow and Edinburgh. It was a long way away from his home and worlds away from the rural quiet of Easter Ross or even the slightly larger world of Dingwall, and it was Johnny's first exposure to industry, big populations, and urbanization. It could have been quite a shock to a country boy, but from his subsequent career it can be guessed that it was a wider world that John MacLennan found that he liked.

Study at the college did not, however, lead to a technical career, for Johnny was interested in neither academic nor technical studies. Yet he wanted more from life than the farming that employed his father and by then his elder brother. The Highlands did not offer a great deal of choice to a young man setting out at the start of life, and it was common for many to join a police force or the army. Many families had traditionally sent their sons out into the wider realms of the British Empire, which still offered the opportunity of colonial service in places like Hong Kong, although the MacLennans had not been amongst these.

They did, however, bless Johnny's desire to join a local police force. It was good employment for a young man from an honest, Christian, and traditional family. It held the romance of a disciplined, manly life in uniform, and it could lead to promotion and a place in society which was unobtainable through farming. It was also the type of career that would appeal to a young man who, like Johnny, had developed views of life and character traits that were strongly conservative. Peter Whyte, who was Johnny's fellow police cadet in Stirling and who became a lifelong friend, described him at this time: "Socially, he was the centre of the party and a bit loud. Some thought him arrogant. He played to the gallery a bit. He was a man's man, a strong character, a disciplinarian and very honest."[4] These were traits that would mark the most visible aspects of Johnny's personality for the rest of his life.

So Johnny applied to become a cadet in the Stirlingshire and Clackmannanshire Police. Evidently he did not wish to join the Ross and Sutherland Constabulary, the force that covered his home region; he had clearly come to prefer the brighter lights he had got used to in Stirling. He was still a bit small for his age and, as the days for his application drew near, he pestered Ron and Anne to measure him against a doorpost in the house. When the local constable measured him, he was still a quarter of an inch short of the 5'8" he was required to reach by the age of eighteen and a half; the police officer knew him, of course, and between the two of them they made sure he met the requisite standard. He was accepted and joined the Force Training School in Stirling in May 1968.[5]

The Stirling force was a small one with well under a thousand officers covering the cities of Stirling and Falkirk, as well as the farming country in rural Clackmannanshire north of the Forth. It trained its cadets in Stirling, so for a second time Johnny lived away from home. The police were not encouraged to fraternize too closely with the community; they had their own club, bar and sports facilities and deliberately didn't mix much in the city, so there was little chance to socialize. The work did not pay very much, so when he had a spare day at home Johnny would work for a little cash on his father's farm.

After passing out of training in October 1969, Johnny was posted in Stirling town as a cadet and he remained there when he made the rank of constable in 1972.[6] Yet, although Stirling was a city that offered far more than he had ever dreamed of in Easter Ross, it was still a small town without a great deal to excite or challenge. Johnny was perhaps beginning to feel that life had more to offer than he could find there. At some point, through colleagues or perhaps advertisements in police journals, he became aware that the Royal Hong Kong Police were looking for recruits to fill their expanding force. They wanted trained and experienced young police officers like Johnny. This was a chance to experience the glamour of colonial policing in the Far East and maybe to earn a bit more pay. It is unlikely that he was aware of much about Hong Kong or its police force, or that he had heard anything of the vice or corruption that were then just beginning to give it such a bad reputation. Even if he had, the lure of the Orient proved irresistible, and on 3 October 1973 he handed in his warrant card and uniform and left Stirling for the last time. By the twentieth of the month he was in Hong Kong.[7]

2

Hong Kong

He would not have known it when he landed at Kai Tak Airport, but John MacLennan was arriving in a Hong Kong that was beginning to emerge from its colonial chrysalis and transform into the city it is today. But as the police coach drove MacLennan and his fellow police recruits out of the crowded airport and through the congested Kowloon streets, change was not the first impression the colony would have made upon him. To a newcomer, Hong Kong was, and still is, an awesome shock to the senses. Landing was itself an experience that always staggered new arrivals: as aircraft came in to land, they rocked and roared mere feet above and between the buildings of the city, then banked sharply right, swooping down to land suddenly on the single runway that jutted out into the harbour. After disembarkation came the noise and smells of the crowded arrivals hall, where crowds jostled and shouted in raucous Cantonese. It was a sensory tsunami for a young man from a quiet Highland village.

Quiet and order were restored as the coach was carried by ferry across the majestic harbour to enter the different world of Hong Kong Island, which still bore touches of Edwardian elegance.[1] Their destination, the Police Training School at Aberdeen, was on the south side of the island in a secluded corner where recruits could be kept isolated from the moment they debussed.

The school was run on rigidly formal, old-fashioned lines and aimed to fit the four intakes of recruits it trained simultaneously into their place in the hierarchical society of Hong Kong. Not much had changed yet in the way the colony was run. Its structures of political and social control were in many ways living fossils that had survived from the old imperial ways of doing things, well after most of the rest of the British Empire had faded into history. The police were far more numerous and visible on the streets in the colony than they were back in Scotland, but when John MacLennan joined the force in 1973 its structures and methods were little different from those with which he had been familiar.[2] In the colonies, however, there had to be greater emphasis on the maintenance of control. In the Hong Kong of the time, it was generally accepted that there was a good deal of "slapping about" of suspects, both by expatriate and local officers, the latter in part motivated by the old Chinese idea that a person had to be brought to kowtow before authority to indicate remorse.[3]

Methods of detection that are nowadays commonplace either did not exist at the time or were unavailable in Hong Kong, where the government was notoriously unwilling to spend money and kept the force badly under-equipped. There were as yet no radios or scenes of crime equipment, so, for instance, there were no paper bags issued to preserve residues of gunpowder and thereby provide evidence for the firing of a weapon. The government even refused to provide the police with typewriters. Very few cars were available and transport was often by ancient Land Rover or long-nosed Bedford J3 truck.[4] The revolvers issued to the force fired .38 rounds of a very low power, partly to avoid casualties on the street. So weakly powered were these weapons that police officers firing their weapons could not be sure of downing an adversary; rounds from their revolvers would not always pass through two layers of plywood or the rear window of a car. Many police weapons were badly functioning and the ammunition issued for them was often so old that the bullets would drop out of the cases before they were loaded.[5] The force made the best of what it had, and there was an emphasis on getting the job done, on putting away criminals rather than observing the rights of suspects, and on not being too squeamish about how this was done.[6]

Many of the old hands in the force were officers who had originally come to Hong Kong as other parts of the Empire became independent, men who had started their careers in Palestine, Malaya, West or Central Africa or in the Pacific Territories. As a result, the police tended to be cliquish. Old hands drank together in groups according to their origins: Scottish and Irish policemen, the "Afrika Korps" of ex-African colonial policemen, and "Cocoanuts" from the South Pacific. Members of Special Branch stayed slightly apart.[7] All of them resented those drafted in over their heads from outside. Yet, when confronting the world, the force put up a united front. Those who did not conform, who rocked the boat or discredited the force, were not made welcome and did not last long.[8]

All the senior officers were still expatriates, although able Chinese officers were now reaching superintendent rank. John MacLennan, as a probationary inspector, already held a rank far senior to the one he had left behind in Stirling, and he would spend the rest of his service commanding non-commissioned officers and constables who were Chinese. The first part of his training in Aberdeen was to learn the language.

The force was headed by Commissioner of Police Charles Sutcliffe, a wartime soldier who had become a colonial policeman in Tanganyika.[9] His headquarters were in Arsenal Street on Hong Kong Island. Under his command fell the police districts into which the colony was divided; Hong Kong Island, with its headquarters on Hollywood Road; Kowloon, headquartered on Argyle Street near the end of the Kai Tak Airport grounds; and the New Territories, with its headquarters at Tsuen Wan. The fourth district, Marine, operated a fleet of launches which patrolled Hong Kong's waters.

Each district was commanded by an assistant commissioner and was divided into divisions, and each neatly matched the geographical and social divisions of the colony. Hong Kong Island was the most colonial and European district, the place of government and the centre of financial business. Crime rates were lower here, except in the red light district in Wan Chai and the Chinese settlements in Eastern District.

Across the harbour, Kowloon was the hub of the Chinese population and its packed streets contained many of their businesses and most of the tenements in which they lived. Around Kowloon's edges clustered squatter shanty towns, constructions of wood, tin, and tarpaulin. On the upper floors of the tenement buildings in Jordan and Yau Ma Tei, vice establishments catered to the local population, more numerous by far than their equivalents in Wan Chai. Policing in Kowloon was a much tougher proposition than on Hong Kong Island. Crime was often viciously violent, the number of vice establishments of all types was enormous, and the law was difficult to enforce. In 1973, the levels of violent crime here were rapidly rising and the Chinese population felt neither safe not protected by the police. Police officers stationed in Kowloon needed to be tough and sharp to survive.

According to the treaties imposed on the Chinese in the nineteenth century,[10] both Hong Kong Island and Kowloon were irrevocably British, but north of the aptly named Boundary Street, that ran east to west across the peninsula of Kowloon, lay the New Territories. The British had extracted this addition to their possessions only under a ninety-nine year lease, which was due to expire in 1997.[11] The urban sprawl of Kowloon spread across Boundary Street, but north of the line of hills that included the famous Lion Rock, the New Territories were largely rural. There were a few small market towns and many villages here, with a population that was still in many places working on the land or the sea, but whose exodus to the employment of the urban areas was already well under way. Much of the New Territories was governed by a mixture of colonial and traditional Chinese law. Its villagers ran their own affairs and were in some of them almost inviolable. Their leaders were powerful figures of whom government wisely took note if it wished to avoid trouble. Policing here called for different skills: tact, patience, a steady hand, and a knowledge of local customs. This was a quieter place, although not at all one free of violence and vice, for organized crime ran deep here. It would be fair to say, though, that police officers who spent their careers in the New Territories were not usually those marked out for a stellar future.

* * *

All this was much as it had been in the three decades since the end of the Second World War. There had been a great growth in population and wealth since then, but little reform.[12] By the time John MacLennan arrived, however, reform was in the air everywhere, embodied in the towering figure of Sir Crawford Murray MacLehose, the governor of Hong Kong, who was to remain in office for just over a decade after he arrived in the colony in November 1971. He was one of the most remarkable governors in Hong Kong's history.[13] *The Times* obituary for Murray MacLehose (he didn't use his first name) was to describe him as the "last of the great pro-consuls", and he dominated Hong Kong from his arrival.[14] He was a Scot, though a lowlander from Glasgow who later settled in Ayrshire, rather than a highlander like MacLennan. A very tall man (he was well over six feet), well built and upright in bearing, he towered over the local population and most of his British staff. His physically imposing stature matched perfectly his dominating, energetic personality.

When he arrived, MacLehose already had a very clear idea of the policies he wished to follow in Hong Kong, and once he had enunciated them he ensured that he was personally involved in much of the detail of their implementation. Little would happen in Hong Kong in his day without at least his knowledge. He was an intimidating superior and a natural autocrat, and, as the years passed and his hold on Hong Kong's government grew stronger and stronger, many found him a hard master. He was a man admired and feared rather than loved, and was thought of by his officials and the public to be a tad prudish and straight-laced.[15] Ominously for what he was about to face, some also considered him prejudiced against homosexuals.[16] The colony gave MacLehose the nickname "Jock the Sock", a reference to the Scottish word "hose", or "sock".[17] He was also known as "Big Mac" and, more irreverently, as "Panty Hose".[18]

Foreign Office records reveal that in November 1971, before his departure for Hong Kong, MacLehose briefed the officials there about what it was he was setting out to do: "My object in Hong Kong must be to ensure that conditions in Hong Kong are so superior in every way to those in China that the CPG will hesitate before facing the problem of absorption."[19] This was eight years before Deng Xiaoping's assumption of the reins of power in Beijing led to the opening up of the Chinese economy. In 1971, however, it made a good deal of sense. The policy upon which Sir Murray was determined had the added advantages, first, that it would very appreciably improve the lives of Hong Kong's people, and second, that it would prevent the social unrest that had so scarred the colony in the 1960s.

Building on the plans and initial progress made by his predecessors, MacLehose energetically drove on the development of the colony. Infrastructure, housing, social policies, and culture all benefitted from his attention. Hong Kong became one enormous construction site and in the decade that was to follow, its modern shape emerged.

The police were not left behind in this era of renewal and growth. Two state-of-the-art police command centres would open in 1978 and the force was strengthened, so that by 1979 it would have an establishment of 20,691.[20] New police stations were planned for divisions in all police districts. Training would improve and modern policing methods would be introduced, with money at last provided for improved equipment and transport, increased pay, and better accommodation and welfare facilities for police officers and their families. The decade promised to be a very exciting time for a young officer like MacLennan to start a career in Hong Kong.

3

Corruption

Despite this promise of a golden future, when John MacLennan joined the force in 1973, "Asia's Finest" was not a title he would have heard many employ. He was much more likely to have heard some insulting version of the label "the finest police force money can buy" bestowed upon it in 1980 by the satirical British magazine *Private Eye*.[1] At least until that year, and in some of its parts for years after that, the RHKP was widely regarded as corrupt in root and branch. In 1973 it was only just beginning to shake off a very tawdry past.

In this, the force was unfortunate in that being so obviously in the public eye made it a scapegoat for the opprobrium deserved by almost all layers of Hong Kong's colonial apparatus. As Deputy Commissioner of Police Christopher Dawson put it on 20 November 1973, in a speech in which he complained of the "smears, insults and denigration" that he saw being heaped upon the force: "Some people say, rightly or wrongly, that society deserves the Police Force it's got."[2] Hong Kong society was as corrupt, if not more so, than the police force that served it.

In this respect, the British colony had from its inception assumed a feature which, among the Chinese population, and in particular its commercial elements, had always been considered part of the natural order of things. In the business community, corruption was regarded as one of the glues that held transactions together and was, counter-intuitively, considered an aid to the swift and efficient conduct of affairs. A bribe would be offered as routine and was priced into business transactions. As Jack Cater, commissioner of the Independent Commission Against Corruption, put it in his annual report for 1975: "'Hong Kong's business has been built on the commission system', I have been told. And, no doubt, there is some truth in that statement."[3]

Some British colonials took to this system readily, others did not. Many expatriates who made their lives in the colony could live and work oblivious to, or only vaguely aware of, the graft affecting the Chinese population, for bribes would rarely be demanded from a foreigner who might cause trouble. Most British officials would not have dreamed of demanding a bribe to perform their functions, and applied the regulations they administered to the best of their ability, albeit that this was an ability limited by the fact that they were usually guided by the advice and actions of their Chinese subordinates. Some expatriates, however, across all departments and walks of life, were not averse to accepting the gifts and hospitality that enabled them to turn a blind eye to the more direct peculations of their inferiors. Others were paid off discreetly in a regular fashion and a few were themselves actively corrupt. Some British officials actively used their offices to acquire corrupt payments and such men could be found even in the Legal Department, which worked so closely with the police that a suspicion of collusion was not always ill-founded.

In contrast, in the lives of the Chinese who made up the vast majority of the population, corruption was a daily fact of life. A sweetener was necessary for every transaction, licence, permit, or official act involving a Chinese person. Firemen, for instance, would call whoever reported a fire and demand a bribe before they would consider arriving on time to put it out; the stock Cantonese phrase they used on such occasions, *mo soi mo soi* (no money no water), was a standing joke in the community.[4] Even the provision of bedding and treatment in a government hospital would require a bribe to the nursing staff. There was no hope of redress, for the Chinese population could not appeal against extortion to the very authority that was operating to fleece them.

The few expatriates who were fully aware of the true state of affairs were either corrupt themselves or had been forced to confront the fact of corruption because they were considered so low down the pecking order that they were safely exploitable. In 1973, the latter sort included ex-missionary school supervisor Mrs Elsie Elliott, who had first discovered the way things were when she applied to re-establish a school that had occupied licensed premises on Prince Edward Road in Kowloon.[5] She had no means to pay the bribe her predecessors had found necessary to obtain certification that the one fire escape built on the side of the school was in official theory the two required by fire regulations.[6] Not that she would have paid a bribe in any case, and resisting this small piece of official venality set her off on the lifelong fight for the Hong Kong Chinese underdog that would make her a much-loved personality and a scourge of the corrupt and criminal.[7] She was a small, slight and, at a distance, homely sort of woman, but she was fearless, her backbone was of steel, and when aroused by injustice her eyes flashed fire and her tongue was sharp. She was, however, one of a very few who tried to draw attention to the way things were.

Nevertheless, it was corruption in the police that caused the greatest concern due to its effects upon the government and the security of the colony. As investigations proceeded during the 1970s, it became clear that corruption was frighteningly extensive, all pervasive in fact. Jack Cater described how police corruption functioned as a system in an inflammatory speech he gave to the Hong Kong Rotary Club in 1977:

> Every police division has at least one syndicate with many hundreds involved. Hawkers pay several hundred thousand dollars a day in bribes [...] Each syndicate is a protection racket. A broad base of contributors (drug divans, sex dens, etc.) pay to a collector who pays the police-appointed "caterer", who distributes the money [...] Revenue comes from drugs and gambling. Protection is given from prosecution and prevention of competition given. Detective Station Sergeants are the key organisers. There are sub-collectors, head collectors, a chief collector and an accountant [...] Each syndicate has different victims, eg: the Traffic Police syndicate leans on Public Light Bus drivers; the Wan Chai syndicate extorts money from hawkers.[8]

Until 1972, the station sergeants to whom Cater referred were known as staff sergeants. Each of the four police districts had one uniform and one CID staff sergeant class I, the most senior of the district's rank and file. Beneath these in each police division there was one uniform and one CID staff sergeant class II (so before 1972 there were four of these in Hong Kong district, four in Kowloon, and six in the New Territories, but none in Marine). Before 1972, the staff sergeants had been tremendously powerful and formed an "interest group" that met informally to coordinate corruption, and their power only began to be broken from that year.[9]

The money collected by Chinese staff sergeants and their successor station sergeants was shared out across the syndicate and was delivered every month in unmarked envelopes to the desks of expatriate police officers. Jack Cater did not specify who, in his view, provided the collectors and accountants, but for want of alternatives it is clear that they were members of organized criminal gangs. In Hong Kong, that meant the triads, the traditional Chinese secret criminal societies, the local equivalent of the Mafia. Although the RHKP had an anti-triad unit, the Triad Society Bureau, and membership of a triad society was an offence punishable by a prison sentence, senior Hong Kong police officers regularly played down the strength and activities of the triads, in part, no doubt, to deflect attention from the symbiotic relationship they enjoyed with them.

Corruption was often described by the police as a "bus" (Elsie Elliott characterized it as a "wagon"). Kevin Sinclair, a Hong Kong journalist who curried favour with the police and who in 1983 wrote *Asia's Finest*, the semi-official account of the force, and who was a man much in their pocket and usually happy to be a channel for whatever line they wished to give the public, described the system succinctly:

> Within the Force it was referred to as "the bus". You could "get on the bus" and quietly pocket the brown envelopes containing untraceable amounts of cash which appeared mysteriously in your

> locker or desk. You could "stand beside the bus" and watch it go by and refuse to accept corruption payments though you knew graft was common. Or you could "stand in front of the bus" — report corruption and try to stop it — with predictable results. Many got on the bus. Most just stood and watched. Few stood in front of it. Part of the indifference to corruption was that it was efficient. It got results.[10]

His final remark needs some explanation, which he gave in a later book, *Asia's Finest Marches On*, writing there that the five dragons, the staff sergeants who ran the divisional syndicates, used a large amount of their illegal proceeds to fight crime, by, for instance, using it to pay informers.[11] On the face of it, this is an unbelievable remark, but it is one borne out by police officers of the time, who relate that the force was so badly funded that the only way to issue a reward, for instance, for the apprehension of the murderer of a police officer, was to use illegal funds.[12] Even items as mundane as typewriters and the salaries of the typists hired to use them (the staff sergeants were forced to hire them as they themselves were mostly illiterate), as well as the salaries of CID Room boys (civilian orderlies employed in the stations), had to be paid for in similar ways.[13]

Some expatriate police officers progressed from getting on the bus to driving it, and made a career out of exploiting each post they occupied. Especially lucrative was the sale of promotions and appointments. Once the system got fully going, and it had done so by at least the 1960s, it became self-perpetuating, as corrupt officers ensured that honest subordinates were not promoted. Like chose like, so that eventually a large part of the hierarchy of senior officers (or at least those who were long-term Hong Kong officers) was corrupt. It was in the interest of corrupt senior officers to suppress or remove any junior officer who showed signs of bucking the system, for the obvious reason that they could make no money from them. Worse still, honest officers would endanger the whole system by fighting it or by going after the criminals it protected.

The result for those who tried to stand in front of the bus was predictably dire. Elsie Elliott, who by the '60s had become a magnet for anyone run over by the bus, became involved in at least two cases of officers who had tried to do their duty and suffered for it. One of these was Alan Ellis, a young police officer who had been awarded the prize for best recruit on completion of his initial training only to lose his job shortly thereafter. He told Elsie that this was because he had refused to conform to corruption in his first post in Mong Kok, where he had turned down the envelopes of HK$500 offered him through a janitor by his staff sergeant. At one point, Senior Superintendent Peter Godber, who later was to become notorious, had also tried to bribe him, but Ellis took the money he had been given to his boss, who persuaded him to withdraw the resignation letter Ellis had handed in with the cash.[14] The next senior officer up the chain, however, made it plain to him that his contract would not be renewed. After that, he had been moved to the New Territories and from there was forced out.[15]

***

One final example will illustrate how the system worked. Inspector Peter Crush was struck off police strength only the year before John MacLennan arrived in Hong Kong. He had joined the force in 1965 and soon acquired a reputation as a man too honest for the system to tolerate. When, within three weeks of leaving training, he arrested three heroin dealers, the disquiet of his superiors was made obvious to him. Initially posted to Sham Shui Po in Kowloon, he was very swiftly transferred to the Traffic Division because, according to his divisional superintendent, of his "exceptional keenness and powers of observation", but really because he would neither get on nor stand by the bus. In 1967, following an initial two-week cadre course for probationary inspectors at the Police Training Contingent (the riot training school at Fanling, a town near the Sino-Hong Kong border), he was given "an absolutely damning report" by its commandant, who just happened to be Peter Godber, who cited "immaturity" and "lack of leadership potential" to damn an officer he knew had already stood in front of the bus. Almost immediately, the riots caused by the Cultural Revolution broke out in the colony and those on training at Fanling were deployed. On one occasion, Crush was on patrol with Gurkha soldiers at the dangerous police post at Sha Tau Kok, where five constables had been killed by small-arms fire from across the border, and his patrol came under attack from Chinese militia, who threw dynamite "fish bombs" at the patrol.

> When I finally finished this riot-company posting, which had been extended from the usual three months to nearly six months by the emergency, my Company Commander read me an absolutely glowing report about how I "had matured under fire" and how my leadership skills had improved immensely.

Godber, however, forced his commander to change the report and a much toned-down version went into his record of service.

Crush was then transferred repeatedly to non-police station posts in which he could take no enforcement action against drug dealers or operators of opium and gambling dens, or do anything which would upset the protected rackets. On one occasion, he raided a large street gambling den that he stumbled on while walking around the streets when off duty. This was in the Wong Tai Sin Division, where he was not serving but where he had been allocated staff quarters. This caused a tremendous fuss, initially because "the establishment" thought he might have done it in order to "squeeze it". Crush never went to great lengths to hide his homosexuality and, when suspicions arose and were mentioned by his superiors, he made it clear to them that he resented the interest they took in it. As a result of all this, during his sixth year of service and when briefly posted to a police station to engage in routine police work, he was placed under the command of an officer junior in rank to him. He protested about this to his commanding officer but to no avail. In 1971, he realized that he had no prospect of promotion and resigned from the force of his own accord.[16]

It was impossible that any senior officer whose career had largely been in Hong Kong, and who had not been posted in from outside the colony into a senior position late in career (as some were), could have reached the top without either being on the bus or standing by it. Henry Heath, who had joined the Hong Kong Police in 1934, became commissioner of police in 1959 and remained in post for seven years.[17] Heath, a man who was described as being unable to see any evil in his fellow police officers, was reported as saying in 1966:

> I would say that there is corruption in the Police Force, but that there is corruption in other Government departments and indeed in commercial life and, in fact, pretty well every walk of life here in Hong Kong [...] I would say this, that in terms of money the Police Force is probably not the worst, in spite of the fact that it is the biggest section of Government.

He added that the police needed bribes to pay informants.[18]

Any countermeasures taken had been largely, perhaps deliberately, ineffective, fig leaves for an overall tolerance of crime. An Anti-Corruption Bureau was set up inside the force in 1948, supposedly given direction from 1956 by a Standing Committee on Corruption chaired by a principal crown counsel, but it was toothless and soon became moribund. It was revived for a while in 1961, but spent its time publishing reports.[19] In May 1971, Governor Sir David Trench finally began effective action, enacting the Prevention of Bribery Ordinance, Cap. 201.[20] This gave teeth to those fighting corruption, for it made it an offence to have unexplained wealth in excess of that which could have been accumulated through a salary or other bona fide means. So when Trench left office in 1971, he left behind him the means to fight corruption, although he had been unable to do the job himself. His successor Sir Murray MacLehose was not long in post before he was given good cause to deal with the problem. During his first year in office came the arrest of Superintendent Ernest-Percival "Taffy" Hunt, whose flagrant flaunting of a lifestyle way beyond the reach of his salary led to his investigation.[21]

The commissioner of the day, Charles Sutcliffe, had joined the force only in 1960 in the rank of assistant commissioner and so had been unaffected by the "bus". He gathered around him a small group of those on whom he could rely: Deputy Commissioner Christopher Dawson, the head of Special Branch; Chief Superintendent James Morrin, shortly to be appointed to head the Anti-Corruption Office; and Superintendent Norman Whitely.[22] Roy Henry, who had been commissioner of police in Fiji, was brought in as senior assistant commissioner, Operations in early 1973.[23] Their first target was Hunt, who was prosecuted for possession of HK$5 million and sentenced to a year in prison.

Sutcliffe then began to go after Hunt's associate, Peter Godber, who was by then a chief superintendent. After a tip off, mountains of cash were discovered in bank accounts held by Godber along with logbooks that traced that cash back to its source.[24] Godber and his wife then fled Hong Kong.[25]

MacLehose moved swiftly to stem the public outcry and appointed a Commission of Inquiry, with senior judge Sir Alastair Blair-Kerr at the helm, tasked to look into both the circumstances of Godber's escape and to review previous efforts to stamp out corruption in the colony.[26] Blair-Kerr's two reports were sobering. Sir Alastair found that the public believed that corruption existed in large areas of the public service and that senior government officials were either unaware of it, connived at it, or participated in it.[27] MacLehose was surprised and appalled by both the Godber affair and by the Blair-Kerr reports. He confessed in his annual report to London that October that "the suspicion of corruption on a more extensive scale was better grounded than I had personally realized."[28] He could see that he had to do something were his programme of modernizing Hong Kong to have any hope of success. He flew to Malta to meet Sir John Prendergast, the retired head of Hong Kong's Special Branch, to ask him to come back to implement what he had in mind; Sir John agreed.[29]

On 17 October 1973, three days before John MacLennan joined the Police Training School, Sir Murray MacLehose rose in the Legislative Council to announce the formation of the Independent Commission Against Corruption, the ICAC. He appointed Jack Cater as its commissioner and Sir John Prendergast as its director of operations.[30] Its task was to be nothing less than the removal of the canker of corruption at the heart of Hong Kong. It would be given draconian powers of operation, search, and detention, powers beyond anything possessed by the police. From the first, the ICAC was hugely resented by the police, at whose officers it was to be targeted and a central part of whose crime-fighting role it would usurp, but MacLehose had now provided the men, the legal powers, and the political backing to carry forward what Trench had started. Within a decade, the ICAC would cleanse much of the institutionalized corruption from Hong Kong. It was not, however, going to be an easy fight.

4

Amnesty

John MacLennan did not shine at the training school in Aberdeen. His training report stated that his examination results were poor and his knowledge of professional duties barely adequate. "An officer with limited potential. So informed." It hadn't helped that at the start of training he had broken an ankle, but there were things about his character which clearly irritated his instructors, who reported that he showed stubbornness, was "overly-concerned in matters not involving him", and had a desire to draw attention to himself.[1]

MacLennan did, however, make a few friends among his fellow trainees, including Felix Muller, who would later live close to him in Ho Man Tin, and Christopher Burns.[2] He was not a man who made friends easily, rather one who made a few close friends and stuck to them, as he had in Scotland. He also seems to have made an enemy of a fellow Scot, the rough and ready, as well as very blunt, Angus "Gus" Graham, with whom he was reported to "have had words".[3] When he next became involved in MacLennan's life, Graham would show a strong motivation against homosexuals; perhaps he picked up some subliminal signals he didn't like about John MacLennan when they first met.

The training report had also commented that MacLennan had shown an interest in the rank and file on his course. This was an odd remark to make. He would have had only limited contact with any Chinese recruits, who were accommodated at the far end of the school and trained separately. Expatriates were brought together with the squad of Chinese policemen with whom they would pass off the square only at the end of training and it was not customary for the two groups to interact, let alone socialize. Whilst this is perhaps a totally straightforward comment, it may also have been a coded one, for it would not be long before MacLennan showed that he was attracted to Chinese men in ways other than the professional.

A seemingly minor incident may have been the cause of the remarks in his report that he had a tendency to interfere in matters that were not of his concern. While in the senior stage of his training, he went to the airport to meet Peter Whyte, his old friend from Stirling, who was arriving in Hong Kong to start the junior phase of training. Whyte arrived with a batch of recruits that was so unusually large, thirty-nine new officers, that the *Hong Kong Standard* sent a reporter to meet them at Kai Tak and they were photographed getting onto the bus. MacLennan accompanied them back to the Police Training School, warning them en route of the usual initiation planned by the senior squad, who by custom pretended to be instructors to give the new recruits a hard time. When the new recruits debussed at the school, they were duly met by the seniors. Iain Grant, another Scots recruit who had been on the bus, told them to "f...k off" and went to bed, leaving MacLennan to get a ticking off for interfering with the traditions of the training school.[4]

MacLennan passed out of training in May 1974 and, with Christopher Burns, was posted to the Kwun Tong Division, which covered some of the east side of Kowloon (the station was in Junk Bay Road, not far from Elsie Elliott's school for the children of squatters).[5] He was allocated a room in the Kwun Tong inspectors' quarters.[6] In the photograph in his membership card for the Hong Kong section of the International Police Association, which he joined on 1 August 1974, he looks a steady, if rather stolid and serious young man.[7] He seems to have done better at Kwun Tong than his training report might have led his superiors to expect, and at the end of that December he was well reported on by his superior, Chief Inspector Jock Atkinson.[8] He also received the formal appreciation of the district commander of Hong Kong Island for assisting in the arrest of persons wanted for robbery and homicide.

The next stage of a police officer's career was riot training at the Police Tactical Unit (as the Police Training Contingent had by then become) in Fanling. MacLennan was sent there in January 1975. During this course, he was found guilty of a trait rather typical of many junior officers, that of being easily parted from his kit, and he received a reprimand for losing his pack set.[9] When he passed out from Fanling in February 1975, he was attached for a while to Kowloon District Police Headquarters before being returned to Kwun Tong. In July that year, he did a tour of duty with the Emergency Unit for East Kowloon, obtaining a good report that Christmas when his attachment ended.[10]

The pay of a junior inspector at the time was under HK$2,000 a month, and John MacLennan did not have much to spend, so during 1975 he took a part time job teaching English in Causeway Bay, something uncommon at that time for a police officer.[11] In what off duty time he had, he went about a good deal with Christopher Burns, crawling the Kowloon bars and occasionally paying female prostitutes for sex, but he did not spend all his salary and managed to save a little every month. Burns thought him a womanizer and liked this aspect of his otherwise conservative character. He found MacLennan a stickler for punctuality, a fervent monarchist, and a man very proud of being in the RHKP, which he would defend against detractors. He was always well dressed in jacket and tie, or at the most informal in a safari suit, and he wore a kilt for occasions in the mess. He would listen to tapes of bagpipe music, played at a very loud volume. Winston Churchill had always been MacLennan's hero and he would do rather good impressions of him when drunk. Some found him a touch arrogant, even self-obsessed.[12]

This was only one side of his character, however. He had a softer side. He wrote home weekly to his family and would send them presents and, when he could, gifts of money. His mother remembered that he always wrapped the presents himself and would never let the stores wrap them for him.[13]

Chris Burns and MacLennan's boss, Chief Inspector Jock Atkinson, later recalled that at this time he was known to take women home overnight to the quarters at Kwun Tong, and that, although these were all, as far as they could tell, prostitutes, he did have three longer term relationships they knew of with women who were not in the sex industry: one was a Chinese dance girl; the second was an army nurse; and the third was a

Filipina maid. Felix Muller thought that MacLennan only had sex with "sluts", not with decent types, but remembered him being markedly homophobic and declaiming that homosexuals should leave Hong Kong "because the law is the law".[14]

However, beneath what was perhaps a carefully cultivated veneer of conventional heterosexuality, John MacLennan's homosexual side was beginning to force its way to the surface. It was around this time, and very much in secret, that he was drawn at last to act upon the attractions he felt to others of the same sex. There is no evidence that before 1975 he had acted upon such attractions. It is clear, however, that in Hong Kong he came face to face with Chinese men probably for the first time in his life, and found that he was attracted to them sexually. When drink loosened his inhibitions, he began to seek them out for sex and later for companionship. In this hidden life, he found young men in whom he could confide and with whom he could have fun, free of the inhibitions of the life he led on the surface.

The first credible evidence of this is the testimony of a young man of mixed Chinese and Filipino race who was known in gay circles as "Slasher" George, a nickname he had acquired from the scars on his arms that testified to his sad history of slashing his wrists.[15] He and John MacLennan met in 1975 while swimming at Repulse Bay on the south side of Hong Kong Island, at the time a place where homosexuals looked for other men. They began to see each other and kept their friendship going, meeting occasionally over the next five years and sleeping together in MacLennan's quarters. When he gave an account of their relationship to radio chat show hostess Aileen Bridgewater in 1980, George was about nineteen or twenty, which would put his age at fourteen or fifteen-years old when he met MacLennan. He was openly gay but not on the game and he went to bed with

MacLennan because he liked him rather than to make money from him. He came to realize, he told Aileen, that John was bisexual, and he thought that he never paid for sex, but only went to bed for company with those he liked.[16]

Slasher George was wrong in his belief that John MacLennan did not pay for sex. When the drink or the need took hold, he looked for sex where he could find it, and, for a police officer who could not be seen in bars picking up a boy, the street was the easiest option. Sometime in the middle of 1975, MacLennan picked up a nineteen-year old named Peter Sung Chung-wah, a prostitute who worked the Tsim Sha Tsui area and who that day was loitering outside Chungking Mansions on Nathan Road. On this first occasion, MacLennan took a room in the nearby Holiday Inn and paid Sung HK$100 for sex. Some months later they met again on Middle Road, which was in the same area, and went together to the Lee Garden Hotel, where this time Peter was paid only $50.[17] In the next three months, they repeated the tryst on another three occasions.[18]

* * *

While John MacLennan was exploring his own nature and getting his feet under the table in his new post in Kwun Tong, Hong Kong was beginning to discover the extent of the corruption in the force that he had joined. Chief Superintendent Peter Godber was extradited from Britain to Hong Kong in 1975 to be put on trial. He was sentenced to four years imprisonment and a fine of HK$25,000, a tiny fraction of the HK$4 million he had been found to have stashed away.[19] Charles Sutcliffe had got his man, though he did not have the satisfaction of seeing this himself, for the year before he had handed office to a new commissioner of police, Brian Slevin.[20]

Feeling the noose tightening, some of the key criminal elements in the force began to flee. These included the most powerful of the syndicate dragons, Station Sergeant Lui Lok, known as the "$500 Million Man", who during 1974 fled to Vancouver then Taiwan, taking with him two other dragons, Station Sergeants Nan Kong and Ngan Hung.[21] Twenty-two suspects were listed as fleeing Hong Kong the next year.

During 1975, the ICAC was able to launch its first big trials. During that year, 218 prosecutions were launched (96 of government officials, the rest of members of the public), of which 136 resulted in convictions.[22] The courts ordered that a total of $10,297,456.19 be paid to the government in fines, restitution, and forfeitures. Sir Murray MacLehose could believe that it really would be possible to eradicate corruption in Hong Kong and its police force within a few years.

The force's morale, however, was beginning to crumble. Had it been led at the time by a popular or admired leader, it is possible that the force might have avoided the disaster which was now only two years away, but it was unlucky that instead its commissioner was Brian Slevin, an isolated, morose, and alcoholic bully whom no one liked and few respected. Slevin had transferred to the Hong Kong Police when the Palestinian Mandate ended in 1949. Those who still remember him now do so to recall incidents such as the time when he walked out on the officers of one division assembled in their mess to greet him for lunch, preferring instead to have lunch alone with the divisional commander. It is also recalled that at the end of his service in February 1979, he arrived late and wearing a Hawaiian shirt in front of a parade of police officers passing out of the Police Tactical Unit at Fanling. He had to be taken away to change, and was so drunk that, when the flag was being lowered, the embarrassed PTU chief instructor had to tell him to turn around to face it. Slevin had reached the pinnacle of his profession only to watch the ICAC dismantle his force and arrest the men he commanded. He was rotting inside and incapable of the leadership the force needed.

During 1976, the ICAC continued to pull various parts of the force to pieces. Their activities shattered the stabilization of crime, based on the illegal markets in sex, drugs, and gambling, that had kept a seeming tranquility across the colony. The police had been forced to clamp down on the vice that had earlier made them and the underworld rich. The ICAC now went after entire syndicates rather than just corrupt individuals. In May, the Wan Chai division was ripped apart. The ICAC arrested five station sergeants and fifty sergeants, all those working in the division, and staff had to be drafted in to keep the division operational. The morale of the force plummeted and the number of resignations shot up. In July, Senior Superintendent Jack English's suicide caused widespread dismay. After two years with the ICAC he had been posted to head Kowloon CID, but had suffered a breakdown over the effect that the ICAC was having on the police. Some said he had been sent to Coventry by his colleagues on his return to the force. He died leaving a suicide note complaining of the aloofness of Police Commissioner Slevin. As the ICAC's campaign forged ahead, it would not be long before the unhappiness within the police force would burst out in public.[23]

* * *

At the start of 1976, John MacLennan was in the final year of his first two-and-a-half year contract. In March, he gained his driving licence and a month later he was transferred to CID, still at Kwun Tong.[24] He was doing quite well now, at worst an average officer, and was showing more qualities than had been detected at the Aberdeen school. His end of contract leave began on 17 October and before he left he received his report for the year from Peter Moor, district commander Kowloon, who called him "hardworking, practical and level-headed".[25] Moor commented on his steady progress, thought him a competent and useful officer, and concluded by recommending both an increment of pay and confirmation in the force.

MacLennan was so encouraged by this that, before departing, he requested a transfer to Special Branch, to take effect on his return to duty. His request was accepted and before he left in October he was negatively vetted to give him sufficient security clearance for the post.[26] We have no means of knowing the reason behind his choice, but given the circumstances at the time it is possible that MacLennan wished to join the one part of the force where he knew he would be unlikely to be confronted with the dilemma of unmarked envelopes or the attention of the ICAC.

MacLennan and Burns left Hong Kong at the start of their leave. They had planned to go home through Egypt and Italy, and a month or so earlier had written to a Brigadier Silvan, the Italian police officer who headed the IPA in Rome, saying that they would be travelling there from Cairo in November and that they hoped for help with hotel recommendations and the chance to meet fellow association members.[27] Whether this all worked out is unknown; we have no pictures of them both at the pyramids or in the Coliseum, and when MacLennan finally reached Scotland later that month, he gave his family presents that had come from Bangkok, so it seems that they had visited Thailand en route.[28]

Back in Scotland, MacLennan spent much of his time at home. When he arrived he found both of his parents in hospital, his father for treatment of an eye complaint that would gradually cause the loss of his sight, his mother with an ulcer. Johnny visited them every day, and when they got home they found he had both decorated and spring cleaned their cottage from top to bottom. He deposited the savings he'd made in his first contract (£1,500) in his Bank of Scotland account in Dingwall.[29] The family had a very happy few weeks together before his brother Ron drove him all the way south to Heathrow Airport to catch the flight to Hong Kong. As he left, John gave Ron all the British currency he had on him, saying: "All this English stuff will be no use to me now."

It was fortunate for him that MacLennan was on leave at this time, for in the last six months of 1976 alone, the ICAC executed 280 warrants against the police. By the end of 1976, it had enforced interdiction, (the suspension of officers under suspicion) against 305 police officers.[30] John Conway, who knew the MacLennan family, and who features later in this account, wrote that John had told his father during this leave that he would not go along with the corruption in Hong Kong, but would fight it when he got back. His father, however, told Ken Bridgewater that Johnny had never mentioned the ICAC.[31] The two stories may be compatible, though seem difficult to reconcile, and of the two the Bridgewater account has more credibility. Yet MacLennan was certainly in two minds about going back to Hong Kong and during his leave he made an application to join London's Metropolitan Police as a constable. He had not warned the RHKP that he was doing this, so when the Met wrote to Hong Kong on 14 January 1977 seeking a reference, their letter arrived only a few days after a letter had been issued appointing him to Special Branch.[32] In the event, MacLennan did not receive confirmation of a post with the Met, so he flew back to Hong Kong in March at the end of his leave and joined Special Branch.

His arrival after the Met's reference check must have been the occasion of some raised eyebrows and a frosty reception from Senior Superintendent Roper, his new boss, who placed him in the Vetting Section that checked government servants.[33] However, Roper was clearly prepared to trust MacLennan, and after a very short time, in the Easter week of 8–11 April, he personally screened him to handle the lists of the Hong Kong Government's known and suspected homosexuals. Homosexuality was reckoned a character defect in vetting terms, so an expatriate inspector was always placed in charge of such work.

MacLennan himself was not on the Special Branch's list of homosexuals and, from the little knowledge of him that Roper had at that stage, he believed that MacLennan was "not a homosexual". In the course of his vetting interview, he asked MacLennan directly about his views on homosexuality, and MacLennan replied that he thought it a vice. Roper noted that he spoke vehemently on the subject, and claimed that he had slept with female prostitutes in Bangkok.[34]

It was only one week later that MacLennan told his boss that he had received an offer of a place with the Metropolitan Police and he formally submitted his resignation on 12 April. Roper was not amused to have had his time wasted in this fashion and on 17 April moved MacLennan from the Vetting Section to serve out his three months' notice elsewhere.[35] In the very short time that MacLennan had been there, however, he had seen two names on a file list, names that later would cause him much trouble. The names were those of Roy Henry, by now deputy commissioner of police, and Chief Superintendent Ron Redpath, head of the Police Public Relations Wing.[36]

MacLennan spent the next few weeks kicking his heels while he was processed out of the force. This did not do him much good, as it left him with time on his hands which he filled by drinking too much. On 1 May, he got involved in a fracas in a bar that came to the attention of his superiors, who noted in his file: "This officer was involved in a dispute in a bar in Tsim Sha Tsui on 1 May; his involvement was unwise and not the sort expected of a responsible Police Officer."[37] MacLennan could be wild at times when under the influence of alcohol.

Either because he was unsure of the reasons for his change of employer or because he did not reveal them, the explanations that MacLennan gave in his exit interview with Miss A.H. Calderwood, chief staff officer (Recruiting and Development), do not all look like those that were really behind his resignation. He told her that he had only intended to have a short term career in Hong Kong, that "the general Hong Kong environment has deteriorated" (likely a reference to the ongoing corruption cases), and that he had been offered a post as a constable in the Met, which he considered more his home ground.[38] Chief Superintendent Haigh of Special Branch, Roper's superior, minuted in June: "Mr MacLennan is a dour young Scotsman who I feel is out of place in Hong Kong and he has obviously come to the same decision."[39]

MacLennan flew back to London to be welcomed when he reached the Metropolitan Police College in Hendon in late June by a telegram from Christopher Burns that read: "Best of luck in your new venture. Chris. Hong Kong."[40] Training at the police college lasted for most of the rest of the year, and seems not to have been to John MacLennan's liking. Perhaps it opened his eyes to the loss of the privileges he had enjoyed as an Inspector in Hong Kong; perhaps something untoward happened during his training. Again, we have no means of knowing what was on his mind. It was a time in the United Kingdom when many were thinking that leaving the country might be preferable to staying. The Callaghan administration was limping to its inglorious end through a series of strikes in public services and private industry. Living standards had been falling with a collapse in incomes at an annual rate of more than eight percent for over two years. In 1977, the car industry crippled itself with industrial action, strikes closed Heathrow Airport, and the fire service withdrew its labour. Riots broke out in several cities.[41] In comparison, Hong Kong must have seemed a haven of frenetic but peaceful progress, a place where people were working hard to achieve a better future, one that seemed in Britain to be getting further and further out of reach.

Whatever the reason for his decision, on 20 December 1977, MacLennan applied to rejoin the Royal Hong Kong Police, stating, misleadingly, that he had resigned previously as his mother had been sick and that she had now recovered. He also said that he had missed the challenges of life in Hong Kong.[42] The staff officer personnel in Hong Kong, Inspector Dick Lidster, recommended his re-enlistment, and he was accepted once more for a second contract of two and a half years.[43]

* * *

Much had gone badly wrong in Hong Kong during the period in which MacLennan was training with the Met. The antagonisms caused by what many of the police felt was an assault on their organization, and what corrupt individuals feared was an assault on their liberty and wealth, had become corrosive.

In early October 1977, 140 police officers from three Kowloon divisions were arrested by the ICAC, charged with syndicated corruption. On 25 October came the arrest of another 34 police officers, including four expatriate superintendents.

This was the spark that finally ignited what was by now a highly combustible situation. There was a mass rally of police in Kowloon and on the same day 300 police officers gathered at Kowloon Police Headquarters to hand in a letter of protest while another 250 massed at Wong Tai Sin married quarters.

Brian Slevin refused, as he would continue to refuse during the crisis, to meet any of his disaffected men, and on 27 October he designated his deputy, Roy Henry, to meet their delegates, thus meriting the nickname he acquired of "the Invisible Man". Thousands of officers gathered that day to listen to inflammatory speeches at the Police Sports Association in Kowloon and when by the next day the situation had still not been defused, a crowd of about 2,000 police massed in Edinburgh Place in the centre of Hong Kong Island to march to police headquarters and confront the commissioner. While negotiations between the agitators and Roy Henry proceeded, a breakaway group marched at noon through the streets to nearby Hutchison House, the headquarters of the ICAC, led by men who were from the large group of interdicted officers suspended from the force. Eight to ten of these broke in and trashed the offices, assaulted the ICAC officers they found there and injured five of them. In the subsequent investigation, despite the availability of camera footage of the incident, prosecutions were only brought against one ex-sergeant, who became known in the press as the "The Lone Raider", although after the governor exerted pressure more were eventually charged and disciplined inside the force.[44]

On 3 November, Slevin banned mass meetings, but the ban was ignored. Over 1,000 police officers met and demanded a strike. Junior officers began to abandon discipline and the numbers of agitators grew. The following day came the first demand for an amnesty and some police began to cease to carry out routine duties. The governor was by now thoroughly alarmed. He called a meeting of the colony's Security Committee for 3 p.m. on 4 November. There on that occasion were Jack Cater; a brigadier standing in for the commander British Forces who was out of the colony; Brian Slevin; Roy Henry; the district commanders of Kowloon and the Island; and Assistant Commissioner Richy Richardson, the director of Special Branch.[45] The governor asked whether the police would obey orders to arrest the ringleaders. Slevin and his subordinates shamefacedly had to confess they could not rely upon that, even with the support of the military. The brigadier seemed to think that he was being asked to take over policing the colony rather than just to assist in arrests, and he too declined to give any assurances. MacLehose suddenly saw an abyss opening up before him. He feared "that we could be on the very edge of a breakdown in law and order." Slevin and his officers unanimously pleaded that the demand for an amnesty be acceded to and that something be done to ameliorate the ICAC's harsh procedures. The governor felt compelled to acquiesce.[46]

There was still some stuffing left in the government, however, and the meeting decided that the date of application of the amnesty would be fixed so as to exclude the ringleaders of the agitation and divide them from the rest. It was agreed, therefore, that the amnesty apply only to offences committed prior to 1 January 1977, save for those for which warrants had already been issued (a provision meaning that officers already interdicted were excluded from the amnesty). In addition, the governor took powers to summarily and immediately dismiss any officer without appeal (strangely, he had not been able to do this before). The amnesty was announced to a stunned colony on 5 November. Police Ordinance, Cap. 231, allowing summary dismissal for any officer refusing to obey an order, was rushed through the Legislative Council on 7 November. From the eighth, the force proceeded about its duty as normal.[47]

The disturbances had shaken Sir Murray's confidence in the force to the very foundations and his future actions were to be coloured by his perception that the RHKP was a fragile organization with members whose morale needed to be fostered very carefully indeed. He knew that the public no longer had any faith in the force and that trust urgently needed to be rebuilt. He would from now on, whenever he could, avoid revelation in the public domain of anything that would further damage that trust. He gave vent to his feelings in a rare personal letter to the head of the Hong Kong Desk at the Foreign and Commonwealth Office, two weeks after the amnesty had been announced:

> The force has improved under Brian Slevin but it appears to be schizophrenic. Operational efficiency and discipline give an impression of one of the best Police Forces in the world. But quite obviously there is a mental malaise with deeply seated and unsatisfactory attitudes and mental reserves on the part of many of the older officers, NCOs and other ranks. I am shocked to find that the police are not like a regiment. Officers feel no responsibility for their men off duty, relations between senior and junior officers are similarly non-existent.[48]

* * *

It was in the middle of this desperate period of chaos and mistrust that John MacLennan reported back to the force.[49] This time he was posted further afield. It seems that those responsible for his career were now unsure of his long-term potential or reliability, and they allocated him to a job in the New Territories market town of Yuen Long. This was a backwater. It was one of those towns not yet undergoing development, and lay amongst malodorous waterways, fish and duck ponds, and marshes near estuaries that emptied out into the fetid and shallow waters of the inaptly named Deep Bay. Not much had changed up there for years, including the corruption that had flourished across the force and which had still to abate in this sleepy hollow.

MacLennan was allocated Room 5 in the Single Inspectors' Quarters at Yuen Long Police Station. He worked initially in the uniform branch, then moved to a stint of duty at the Frontier Control Centre at Fanling.[50] It was here in these unpromising circumstances that John MacLennan's career — and ultimately his life — would begin to unravel.

5

Homosexuality

To understand what happened next to John MacLennan, it is necessary to take two factors into account: the status of homosexuality in Hong Kong; and the case of John Richard Duffy. The first is important as background to what followed. The second was one of the principal causes of the events which transpired.

Homosexual acts were illegal in Hong Kong. When Britain decriminalized homosexuality in 1967, its colonies did not follow suit and the law in Hong Kong remained frozen.[1] There was still great confusion in most minds about the very subject. The word "paedophilia" was not in currency at that time in Hong Kong and in records of the MacLennan case does not occur at all. Sex with youths and even children did not arouse quite the reactions that are common today and, in the minds of those who were not aware of the detail of the law, tended to be lumped together with homosexuality.[2] The result was that the disgust felt by many, particularly by police officers, for the abuse of minors was applied indiscriminately to all homosexual men, no matter how old their sexual partners.

This did not seem to matter overly as Hong Kong was a tolerant place, despite its conservative colonial traditions, one in which even the stuffiest of colonial officials was content to let lie what went on in the privacy of the bedroom. This was important in Hong Kong, where, as virtually Britain's last colony, many who had joined some form of imperial service in order to escape the suffocating conformity of home life had tended to end up. A larger than standard proportion of Hong Kong's expatriate community seems to have been homosexual or bisexual.[3]

Most expatriates did not treat sex as a matter of moral concern. This was of considerable benefit in a colony where ninety-five percent of the population was Chinese, most of whom did not have attitudes to sex stemming from Judaeo-Christian religion. To the Chinese, traditionally, whilst homosexuality was not considered respectable, and long-term male partnerships were impossible due to the filial requirement of producing an heir, sex per se was not subject to religious or moral sanction. Despite the fact that conservative Chinese figures maintained that homosexuality was a western disease unacceptable to the Chinese population, this was not at all the case. There are no statistics for Hong Kong, but as comparisons, according to nineteenth century European reports, Canton (Guangzhou) had more male brothels than female, and a report from 1900 stated that in Tientsin in the north of China there were 35 male brothels with 800 boy prostitutes in the city.[4]

No reliable statistics of cases relating to homosexuality survive prior to 1979, although there is indication that by then cases which were brought to Hong Kong's court usually involved some other crime or were unavoidable due to the public nature of the offence.[5] As one witness puts it, "If you didn't scare the horses, Hong Kong was OK. However, things could get ugly due to the illegality. Rent boys were police informers and involved in blackmail."[6]

The problem was, of course, and this was what had led to the decriminalization of consensual same-sex acts in Britain, that the mere existence of offences on the statute book, and the concomitant lack of any social acceptance for homosexuality, led to blackmail and extortion. This meant that anyone highly or publicly placed, who needed to find an outlet for a same-sex desire, could not do so openly and was forced to find subterranean channels. These channels were naturally open to criminal elements to control and exploit. Most egregious for the government was the problem that anyone who was being blackmailed or controlled in such ways was automatically a risk to the good government of the colony or the security of the state. So the police, and in particular the Special Branch, took an interest, even though they often held only a watching brief. Where they did take action, it was done quietly and in cases such as those involving the blackmail of government servants and important business figures, and the preferred method of dealing with the victims of these was administrative removal.[7]

Male prostitution was to some just another of the vices that could be squeezed. Procurers (pimps) of Chinese boys could provide a useful source of intelligence about their customers as well as a financial reward to the police officers who, in return, lent protection to their rackets and saw off their potential rivals. Generally, the collection of information about this sort of thing was done inside police divisions, but around 1961–62, a more formalized approach was for a time adopted when Superintendent Cadmer of CID Kowloon decided to collate colony-wide information and put it on record. At the time, Inspector Mick Quinn was tasked to create what became known as "the Black Book". He spent some time obtaining information from various divisions and in the process gained the rather unhealthy reputation as a man in the force who knew about "queers".[8]

Quite why this was done remains unclear, but for whatever reason, the work was continued four years later by Superintendent Taffy Hunt at the time of the Star Ferry riots. Hunt sought evidence on homosexuals and hauled them in, holding some for over twenty-four hours, although in the event none were charged. There has been speculation that Hunt was seeking to deflect examination of corruption or that he was seeking insurance policies, gathering favours he could call in against the day when his corrupt activities might be exposed.[9] Quinn was recalled to work with Hunt on updating the Black Book and claimed in 1981 that, when their investigations had revealed persons too senior to be prosecuted, their team had been told to back away.[10] His remarks echoed those from an unnamed source quoted in the press in 1974, which revealed that in 1966 there had been investigation of a homosexual ring involving a number of prominent Hong Kong citizens, which, if exposed, would have been "political dynamite". Statements had been taken, this source said, from teenage youths who had been paid for sex by government servants, well-known businessmen and community leaders. Three European detectives had questioned scores of people and the order to stop had come from "the very top of the Government". The source of these remarks was probably Quinn himself, for it is noteworthy that the source was making these remarks in 1974 to draw attention to the supposed (and in fact spurious) loss of the Black Book.[11] In 1978–79, when he resumed these sorts of duties, Quinn behaved and spoke as if at last he would be able to finish what he had not been allowed to complete before.

One issue concerning the motivation of police officers involved in these investigations is worth noting here. When Hunt spoke to the press later of his investigation of homosexuals, it was to defend himself and his fellows against the opprobrium they had earned through corruption. He maintained that whilst most policemen were on the take, some were also breaking the criminal law by indulging in homosexual practices and that it was these latter police officers who were morally flawed. He was not alone in holding this attitude. In 1978, moral boundaries were fixed in ways that are defined differently today. It would be right to say, however, that most police officers were committed to putting away those they believed were exploiting children or youths. Mick Quinn said the exploitation of children disgusted many, and political interference to protect those guilty of it was greatly resented.[12]

Homosexuality scarcely troubled the courts. Between 1945 and 1975, no adult European or Chinese man was charged with a homosexual act in private.[13] In the latter year, Donald Barton, the district secretary of Sha Tin, and founder of the first Hay Ling Chau handicapped scout group, was tried for gross indecency with a male.[14] The judiciary was generally not comfortable with cases brought by the police which had any indication of entrapment.[15] When cases of buggery came before it, the judiciary refrained from imposing the maximum sentence of life still open to it; in 1977, for instance, a Chinese waiter was sentenced to four years for the buggery of a sixteen-year-old.[16]

In this, Hong Kong was very different from the United Kingdom, where it was the inexorably growing number of prosecutions in the '50s and '60s that had led the establishment to conclude finally that there was a need to decriminalize. In Hong Kong, in contrast, it was not until the '70s that homosexual case numbers began to rise, and then they did so only slowly. In 1972, for instance, there was only one case; the next year, the year when John MacLennan arrived in Hong Kong, there were six. Nine cases came before the courts in 1974 and eleven in 1975. There was a large jump to thirty-one cases in 1976, but this can be seen rather as evidence of the growing police crackdown on vice than of any drive against homosexuality.[17]

Where there was public interest in prosecution, it was in cases where the press could point the finger at the colonial exploitation of Chinese children. One such occurred in 1974, when the *China Mail* caught wind of a scandal at a school. It ran the headline: "School Head A Homosexual, Say Boys" and reported that a Kowloon government school principal and a senior education officer had been accused by students at their school of engaging in homosexual activities.[18] No names were published, however, and no charges brought. The prosecution of officials was avoided if at all possible as it was felt to damage British prestige.

The tiny number of cases involving officials that did come before the courts did so when it proved impossible to avoid them. One such took place in May 1976, five months before John MacLennan went on his first leave. Brian Jenney, a high-flying, young assistant financial secretary of the government's finance branch, and his boyfriend Liu Yiu-ming, a twenty-three-year-old tailor, were arrested in a fracas outside their flat in Repulse Bay.[19] They pleaded guilty to buggery at Western Magistracy on 18 May but they were treated with considerable sympathy. Liu, who had lived with Jenney for about two years by then, had called the police himself in what seems to have been a fit of pique. Magistrate M.H.B. Newell called this "a personal tragedy" for both men and said that he thought homosexuality "is quite natural to you but unnatural to others." He bound the pair over for two years and ordered them to pay HK$200 costs. It then turned out that the Legal Department had made a mess of the case, for buggery could be dealt with only in the High Court, so the proceedings were invalid and had to be set aside. Attorney General Hobley considered that in the circumstances it would not be just to institute a further prosecution.[20]

As a result of this habitual tolerance, a considerable number of senior police officers were widely, but without any real official concern, rumoured to be homosexual. As John MacLennan had spotted in his short tour in Special Branch, one of these was Deputy Commissioner Roy Henry, who seems to have come to Special Branch's attention when he arrived from Fiji in 1973. The allegations did harm to neither him nor Superintendent Redpath of the Public Relations Wing, the other officer whose name MacLennan saw. Though they were widely spread, such rumours were ignored. Homosexual police officers were expected to behave discreetly and the practice of going abroad for sex (which at that time could not lead to a prosecution) was adopted by those known as "MacCowboys" after the closest foreign jurisdiction where this was possible, Macau.[21] Regarding what unimportant officers or junior ranks of the police force got up to, no one really wanted to know, and eyes were usually averted. Some police inspectors were living with their male partners in government accommodation by 1978, although they were careful to be discreet about it, to the extent in some cases of never being seen in public with their boyfriend.[22]

The government, occasionally pressed by London, made sporadic noises about reforming the law, but almost Victorian levels of prudishness and hypocrisy prevailed and, usually hiding behind the conservatism of Chinese members of the establishment who were said to oppose decriminalization, they did nothing. Sir Y.K. Kan, a member of the Executive Council, was reckoned to be a particular barrier to change.[23] In August 1977, rather strangely, Attorney General Hobley even drew up proposals to increase penalties for acts of gross indecency from two to five years, but this proved to be too much against the grain and he abandoned the idea.[24] The government continued to hire and employ homosexuals and didn't seem to mind, not even bothering to publish a policy on the matter. Behind the scenes, it took an unofficial "don't ask, don't tell" line, but attempts within the government to implement a policy whereby its employees could declare that they were homosexual without admitting any actual offence (and so be able to resist blackmail) were frustrated by traditional and religious elements. The police felt that nothing was clear. There was no motivation to prosecute homosexuals but the law had not changed so inaction on their part could be construed as a dereliction of duty.[25]

* * *

The tolerance in this system gave homosexuals some space to meet, find sex, and socialize. There was a lively social circle of house, junk, and beach parties, which could be enjoyed discreetly and privately by expatriates and their Chinese partners and friends.[26] Before 1980, Hong Kong even seemed to be developing a regular party circuit. At the summit of the social scale were the

New Year parties thrown by Christopher "Beppo" D'Almada e Castro at Casa Branca, his large house in Clearwater Bay. Beppo was independently wealthy, a magistrate in Western and Kowloon districts, and threw fabulous parties that people vied to attend.[27] On New Year's Eve, there was a party thrown by Concorde Travels in the presidential suite of the Excelsior Hotel.[28] These circles included members of the police force, some of whom could be quite indiscreet, even wild at times. One inspector was said to go out in drag, and he and another inspector were said to give transvestite parties, at which they showed pornographic movies to large numbers of youths in their flat in Grand Court, Kadoorie Avenue.[29] In some circles, it was fashionable for even some heterosexual officers to be camp; a very smart local officer with much promise in the force led what was known as "the Flying Circus", which would dress in gay fashion and "bomb" various police messes. One of the members of the band was John MacLennan's friend Peter Whyte, who was not homosexual.[30]

By 1978, there was a range of locations in which homosexuals could meet. Whilst most Chinese men had little to do with expatriates, and the bar scene was restricted to those who could afford to pay for it, there was a degree of racial interaction. Some Chinese men sought out expatriates as it was safer for them to find a partner away from their own community.[31] A bar in the Ambassador Hotel and before it the Firecracker Bar in the basement of the President Hotel, both in in Tsim Sha Tsui, were well known gay watering holes. There were small bars in the Yau Ma Tei area of Kowloon that were also known to cater for the gay community.[32] On the Tai Po Road, just outside Kowloon, was the Carlton Hotel, where the manager was gay, male couples were not discouraged, and expatriates, including police officers, could discreetly take partners. The Cage discotheque in Carnarvon Road, also in Tsim Sha Tsui, was a bar run by two Europeans that included police officers among its clientele, including an officer from the local CID, who was alleged to "give protection" to what was a pick-up place in the evenings, one which admitted young boys for free to attract punters.[33]

On Hong Kong Island, every night after seven, the basement Dateline Bar and Restaurant in Wellington Street turned, by an unwritten rule, into a venue where "members", the local word for gay men, could dance together.[34] Especially used on Fridays and Saturdays, there were several gay saunas, including the President Sauna in the basement of the Harbour Hotel in Gloucester Road and the Yuk Tak Che Sauna, a Shanghainese-style bathhouse in Mong Kok, the doors of which closed late at night to allow sex parties to continue in private.[35]

There were various locations for those who wished to pick up prostitutes. Until its closure in 1976, the Cellar Bar in the Imperial Hotel in Tsim Sha Tsui was one of these, as was its replacement, the Waltzing Matilda Inn in Cornwall Avenue.[36] The open streets provided others: the Star Bowl and the Ocean Terminal on the tip of Tsim Sha Tsui were favourite locations for prostitutes to seek clients.

For those who preferred the excitement of "cottaging", or "fishing" as it was known in Hong Kong, there was a series of toilets (known locally as "fishponds"), including a circuit taking in the Hilton Hotel, the public toilet on Ice House Street and Beaconsfield House in Central. Some of the public toilets near the tramlines in Western, the bus terminals in Tsuen Wan, and some restaurants near the Kowloon Walled City were even decorated and provided with cushions.[37] There was a well-used toilet at the east end of the beach at Repulse Bay, at the time the only place where gay couples could sunbathe together and a good place to cruise for sex or a partner.[38]

"Fishing" could be risky, as the police would occasionally try to entrap the men using them by dangling attractive young officers as bait. The police would raid the other locations occasionally. Men feared there was a camera filming the entrance to Dateline, but many went there anyway. The atmosphere was relaxed enough to attract men from places like England, where, despite the decriminalization of homosexual acts in 1967, social attitudes had barely shifted. Homosexual men who could afford to travel might fly in to the colony for a discreet holiday, attracted by the fact that in Hong Kong (unlike in Manila and Bangkok) it was possible to find a partner who was not on the game. The actor Wilfred Brambell, the Steptoe of the BBC comedy series, was one such, and he met his lifelong partner, a Malay man, there in the early '70s while on one of his periodic visits to his friend, RTHK broadcaster Ralph Pixton, who was widely (and rightly) assumed to be gay.[39]

In short, by 1978, there was a tolerable *modus vivendi*. But then came the arrest of Richard Duffy.

6

John Richard Duffy

John Richard Duffy, whom his friends knew as "Richard" or just "Duffy", was a successful thirty-three-year-old solicitor and businessman who in 1978 had been working in Hong Kong for eleven years. He was a man who elicited both hatred and affection, and has been described as "a Robin Hood character".[1] He was openly bisexual, with, if anything, a preference for youths, a man who took innumerable sexual partners and who was contemptuous of the legal restrictions placed upon homosexuals in Hong Kong. In this, and some alleged in perhaps other areas also, he sailed very close to the line, but he did so with much warmth of character and a visible twinkle in his eye. He was, therefore, a popular man to many, although not in the police force, at whom he cocked a continual snook. He had friends across all segments of Hong Kong society, and didn't mind whether he mixed with taipans, barristers, high officials, or the poverty stricken, as long as he found them amusing.

Duffy was a man of some means, who had a yacht on which he could entertain and a villa on the beach on Castle Peak Road, a few miles west of Tsuen Wan, where his guests drank, swam, and waterskied. From 1968, he ran a wig factory named Gilda Fashions in Tsuen Wan and there employed some 3,000 Chinese employees, many of them young men who formed a pool from which he often found sexual partners. His friends soon became aware that he had a source of youths and he was not at all averse to helping them out by supplying them. "Everybody," he said, "wanted in on my supply of male partners. I used to get indirect approaches from procurers, and subsequently certain Europeans in the Colony."[2] He didn't charge for the boys he supplied, but was not at all bothered about their age. He was known by those on the game in Hong Kong to seek boys who were under fourteen years old to supply to expatriates.[3] When interviewed by the police about this, he threatened to publish his diary revealing his high-priced clients, so the police backed off.

Duffy's factory closed in 1972, but he kept up his contacts, and found other sources of boys willing to sell their bodies for sex, for instance pupils from the King George V School. Many people did not have much money in the Hong Kong of the '70s, and selling one's body seemed an easy way to make it.

A chance meeting with Elsie Elliott on a chat show about the Charles Bronson film *Death Wish*, which Duffy and partners were promoting in Hong Kong, led to his offering her help with some of the cases that she took up against the police. This was Duffy's "Robin Hood" side. He defended for free boys who had been picked up by the police in parks, in bars, and on the streets and accused of triad membership. There was a quota system in operation in the force and junior officers needed to fill their allocated totals each month. The easiest method was to arrest those who could not defend themselves, then coerce confessions out of them in the police station. Duffy successfully fought three such charges, pointing out to the magistrate on one occasion that the statement used in the case was word-for-word identical with that used in a case he had defended at another time.[4] This did not, of course, endear him to the police, who believed, wrongly it seems, that Duffy only took the cases to have sex with his clients. He rubbed salt in the wounds he caused by writing letters of complaint to the police and the Legal Department about the conduct of the arresting officers, crown counsel, and magistrates, including criticism of the officer commanding CID Kwai Chung, Inspector Poon.[5]

Living in his glass house, it was foolish to throw stones in this fashion, but some of Duffy's friends were very highly placed indeed. Guests on his yacht included the chief justice, Sir Geoffrey Briggs, and the head of one of Hong Kong's most prominent hongs.[6] One of the photographs taken on Duffy's yacht (one that the police did not locate) had Briggs and this other eminent person standing either side of two boy pipers whom Duffy had "rented" out for the weekend from the Cape Collinson Correctional Institute (a prison for fourteen- to seventeen-year olds).[7] One of them, the photograph did not make quite clear which, had a hand up one of the boys' kilts. The emergence of such a photograph of the chief justice would have caused a shock but would not have been a surprise to many. He was notoriously effeminate; after he retired, reporter Duncan Campbell referred to him in the *New Statesman* as "the effeminate judge who left Hong Kong". He was nicknamed "Brenda" by his gay friends. Many lawyers had no doubts that he was gay, although it was not widely known that he was interested in teenagers.[8] Duffy thus had powerful contacts. He felt he was protected, which to a degree he was, and in the old, pre-ICAC days, he would have remained so.

Duffy's habit of supplying boys and young men to his friends made him enemies in the triad-linked and police-protected criminal procurement organizations operating in Hong Kong. What they did for profit and to gain a hold over their clients, Duffy did for free.[9] They wanted him out of the way. He was also at risk from those he had offended. Chief Inspector Mick Quinn made it clear how notorious Duffy had made himself across the police force:

> Quite a number of persons in the Force were very interested in Duffy not just because of his arrest on homosexuality. It was suspected he had been on the periphery of other offences [...] Every unit in the Force had some time had to dabble with Duffy.[10]

This inevitably brought him to the attention of the ICAC who wanted him to testify against corrupt police officers, but Duffy would not cooperate.[11]

It fell to the New Territories police to take him on, as Duffy lived and operated in, and drew his young men from, Kwai Chung and Tsuen Wan, where New Territories police headquarters was situated. The district commander New Territories, Mike Illingworth, was an old Hong Kong hand, having joined the Hong Kong Police in 1947.[12] He had been left in the New Territories to finish his service and was regarded by his officers as rather old-style and paternalist, but one thing he really disliked, and became very moral in his condemnation of, was the exploitation of young boys. Duffy enraged him.

So Illingworth and his senior staff officer criminal investigations, Chief Superintendent Li Kwan-ha, launched an investigation led by Superintendent Brooks of the New Territories CID.[13] Duffy's high-priced friends made this risky, however, so Brooks waited to pounce until the summer holidays when the chief justice was on leave.[14] On 14 August 1978, Duffy was arrested.[15] The police raided his yacht and houses and interrogated his staff, later claiming to have found photographs of young boys having sex and being abused. Some boys known by the police to be associated with Duffy were taken in for questioning, and Duffy later said that he had admitted the charges thrown at him as he knew the boys in the case were being beaten up.[16] On 23 August 1978, he was committed for trial at Tsuen Wan District Court charged with buggery with three boys aged fourteen to sixteen and with gross indecency with another boy.[17]

Duffy, however, was not going to go to jail quietly. He complained that he had been framed and that the three boys, all from one small area of Kwai Chung, had been coerced; the complaint was dismissed out of hand by the Complaints Against the Police Office. When Elsie Elliott wrote to him to tell him she had been shocked by the sentence he received, he wrote back to her that he had pleaded guilty because "I did not want other boys or people involved, though the motivating reason was my knowledge of my own guilt, and remorse." He told her that the boys had not made any complaint to the police about him but that he could not deny all the allegations without perjury. "He who lives in glass houses," he concluded wryly, "should not throw stones."[18] He wrote to her again subsequently to explain what he had done, having had time in jail to examine his own conduct in the "cold light of day". He had committed offences he knew were against the law, he said, because he thought it public policy not to prosecute where no coercion, assault, or young children were involved. The police had said that his "victims" were innocent fourteen-year-olds who had never had sex before. In fact, he told Elsie Elliott, they had, and the youngest was aged fifteen years, five months.[19]

However, now that he had smashed all his own windows, he could see no reason to stop throwing stones at those who had not protected him, who continued to conduct their affairs without any hindrance from the police, and who occupied high official positions which seemed to put them beyond the law. He squealed, and at length.

What he told his interrogators shocked them. Superintendent Brooks took the material directly to Li Kwan-ha who showed it to Illingworth. He in turn took it straight to Jack Johnston, the director of Criminal Investigation at police headquarters, who informed the Legal Department.[20] Interestingly, Johnston seems to have decided not to inform Roy Henry, who at that point was standing in as commissioner for Brian Slevin, who was on leave.[21] Was he left out through suspicion that he might himself have been implicated or had Johnston an axe to grind against him? There is no evidence, nor is there direct evidence of what happened next, but it is clear from subsequent events that the information then rocketed up through Hobley, the attorney general, to the governor and then to London. It was explosive.

The revelations that streamed out of Duffy's angry memory have never been revealed in full, but he and others leaked sufficient of them that they can be reconstructed in part. He alleged that a very large number of prominent Hong Kong figures were homosexual and that they were involved in various ways in illegal activities. More damagingly, he revealed that some of these men acquired very young boys through triad-linked procurers. He exposed several circles of such men operating independently.

The investigation into Duffy had in any case revealed to the police the names of some of his contacts, as Duffy found out when he was questioned by Officer Commanding CID Kwai Chung, Inspector Poon, who was now more than getting his revenge for Duffy's complaints against him. Poon told him that they had a list of named suspects that included: a superintendent and three inspectors of the RHKP; three members of the judiciary, including the Chief Justice Sir Geoffrey Briggs; an administrative officer in the Hong Kong Civil Service; and a lawyer employed by the Legal Department, who had been accused and had confessed two years before but had not been charged, his crime being that of having had sex with several boys aged under fourteen from the Kowloon New Method School.[22] Duffy heard later that this man had been tipped off by Quinn and had left Hong Kong.[23]

Duffy knew those who had wanted him got out of the way, and he told the investigators of the triad-linked procurers of whom he was aware, in particular of the male prostitute ring run by an ex-police officer named Molo Tsui, which operated out of the man's flat in Westland Gardens, Quarry Bay.[24] Tsui ran a regular 3x2 inch advertisement in the *Star* for a "boy service" bathhouse named "the Sunny Bath House", whose customers Duffy alleged included the editor of that paper. Molo Tsui, he stated, employed a prison officer named Garry to pick up boys at the Star Bowl and the Ocean Terminal complex, and used a taxi driver, Ah Chau or Chow, to collect boys who hung around there late at night. Tsui, Duffy stated, had many boys on his books, whom he would call after receiving an order. A few of them, boys aged fifteen to sixteen, lived with him. He got an introduction fee of HK$50–100 per customer, plus half the boys' fees. Duffy believed he had been imprisoned at some stage for intimidation and had been charged for selling drugs, but that he had been protected by the police.[25]

Most dangerously of all, Duffy gave information concerning a procurer of young boys named Kazi Chow, whom he said was a close friend of Sir Geoffrey Briggs.[26] When Duffy said this to Chief Inspector Mick Quinn, who had now been assigned to the case, Quinn responded that it would be dangerous for him to say that in court.[27] One assumes that Quinn had some idea of how dangerous was the ground on which Duffy was treading here; Chow seems to have been the intermediary between the chief justice and the procurer Molo Tsui, in other words the means by which Sir Geoffrey Briggs paid a triad-linked pimp for sex with youths.[28]

This was far from all of it. Duffy gave the police a list of their own colleagues who he was aware were homosexual.[29] This included the then commissioner of police, Brian Slevin,[30] Chief Superintendent Redpath,[31] and twelve other named officers.[32]

Duffy also gave details to the police of a European who kept a yacht at the Royal Hong Kong Yacht Club in Causeway Bay and lived in a cul-de-sac next to the playground of the Hong Kong Sea School at Stanley with the two Europeans who owned the Cage Discotheque.[33] These, he stated, procured boys from the school and passed them around a group of friends. Other names mentioned by Duffy included those of a senior executive of the Hong Kong and Shanghai Hotels, who lived in the Repulse Bay Hotel;[34] a textbook publisher, formerly of Longmans, rumoured to be a member of MI6;[35] a lawyer who had become a businessman in a trading company;[36] a prominent doctor and member of the BMA;[37] a well-known TV personality;[38] some other TV people;

and a businessman of a property and printing group based in Duddell Street in Central.[39]

All of this was very unwelcome news to Sir Murray MacLehose, who had just weathered the storm unleashed by the ICAC assault on police corruption and was engaged in nursing a very bruised and fragile force back to life. He was in the middle of transforming the physical and administrative structures of the colony and in reopening relations with the Communist Chinese Government. To do all this effectively, he believed that he needed to make a direct appeal to Chinese notions of "righteousness" and probity, and to their respect for "the incorrupt Mandarin". He had awakened the conscience of Hong Kong to embark upon his grand design.[40] Now he was faced with a scandal in which many members of the establishment over which he presided were alleged to be homosexuals involved in breaking the law, worse were the security risks, and worse still were men preying on Chinese boys. Those named by Duffy included two of the four most important figures in the colony: the chief justice and the commissioner of police.

It must have been absolutely clear to MacLehose, from the moment he was briefed on the Duffy case, that none of this could be allowed to become public knowledge. There had to be an exercise in damage limitation and control. Nor was it a vain hope that it all could be kept under wraps. Sir Geoffrey Briggs was due to retire in under four months' time at the end of 1978. Brian Slevin was due to retire within six months. The remainder of those at whom Duffy had so far pointed his finger were not of great consequence. MacLehose had to hope that it would stay that way.

It had always been this way in the colonies, wherever British control was felt to be threatened by a loss of prestige, but the system had its roots in the structures of power and class back home. Sir Murray MacLehose and his senior officials were to prove no exception. It should not surprise that the cover-up that they ensured of the Duffy allegations was effective and, until today, absolute.

* * *

On 19 August, DCI Johnston chaired a meeting to chart the course of action. No one at the time knew whether Duffy's accusation had any validity, although the evidence they had seized at the time of his arrest gave clear leads to some of those he had named. His list had to be tested. The team set up earlier by Illingworth was conveniently at hand to do this and making further use of it would prevent access by any new investigators to the information that had been revealed.

Li Kwan-ha, who was present, made a strong plea that a proper investigation be carried out and that the force be allowed to come down hard on culprits; he believed that the Chinese community was against everything the Duffy investigation had revealed.[41] The senior officers present would have been aware of the way such investigations had been suppressed in the past. They could have had little conviction that this time it would prove any different.

7

Yuen Long

John MacLennan began work in Yuen Long on 25 March 1978. A short time later, he and Matt Handley, who had trained with him in the Metropolitan Police and had come with him to join the RHKP, were both made prosecuting officers in the Fanling Magistracy.[1] Handley got on well with MacLennan, whom he described at the time as "normal, occasionally withdrawn, after whiskey rather excitable and loquacious."[2]

There were things going on at Yuen Long which MacLennan did not like. Manila envelopes containing cash were turning up regularly in his office, the significance of which was clear. This was a practice that was dying out across the force, division by division, and there were few by 1978 where it still continued. It seems that Yuen Long had yet to catch up. MacLennan took the envelopes to the ICAC's Community Relations Office in Sham Shui Po, Kowloon, and handed them to an officer named Anson Che Tak-ying.[3] If this became known, and it is quite possible that in the small world of Yuen Long that it did, it would not have endeared MacLennan to the divisional syndicate or even to his honest colleagues.

Nor would MacLennan's habit of bringing young men back at night to his police quarters have made him popular. It is unclear when he started doing this, or how often he did it, but at some point early in his time at Yuen Long some officers took sufficient offence to report the matter. No official action was taken.[4]

MacLennan had not been long in Yuen Long when the district commander, Mike Illingworth, paid a visit to the division and met its officers assembled in the mess. Something went badly wrong that day and MacLennan made exactly the opposite impression to the one he must have intended to make. Perhaps through a case of nerves or maybe through drinking too much beer at lunchtime, he played up, tried to be the centre of attention and made too much noise. Illingworth recalled "I found his behaviour unusual, slightly effeminate and definitely exhibitionist."[5] Aware, almost certainly, of the earlier reports, he was perhaps looking out for this. Before he left, Illingworth told the divisional superintendent, Ernie Common, to keep an eye on him.[6] It was strange that Illingworth had taken so badly to MacLennan, for at least two other officers in the division at the time appear to have been homosexual and they do not seem to have caused him any unease. Illingworth was known to have two "MacCowboy" friends still serving in the force.[7] Perhaps, as he had failed to act when told informally of MacLennan's bringing young men to his quarters, and rather than mention this, he later covered the lack of official action with the story of the encounter in the mess.

Sometime in July, MacLennan and two other expatriate inspectors from the division, Bob Wilkinson and Rab Nawaz, who had eaten an evening meal at the Better Ole Restaurant in Fanling, decided to finish off the evening with a drink at Bennina's Restaurant in Yuen Long.[8] At the table next to them was an ex-policeman named Ah Keung, who was sitting with three Chinese youths: Lau Wun-man; Tse Kwan-sang; and a third whom Keung came over to MacLennan's table to introduce, David Lau Wai-tong.[9] Lau was seventeen years old and studying in Glasgow, Ah Keung said, and wanted to join the police force.[10] He thought he should meet MacLennan as he was a Scotsman and might be able to help him, and he gave MacLennan Lau's phone number. The boy was staying with his grandmother in the nearby village of Pat Heung.

What happened after that remains the subject of conflicting accounts. According to David Lau, MacLennan phoned him subsequently to invite him for a drink, an invitation which he initially refused, although he later phoned MacLennan back to arrange to meet him in the company of his friend, Lau Wun-man. The three of them ate at the Kaiser Restaurant and, as they left, MacLennan suggested to David Lau that they go to his office to get an application form for police recruitment. David Lau agreed and went alone with MacLennan, who, instead of heading for his office, took him back to his accommodation, where he showered then suggested David Lau do so too. David Lau claimed that after he did this reluctantly, MacLennan took him onto the bed and ran his hands over him, saying "I love Chinese flesh." MacLennan then gave him a pair of yellow briefs to wear, but Lau refused to lie down or to have sex, and left, taking the briefs, but as he did so saying to MacLennan that it was "OK". MacLennan, he said, telephoned him later to apologize.[11]

Some days later, on 8 August according to Lau's account, he mentioned what had happened to another friend, Tsang Kin-ho, who had just returned from studying for a BSc at Huddersfield in the United Kingdom, and who in turn told his father, ex-station sergeant Tsang Shing. Tsang claimed to be revolted by what he heard; "Beasts should not be in the police," he said, and because he believed that David Lau was too frightened to report the incident, he himself reported it to the duty officer at Yuen Long, who that day was Inspector Peter Else.[12] Else rang David Lau and asked him whether he wished to press charges, to which Lau replied that he did, so Else immediately passed the case up to his divisional superintendent, Ernie Common.[13]

The CID was tasked to interview David Lau, who came to the police station with Tsang Kin-ho and made a formal complaint, handing in the pair of yellow underpants, which thereafter for some unknown reason were stapled to the file. At that point, Common informed the district commander, Mike Illingworth, who discussed it with his deputy, Peter Chan, and with Li Kwan-ha, his senior staff officer criminal investigations. Both said they were stunned by the allegation and wanted the issue handled outside the district.[14]

New Territories CID was then within five days of arresting Duffy. Everything they had so far discovered about him had placed his activities and contacts outside the district. Now, an allegation of homosexuality had apparently surfaced involving one of the district's own junior officers, a man whom Illingworth had already decided was suspect. Chan and Li were not about to see such a case dealt with lightly, nor did they wish at such a time to be seen to be doing so, and they advised Illingworth (who needed little persuasion) to refer the matter to police HQ in order to have it investigated by someone who did not know MacLennan.[15]

At police HQ, Richard Quine, then director of Criminal Investigation, was apprised of the case and appointed Chief Inspector Norman Rich, who was at that point serving in the Interpol Bureau, to investigate.[16] Quine was reckoned to be "the Robert McNamara of the Force, cold and calculating, interested in statistics rather than murder."[17] It is likely that to him this was just another case to be dealt with and that he had interest in John MacLennan neither as a man nor as a young officer in the force. Rich was perhaps not the best person to have been detailed to investigate the case, a man regarded by contemporaries as neither the brightest officer in the force, nor one with the greatest strength of personality. An indication of this was that Rich seemed to think, or so he claimed later, that he was conducting only a preliminary inquiry.

MacLennan was interviewed by Rich on 11 August and vehemently denied the allegations. He said that David Lau had stood at their table and asked how to be recruited into the police force. He claimed to have made enquiries with the Recruiting Office on Lau's behalf and to have telephoned him about that (the Recruiting Office could neither affirm nor deny this). He had not taken Lau back to his room. Rich searched MacLennan's quarters, and found that he did not normally keep yellow underwear, a fact confirmed by the laundry amahs of the station, who said they had never seen yellow underpants in his room.[18] When Rich interviewed David Lau, the boy did, however, seem to know the layout of MacLennan's room, but he himself muddied the waters by telling Rich that the incident had been reported without his knowledge, that he wished to continue the friendship he had made with MacLennan, and that he was prepared to overlook what had happened in the flat. He added that he knew that his friend Lau Wun-man was a triad member, though he denied being one himself.[19]

Rich also ascertained that Tsang Shing had been a station sergeant who had served in the police from 1950 to 1976, although he failed to draw any inferences from this and did not mention it in his report. In fact, Tsang had been one of the nine station sergeants of the Wan Chai division arrested by the ICAC in 1976.[20] Rich was unable to get anyone in Yuen Long Division to locate Lau Wun-man for interview and by the end of August David Lau was also out of reach as he had flown to Scotland. As emerged later, Rich could be severely criticized for six areas of his work: he did not inquire how the first statement had been taken from David Lau and whether he was shown MacLennan's quarters then; he did not compare David Lau's two earlier statements; he did not ask David Lau to take him to MacLennan's quarters; he relied on familiarity with the quarters to prove guilt; he did not make enough effort to find Lau Wun-man; and he did not investigate the possibility that there was an attempt being made to discredit MacLennan.[21]

* * *

There are a number of things that raise doubts about the Yuen Long incident. Ex-Station Sergeant Tsang's involvement is suspicious; it is highly unlikely that a man who had lost his job through an allegation of corruption would have acted for the good of the force that had expelled him. David Lau's connections were not discovered by Rich; Duffy wrote later to Elsie Elliott to tell her that he had been informed that David Lau was the nephew of a Chinese CID police officer who was a friend of Chief Superintendent Redpath, and that this man had instigated the complaint because MacLennan had investigated something connected with him.[22] This cannot be substantiated, but it became clear in the course of investigations for the later inquiry that David Lau's statements were inconsistent and did not hold water.

Lau had been unable to estimate with any degree of convincing accuracy the number of steps leading to MacLennan's flat and got the location of the flat wrong. In what were eventually to be three statements, he changed his mind about the number of telephone calls he had made to MacLennan and how he had met MacLennan for the second time. He had also altered his story about what had transpired in the flat, confusing his willingness or not to lie down on the bed and the order in which the two were said to have showered. His description of the cupboard in the flat containing underwear did not bear relation to reality. There was also the matter of his attitude to MacLennan; he had said he wished to remain friends but yet had reported him and said that he wished to save anyone else from being caught by him.[23] In addition, when Lau Wun-man was eventually located (he went into hiding and had to be arrested in 1980) he denied being a triad member, alleged that someone was trying to set him up and gave evidence that conflicted with David Lau's. He claimed to be in dispute with David Lau, who, he said, was chasing his sister.[24] Lau Wun-man proved to be an utterly unreliable witness and Elsie Elliott received information that he was a known member of the Wo Shing Wo Triad Society.[25]

On the other hand, some of the story that David Lau related was clearly true. There had been a meeting at the Bennina Restaurant as well as subsequent contact. It is not possible at this distance to provide a true account of what happened, but it seems likely that there was some form of a set-up by ex- and serving policemen in Yuen Long intent on using what they could see was

MacLennan's weak spot to get rid of him. David Lau was set to "hook" John MacLennan and was then pressured into reporting an expanded version of what took place.

If the meeting in the restaurant was indeed a set-up, one of MacLennan's fellow police officers who was with him that night must have made sure that he came there after the session in the Better Ole. Of the two, Bob Wilkinson, who was known throughout his service by the nicknames "Uncle Bob" and "Gentleman Bob", and never once drew his weapon in thirty-four years' service, is the less likely candidate. He was never known by his friends even to swear.[26] Inspector Rab Nawaz is the only alternative conspirator. It is alleged that later in his service he was discovered by a subordinate selling Frontier Closed Area permits to unentitled persons at Tak Kwu Ling police station. Some years after that, it was alleged that he was involved in a sexual assault on a male behind the Mariners' Club in Tsim Sha Tsui.[27] Of the two officers who accompanied MacLennan, Nawaz's record makes him more suspicious.

Why this set-up should have been arranged is impossible to say. Perhaps it was connected with MacLennan's visits to the ICAC office and his revelation there of the envelopes stuffed with cash he was being given. Perhaps he had inadvertently trodden on wrong toes in the division or, as he himself later suggested, in the village of Pat Heung. MacLennan may have left himself vulnerable to an allegation.[28] But if the story that MacLennan had taken David Lau to his room was untrue, as it seems, then the substance of the accusation was false.

Rich submitted his report to police HQ on 9 September. The evidence, he thought "had the ring of truth" but fell "short of proving the allegation beyond all reasonable doubt."[29] His report, with the yellow underpants still attached to the outside of the file, progressed steadily up the police hierarchy. On 12 September, DCI Quine minuted that the story had a ring of truth but that there was insufficient evidence to proceed. However, as the case concerned a police officer, he passed it to the director of public prosecutions (without, it seems, informing Roy Henry, at that time acting commissioner).[30] As he did so, Quine, perhaps prompted by Illingworth, also made a connection with Duffy, saying that the DPP should be consulted "bearing in mind the recent Duffy case. Incidentally the possibility of a link has not been overlooked, but apparently Duffy and MacLennan do not know one another."[31] Ray Astin, who was then acting DPP, wrote back on 20 September that although there was a *prima facie* case of an attempt to procure an act of gross indecency, there would be no prosecution, as David Lau, the only witness, was unavailable.[32] The attorney general, Hobley, confirmed this line.

At this point, the file was sent to the team which had investigated Duffy, presumably to see whether there was any other information on MacLennan to back up a charge, but there was nothing and they returned the file to police HQ.[33] Now sure that no useful purpose would be served by pursuing a criminal case, Quine sent the file to the Police Personnel Branch for it to consider disciplinary action, although he said that he saw no ground for the termination of John MacLennan's contract.[34] Commander personnel, Alistair McNutt, was of similar mind and recommended that Illingworth interview MacLennan and warn him that his contract would be reviewed before it ended in September 1980.[35] McNutt took the precaution of consulting Richard Smallshaw, MacLennan's old divisional superintendent in Kwun Tong, who was surprised that it had been suggested that MacLennan was gay, as he'd never seen anything in his character to indicate homosexuality. He said it was his view that MacLennan had a stubborn streak, but one he thought more of an advantage than not.[36]

Since the 1977 police disturbances, the governor had persuaded London to draft in British officers to reform the handling of personnel issues and to bolster the force. MacLennan's file now went to the two principal of these. John Over, director of management and development and an ex-British police officer, saw the file on 17 October and agreed with Quine and McNutt. The next day, Over's superior, Major-General Corran Purdon, deputy commissioner of police in charge of administration, read the file, and minuted that he agreed with all the advice given so far.[37]

With these recommendations affixed from every officer in the chain, the file was then passed by General Purdon to Roy Henry, who was standing in for Brian Slevin. Henry read the file on 19 October, and, noting that MacLennan's divisional commander had not so far been asked for his view, he sent the file over to Tsuen Wan for Mike Illingworth's comment.

The day that Roy Henry read the file was the very day that Duffy at last appeared in court. He had spent three months in custody giving information to Brooks's team and he now pleaded guilty to four charges of buggery and three of gross indecency.[38] Justice O'Connor, presiding, said that he had to have regard for public opinion and sentenced Duffy to three years' imprisonment. This was despite an oddly worded plea in mitigation by Duffy's barrister, Charles Ching, QC, who told the court that Duffy was a social crusader and added that in any case "to send a homosexual to prison is like sentencing an alcoholic to a period of confinement in a bar."[39]

Illingworth had not changed his mind about MacLennan and the details revealed in the Duffy investigation made him if anything less inclined to take a soft line. The month before, on 1 September, he had been sufficiently concerned at what had been uncovered to write Roy Henry a minute entitled "Indecency and Violence", demanding that the procurement of minors be thoroughly investigated. He had written:

> Arising from this [the Duffy] inquiry, certain information concerning homosexual activities has come to light which tends to indicate that these are fairly widespread throughout the Territory amongst all stratum [*sic*] of society; furthermore it's clear that these abominable offences go beyond the stage of consenting adults, minors are being procured or being induced into such offences and this cannot be allowed to continue. Very adverse public reaction can be anticipated as and when this situation comes to light, or is more fully appreciated, and there is already plenty of talk and gossip. I strongly recommend that these offences be thoroughly investigated with a view to eradicating these undesirable practices, which are not acceptable anywhere in the world.

Roy Henry had read this minute, discussed it with Jack Johnston (who had just taken over from Quine again as DCI) and asked to be kept updated, although it seems that he was not fully briefed on the Duffy case.[40] He could have had no illusions but that Illingworth was breathing down his neck about the issue.

So when, in the following month, Illingworth returned the file with a note demanding that John MacLennan be dismissed or at the very least be taken out of his district, Roy Henry could not have been surprised. Illingworth wrote of the view that he had taken of MacLennan when they had met in the Yuen Long mess, stating that "MacLennan is in my view a homosexual [...] Nothing is to be gained by keeping him to go through all this again in 1980" (i.e., the next time his contract was up for renewal). He added that he certainly would not want him in his district or in the police quarters he occupied. He made it clear that he did not see this just as a case of homosexuality but of the exploitation of youths, and that he connected MacLennan's case with Duffy's. As he put it:

> I would add that the law in Hong Kong and not what it is in UK is relevant. Amend the law in Hong Kong and the situation in this particular case would not have altered (any more than it did for Duffy) assuming we were to adopt the UK statute.[41]

In the UK, the age of consent for homosexual activity was twenty-one.

More surprising than Illingworth's recommendation was what Roy Henry did next, for, despite all the other recommendations he had received to the contrary, he complied exactly with Illingworth's wishes, and on 28 October instructed General Purdon to terminate John MacLennan's contract. Purdon was told not to give MacLennan any reason for his dismissal. It was contractually possible to do this, but it was a very rare course of action to take, and Martin Rowlands, the secretary for the Civil Service, whose department was entrusted with the task, could remember only one other example of it being done.[42] MacLennan was to be dismissed at a month's notice, not told why, and given no chance to defend himself.

Even Mike Illingworth was surprised at this. He later revealed his reaction when he had read on the file that MacLennan had been summarily dismissed: "Well, if you are going to dismiss somebody, you can't just dismiss him out of hand, you've got to have good and valid reasons and this doesn't seem to have been gone into at all from subsequent sight of the file."[43] Roy Henry was an officer liked and admired in the force, and no informant has been able to give any other instance in which he acted so out of character and in such a brutal fashion. Why did he do it?

In a later statement, he gave a series of what seem like obvious excuses for what he'd done. He said that he had known Illingworth since February 1973, that he valued his judgment as a leader of men and recognized his ability to wisely apply policies in the New Territories. He rather unbelievably stated that he regarded Illingworth's minute as indicating that MacLennan had character weaknesses, not particularly that he was homosexual, and then contradicted himself by saying that he felt the New Territories people were puritan and would criticize the force if it were seen to sweep accusations of homosexual acts under the carpet. He tried to make much of the fact that an officer knew that his terms of service allowed him to be terminated, and concluded that he believed MacLennan's dismissal was in the force's and MacLennan's own best interest.[44] He later added that he believed at the time that MacLennan would be able to appeal against his decision.[45]

Roy Henry was a fine police officer, who had brought the force through the disturbances of 1977 with little help from his commissioner, Brian Slevin. In his own time as commissioner (a post he would hold from 1979 to 1985), he would set in train the reforms that made the force the fine organization it is today. Comment upon him from colleagues and those who knew him personally is almost universally favourable: "Roy Henry was seen as a successful reforming Commissioner, a great improvement on Slevin, in whom senior officers had lost confidence and who drank."[46] Widely liked and almost universally admired, Henry has been described as "a relaxed, nice man who talked to subordinates".[47] He was not corrupt and he took pains to get on well with all ranks of the force. It is difficult, if not impossible, to find a police officer who will criticize him.

There is no doubt, however, that Roy Henry was homosexual. This was a matter widely rumoured at the time and as widely ignored (although the force ambiguously christened him "Roy the Boy"). It did, however, make him vulnerable. Although in his early days in Hong Kong he did his best to behave discreetly, his reputation had come with him from Fiji and from his earlier service in Malaya and Sarawak. The chief justice, Sir Geoffrey Briggs, whom Duffy had accused, had been in Borneo as a puisne judge while Henry was commissioner there from the '50s to the '60s. There were officers in the RHKP who had known him before, one of these unfortunately being Chief Inspector Mick Quinn, who was currently working for Mike Illingworth in the New Territories, employed in the team investigating homosexuality. There were fears that Quinn would try to smear Henry.[48]

When he first arrived in Hong Kong, Roy Henry had needed to tread warily, although he was less discreet when travelling abroad. He was seen in Penang in November 1980 accompanied by his boyfriend of the time, a thirty- to forty-year old Chinese man who was a cook at a hotel there. Also there then was a retired police officer named Roger Smith, who had shared a bungalow with Henry in the Sarawak Police and recounted how they had swapped partners in the middle of the night. Smith had visited Roy Henry several times in Hong Kong and had been briefed by him to touch no one in Hong Kong due to the prominent position Henry held.

Homosexual circles in Hong Kong had no doubt that Roy Henry was one of their number. Some gay men from Hong Kong saw him at a gay haunt at Pagsanjan Falls near Manila in the Philippines, where there were many young boys for hire. They would come and sit on the steps of the bungalows waiting to be taken up, and would push the boats up to the falls.[49] Some members of Hong Kong's homosexual community knew men who had slept with him.[50] As a result of this, although gay circles did not come across Roy Henry in Hong Kong, they were aware of him and christened him "Ro Ro".

Later, when the dust of the MacLennan affair had settled, and he had in effect been publicly outed by it, he became less careful. John Slimming, director of information, had served in Borneo with Roy Henry. Informed that his deputy director, Johnny Johnston, had seen Roy Henry driving a Chinese boy around in his personal car, Slimming exclaimed in exasperation "I've told him never to do that."[51]

Roy Henry died in 1998, leaving no available record of his thoughts, so we are left with the need to suggest possible motivations for his dismissal of MacLennan. Knowledge of the circumstances that would have affected him at the time is vital here. Firstly, Roy Henry was an officer who had been parachuted in, as it were, at commissioner rank from outside the force (in his case from Fiji), above the heads of men like Illingworth and Blackburn, who had served in the force all their lives. This kind of situation was notorious for causing resentment, and it is quite likely that Illingworth did not look favourably on Roy Henry and that he might have been expected to take advantage of any opportunity with which he was presented to do him injury. When the MacLennan file arrived on Roy Henry's desk, Illingworth was conducting something of a campaign against the exploiters of young boys. Roy Henry knew of the rumours circulating in Hong Kong that he was gay. Opposing Illingworth in this matter might have given him the opportunity of raising Henry's own proclivities as a reason for his failure to act. Henry was on very thin ice here, and a speedily decisive removal of a cause of possible accusation would perhaps have seemed the wisest course.

Secondly, the MacLennan case had arisen at a time when the Duffy investigation had begun to cause ripples. Henry took his fateful decision about MacLennan only nine days after Duffy's conviction. Henry knew that Duffy had information about him, but he could not know what Duffy had said, or what he might yet say, so was unable to guess what Illingworth now knew. The fact that Illingworth and Johnston had not fully briefed him on the Duffy case could be taken as an indication that they wished to keep him out of it, probably because he himself was an object of their suspicion. So Henry, a homosexual officer whose career was perhaps being put at risk by accusations made by Duffy, might well have considered it safer not to make an enemy of the man who had arranged Duffy's successful prosecution.

Thirdly, both the Duffy and the MacLennan cases had come to light at exactly the wrong time for a spotlight to be shone on Roy Henry's own sexual orientation, for he was being considered as the successor to Brian Slevin, who was due to retire as commissioner in March the following year. Henry must have had real doubts about whether he would get the job. Although he had been cleared by Special Branch vetting when he arrived in Hong Kong in 1973, he knew that his name remained on their files and that this fact would be known to Sir Murray MacLehose, in whose hands the appointment would rest.

MacLehose had not taken to Roy Henry and is quite likely to have made that clear. Despite Henry's good work in the Godber case and in his personal role in negotiating with the police agitators in 1977, MacLehose considered that he was a man "too friendly with everyone".[52] Neither Sir Murray, nor the officials he briefed in the Foreign and Commonwealth Office, believed that Roy Henry had sufficient stature to carry forward the reform of the force. The head of the Hong Kong Desk in London minuted: "There are reservations as to whether Mr Henry is of the right calibre for the job, although he would be a popular choice with the Force."[53] Jack Cater did not rate Henry highly, commenting that "it was alleged that he showed weakness".

The governor had already told the FCO that he considered Henry "was not the ideal selection for the job",[54] and so London had started to canvas for alternatives. In a meeting that MacLehose attended at the FCO on 16 August 1978, five candidates from Britain had been reviewed, and Sir Murray's top choices turned out to be Sir Colin Woods, the inspector of constabulary, and Sir Kenneth Newman, chief constable of Northern Ireland. Neither was to prove available, leaving Henry as the choice by default. The governor was still unhappy. Roy Henry's appointment would be acceptable in Hong Kong, he opined, "but he would not be seen as the man to tackle fundamental problems." In the event, no one else suitable could be found and the decision to appoint Henry was made on 24 October, although it was not announced immediately. Henry was unlikely to have been aware of that fact when reading the MacLennan file, for right up to the last minute the UK authorities, unaware that a decision had been taken, were continuing to search for candidates in Britain.[55]

In Roy Henry's mind would have been the realization that consideration for the post of commissioner would necessitate another official look at his sexual orientation. A light vetting had been carried out when he moved to Hong Kong, and another was in fact carried out some time during 1978 before he was appointed.[56] With the commissioner's job in the balance, now was not the time to have the boat rocked or for Henry to become involved in cases that might cast him in a bad light.

So Henry resolved to make the decision to dismiss John MacLennan, whom he had never met, and not wait three days for the return to duty of Commissioner Brian Slevin. This in itself is odd, not something that an officer acting in the absence of his boss would be expected to do. Henry clearly wanted the issue out of the way. One might conclude that he was not motivated by any interested in John MacLennan as a man, nor concerned about any fuss MacLennan might make during an appeal. He was, it seems, motivated by concern for the trouble that Mike Illingworth might make, and the damage that might do to his career.

8

Appeal

Throughout the three months during which he was under investigation, John MacLennan continued with his duties in Fanling, miserable, humiliated, and unsure of his fate. There was to be no reprieve offered him by Brian Slevin when he returned to duty, for the commissioner signed a minute to the secretary for the Civil Service on 6 November requesting MacLennan's termination with one month's salary in lieu of notice, with his end of service to be fixed at a date fourteen days from the issue of the letter of notice. The Civil Service Branch objected to the provision that no reason was to be given MacLennan for his dismissal, so it was agreed that he would be told verbally of the cause by a senior officer.[1] It was not until 14 November that they got around to issuing the letter and only on 20 November was MacLennan summoned to police HQ to be told by the senior staff officer personnel, John Mansell, that he was to be dismissed.[2]

Mansell duly informed MacLennan that the Yuen Long complaint was the sole reason for his dismissal. MacLennan responded passionately that he denied any guilt. Dick Lidster, who had only hired MacLennan back into the force the year before and was present at the interview, took him into his own office and told him that although he had no right of appeal under section 10 of Colonial Regulations, he had the right to petition the governor.[3] How he was to do that was not made clear, and that was all that was said to John MacLennan on that day. Disconsolate, he returned to Yuen Long to find that he had lost his job at Fanling and had been posted to Kwai Chung for temporary duty in the District Command and Control Centre. He had just two weeks left to serve.

Despite the shock, MacLennan rallied. He did not dissolve into self-pity, but immediately began to ferret out every possible path open to his reinstatement. He had little time if he was to prevent his deportation from the colony. He turned first to a friend, Chris Burns, and together they arranged to meet their boss from Kwun Tong days, Chief Inspector Jock Atkinson.

MacLennan also turned to the magistrates in whose courts he worked as a prosecutor at Fanling. Both were sympathetic characters who were known for their concern for the underdog,[4] and he consulted Magistrates Henry Daniell and Patrick Rattigan on two or three occasions.[5] He told them of his dismissal and that he wanted the Yuen Long allegation to be heard in court. Regrettably, MacLennan muddied the waters here by adding that he had seen the list of suspected homosexuals during his time in Special Branch and he went so far as to mention the names he had seen. Daniell had liked John MacLennan while he worked in his court and thought him a “very loyal, straightforward, blunt

Scotsman who was not terribly bright." He agreed to help him as he felt that he had been shabbily treated. He did not consider him gay, which was just as well, for he was not warm towards homosexuals. He had earlier lodged complaints about police officers getting drunk then sexually exploiting cadets from the Police Cadet School in Fan Gardens, Fanling.[6] Rattigan recalled that MacLennan was really distressed when they met, bordering on crying and wondering what he was going to do in such a short period as was left to him.[7] Rattigan did not believe the Yuen Long accusation for he found it "extremely hard to believe he was that kind of person".[8]

Of the two of them, it was Daniell who drove the small campaign that now developed. He had the bit between his teeth and contacted Father McGovern, who was a member of UMELCO, the body that oversaw the Complaints Against the Police Office, telling him he believed there had been a frame up.[9] He also telephoned Mike Illingworth, whom he found "unhelpful [...] I got the impression that he wanted to wash his hands of it and let him go without fuss."[10] Illingworth, alerted by Daniell, telephoned Eric Blackburn, director of Personnel and Training, who had been on leave during the earlier handling of the case, to warn him that Daniell, Rattigan, and Father McGovern were now involved.[11] By now, Daniell was trying to reach General Purdon, who was Blackburn's superior, although he did not get through at first, but instead spoke to Purdon's deputy, John Over, who was surprised at the call. Daniell, Over felt, was "obviously very emotional, surprisingly so for someone who was apparently a judge."[12] Over got General Purdon to ring Daniell back to ask him to put his information on paper.[13]

Perhaps as a result of Daniell's advice, John MacLennan was now in contact with the legal firm of Hampton, Winter and

Glynn, which often handled issues involving police officers. His solicitor, Stephen Llewellyn, drafted for him both a memorandum of appeal and a petition to the governor, although in the event the latter never needed to be submitted. MacLennan did not tell his solicitor that he believed he had been set up nor of his work with Special Branch, but he did instruct him that he wanted to face a disciplinary hearing or a criminal trial.[14]

Ironically, in ringing Eric Blackburn, Illingworth had brought about a reappraisal of the course of action he had initiated. Blackburn was an old Hong Kong hand, and a very powerful figure in the force. It was not for nothing that he was known as "Black Eric" or "the Prince of Darkness", the force's disciplinarian and "hatchet man", the senior officer tasked routinely with carrying out the unpleasant tasks of getting rid of people and "saying no" to appeals.[15] He was widely respected, feared even, but not much liked. Older officers such as Illingworth were contemptuous of him, labelling him a "jumped up ex RMP corporal".[16] At the time, Blackburn was in the invidious position of having been superseded by General Purdon and John Over, with whom there was an undefined overlap in responsibilities. In effect, Blackburn had found himself working under both Purdon and Over, and it is unlikely that this was a situation to his liking. It is clear that at times he managed personnel affairs with only a nod in the direction of his nominal superiors. He was, however, the expert in the sort of matters now affecting John MacLennan and he could see that the case had been badly handled. He was not in the slightest interested in saving Roy Henry's face, and, in what transpired, he didn't even bother to inform him of the outcome. He was probably particularly unhappy that outsiders had begun to interfere in his area and he could see the danger to the force's image were details of the case to become public knowledge. Blackburn would from now on work to unravel the mess that Roy Henry had created, but it would not be to the benefit of John MacLennan.

Blackburn instructed Senior Superintendent Mansell to advise MacLennan of his route to make an appeal. This was sensible, and when General Purdon received the letter from Magistrate Daniell and called both Blackburn and Mansell in to discuss the case, Blackburn was able to tell him that he had already put in train steps leading to an appeal.[17] On 24 November, Mansell and Lidster once again interviewed MacLennan and told him to forward an appeal through the commissioner to the civil secretary. MacLennan immediately submitted to them the memorandum of appeal his lawyers had drafted, demanding a written reason for dismissal and trial. He denied in this document that he was homosexual and claimed that this was proven by the fact that he had been vetted to work in Special Branch, where he had seen Roy Henry's name on the list of suspected homosexuals. He pointed out that Colonial Regulation 59 (1) obliged the governor to ensure that an officer was "informed of the grounds upon which his retirement is contemplated" and to give an officer the "opportunity to make representations".[18] Mansell passed the appeal to Blackburn, who decided that the grounds for termination were tenuous and advised General Purdon accordingly. Purdon decided that MacLennan had to be reinstated.[19] He told Blackburn to inform the civil secretary and to tell Commissioner Slevin about MacLennan's remarks about Roy Henry, and when Blackburn had done this, Slevin docilely agreed to the reinstatement.[20] On 27 November, General Purdon interviewed MacLennan to tell him he was recommending his reinstatement.[21]

Unfortunately, the other wheels that Henry Daniell had set in motion continued to turn, and he carried on contacting powerful people. His next call was to Martin Rowlands at the Civil Service Branch, whom he told that he thought it wrong that MacLennan had been given no reason for his dismissal.[22] Rowlands professed himself sympathetic, and seems to have been so, as in the next few days he reviewed the case and decided that the termination had been unfair, based as it had been on unsubstantiated allegations that were, in any case, not of a very serious nature. He told his deputy, A.J. Hunter, this some time after 29 November.[23]

Daniell also telephoned Elsie Elliott,[24] who went up to Fanling on 28 November and had lunch at the Jockey Club with the two magistrates and Father McGovern. The magistrates (not, it should be noted MacLennan) told her that MacLennan had seen a list of suspected homosexuals in government employ. They later claimed not to have mentioned a name, although Elsie and McGovern recalled hearing Roy Henry's name (Father McGovern thought later they might have jumped to that conclusion as the rumours about Henry were so common).[25] The magistrates "thought that this had become an embarrassment or a threat. The implication was that they were sacking him to get him out of the way."[26]

Left alone with Daniell by the other two men, she was then introduced to John MacLennan, whom she later described from their single meeting as: "a typical dour Scot, simple, down-to-earth, the kind of person we need in the police in Hong Kong" and "a little naïve and not too clever, but honest and decent."[27] MacLennan told her that he blamed triads for the affair in Yuen Long and thought that the young Chinese man concerned had been induced to lay charges.[28] She told MacLennan and Daniell that she would write to the governor. Why John MacLennan let her proceed with this, when he had been told the day before by General Purdon that he was to be reinstated, is a mystery. He seems to have told her that Purdon had given him hope of his receiving justice but that reinstatement was not in his hands. This was technically correct, so perhaps he had misunderstood or doubted what Purdon was telling him. Elsie Elliott was a redoubtable woman not easily deflected from any course of action she had set her mind on, but MacLennan should have had the sense to point out to her that now it was unnecessary to involve anyone as eminent as the governor.

Unfortunately, he did not. As both Elsie Elliott and Magistrate Daniell assessed, he was not a particularly intelligent officer. It is very probable that he had no idea just who Elsie Elliott was, or of her direct access to Sir Murray MacLehose, or of her potential to cause explosive reactions in the police and Civil Service.

As soon as she got home, Elsie wrote to the governor. She kept a couple of typists fully employed with her political and activist work, so her letter writing was always swift and voluminous. Murray MacLehose was well used to receiving letters from her. In her letter, she had some of the details in the case right, others she did not. She told the governor that she had been called in by Magistrates Daniell and Rattigan and that MacLennan intended to take legal action for slander having been unable to see either Slevin or Purdon (this was incorrect). She related that the magistrates had grilled him after their courts closed until 8 p.m. (they later denied saying this) and that "they were convinced he was innocent, and that he was not in the least likely to be a homosexual at all." She said the magistrates had looked for a motive and that "they did discover that on his first term in Hong Kong it was his duty to investigate homosexuals. They feel that he must have investigated some high policeman who now wants to get him out of the way." She did not, however, mention Roy Henry's name. She made it clear that she had been given to understand that the magistrates believed there had been a frame up.[29] Elsie delivered this bombshell to Government House by hand that night. Father McGovern rang the governor's social secretary to ensure that the letter was read.[30]

MacLennan was at the time at a meeting with Chris Burns and Jock Atkinson, so it does seem that he was unconfident of General Purdon's successful cancellation of his dismissal. He told Atkinson that in his time in Special Branch he had seen something which he described as "political dynamite" that "could blow the lid off the Colony", although he did not specify what he had seen as he said it was "more than his life was worth to talk about it." He told Atkinson of his conversation with Elsie Elliott.[31]

The governor read Elsie's letter the next morning. Unsurprisingly, things moved swiftly then. He rang both Rowlands and Purdon to say that he was not at all happy that no reason had been given MacLennan for his dismissal (Elsie Elliott had got that partially right; the governor had missed the sentences in her letter where she told him that he had been given a verbal reason after he protested). He thanked Elsie by return of post and said he was looking into the matter.[32]

The police now reacted fast. Eric Blackburn contacted Hunter of the Civil Service Branch and met him at 2.30 p.m. that day to tell him that the police wanted to reinstate MacLennan as the evidence in the case would not hold up on appeal and as Daniell, Elsie Elliott, and the governor were now interested. They both agreed that MacLennan be reinstated forthwith. That afternoon, Blackburn called MacLennan to his office and told him that his appeal was under active consideration and that his reinstatement would come within days. Blackburn was forced to lower himself to ask MacLennan to prevent his friends from making further representations to the governor.[33] Sir Murray had passed on a copy of Elsie Elliott's letter, so Blackburn would very much have resented that MacLennan appeared to have told Elsie Elliott of his sight of the names in the Special Branch file.

Reinstatement did not take even the few days that Blackburn had indicated. With the governor now interested, what had taken three months to come to pass now took one day to unpick. Still on 29 November, Alasdair Sinclair of the Civil Service Branch issued a letter cancelling MacLennan's dismissal, once again giving no reason, but adding "Any personal inconvenience or distress which my earlier letter may have caused you is regretted."[34] Although the cancellation was by now a *fait accompli*, Secretary Rowlands wrote the next day to the governor to say that they wished to reinstate MacLennan and recommending they do so swiftly. The governor agreed.[35]

On 1 December, Blackburn interviewed John MacLennan and issued him the letter cancelling his dismissal. He told MacLennan that he would be transferred to Kowloon City Division and would henceforth reside in Ho Man Tin. He made his feelings about what had happened and what he believed MacLennan had done very clear. He warned him he should "carefully weigh in the balance the possible effect of recent events on his career and decide whether or not he was well suited for a police career in Hong Kong." He made MacLennan understand that he regarded him as disloyal for going outside the force for help. MacLennan came away in no doubt that he had been given the message that he should not be surprised if he did not get promoted, and that this was because the governor had intervened on his behalf.[36]

So MacLennan was reinstated, but in the process he had ruined himself. He could not have realized at the time quite how bad his position had become, but he did know that he had been badly compromised. Blackburn's direct speaking at the final interview could have left him with little doubt. MacLennan rang Magistrates Daniell and Rattigan to inform and thank them, and later rang Elsie Elliott for a similar reason. He told her that the force had very badly disliked her intervention. They both agreed that they would not contact each other again, although by then, unfortunately, Elsie had posted him a copy of the reply the governor had sent to her letter.[37] They stuck to this, and in the event Elsie Elliott was never to meet John MacLennan again. Save for an exchange of Christmas cards that year, they had no more contact.[38]

Before leaving the Yuen Long incident, one more event remains to be reported. It may seem incredible that a man with such a sword of Damocles hanging over him should have done anything as dangerous as to pick up a male prostitute or have sex with an unknown man, but from the evidence of a youth named Bobby Po Yau-chuen, it seems that this is exactly what John MacLennan did. Perhaps it was on a night when he had drowned his sorrows in drink, or when he was feeling particularly low and needed comfort. Whatever the cause of the occasion, before the decision had been made to move him out of Yuen Long, MacLennan came across Bobby Po in Cameron Road in Tsim Sha Tsui. The boy was a curly-haired nineteen-year-old, who supplemented the meagre wages he earned as a plate metal worker by hustling on the streets, where he had the unattractive nickname amongst his fellow hookers of "Big Mouth Woman".

John MacLennan picked him up and took him up to Yuen Long by taxi and they spent the night together in his quarters.[39]

* * *

The elements of the tragedy that would unfold through the following year were now in place. Some of those elements were indubitably of John MacLennan's own doing. It could not be denied that his relationship with Slasher George and his sexual bouts with Peter and Bobby were acts committed of his own free will.

The other elements were, however, a tragic coincidence of circumstances beyond MacLennan's control. He had in all probability been set up in Yuen Long. He had then unwittingly become the victim of two senior officers who had little or no interest in him but were pursuing interests of their own. He had been saved from dismissal at the cost of the creation of enormous enmity among some very powerful and vindictive officers at the top of the force.

This had not been John MacLennan's doing. He had not asked Elsie Elliott to intervene, nor, before she suggested it, had he sought the involvement of the governor. He could have had no idea of the effect that Elsie's intervention could have. He had not told Elsie Elliott of his sight of the names of suspected homosexuals in the Special Branch file, but the magistrates had.

The attempts by Daniell and Rattigan to help John MacLennan by enlisting Elsie Elliott to his cause had set in train a sequence of events that was now inexorably leading to his death.

9

The SIU

By 23 August 1978, the New Territories District had assembled a team to follow up Richard Duffy's allegations and the information they had already acquired from the investigation that had led to his imprisonment.[1] At first, the unit was held on the New Territories establishment, but its work was closely monitored by police HQ and it was the DCI, Assistant Commissioner Jack Johnston, who christened the team the Special Investigation Unit.[2] Superintendent Bob Brooks, the second-in-command CID New Territories, and the man who had investigated Duffy, was placed in charge.

Brooks was a dour Scot from Kirkaldy, a grey man who has left little trace in the records and of whom few have any clear memory. Kemal Bokhary, who represented his unit at the inquiry, thought him "an extremely able officer", but one police source describes him as "steady, unimaginative, dull". To another police officer, he was "not a bad bloke" who liked his whisky.[3] The *South China Morning Post* has a photograph of him taken in March 1980 that shows him bespectacled and with a double chin, the sort of unobtrusive man who would not be noticed in the street. Aileen Bridgewater, however, thought him sinister: "Brooks is a thug, a tough hard man who would have no mercy."[4] Brooks was adept at using his ordinariness to fade into the background and preferred to let his subordinates attract attention. At the inquiry, he struck solicitor Murray Burton as the kind of man who "kept himself clear, invisible, delegated Mick Quinn to do the dirty work and allowed others to take the flak."[5] Quinn himself described Brooks as "a person who is very abrupt, very straightforward", one who "did not, I think initially, like mixing with the homosexuals."[6]

Brooks asked for Chief Inspector Mick Quinn to be brought in to act as his second-in-command. Quinn was just leaving his job as divisional detective inspector Shatin and was about to be posted to CAPO. He did not want the SIU job, but his earlier experience with Taffy Hunt and the Black Book had not been forgotten.[7] He was a more vivid character than Brooks, an overweight Liverpudlian Irishman whose hard drinking showed in his complexion.[8] With twenty-seven years as a police officer, he was an "old school" cop,[9] one not averse to the techniques of violence and intimidation that were only just beginning then to seem unacceptable. Kemal Bokhary described him more gently as "a police officer who knew nothing of how to be diplomatic but of the type that people would want on the case if, for example, a loved one of theirs was kidnapped", and recalled that he had suffered a severe injury to his hand in the line of duty during the 1966 disturbances.

One police source describes Quinn as "an old style Police Officer and not very bright",[10] but he was intelligent enough to present himself differently as circumstances demanded. He showed this in his public appearances, giving the minimum of respect to those he considered unimportant, but prefacing many of the replies he made to the questions of the most important with a carefully placed "Sir". This did not wash with John Beveridge, the counsel to the inquiry, who was recorded as saying with a sarcastic smile that "Quinn is just an honest Irishman".[11] Nor did it impress one who knew him who summed him up as "a Liverpool bully"[12] while another described him as "a real nasty piece of work".[13]

There was indeed a darker side to Quinn, which he did his best to hide from official notice. Elsie Elliott had crossed his path before in the aftermath of Hong Kong's 1966 riots, which she had been accused of inciting. Asked whether she had "a vendetta against him?" she replied, "Oh no". Elsie had heard that the injury that Quinn had suffered in the disturbances was caused by a rioter who cut off part of one of his fingers, and that when the man was brought into custody, he was left alone in his cell for a time with Quinn, who exacted a bloody recompense for his lost digit.[14] One of his nicknames — "Fingers Quinn" — originated in this incident.

Peter Crush described him as "an Irish thug with a reputation as a squeezer who got himself posted from DDI post to DDI post to enable himself to make money." Crush also believed that Quinn had an animus against homosexuals. A barrister friend told Crush that he met Quinn in the mess at Kowloon City Police Station after he was posted to the SIU, where Quinn told the barrister that he "was going to have fun doing a bit of queer bashing in his last few years", although, he added, clapping the lawyer's back, that the lawyer didn't have to worry as he would not touch his friends.[15] Quinn had relished his time hunting homosexuals in the sixties and had resented being prevented from prosecuting them. He also nurtured a grievance that gay senior officers in the police force (and he apparently named Roy Henry here) had prevented his promotion and shunted him into the backwater of CAPO.

Over the weeks from August to September 1978, as the SIU team assembled, those who were already present took part in the interrogation of Duffy. Initially, the SIU was given a substantial commitment of manpower: Brooks and Quinn were joined by two inspectors, one of them the Scotsman Gus Graham, who had crossed swords with John MacLennan during training, the other Chinese, Inspector Stephen Tin Chat-man. Eleven (later twenty) rank and file were gradually posted in.[16] An inspector was also seconded to the unit from Special Branch.[17]

Gus Graham appreciated neither the unit's work nor all of his fellow team members. He did not like Quinn, whom he regarded as too old for the job and someone who spent too much time in the bar. He gossiped with another officer that Quinn had leant on a crown counsel to deal improperly with a death in police custody and alleged that he cut corners.[18] At the inquiry, Graham would vehemently deny that he had said this, accusing the officer who had said it of being a homosexual and a liar (the officer was certainly not the former).[19] Others did not much take to Graham. Officers in the force thought him "a nutter" and not very bright.[20] Barrister Conrad Seagroatt thought him "a nasty piece of work". Graham was certainly antagonistic towards homosexuals, as his evidence at the inquiry revealed; he stated that "Hong Kong had always been considered a haven for homosexuals and it was the job of the SIU to purge them out."[21] Even Brooks had to admit that Graham's views of homosexuals were strongly adverse; he carefully told the inquiry that his own feelings were "a little less stringent" than Graham's on that subject.[22]

The SIU was not, save in perhaps Quinn's eyes, a popular posting; those ordered to join it did not relish the idea of tracking down homosexuals, particularly their colleagues or others in government service, and divisions were unwilling to send the unit their best men. Brooks and Quinn complained about the quality of those they were sent, many of whom they described as rejects. As Quinn put it, the SIU usually got "the lame and the weary and anyone they wanted to get rid of [...] including myself."[23] This was not a team that was going to operate with subtlety or much understanding of the gay community. There was from the start a large deal of open prejudice against homosexuals among its members, and their work, for which they felt distaste, served if anything to reinforce that.

* * *

On 4 September, the team was moved down from its temporary location in Sha Tin to police HQ, where it was placed under the command of Chief Superintendent "Big Bill" Ross, chief staff officer of the Special Operations Group (the SOG), who reported directly to DCI Johnston.[24] Ross was a Glaswegian, an old Hong Kong hand and a rugby player. He was an officer with a good reputation in the force.[25] Johnston briefed Roy Henry about the establishment of the unit, although the latter would later claim not to have known of it and seemingly kept his distance from the start.

It was Johnston, therefore, who tasked the SIU and he did so verbally; there was no instruction placed on paper at this stage.

The unit was to go after the procurers of young boys, but only in conjunction with, and on the advice of, the acting director of public prosecutions, Neil MacDougall.[26] The government was using the Legal Department to keep a firm grip on the choice of targets pursued by the SIU in what now became known as Operation Rockcorry. From the start, the SIU was restricted from investigating individuals whose exposure might have embarrassed the colonial establishment. Although the unit owed its existence to the information given by Duffy, it was not allowed to investigate those he had named. At no stage was its target list allowed to include the names of either the chief justice or the commissioner of police.

Gus Graham accompanied Brooks and Quinn to the unit's initial briefing by MacDougall, a briefing also not accompanied by any form of paper record. He recalled that the DPP told them that they were to target procurers. The problem with investigating such men was the difficulty of acquiring evidence that would hold up in court. The clients of procurers were likely to be "wealthy people in prominent positions who would not be likely to give evidence."[27] Those important people were not to be questioned speculatively. That put the SIU in a bind, one that the unit was never able to escape.

Quinn's view of what the SIU were being tasked to do sprang directly from the DPP's briefing, although it expanded upon it: "We were tasked with obtaining information on what was happening in the homosexual fraternity in respect of the exploitation of young boys."[28] He believed that these instructions came down from the top, he imagined (wrongly) from the commissioner himself. Neither Brian Slevin nor Roy Henry seems to have been involved in tasking the unit. Quinn understood that they were instructed to pursue a wider pool of targets than that described by Graham, one that included procurers, those who were security risks, and blackmailers. Blackmailing, to Quinn's mind, was "very rife in Hong Kong; I mean the most heinous offence of the lot is the blackmailing aspect to the homosexual set-up."[29] From Quinn's account, the SIU was not targeting those who were merely consenting adult homosexuals.

Yet, right from the start, the team did not restrict its operations within these very limited parameters and widened the net to take in all the homosexuals about whom they could acquire evidence in Hong Kong. These were very few at first, for the SIU knew very little about the gay community and, other than Duffy and the procurer he named, Molo Tsui, who seems to have been a CID informer since the fifties (and had later been controlled by Taffy Hunt), they had few sources immediately available to tap.[30]

> Well, the position is this, that we had little or no information whatsoever on homosexuals in Hong Kong. Nobody bothered with it at all. Nobody had a clue what was going on. Everybody knew that there were homosexuals in Hong Kong but there was nothing such as this, these Black Books. Now, when we first started we were getting masses of names, information; Police Officers were coming up and saying: "So-and-so is" and passing on such information. Anybody who gave information got named on a sheet, and if he cropped up often he was investigated.[31]

Police HQ did not help, for at first it ruled out providing the unit with the Black Books of which Quinn spoke, despite the fact that they were records which he himself had compiled and revised over the previous decade and a half.[32]

The SIU's lack of focus was not improved when it was tasked in January 1979 to look into call girl rackets; a female inspector,

Mia Thomas, was posted in to handle this.[33] By the next month, it was realized that they had run into something of a dead end. The unit had contacted a few homosexuals known to them, but even though they told these that they were not conducting a witch-hunt, "a complete panic ensued, everybody shut off."[34] The unit had been "out every night of the week" visiting homosexual haunts and detectives had gone under cover. "We had toilet patrols, we had the men going in toilets nightly and daily, and the beaches, we were paddling the beaches at weekends, photographing homosexuals."[35] They had put informants into drinking holes and

> put police officers into bars to mix with homosexuals [...] One detective was very upset about being tapped up by these [...] The detectives had to dance with these homosexuals, which the detectives didn't like doing — they had to get up and do the twist with these boys, which they objected to — it had never been done before.

No policeman, according to Quinn, ever went so far as to offer anyone sex, but the unit did arrange an agent provocateur to offer eight- to fourteen-year-olds for a yacht party. This scheme progressed as far as the hiring of some boys to act as bait, but there was a leak and no junk turned up at the Star Ferry terminal to embark them.[36] Despite all this effort, the SIU made no arrests.[37]

In one area alone were the SIU successful and that was in the recruitment of an informer. They were given, almost on a plate, the identity of a homosexual police officer who really did have a good deal of information to give about the gay community and who was prepared, through fear of losing his job, to give it. This was Inspector Michael Fulton.[38] His recruitment was something else that can be laid at Duffy's door, for after his arrest Duffy typically riled the Kwai Chung CID by telling them that one of their own was homosexual. His interrogators discovered that Fulton, who was not actually stationed in Kwai Chung but in Kowloon City, had attempted to see Duffy, and they put two and two together.[39] Gus Graham was aware that Fulton was gay; he seems to have been keeping a mental list of the homosexuals he had recognized during his service. Recognition would not have been difficult in Fulton's case, as so obvious a homosexual was he that even heterosexual police officers called him "Mother Fulton".

Fulton had been living for some time in police quarters with his boyfriend, Raymond Lam Wai-man. When they had met in 1977, Fulton was twenty-seven and Lam was an eighteen-year-old prostitute.[40] Fulton was promiscuous and carelessly open in his behaviour, a habitué of the gay watering holes and a friend of many prominent gay characters. He had known Duffy since about 1976 and had been once to his boat. He had also been introduced to Molo Tsui.[41] He had, alleged Quinn, the sad ambition of being "accepted by the upper-crust gay community and getting an invitation to their annual Christmas Party."

Mike Fulton was a likeable, good looking, highly sociable, but soft and malleable man who was highly strung, nervous, and easily confused. Even one of his closest friends, Inspector Mike McDaid, described him as "frightened, garbled, irrational", a man who "found it hard to differentiate truth from fiction, would comply under pressure without thinking of alternatives, extremely disturbed and anxious."[42] Quinn later described him as "very timorous".[43] Fulton was, sadly, just the sort of man whom intelligence operatives target as sources and it was all too easy to indicate to him that if he refused to give information, his career would be on the line and maybe worse.

At first, Quinn, who handled him, did not even have to lean too hard; "I mean there is no question of my browbeating to get this information from him, he was willingly telling me."[44] Quinn was not being truthful here, as he and his superior, Brooks, employed the age-old technique of alternating intimidation with seeming bonhomie to extract what information they could. One day Brooks would play the avuncular soft cop, Quinn the hard man, another day they would exchange roles. They promised Fulton immunity if he would sign a statement saying that he was gay, despite the fact that they had no power to do so. This was a step too far even for Fulton and he would not place a confession on paper.[45] In October 1978, they warned him that they had statements from two boys who claimed to have slept with him and which they could use against him if he ceased to cooperate. In what was to become a typical SIU *modus operandi*, only one of these boys had actually slept with Fulton, the other had not. From the very beginning, the SIU seemed not to make much distinction between true and false information, and saw no obstacle to manufacturing as much, if not more, evidence than they actually uncovered.[46]

Once it was clear that they would be able to make use of Fulton as an informer, Brooks and Quinn reported the matter to his superior at Kowloon City, Assistant Divisional Superintendent David Hodson.[47] This formality completed, they arranged their initial "meet" at the Sha Tin Heights Hotel, the first of what was to be a long series.[48] Fulton was very worried by this and summoned up courage to ask for an interview with his divisional superintendent, Jack Trotman, telling him that he was gay and that the SIU had asked him for information.[49] Trotman, was a decent, tolerant man and told Fulton that his sexuality was his own affair, that if he wanted help he should come to him, and that he should make sure that he looked after his service revolver if he invited men to his flat. He then took his agitated subordinate for a drink.[50]

Yet Fulton did not make use of this offer of help to stand up to the SIU or to stop their pestering him. Quinn described to the inquiry how useful Fulton was to the unit; at the time, he was their only source of hard intelligence about the gay community. What that meant became clear at a meeting at the Imperial Hotel in October 1978, when Fulton gave the SIU a list of names of 122 gay men he knew.[51] With the list were pen pictures for each man. He also handed to them a written brief on what he knew of the gay scene in Hong Kong. He gave them the names of two other police officers who were living with their boyfriends in police quarters, as Quinn put it, "paying the Government rent for the boys living there."[52] One of these had been Quinn's subordinate at Sha Tin, although Quinn had not realized then that the man was gay. The SIU subsequently tried to turn both these officers into informants but failed; "We got very little. In comparison, Fulton was 10,000 per cent."[53] Fulton also told the SIU that Roy Henry was gay.[54] He was, however, unable to give them any information at all about procurers or blackmailers.

* * *

Ross was not sanguine about the possibility of success in any of the SIU's investigations and rapidly reached the conclusion that the unit's work was a waste of time and resources. In an interim report he wrote in December to Paddy Clancy, he said that they were approaching the Duffy case from four angles: the identification of homosexuals; the identification of their haunts; the debriefing of Duffy's boy partners (who had been kept in "protective custody" in a hotel for over a month after Duffy's court hearing); and the establishment of sources inside the gay community.[55] Despite this widening of the SIU's remit, there had been no concrete results, and he complained that the SIU had not even been given the Black Books.[56] His plea resulted in the supply of the books, but the information they contained was found to be out of date. The books were also found to be an inadequate way to keep records so by April of the next year they were returned to the Central Records Office.[57]

Only one SIU source continued to be productive. Mike Fulton was posted to police HQ in January 1979 to work in the Research and Analysis Division of the Criminal Investigation Bureau. His boss, Superintendent "Bash" Merritt, found out that Fulton was gay in his first two weeks in post and told the head of CIB, Senior Superintendent John Clemence.[58] Both felt that Fulton should not have been placed in such a sensitive post, but the CIB was part of Bill Ross's SOG, and he told them to keep Fulton as he was an agent of the SIU.[59] As a result, Brooks and Quinn carried on unimpeded, pumping Fulton for information when they met at watering holes that included the Hilton Hotel.

By the end of that month, it was clear that the unit was making no progress, and it began to be run down. Brooks went on six months' leave on 28 February and it was planned that he would join CAPO on his return, which left Quinn in charge. By then, only seventy-five percent of the SIU's work was focused on homosexuality, the remaining twenty-five percent of their time being spent on other issues, including the investigation of Vietnamese call girls.[60] Staff began to be posted out to more useful tasks; Miss Thomas and Gus Graham departed and some of the rank and file were sent to the Marine Police to help with the influx of illegal immigrants. In April, the SIU submitted five files to the Legal Department recommending prosecution, including one on Molo Tsui, but no action was taken.[61] Quinn was left for the next four months with only two detective constables, all three of them twiddling their thumbs, and he planned to go into hospital for a routine operation in July.[62]

The SIU had been a failure. It had made no arrests. From the governor's point of view, however, the unit had done its job. He could tell London that Duffy's evidence had been probed and that no further scandal had been uncovered. Sir Geoffrey Briggs had left the colony at the end of 1978 and Sir Denys Roberts was now chief justice. Brian Slevin was in the last stages of retiring, and was replaced by Roy Henry in March 1979. London had not understood why the governor had let Slevin, who was widely blamed for the collapse in discipline in 1977, linger so long.[63] However, speedy dismissal was not Murray MacLehose's way of dealing with problems. He would neither affix public blame to subordinates nor indicate by sacking them that he no longer placed trust in them. This would have been to admit that there had been a mistake, and that was bad for prestige. Rather, he would allow those who failed to finish their term and go, either into oblivion (like Slevin), or upwards to a well-funded and honoured semi-retirement (like Briggs).[64] No trace of Duffy's allegations had surfaced in the media. Scandal had been averted. The governor could be cautiously optimistic when he submitted his annual report for 1978, although it is clear that he still feared the fragility he had faced in the force the year before:

> The complete cure of the Force will take time; but time is on its side as the quality of the young intake into both constabulary and

> inspectorate over the past five years is high. The more dubious elements are gradually leaving, and there is an excellent lot of young officers at the mid-levels [...] In retrospect, I am inclined to see the near-mutiny as a regrettable, violent and perhaps inevitable passage in the process of transforming the Force from a colonial militia into a modern constabulary — a process that has progressed far and fast.[65]

10

Pursuit

Amidst all the SIU's rather aimless thrashing about, something occurred which, whilst at the time seeming unimportant, assumes significance in the light of the events that followed. In December 1978, the SIU was instructed to target John MacLennan. They reviewed the Yuen Long case file and made inquiries to follow the case as it had been left by Inspector Rich. On two separate days, 7 and 12 December, Sergeant Leung was sent by the unit to dig around in Yuen Long.[1] Nothing was uncovered and the SIU could find no further evidence that MacLennan was homosexual. The nature of MacLennan's case had had nothing to do with procurement, blackmail, or security. Why did they take it up again?

An explanation might be offered that the officers in the SIU were in the main from the New Territories, and so were very much Mike Illingworth's men. Illingworth made no bones about what he felt about MacLennan's reinstatement; he was, he said, "saddened and had strong feelings about the misguided and ill-informed senior officers who reinstated MacLennan on appeal."[2] Brooks had been aware of the Yuen Long case while he investigated Duffy. When MacLennan's file had been referred to the SIU in September, it had been read by Brooks, Quinn, and Graham.[3] An animus against MacLennan might have been expected. This does not, however, account for the fact that in December they were instructed to take up the case again.

The creation of the SIU gave police HQ a tool to use in any case involving homosexuality, a tool of which senior officers involved in the Yuen Long incident had indeed made use in September, within a week of the SIU's move to Arsenal Street. Now, senior officers in police HQ decided to do so again. Bill Ross was asked by Eric Blackburn to continue the investigation into MacLennan.[4] Ross took this as an order.[5] Blackburn told Ross the fact that MacLennan had revealed Roy Henry's name during his fight to be reinstated.[6] Blackburn had no "normal duties" to pursue in this matter. There is only one reason why he could have given such an order to the SIU, which is that he intended to have MacLennan removed from the force. Nor was this occurrence in December 1978 an isolated event. He was to pursue this course of action throughout 1979.

The SIU has been blamed for going after John MacLennan through prejudice and ill will. It did not. The SIU was ordered to do so. What was to happen to MacLennan over the next year was not at all random or coincidental, but planned.

At a meeting at the Kowloon Bowling Club in January 1979, Quinn for the first time put John MacLennan's name to Fulton, saying that MacLennan had "pulled strings, dropped names and played dirty."[7] This was despite the instructions Brooks had given his target meeting on 2 January that procurers and prostitutes were their top targets.[8] In the event, Fulton knew nothing about MacLennan, but the pressure from above was evidently still on to get results about the latter.

Paddy Clancy later recalled that the Personnel Department again asked Ross to have MacLennan investigated in February 1979.[9] As a result, when Quinn submitted a progress report on Operation Rockcorry that month, he included a paragraph on MacLennan. All he could find to say, however, was that no evidence had surfaced and that the only suspicion about him was the Yuen Long incident. Quinn had been fed a piece of gossip by Duffy, whom he continued to interrogate in prison, and separately by Gus Graham, that MacLennan was "basking in the limelight of his victory over Police Headquarters," that he had claimed that his knowledge of homosexuals in high places had got him off and that he had attended several victory parties, one hosted by Magistrate Daniell.[10] There is no evidence that any of this was true. Quinn wrote on MacLennan's file that he was "brass-necked and arrogant for challenging his dismissal." Ross indicated the true chain of authority in this matter by telephoning Eric Blackburn to pass on the detail in this report.

* * *

Unaware of all this, John MacLennan started duty in CID at Hung Hom, a subdivision of Kowloon City Division, in December 1978.[11] His immediate boss there was already known to him, for it was Iain Grant, whom he had met first in 1974 when greeting Peter Whyte at Kai Tak Airport. Not long after MacLennan arrived, the whole station moved to a new building in Ho Man Tin, whilst retaining responsibility for Hung Hom. MacLennan was given command of a small reserve team of Chinese detectives. Their work was routine: they forwarded to the Commercial Crime Bureau forged HK$500 notes that the public had handed in; they investigated shoplifting, minor thefts, and assaults; they occasionally made arrests when more serious crimes were involved, then processed those arrested up the chain. These were unexciting duties that did not put MacLennan or his men at any abnormal risk. MacLennan settled in well and Grant liked him, although he did not think he was a flier, nor the sort of officer to set the world on fire. He had occasionally to be chased for his work.[12] The job was, however, real policing and it gave John MacLennan a respite after the distress of the previous months.

MacLennan found that he was among friends at Ho Man Tin. Felix Muller, who had joined the force with him back in 1973, was living in the same flats, and with Muller he made a small circle with which to socialize. One friend of the time recalled that he was not so close as to be a real friend, rather more of a steady acquaintance, flamboyant and loud, unusually demonstrative in that he would hug women when they met.[13] Iain Grant joined them for a drink sometimes, as did MacLennan's old friends Peter Whyte, Nick Angell, and Chris Burns. MacLennan, like many other police officers of that time, drank a lot and kept a large selection of alcohol on shelves in his quarters. The circle would meet in each other's flats or go out drinking together. When out on the town and too full of alcohol, MacLennan could be as wild as before. One friend remembers an incident redolent of that which had given MacLennan a black mark in his file in 1977. One night on Nathan Road in Tsim Sha Tsui, he picked a fight with a man, suddenly shouted "he's got a gun", then ran away.[14]

This sort of behaviour did not make him popular with all those living at Ho Man Tin. Mrs O'Connor, who lived some thirty yards down the corridor from MacLennan, described him as "a crazy guy who got drunk a lot". Her husband, Inspector Paul O'Connor, was kinder. He used to drink with MacLennan (perhaps the source of his wife's antipathy), thought him an extrovert, and liked his Churchill impression. The thought that MacLennan had any homosexual tendencies never crossed his mind.[15]

Such tendencies remained well hidden from MacLennan's police friends, none of whom considered him gay. Iain Grant, whose wedding MacLennan attended in October along with many other expatriate inspectors, had heard of the Yuen Long incident but dismissed it out of hand; the image MacLennan presented was the exact opposite of what he would have expected were the reports to have been true.[16] MacLennan continued to take female prostitutes back to his quarters and if anything did his best to make sure that this was noticed. Grant recalled an occasion when he was called by a sergeant to see a somewhat ugly looking female prostitute in the CID room. She had been brought in from Tsim Sha Tsui by MacLennan, who alleged that she had stolen his alarm clock some time before when he had brought her back to his quarters to have sex and had refused to pay her. "She was so unattractive that any normal bloke would have not wanted to confess he had a sexual liaison with her." Grant thought that MacLennan was intending to show off his heterosexuality; when teased about it, he blustered and dismissed the whole thing with a wave of his hand, without any sign of shame or shyness.[17]

A multi-faceted, perhaps divided, character, emerges from accounts of this time. Given MacLennan's self-conscious conservatism, he must have found the different parts of his life very difficult to reconcile. He was hiding something more serious than occasional sex with ladies of the night, for, some time during the year, he began a steady relationship with the wife of a wealthy

Hong Kong merchant, whose office he had visited to investigate a burglary. He kept this affair utterly secret, despite the fact that his mistress lent him a silver-grey coloured Volkswagen Beetle to use for their trysts on Hong Kong Island, where she lived. He had sold the old car he had owned when he was moved to Ho Man Tin.[18] None of his friends was ever aware of this affair.[19]

Nevertheless, the events of 1978 seem to have burst the dam that had until now mostly inhibited MacLennan from giving rein to the homosexual side of his nature. One of his drinking holes was the Waltzing Matilda Inn (a bar known to regulars later, though not at the time, as the Wally Matt) on Cornwall Avenue, Tsim Sha Tsui. There were two bars in the area with the same name, the other being the Waltzing Matilda Arms in Cameron Road, but it was MacLennan's bar that was frequented, by boys on the game and the European tourists who came there to pick them up. These prostitutes had moved their trade to the Waltzing Matilda Inn after their old pickup place, the Cellar Bar at the Imperial Hotel, had closed a few years before.[20] In the early evening, the Waltzing Matilda Inn was a place where expatriates could find English beer, but later, after 10 p.m., they would have to avert their eyes from a different type of clientele. It was a small and sleazy place, the tiny bar on one side and the opposite wall partitioned into cubicles with tables.

The Waltzing Matilda's bar tender, Dick Stanford, was both gay and a police informant, not that the police needed to be told much about the bar, as many younger police officers were regulars there. Stanford kept them in the picture about the men who frequented the place. He told the SIU that he thought MacLennan was a man with two characters. The first was always in evidence when colleagues were around, when he behaved in a very superior, standoffish, fashion and particularly when he had taken a few drinks, MacLennan would become "bombastic, pompous and colonial" with the Chinese staff. When alone, however, or not with those who knew him, he was a friendly man who tried to engage the Chinese waiters in conversation. Stanford guessed that he was a closet homosexual.[21]

Now more frequently than before, MacLennan began to take male prostitutes back to his quarters. Although the evidence is in its detail unreliable, it seems that while crossing the harbour by ferry one day he came across Bobby Po, the boy whom he had taken back to Yuen Long the year before. They hooked up again and went to what Bobby thought was the flat of a friend in Ho Man Tin, but which seems more likely to have been MacLennan's.[22] They met again several times for sex, and on one occasion, either in the Waltzing Matilda, or more likely at Tsim Sha Tsui pier, Bobby introduced MacLennan to Jimmy Cheung Kwan-ching.

Jimmy was a twenty-five-year-old garment factory worker, bisexual and married with a daughter, who had arrived in Hong Kong from China only six years before. He had become a prostitute in 1977, when he had been introduced to sex at a tea party by a pimp named Eddie and found that he liked it. He worked for several procurers, including Eddie, who had taken him to a wooden hut in Diamond Hill for his first encounter with a Chinese man, and for another called Lo Leung ("Old Lady"), who pimped him to a tourist in a Tsim Sha Tsui hotel. MacLennan took Jimmy back to Ho Man Tin and he featured irregularly in his life during the year; they met on some five occasions and had sex three times, something Bobby seems to have been jealous about (the fees he forfeited no doubt had something to do with that).[23] Bobby did not let his feelings prevent his seeing MacLennan as well, and he visited him occasionally on Saturday nights at Ho Man Tin, being paid HK$50 each time.[24]

Another prostitute about whom there is convincing evidence that MacLennan met around this time was Peter Sung, whom MacLennan had first come across in 1977. They now crossed paths again and Peter visited the Ho Man Tin flat about four times, charging MacLennan HK$50 or $100 each time, but giving MacLennan sex for only HK$20 on the last occasion, as by then he had begun to think of him as a friend and fancied him. Peter knew the Ho Man Tin flats well, as he claimed to have two other customers there. The last time he visited MacLennan, which was in about August 1979, he took a friend with him named Alan (his full name is not recorded), whom he wanted to introduce as a potential boyfriend. In doing this, there is no doubt that Peter Sung was trying to do both men a favour. Alan stayed the night.[25] He was rather sweet, a twenty-one-year-old hotel masseur who was conflicted about his sexual orientation and who was in denial that he was gay. He later stated that he and MacLennan slept together for only three hours that night. They had stayed up late discussing life and philosophy, and they had not had sex. John MacLennan drove him home early in the morning.[26]

* * *

By mid-1979, it was beginning to look as though the pursuit of homosexuals in Hong Kong had been a temporary aberration. The gay community began to feel that it could set aside its fears and settle back into the ways of life it had followed comfortably in the past. The SIU was apparently on its last legs and was no longer conducting inquiries.

John MacLennan had never been part of Hong Kong's gay scene and had not gone to Dateline or the big gay parties, so he could not have been aware of the gradual easing of tension around him, but his own situation also seemed to be improving. He had, he could begin to imagine, survived the Yuen Long incident, had settled well in his new post and had started to live life again. He may even have begun to consider that he might, perhaps, have a career ahead of him in the force.

This increasingly rosy picture was about to be proved an illusion. Eric Blackburn had not forgotten the man who had made a fool of the force and whom he had failed since to expel. More ominously, in Stanley Prison John Richard Duffy was still fuming about the injustice he felt he had suffered by being the only man picked upon for prosecution. He was about to have an application to appeal his three-year sentence denied. The furies that this would unleash would give Blackburn another opportunity to destroy John MacLennan, and it was one he would take.

The final element in this noxious mix was now on its way to Hong Kong, for a new attorney general had just been appointed, and he had resolved to apply in full the laws against homosexuality. Hong Kong's gay world was about to be placed under siege.

11

The Honourable John Griffiths

John Hobley retired from the post of attorney general in May 1979 and, contrary to longstanding custom, the governor asked London to find a replacement from the United Kingdom. The post was an important one, its incumbent ranking eighth in the colony's order of precedence. Sir Murray felt that there was a need for a new broom in the Legal Department and that such was unlikely to be wielded by anyone promoted from the 150 or so lawyers within it.[1] When Lord Carrington, the foreign secretary, visited the colony that summer he was briefed that the appointment was considered "an experiment".[2] It was not to prove a successful one.

The new man came with a high reputation and must have seemed to MacLehose to fulfil all his specifications. John Griffiths was a London silk, with a good name and a fine practice in 2 Crown Office Row Chambers.[3] He had been made a recorder in 1972 and had worked in Hong Kong before, appointed as prosecutor in 1977 in the abortive opium and heroin trafficking case against Ma Sik-yu ("White Powder" Ma) and his younger brother Ma Sik-chun ("Golden" Ma).[4] Griffiths was a tall, attractive man with an impressive mind, a razor sharp memory, and a persuasive tongue, something of an actor manqué (he had played Shakespeare once with Michael Hordern). He was well read, cultured, and had a charm that was highly attractive to some women, whose company he enjoyed.[5] The other sides of his character would make themselves known only after he was in post. Sir Denys Roberts, the chief justice, would later describe him as "a good looking but rather excitable man" who did not enjoy situations in which "endless patience seemed to be required".[6]

Before travelling to Hong Kong, Griffiths took time to prepare himself for his new role. Two of the issues that were flagged up to him at the start were the colony's anomalous position on homosexuality and the abuse of children that was occurring there. He was briefed on these by the deputy undersecretary at the foreign and commonwealth office, who doubtless made him aware of some elements of the Duffy case and the doubts about Sir Geoffrey Briggs and Commissioner Brian Slevin.[7]

Paedophilia was in the news in London at the time and in a way that involved the Foreign Office. Since 1975, the activities of the Paedophile Information Exchange, or PIE, had caused growing concern. It had worked hard to link itself with the country's young gay rights groups as well as with civil liberties organizations, such as the National Council for Civil Liberties. It succeeded so well that in the years 1979 and 1980 it even managed to extract a grant of £70,000 from the government.[8] By then, a reaction had already begun and in 1978 the Metropolitan

Police raided PIE's offices and brought to trial five of its leading members, who were convicted of promoting contacts between adults and children in the organization's magazine, *MagP. I.E.* What was not known at the time, but would have been embarrassingly clear to the senior officials in the FCO, was that a sixth man, who went under the name of Peter Henderson, had not been charged along with his fellows, for this was in reality Sir Peter Hayman, who had served in MI6 and had been both British minister in Berlin and high commissioner to Canada. Not only was Hayman a member of PIE, but he had been separately investigated in 1978 for leaving a parcel of obscene material on a London bus.[9]

When the deputy undersecretary briefed John Griffiths, the FCO and the security services were managing to keep all this under wraps, but they must have viewed with alarm the possibility of scandals involving the abuse of children breaking out in Hong Kong. The likely drift of the briefing would have been for Griffiths to be aware, to exercise discretion, and above all to keep any cases out of the public arena.

Griffiths also arranged to meet Neil Duncan, a campaigner for the Movement for Homosexual Law Reform, which was seeking to amend Hong Kong's law. He lunched with a group of Hong Kong journalists, including Derek Davies, the highly influential editor of the *Far Eastern Economic Review*, the leading political and economic English language journal in the Far East at that time.[10] It is not known exactly what these told him, although one might surmise that Derek Davies, who was a very well-informed man, bent his ear about the lack of prosecutions of powerful men following the Duffy case and the widespread rumours in Hong Kong about judges, law officers, the two police commissioners and others. All these would have been linked, perhaps, with clear indications of journalistic revulsion at the exploitation of children.

Griffiths does not seem to have had much sympathy for the homosexual cause. Some of those who got to know him believed him to dislike homosexuals.[11] Nevertheless, he later made public his view that there was sense in amending Hong Kong's law to bring it in line with that in force in England and to remove the vulnerability to blackmail it created. There is no doubt, however, that Griffiths flew out to Hong Kong believing that there was a problem with the law and its enforcement, and that he would need to sort things out. The briefing he received in the FCO must have been alarming and had been reinforced by the information given him by the very knowledgeable Hong Kong journalists he had met. It could therefore very well have been the case that John Griffiths framed the policy he was to adopt in Hong Kong with the very moral intention of dealing with abusers of children. Unfortunately, it does not seem that he made much, if any, distinction between cases of paedophilia and cases of homosexuality involving consenting adults. It does not seem to have occurred to him, or, if it did so, to have worried him, that in seeking to enforce the law he would be ensnaring in his net not only child abusers but otherwise inoffensive homosexuals.

* * *

Soon after his arrival in the colony, Griffiths asked Neil MacDougall, still the acting DPP, about the Hong Kong Government's policy on the prosecution of homosexuals. MacDougall told him that in effect there was no policy and that prosecutions of homosexuals were very rare. Griffiths then asked whether there were old files extant for which prosecutions had not been mounted, as he wanted the law enforced. The DPP was not in possession of the facts and so asked police HQ, which passed his request down to Bill Ross.[12] One of the Legal Department's lawyers, Gary Alderdice, was sent to the SIU's office to collect what files they had.[13]

It was about then that Quinn heard that the new attorney general was setting about reviving investigations into homosexuals. Sometime in mid-June, he called Mike Fulton to meet him at the Wine and Cheese Bar on Hennessy Road, Wan Chai, and told him that the new AG was reviving the SIU's work. Quinn added that Griffiths was "not an ex-government man and he doesn't realise that some dogs are better left lying." Interestingly, in the light of what was to emerge later concerning an Australian procurer named Ian McLean, on this occasion Quinn told Fulton of

> a man offering drugs to European children, I think he specified European children, at the Island School in exchange for, for favours, which I took to be homosexual acts [...] He also gave me the names of certain businessmen thought to be using procurers.

These were men whom Fulton did not know.[14]

Quinn also decided to have another talk with Duffy. When Quinn saw him in Stanley Prison on 19 June, Duffy warned him that he was preparing a petition to the governor in which he was going to name prominent homosexuals. This information was passed straight up the chain of command, and that day Roy Henry wrote to Sir Jack Cater, who was now the chief secretary and had been knighted that year, telling him that Duffy's petition was on its way.[15]

It is also clear, although the Legal Department did its best subsequently to draw a veil over the impetus given by the attorney general to investigations of homosexuals, that other approaches to the issue were being given consideration at the same time. This included the vetting of government personnel. In response to this, the director of Special Branch advised on 7 June that there was a need for caution in using his files for making lists of homosexuals as the allegations they were based on were insufficient to provide proof.[16] Commissioner Henry minuted his agreement with this view on 8 July and directed his deputy commissioners to ensure that they did not make use of Special Branch files alone.

On 29 June, Griffiths received a document that dramatically confirmed his view that homosexuality was an issue that needed urgent attention. Frustrated in his appeal for a reduced sentence, Duffy tried to have his draft petition sent out of Stanley Prison to his solicitor. It was intercepted by the prison authorities and rapidly made its way through the Security Bureau to the attorney general's desk. Its contents were even more of a bombshell than the information Duffy had given the SIU the year before. Much to Murray MacLehose's dismay, when he was given the draft petition on that same day, he saw that the departure of Briggs and Slevin had not brought the end he had hoped to the Duffy affair.[17]

Although no copy of what Duffy alleged has ever been made public, it is clear that he made allegations that were highly damaging to the government, allegations that were new, and which implicated figures still prominent in the colony. From subsequent events, it can be inferred that the new list included the current chief justice, Sir Denys Roberts, the current commissioner of police, Roy Henry, and the head of another of Hong Kong's uniformed services.[18] Confirmation of this appears in a brief written by the crown solicitor for the governor in the following year, which stated:

> [the Duffy] draft petition contained general and unsupported allegations against many prominent personalities including the past and present Chief Justice, the past Commissioner of Police, Mr Slevin, and also the present Commissioner of Police.

It went on to mention that both the chief justice and the director of prosecutions, Neil MacDougall, had been made vulnerable by Duffy "in relation to wild and unsupported allegations of homosexuality and supposed links with their professional behaviour in some instances."[19] Duffy also alleged that Roy Henry and other police officers were protecting the procurer Molo Tsui.[20]

From his subsequent correspondence with Elsie Elliott, it is clear that Duffy also used his petition to fill in a lot of the detail he had left out of the information he had given the SIU in 1978. He had used his time in prison, where he was well looked after by his triad acquaintances and was having so much sex that he contracted a venereal disease, to ferret out information he had not known before. One of his sources was an Inspector Greaves, who was serving a sentence in Stanley Prison for aggravated burglary.[21] He had told Duffy of policemen involved in the narcotics trade and of homosexual inspectors who picked up boys at the Cage Disco and took them back to police quarters at Wong Tai Sin.[22] It is highly likely that he also gave information on highly placed individuals in the business world, but he was too careful to tell Elsie Elliott or anyone else of these and no record remains as to who they were.

This information was a nightmare in terms of what it said about law and order, the administration of justice, corruption, and the connections of highly placed colonial officials and business figures to triad-linked procurers. It also revealed the potential for very serious breaches of state security. The naming of the chief justice was doubly problematic here, for until the previous year he had been chief secretary, the governor's right-hand man, privy to all the secrets of government policy and personnel. The revelations Duffy seems to have made about the exploitation of young boys, however, seem at no stage to have been given much consideration, and there is no evidence that there was ever an attempt to find or give justice to the victims.

Fears of security leaks could not have come at a worse time, for the governor was then deeply involved with a security scandal involving the British security services at Little Sai Wan, an old RAF station on the east of Hong Kong Island. This was a listening post, part of Government Communications Headquarters Cheltenham, that supplied the British and their American allies with information about the Peoples Republic of China. An ex-intelligence officer, Jock Kane, who had been stationed there and had failed to gain official attention with internal complaints, had gone public in 1978 with allegations of security failures at the base. At the end of that year, Prime Minister James Callaghan had been forced to announce an inquiry.[23] The security breaches badly embarrassed GCHQ's relations with their American counterparts.[24] The next prime minister, Margaret Thatcher, would be forced to make a public statement denying all this in 1980.[25] The scandal revealed the links between corruption, the triads, and foreign intelligence agencies.

Nothing appears in the public record to indicate that Duffy's allegations involved state security. There is, though, one hint in existing documents to show that the possibility that there had been a security breach did not go unconsidered. On 24 July, the commissioner of police reported to Sir Jack Cater that

Special Branch officers had expressed interest in visiting Duffy in prison. Their interest was "in connection with Duffy's contacts with Russians"; it was somewhat vague. However Duffy was uncooperative so in fact Special Branch did not interview him.[26]

There is one other possible indication that there was some issue affecting state security at the time that has yet to be revealed. There is an unusually large number of FCO files listed in the National Archives as covering the period 1979–80 but which remain embargoed for periods of forty or more years. Some of these relate to Roy Henry and Sir Denys Roberts. Files on identical subjects, both for years before and after this period, have not been similarly embargoed. The only file on the case in the Hong Kong Public Record Office that is not just full of press cuttings is also embargoed.[27] One can only speculate as to their contents.

Whatever security concerns were in Sir Murray MacLehose's mind at the time would only have served to supplement considerations similar to those that had applied when Duffy's first set of allegations had surfaced the previous year. There remained an absolute necessity of preventing any of the allegations surfacing in public. There also remained a lesser requirement to investigate the truth of what Duffy had said. This time, however, there was also a need to make sure that London was convinced that everything was being done to deal with the problem. The emergence of allegations that were worse than those of the previous year would not have given the FCO much confidence that the matter had been dealt with thoroughly. A more formal response was required, and yet one that remained under the governor's control.

In conference with Sir Jack Cater and John Griffiths, MacLehose directed that the new allegations be investigated by the team that had worked on the case before. The SIU was to be revamped and was now to report directly to the attorney general.[28] Quinn, still its commander, was told of this in hospital by Bill Ross, who instructed him to start work by once more interviewing the witnesses whom the SIU had identified earlier. Once out of hospital, Quinn went to see Neil MacDougall, who told him to resume action on the five files that had earlier been handed to the Legal Department for possible prosecution.

Neither MacLennan nor any of the powerful people now named in the Duffy petition were named in these files; instead, they included the one procurer Duffy had mentioned, Molo Tsui, and others whose names had emerged by chance in the earlier investigations. Now, however, from what MacDougall told Quinn, it seemed that the rich and influential were no longer to be to be off limits. Quinn told MacDougall that when he had investigated similar allegations before, and had found names of prominent suspects, his inquiries had been blocked. MacDougall said that this time they were to proceed.[29] Quinn was delighted to hear this, but pointed out to the DPP that if they were to take action against all those named in the files "it would open a Pandora's box". MacDougall replied "Go ahead — everybody", a response that would later became another subject of dispute. MacDougall would deny declaring open season on the gay community and refuted Quinn's statement that he had said that the "lid was off investigations into homosexuals". Yet Quinn was quite clear about this and his later behaviour gives credence to at least his belief in what he said he heard that day. Although the DPP and

Quinn were to disagree about the policy of "gloves off" regarding the gay community, and that "even consenting adults [were] vulnerable to prosecution", both men remained in agreement that MacDougall had instructed Quinn to get more information on Molo Tsui and other suspected procurers, and promised immunity from prosecution for any witnesses giving evidence against these.[30] The DPP allocated a crown counsel with whom the SIU could deal directly. Initially this was Gary Alderdice, later it became Senior Crown Counsel Joe Duffy.[31]

Quinn asked for more manpower to take on the increased workload he foresaw, so the DPP requested this from the attorney general. Immediately, Inspectors Graham and Tin were drafted back to the unit and a new inspector, Craig Loughrin, was posted in.[32] DCI Paddy Clancy asked Peter Moor, who had once been MacLennan's district commander in Kowloon and was now deputy commissioner operations, to take the unit onto the establishment of police HQ in the New Territories District. Rank and file began to be posted in.[33]

The fact that Quinn took at face value MacDougall's direction that there were no longer restrictions on his investigations was borne out by complaints that soon reached the attorney general from some of those Quinn began to intimidate, or to try to intimidate. Foolishly, Quinn started to throw his weight about with members of the Legal Department, ensuring that his conduct would get back rapidly to the AG. Magistrate J.G. "Blue" Wilson was an Australian magistrate who for many years presided over a court in Causeway Bay and was much loved by the public for his defence of those he saw as underdogs; this, of course, did not endear him to the police. It was well known that he was gay but no one had, until now, even passed comment on this fact.[34]

He had the misfortune to bump into a very drunken Quinn at a farewell party for a police superintendent in Kowloon. Quinn lurched up and blustered loudly: "I know about your boyfriends and I am going to get you." Blue Wilson was not the sort of man to take that lying down and took a swing at Quinn, then stormed off to see the attorney general to lodge a complaint.[35] Others were less robust. Michael Bunting was a homosexual Legal Department barrister upon whom Quinn had his eye.[36] He complained to his colleague Gary Alderdice that he had been approached by Quinn, who told him that he was going to get a case against him and that he should either leave town before he was put on the stop list or take immunity in return for informing on homosexuals. Quinn also made ridiculous allegations that Blue Wilson had had sex with Molo Tsui. While Wilson's response to some of Quinn's allegations was "tell Quinn to get fucked", Bunting was not made of such stern stuff and fled to Bangkok.[37]

While Quinn set about resurrecting the SIU and throwing large rocks in the homosexual pond, the governor continued to involve himself in the issues surrounding the investigations. On 12 July, Griffiths sent him the result of his department's perusal of the SIU files, then went to Government House to discuss the matter, telling the governor that he "felt there was a public perception that there had been a cover up of homosexual cases," an opinion which he seems to have garnered from his lunch in London with Derek Davies. He also informed MacLehose that the SIU had a homosexual informant inside the force and that it was Inspector Fulton.[38]

So informed, the governor summoned Commissioner Henry and put to him Duffy's allegations about his sexual orientation, showing him the draft petition. He "strenuously denies them", he reported to London, and MacLehose seems to have taken these denials at face value.[39] Presumably he did the same with Sir Denys Roberts, the chief justice, although this is not recorded. Sir Murray did not initiate further inquiries into either man and contented himself with instructing Henry to follow up the cases now being revived by the SIU, specifically mentioning that of Molo Tsui.[40] Yet it seems that the governor did not now totally trust his commissioner, for two days later he instructed Griffiths to pass a message to Bill Ross to expedite the case against Molo Tsui. Griffiths added to this instruction his own caveat that he wished to be informed of any civil servant who came to the attention of the SIU.[41]

Within two weeks, Molo Tsui had been arrested. Of the other four named in the files, one suspect was by then in Sri Lanka and could not be extradited. A second was arrested but never named in public and escaped prosecution. This was Ka Sze (Kazi) Chow, Sir Geoffrey Briggs's old link to Molo Tsui, who agreed to give evidence against Tsui in exchange for immunity; it would have been dangerous to put him in court to tell of what he had known.[42] The remaining two were arrested: one was Gordon Huthart, the owner of a discotheque; the second was a crown counsel from the Legal Department, Howard Lindsay.[43]

Lindsay had been targeted following information received earlier from a prostitute informant nicknamed "Mars" (a boy named Kwan Kit-sang), who had claimed to have slept with a man named "Howard" but could not give his surname. Now in July, Mike Fulton supplied the name when he met Quinn and Graham once more at the Wine and Cheese Bar.[44] Lindsay would be prosecuted in the Western Court that November by Kemal Bokhary, charged with four counts of indecency, but it would be ruled that he had no case to answer as he managed, in a defence he conducted himself, to discredit the prostitutes he was alleged to have paid. He would demonstrate to the court that they were confused in the dates they had given, were connected with drug trafficking and had tried to blackmail him. Magistrate Mackenzie-Ross would declare them to be "of bad character".[45]

Lindsay would nevertheless lose his job in the Legal Department, forced to resign by the attorney general in person immediately after the case, and would have to leave the colony. He felt badly aggrieved. He had, he thought, been victimized, although he did not deny being gay and it seems that he had slept with at least some of those brought in evidence against him. He alleged that Quinn had told him that the SIU wanted to prosecute him as they were pursuing police officers and that it was only fair that they go after a lawyer from the Legal Department to maintain the balance.[46] A sour note in the affair was that the attorney general had granted immunity from prosecution to Kwan Kit-sang and an Indian boy, Hodson Hussain, alias Colin White, the two prostitutes who testified against Lindsay, in an attempt to procure a conviction of a member of his own staff.[47]

There was no way that the SIU could pretend that their prosecution of Howard Lindsay had anything to do with Duffy, procuring, blackmail, or security. Nor was there anything of that nature in their case against Gordon Huthart, who was arrested on 9 August on fifteen counts of buggery, assault, criminal intimidation, and possession of two types of drugs. He pleaded guilty to lesser offences and was jailed for eighteen months (although he served only seven of these).[48] He told Elsie Elliott that he had been forced to admit to these false charges as the SIU had threatened him they would bring more charges attracting a five-year sentence.[49]

Huthart had been on the SIU's list since 22 December 1978, when he and his partners (some of whom were alleged to be involved with triads) opened Disco Disco on D'Aguilar Street.[50] He was the scion of a prominent and rich commercial family, his father the managing director of Wheelock Marden, the company that ran Lane Crawford, which operated the most prestigious department stores in town. Gordon Huthart was openly, loudly and defiantly gay. He had been involved in the burgeoning disco scene in New York and was the first to bring it to Hong Kong, creating a glitzy, modern, and highly stylish disco where the rich and glamorous could mix and show themselves. Top actors, artists, the rich and those who wanted to be any of these things flocked in night after night, and the younger, wealthier parts of the gay world did so too.[51] Huthart was, in effect, the initiator of Hong Kong's nightlife in Lan Kwai Fong. He was also foolishly brave in poking two fingers at the police, probably relying on his connections to protect him.

When Disco Disco opened, its weekend evenings were unofficially but heavily gay. Huthart was acquainted with Molo Tsui, who used his disco to pick up young boys, and when he was arrested he was offered immunity if he would testify against the procurer. Typically, he refused "in an offensive manner".[52] Like Lindsay, he had, of course, no connection with procurement, blackmail, or security. The SIU took down with him a security guard at his disco, Yuen Pak-hoi, who they alleged had attempted to intimidate their witnesses against his boss.[53]

What happened to Molo Tsui was less straightforward. Arrested on 2 August and charged with two counts of buggery, two of gross indecency, and four of procuration, Molo Tsui then disappeared from view, remaining in police custody for a solid eight months until he appeared in court.[54] Whatever information he gave to the police in that period, there is record of only one name that emerged from his "interrogation", that of Sunny Chan Chi-fong, who, Tsui said, was "the biggest procurer in Hong Kong". This was nonsense; Chan was a minor figure, subordinate in some way to Tsui, a man who ran a "relaxing massage service", which he advertised in the *Sun* newspaper as "New Way Massage", or rather had done so until the arrest of Molo Tsui, when the advertisements stopped immediately.[55] Chan was not arrested.

Sunny Chan was not alone in advertising his services openly in the press. Molo Tsui marketed his prostitutes as part of the Sunny Bath House in the *Star*.[56] Eventually, on 3 March 1980, the local press reported that fifty-three-year-old "jewellery broker" Tsui Kwok-wah had been given eighteen months after being convicted on eight counts of procuring gross indecency. At his trial, he was found not guilty of three counts of buggery and of seven of committing and procuring gross indecency, because the crown offered no evidence on these charges. It is perhaps of note that the crown counsel who prosecuted Tsui was Warwick Reid, who was to be jailed in 1990 for corruption.[57] At the trial of this man who had been supplying young boys to expatriates since the 1950s, it was preposterously stated that only one of his "victims" had been aged under sixteen.[58] Duffy later wrote to Elsie Elliott to tell her that the police offered no evidence against Molo Tsui on the buggery charges despite the facts that they had evidence that he had supplied boys, and that no evidence was brought out to show that he lived by procurement. Tsui had been allowed to plead guilty to charges with a maximum penalty of two years.[59] Prosecuting Molo Tsui was dangerous, for he knew who his clients were and they were now vulnerable. He had leverage and there were indeed parts of the police force that were protecting him. He had been highly useful, and of course profitable, to many officers over nearly twenty years, and his usefulness was not yet over, for the SIU were to make use of him again in their campaign to amass evidence against John MacLennan.

* * *

Just four prosecutions were not much to show for all the SIU's work. It is notable that only one of these prosecutions, that of Molo Tsui, possessed any relevance to Duffy's allegations. There was pressure to do more and to get a return on the now heavy investment of resources allocated to the unit. By the end of August, its staff included one chief inspector, three inspectors, and ten rank and file, plus an interpreter and a typist. Police HQ now planned to expand the unit to comprise a superintendent, two chief inspectors, four senior inspectors or inspectors, thirty rank and file, and nine civilians.[60] Superintendent Bob Brooks came back to Hong Kong on the 14 August, his posting to CAPO was cancelled and he once again took charge of the SIU.

The problem for the SIU was that they were still at a loss for leads. As it had been when first formed in 1978, the unit was left to thrash around looking for targets. They had no safe way of getting close to the important people whose names Duffy had given in 1978 and they did not have the list of those he had more recently named. Surprisingly, as the unit had been reformed supposedly to follow up on the leads in Duffy's petition, the SIU was not given a copy of that document. Quinn went to Stanley Prison on 14 August to try to obtain one, and almost succeeded, as he gave Duffy some form of guarantee against further prosecution in return for a copy. This guarantee was to become a subject of much dispute later, as there was no legal authority for its issue. Quinn claimed that Paddy Clancy had passed him the authorization, but Clancy denied it. In any case, Quinn was thwarted by the prison authorities, who seized the copy of the petition that Duffy gave Quinn before the latter could spirit it out of the prison.[61] The following day, Clancy prevailed upon the chief secretary, to whom he had been forced to go direct, to clear the release of the petition to the SIU, but he received a copy only over the objections of the attorney general.

On 20 August, Roy Henry sent his initial report on Operation Rockcorry to the governor and a meeting was convened at Government House on the 28th.[62] Present were the governor, the chief secretary, the attorney general, the commissioner of police and his deputy operations, the DCI and Chief Superintendent Thorpe of Special Branch. The meeting reviewed a formal guideline for Operation Rockcorry drafted by the attorney general, to which the governor gave his imprimatur by reading it to the meeting himself. They agreed the increase in the SIU's strength demanded by Roy Henry and gave priorities for the operation. These were to be: procurers; the abusers of the young; and government servants involved in law enforcement. This time there was no mention of blackmail or of security, although the latter was presumably covered by the inclusion of government servants.[63] A formal directive for Operation Rockcorry was issued in a letter written to Roy Henry by the attorney general on 31 August, which became known as the SIU charter.[64] John Griffiths expanded in this upon what the meeting had discussed. He personally altered the provisions the meeting had agreed involving government servants. The targeting priorities he now directed were:

Primary target — procurers "those who profit from procuring".
Second — abusers of young boys "say of the age of eighteen or under", or the mentally or physically disabled.
Third — homosexuals "against whom credible evidence emerges during other investigations; by credible evidence I mean the direct evidence of persons directly concerned or with personal knowledge of what occurred, as opposed to hearsay, gossip, or mere suspicion."
Fourth — in response to a complaint by the public.

Griffiths went on to say that leads should only be followed concerning anyone whose name emerged as an alleged practising homosexual if it would lead to the prosecution of a procurer or abuser of young men. He made an ominous distinction here; leads regarding members of the judiciary, the attorney general's chambers, of other lawyers in practice in the courts, or of the police, should be followed up as "it is unacceptable to have those charged with the enforcement of the law themselves to be deliberately breaking it." He concluded:

> It is I suppose possible that leads may appear pointing at very senior Police Officers or, similarly, members of my chambers. These should be reported to me personally at once and I will decide the manner in which enquiries will proceed — to do otherwise would place more junior Police Officers in a difficult and invidious position.
>
> Lastly, it may be that credible leads appear pointing to senior members of the Government service. In deciding whether or not to pursue them, such cases must be considered on an individual basis, bearing in mind the position of the suspect in government and all the other circumstances.

The letter appointed the acting DPP, Neil MacDougall, and Warwick Reid to advise on legal issues for Operation Rockcorry. It also demanded that the attorney general be kept informed of all investigations.

The SIU charter could, and later would, be attacked for being both too wide-ranging in the scope of its targets and discriminatory in its application. All homosexuals could now be considered potential subjects of investigation, for there was an inherent conflict between the AG's third priority of target, homosexuals in general, and the caveat he included later in the charter that leads concerning them should only be followed up if they would lead to abusers or procurers. Until leads were followed, how could any police officer know where they would lead? In practice, it was indeed now "open season" on homosexuals.

The charter also created two classes of discriminatory exemptions. The first exempted practising homosexuals in government service from whatever benign neglect might still be afforded the rest of the homosexual population. Their holding any form of government position now made them targets. For the first time, it could now be said that an officer like John MacLennan was a legitimate object of concern. The second, more egregiously, exempted senior members of the government service from automatic investigation by the SIU. John Griffiths included this, he explained, to relieve junior police officers of the "difficult and invidious" decision to investigate their superiors. In effect, however, he had placed himself in the position of being the sole judge of such issues. Whilst colonial authority had usually behaved in this way in the past (it had certainly done so, and would continue to do so, in the Duffy investigations) such a brazen formulation was unique. It could not be supported either in law or in the public domain. Any revelation of this policy would have an effect precisely opposite to what Griffiths claimed he was seeking, which was to overturn the perception that there was a cover-up of homosexual offences involving the powerful.

This would not be the last occasion in the MacLennan affair on which John Griffiths would arrogate to himself powers and authority better left to the usual machinery of government and the law. From now on, his personal involvement in the homosexual witch-hunt that he had set in train would become more and more marked. For now, however, he must have been gratified with the way things were going, as the Duffy petition had given him the means to do what he had always intended, which was to apply the law to homosexuals in Hong Kong. Yet inserting himself so directly into this morass was unwise, for it ensured that the campaign he was now unleashing would not only damage its victims but would also come back to discredit him.

12

Set-Up

It did not take long before John MacLennan's name reappeared in the SIU's reports. The police were to claim that he "came to the notice of the SIU."[1] This assertion is unsupportable, for the circumstances make it plain that the SIU went out to find information about MacLennan, and that initially what they were able to dredge up was insufficient to justify further investigation. There is no mention here of their receiving an order to do this, but this was the same unit which Assistant Commissioner Blackburn had ordered to investigate MacLennan six months before and the order had not been rescinded.

The first piece of information that the SIU placed into the slowly forming jigsaw of their search to incriminate John MacLennan was later subject to so much obfuscation that its truth, or otherwise, is impossible to assess at this distance. On 3 August, Quinn and Graham met Mike Fulton at the Wine and

Cheese Bar. Gus Graham was to allege that during this meeting, Quinn went off to the toilet, and Fulton then told him that MacLennan had attempted to pick up his boyfriend, Raymond Lam, at the telephone box in the foyer of the Ho Man Tin quarters, where they all lived. Lam had been about to use the payphone when MacLennan had offered him the use of the phone in his room. Lam purported to believe this was a sexual ploy, one he didn't accept.

Fulton, however, was to claim that, although the event had taken place, it was Quinn who told him about it and that he himself had not told anyone of it. Plainly this was impossible, unless Raymond Lam had himself informed the SIU, something that was perhaps a possibility, but one of which there is no suggestion in the record. Fulton later suggested that the phone must have been tapped, which was a nonsensical suggestion as the supposed pickup was done face to face, not on the phone. The most common sense conclusion here is that Fulton did indeed tell Gus Graham this snippet about his boyfriend but that he later regretted saying it. The SIU were putting pressure on him at the time. Despite the fact that he had just brought Quinn a gift when he returned from holidaying in Malaysia, Fulton had found his handler in one of his hostile moods. Quinn had accused him, falsely, of taking a fifteen-year-old boy into the flats by the back stairs, an event of which he claimed to have a photograph.[2] Although the incident involving Raymond Lam was itself of little importance, nevertheless Quinn reported it to Bill Ross, who thought it worth informing Paddy Clancy.[3] The hierarchy, it seems, was still demanding reports on John MacLennan.[4]

Quinn next tapped up Dick Stanford, his source in the Waltzing Matilda, but all he could contribute was that MacLennan was bouncing cheques in Joe's Bar (not his bar, one should note, but the one across the road) and that he was "keeping the company of — or at least being friendly with — male prostitutes, as well as frequenting gay haunts like the Ambassador Hotel and the Tsim Sha Tsui Star Ferry concourse." How Stanford, standing behind the Waltzing Matilda bar, was supposed to have known this is unclear, but Quinn passed the information up the line to Clancy. Quinn tried to spice this up with his own input. He had, he said: "seen MacLennan at the bars, we knew that MacLennan was drinking heavily."[5] Both he and Clancy felt that the information they had gleaned so far was "too gossipy" to take to the Legal Department.[6] All this would have been risible had it not revealed the very sinister intention behind their actions.

In the autumn of 1979, whatever luck had hitherto remained to John MacLennan finally ran out. A series of events now ensued that was to provide the police with real evidence with which to proceed against him. The evidence that the SIU now uncovered, purely by chance, was real.

The information that emerged then was sufficient to bring MacLennan before a court. It originated from a man MacLennan did not know, a detective police constable named Liu Man, who had been posted into the SIU in September 1978. He was, it seems, one of those "rejects" bemoaned by Chief Inspector Quinn. When he first arrived in the unit, however, Liu had seemed to be talented and effective. Quinn liked him, describing him later as:

> One of the younger, more brilliant types to join us. He was outstanding in that he could speak very good English, he appeared to have a very good record and he knew the Tsim Sha Tsui area very, very well.[7]

Unfortunately for all concerned, Liu, although married, was a man who carried on clandestine affairs with men. Given the *raison d'etre* of the unit, it was strange, but nevertheless the case, that no one seems to have thought to vet the officers posted into it in terms of their sexual orientation.[8] Liu had been having an on-and-off affair with Peter Sung Chung-wah since 1971 and was occasionally still sleeping with him when John MacLennan first paid Peter for sex in 1976.[9] DC Liu later claimed that he had first met the boy at Victoria District Court in 1977, when he himself was being prosecuted for corruption by the ICAC (he was acquitted when the witness failed to appear), but he probably selected this date because Sung had been a youth aged fifteen when they had actually met.[10]

Sufficient doubts about Liu had arisen in the SIU by December 1978 for Superintendent Brooks to send him back to Kowloon City. He was suspected of leaking information to gay acquaintances in the Dateline Bar and gossip of his relationship with a young man was circulating. When interviewed by Quinn before his departure, Liu denied that he was homosexual, blamed drink for his behaviour, and alleged that there was a gay vendetta against him. The following year, Quinn saw Liu in bars frequented by Europeans and asked him to report any information he had on the gay scene, which Liu did not do.[11]

Inspector Tin would claim that when Quinn began to pull the SIU back together again after June 1979, he had his team extract what information they could from the prostitutes they knew, and from this Liu's name surfaced in connection with an allegation that he had solicited a boy for HK$1,000.[12] This was intrinsically unlikely to have been true (the sum of money was unrealistically high) and Tin was forced to admit that he had found Liu targeted as a homosexual in the SIU card index when he rejoined the unit. It seems that Liu was a target from the resumption of the SIU's work, and the unit put pressure on him to provide information about homosexuals by threatening to tell his wife about his sexual activities;[13] Quinn would later admit that the SIU had exerted such pressure.[14] Not that this was particularly wrong or out of the ordinary; it was, after all, what the unit was for. From September to October, the SIU continued to pile pressure on DC Liu, who became a very frightened man, for he did not really have any information to give to get the SIU off his back.

By the autumn of 1979, the SIU had still come up with nothing with which to incriminate John MacLennan. They, too, were feeling the pressure, as the powerful officers to whom they reported in police HQ were not content that all they had been fed so far was irrelevant gossip. Despite the fact that they had real evidence that three other police inspectors were homosexuals, the SIU had been forced to concentrate on MacLennan and his name remained top of their list of targets.[15] Paddy Clancy was breathing down their necks and demanding daily briefings.[16] In response, Brooks and Quinn were reduced to an attempt to manufacture evidence.

They initiated this at their next meeting with Mike Fulton on 24 September. This time the SIU team included Inspector Norrie MacKillop, who had just joined the unit as its administrative officer.[17] What they wanted, they told Fulton, was for him to introduce someone he knew was gay (they had the nerve to suggest that this might be Raymond Lam, Fulton's own boyfriend) to meet MacLennan and report back what happened. Fulton had no doubts that what they meant by this was that he was to attempt to set up MacLennan with a gay man with whom he might have sex, so providing the SIU the evidence they needed for a prosecution. Brooks told Fulton they had to arrest MacLennan, who was "a bad bastard and a danger to the gay community", although he could not explain what it was about MacLennan that made him so dangerous.[18] Back at police HQ, Brooks and Quinn briefed Paddy Clancy on what they had done, although they later claimed they had told him that they merely asked Fulton to "become friendly" with MacLennan.[19]

Even for Mike Fulton this demand was too much to stomach, and although he seems to have told Brooks and Quinn that he would comply, he resolved not to do so. What he was too frightened to reveal to his handlers was that he had decided the month before to call a halt to being an informer. On 28 August, he had consulted a solicitor named Claypole from the firm of Haldanes and told him that he was being intimidated by the SIU.[20] Yet even at this stage he could not find it in him to break free, and he would agree to meet the SIU twice more.

At the Imperial Hotel on 3 October, Fulton told Brooks that setting up MacLennan was a hard thing to do and that he hadn't managed it yet. The SIU was not to be deflected so easily, and six days later Fulton was called back to be told he had been stringing them along and that they now wanted evidence on MacLennan. They had, they said, been keeping Fulton "in cotton wool till now", but that would end if he did not do what they wanted and their original agreement to protect him from dismissal would no longer stand. They left Fulton in what was an "obviously emotional" state. He believed he had been told to commit a crime and he now once again sought help. He explained his difficulties to two friends, Inspector Mike McDaid and his wife, and together they drafted a memorandum to the commissioner of police.

McDaid delivered this personally to police HQ on 10 October, so effectively ending Fulton's role as an informer.[21] That day, Clancy told Peter Moor, the DC (Ops), that Fulton had alleged he had been told to set up MacLennan.[22] Although there is no record of this, it is highly likely that this information, or some version of it, was passed swiftly up the chain to the attorney general and the governor (although the latter certainly was not made aware of the detail of Fulton's allegation until February 1980).[23] Fulton saw his solicitor again and was advised to request an interview with the commissioner of police, which he did not do.[24]

The SIU's attempt to set up John MacLennan was to be one of the subjects of greatest dispute in the affair, and all those members of the unit involved would deny that Fulton had been told to bring it about. Mick Quinn was to give the CAPO interviewer who talked to him the next year two different versions of what happened at the meeting in the Imperial Hotel, firstly denying that they had made the demand of Fulton and finally saying that he had left the meeting before Brooks told Fulton what to do.[25] Fulton, however, was never to waver in his allegation that he had been asked to set up MacLennan. It has to be remembered, however, that whatever the rights and wrongs of this issue, the set-up planned by the SIU never occurred. The importance of the set-up lies in the way it demonstrates the lengths to which senior police officers were prepared to go to get rid of MacLennan.

* * *

The lack of evidence against MacLennan, however, was about to be remedied. The SIU continued to bear down on DC Liu Man and he was brought in for interview on 2 October.[26] They told him that they wanted names and he panicked. He invited his sometime lover Peter Sung to tea and told him that he was in trouble, that he needed to feed the SIU some tidbits to prevent their revealing his nature to his wife, and begged for his help. He asked Sung to give him names of some of his clients who were government officials and police inspectors. Sung refused at first and told Liu to ask "Wicky" (Ricky Kwok Siu-keung, another male prostitute with whom Liu Man had had sex). Liu kept contacting Sung and was eventually forced to bribe him with HK$500 to pay off loan sharks who were harassing him. In return, Sung gave him the names of two of his clients, "John the ICAC man" and "Colin the Whipper".[27] Why John MacLennan should have been identified by the nickname "John the ICAC man" is unclear, but from the statements of other prostitutes it does seem that the nickname was the one by which the boys knew him. Perhaps MacLennan himself told them some fanciful story about his work. "John the ICAC man", Peter told Liu, was a police inspector living at Ho Man Tin who was also known to prostitutes as "Inspector John who later went to work for the ICAC". He handed John MacLennan's telephone number to DC Liu.

"Colin the Whipper" turned out to be Colin Logan, an ex-army officer then employed as a civil servant in the Security Bureau, a man who some found to be "very conventional, even self-righteous", others "a friendly affable chap",[28] but who in reality was a sadist who was in the habit of paying prostitutes to be whipped.[29] The going rate was HK$20 per stroke and he would give up to ten strokes at a session. Peter Sung also passed Liu the names of two male prostitutes, the first being that of Alan, whom he had himself introduced to John MacLennan, and the second that of Michael Tsang Fan-tsun.

On 16 October, Liu took Peter to meet Inspector Tin at the Hong Kong Hotel, gave Tin the names he had extracted from him and left the SIU to take him into custody. Locked up over two days, Sung gave information that included his sessions of sex with John MacLennan, the names of twelve male prostitutes he knew were working in Tsim Sha Tsui and the identities of two or three of his European clients. He was unable to remember accurately the dates on which he had met MacLennan; like all the prostitutes involved in the case, he kept no diary, and it was impossible for him to remember precise dates, times or even locations; he was to give a series of muddled accounts of these over the next few months. Nevertheless, he did provide accurate details of MacLennan's flat in Ho Man Tin, he did have a record of MacLennan's telephone number, and his account of having sex with MacLennan in the Lee Garden Hotel in 1977 was found to be correct when checked against the hotel register.[30]

The SIU had been handed on a plate the information they had been seeking for so long.[31] They probably could not believe their luck. It had been only six days since they had lost their major source when Fulton blew his own cover. Now they were in possession of MacLennan's telephone number in the notebook of a male prostitute. Whatever skullduggery, driven by illegitimate motivation, they had had been involved in before was now an irrelevance. From this moment on, the investigation into MacLennan was a legitimate one, for it fell both within the law and the attorney general's charter for the SIU. The unit, however, was not about to mend its ways or to conduct an investigation with wholly legitimate methods.

* * *

On his second day in custody, in return for immunity from prosecution, Peter Sung identified MacLennan's photograph and signed a statement incriminating him. Over the two days Sung was held, Inspector Tin set about tracing the contacts he had given.[32] On 17 October, Alan was brought in and questioned about his relationship with MacLennan. Although he admitted to sleeping one night on MacLennan's single bed, he refused to state that he had taken part in any homosexual act.[33] The next day, the SIU arrested thirty-six-year-old prostitute Michael Tsang, who was induced to state that MacLennan had picked him up in Tsim Sha Tsui in December 1978 and had taken him to his flat for sex.[34] Inspector Tin claimed to have found MacLennan's telephone number in Tsang's notebook, but the entry was a later insertion and did not match the date when Tsang claimed to have met MacLennan.[35] Tsang would later fail to identify John MacLennan's photograph and would not be able, even approximately, to describe his flat.

It appeared, too, that his statement had been tampered with. On the first statement he made, which was dated 18 October, an unidentified officer in the SIU noted in pen that John MacLennan had not been living at the address given by Tsang on the date that he said he had visited there. A second statement was made which altered the date of the sexual encounter to match the address. It is clear that Michael Tsang had given the SIU the information they required. Tsang's advanced age for a prostitute also militates against the veracity of his statements. It is unlikely that MacLennan, whose taste seems to have been for younger men, would have been attracted enough to pick up a man of thirty-six. Michael Tsang had never met John MacLennan.[36]

Peter Sung now created a short career for himself as an informer, handled by the SIU's Sergeant Leung. From mid-October to the following February, he met Leung on about thirty-two occasions and was given between HK$20 and $30 each time.[37] Leung called him "an informer of a very rare kind" due to his cooperative nature.[38] The information he had first given led to the opening of an intelligence file on John MacLennan on 25 October. Quinn initiated this by writing a report "to confirm that MacLennan is a practising homosexual and to give consideration to the issue whether the SIU should continue an in depth inquiry into his background with a view to establishing further evidence against him or to proceed to trial with the available evidence." Quinn called for the Yuen Long file and wrote:

> The only suspicion against him [MacLennan] was the New Territories incident. Reliable sources, however, indicated that MacLennan was basking in the limelight of his victory over Police HQ and he claimed it was his clandestine knowledge of top homosexual personalities that had forced the Government to reinstate him [...] It is fairly apparent from fresh information obtained by SIU that MacLennan is homosexual and was extremely fortunate to avoid prosecution in the original complaint. It is extremely unfortunate, having terminated his services Government was forced to reinstate him. I consider MacLennan brass-necked to say the least in having the temerity to contest the termination. This action indicates the type of person we are dealing with. His arrogant character reveals itself in his efforts to influence the SSOP. (Senior Staff Officer Personnel) at the time of his termination of contract by inferring he is well aware of homosexual fraternity within Government [...] MacLennan can still be charged with buggery and gross indecency.

Brooks supported this, adding that "there is more than sufficient evidence to proceed against MacLennan."[39] The next day, he took the file to Bill Ross and together they walked it into the office of Paddy Clancy, who in turn took it straight to Peter Moor. The latter directed that, if the evidence proved substantial, both

MacLennan and Colin Logan should be charged, and ordered that the case be taken further.

Despite the seeming cooperation of Peter Sung, the SIU had little to show so far from the leads he had given. Sung's information was, of course, incriminating, but Alan was not a prostitute and had resisted pressure to give evidence against MacLennan (he was never to do so). All the SIU could get him to state was that at some point he had given three "happy endings" to unspecified customers whom he was massaging in the hotel where he worked. He would later refute even this and would say that he had been coerced into saying so by Inspector Tin.[40] The only other witness, Michael Tsang, had all too obviously needed to be steered to state the right things. More evidence had to be found.

On 1 November, Eddie Chu Wai-kwong was brought in.[41] This was the Eddie who had introduced Bobby Po and Jimmy Cheung to prostitution. He was both pimp and prostitute himself. Now, he gave a statement to the SIU claiming that he had been paid for sex with John MacLennan. There was nothing in reality to connect the two of them, save for a remark by Dick Stanford, who said that he remembered MacLennan being curt with Eddie one night in the Waltzing Matilda and "it seemed he knew him". Eddie gave a second statement, similar to the first, on 8 November, but then made himself scarce and was never again located.[42] There is no reason to think that he had been to bed with John MacLennan.

The SIU were on firmer ground with Jimmy Cheung. Asked by Inspector Tin about "Inspector John", he initially refused to admit that he knew him — he later said that he considered MacLennan a friend and did not want to incriminate him — but

Tin exerted pressure and Jimmy signed a statement confessing that he had been paid by him for sex. He gave Tin a card with MacLennan's telephone number.[43] Jimmy Cheung was something of a tough character, and he would later retract the statement he had given the SIU, saying that it was "false" and he would denounce the SIU for "protecting" prostitutes in Tsim Sha Tsui in return for information. He later stated that he had first met Inspector Tin at the South Kowloon Court, where he had been charged with soliciting, and Tin had asked him if he knew an "Inspector John" who lived in Ho Man Tin. Jimmy had told him he did not, but about three weeks later he had been arrested, and on that occasion he had given the statement that he had had sex with MacLennan. Tin had told him that he would not be responsible for his safety if he failed to give him the information he wanted, "even if I were chopped to death outside".[44]

Peter's list of prostitutes seems to have been randomly constructed and certainly was not aimed by him at incriminating John MacLennan. However, he and the fellows he dragged into the case were very swiftly aware that the SIU was targeting MacLennan, and while those who knew him did not want to do him harm, those who did not know him had no compunction about making false statements. One of the latter sort was Sun Kam-hung, known to his friends as "Lula", a thirty-one-year-old prostitute, who was persuaded to state that he had met MacLennan in the Waltzing Matilda and then had gone back to Ho Man Tin to have sex with him. He would later claim that he had been beaten into saying this by the SIU.[45] Confronted with this allegation, Sergeant Leung would admit that there had been a scuffle; Lula, he said, had struggled and become "a bit crazy", so he had to be handcuffed before he was taken to the police station.[46] Lula was badly in debt to loan sharks and so was vulnerable to pressure. He had information on other government servants whom he serviced in Tsim Sha Tsui, but it seemed to him that the SIU was not interested in them. The story he gave in his statement about John MacLennan did not hold water, and he was later to prove unaware of the layout of MacLennan's flat. He would retract his evidence in entirety. There is no real indication that he knew John MacLennan.

Jeff Tso Yuk-kwong, another prostitute who featured on the SIU's initial witness list, was not brought to the station to give his statement, but was interviewed by Inspector Tin at the home of his boyfriend, Dick Stanford.[47] Tso was a twenty-five-year-old with eleven previous convictions for burglary, theft, wasting police time, and membership of a triad society.[48] His previous convictions made him vulnerable to pressure, as did the fact that his lover, Stanford, was on the SIU's target list himself, despite the fact that he had been working for them as an informer.[49] Tso would consistently fail to identify MacLennan's photograph and was to describe a totally different man. He gave a total of three statements that he had been paid for sex by MacLennan, but in a fourth statement he would admit that all the previous statements had been false. Tin, he said, had threatened him with an accusation of triad membership. He confessed that he had lied to assist the SIU and to throw them off the trail of another police officer at Ho Man Tin who really was his client.[50] He did not know John MacLennan.

Moor was told of this progress and on 16 November ordered the SIU to open a prosecution file.[51] It was still a very shaky case. A lawyer like Howard Lindsay, who evaded the charges brought against him by attacking the character of the witnesses and the confused chronology they provided, would have pulled the evidence to pieces. The witnesses against MacLennan were all prostitutes, none of them remembered times and dates, and all of them were to change their minds as time went by about the details they had given. Only two of those so far named as having had sex with MacLennan — Peter Sung and Jimmy Cheung — had actually done so. The other witnesses were all false: Michael Tsang, Eddie Chu, Lula Sun Kam-hung, and Jeff Tso had all lied to comply with SIU instructions. The unit would find more witnesses later, but all but two of those would be false as well.

The Legal Department had doubts that a charge would stick, as Warwick Reid made clear to Brooks when they met on 20 November. He demanded further corroboration, so the SIU went back out to look for more boys and pulled in Bobby Po, "Big Mouth Woman". He was shown MacLennan's photograph but refused to identify him, at which point, he would allege, he was hit by Sergeant Leung and threatened by Inspector Tin that he would be charged with blackmail and intimidation unless he gave the information they wanted. Tin also told him that Jimmy Cheung would give evidence that he knew MacLennan. At that point Bobby Po gave in, identified the photograph and gave a statement saying that he had had sex with MacLennan on three occasions.[52] This was sufficient to satisfy the Legal Department, and when Moor saw the attorney general and Neil MacDougall on 30 November, he got the green light to proceed. He told the SIU to request a search warrant for MacLennan's flat from South Kowloon Magistrate's Court.[53]

The SIU was very careful to take each step only on the direction of those further up the chain of command, a chain which reached all the way up to the attorney general. So although the order had already been given to prosecute, Brooks went back to his superiors to confirm an order to arrest MacLennan. On 3 December, he and MacKillop saw MacDougall, who acquired the attorney general's decision to arrest first Logan on 5 December ("for security reasons"), then MacLennan. Clancy informed Moor of this.[54]

The last witness from Peter Sung's list was finally located by the SIU on 12 December. This was fifteen-year-old Ricky Kwok Siu-keung, who gave a statement acknowledging that he had slept with MacLennan on several occasions in Ho Man Tin.[55] Ricky was an extremely attractive boy, of whom the other prostitutes, who knew him as "Wicky", were jealous. It was said that he had only to walk down half the steps into the Cellar Bar to attract a customer, and he never needed a pimp. He was vain, capricious, and only put out for cash, although he liked the sex, the attention his punters gave him, and the money he earned, which was enough to allow him to live extravagantly. He told his friends that he wished there were forty-eight hours in every day so that he could pack in more punters, and he passed to the other boys the customers he didn't fancy or have time for. He was totally uneducated, although he had picked up some English from his clients, and had gone on the game after his uncle had buggered him when he was twelve. He had found he enjoyed it. His friends believed he had been one of Duffy's boys. He had slept with John MacLennan.[56]

Ricky Kwok's was to be the last piece of substantial evidence the SIU assembled. Brooks got Bill Ross's permission for CID to conduct surveillance three times on MacLennan, but nothing was noted except for the late nights he kept. On 13 December, MacLennan was placed on the watch list at Kai Tak Airport.[57] As

Logan's case only reached the courts in December, it was decided to let the MacLennan case tide over until the new year. Then, on 3 January 1980, senior Crown counsel Joe Duffy, standing in for Warwick Reid who was on leave, passed to the SIU the attorney general's instruction that they were to prosecute MacLennan for eight counts of gross indecency with five prostitutes.[58] By 11 January, Brooks was ready. In his presence, Bill Ross rang Jack Trotman, MacLennan's Divisional Superintendent, and ordered him to have John MacLennan report to his office at 10.30 a.m. on 15 January for arrest by the SIU.[59] The charge sheet was to be:

> Michael (Tsang) — gross indecency — a false charge.
> Jeff (Tso) — gross indecency — a false charge.
> Bobby (Po — Big Mouthed Woman) — gross indecency.
> Lula (Sun) — gross indecency — a false charge.
> Wicky (Ricky Kwok) — gross indecency.

By then, the SIU had been forced to set aside the other witnesses they had accumulated earlier; Peter Sung, Jimmy Cheung, and Eddie Chu had been caught attempting to blackmail Colin Logan and so could not be produced as credible witnesses in court. Alan was still steadfastly refusing to admit any homosexual relationship with MacLennan.[60] They could by no means have been sure of success.

13

Stumbling Blocks

As the final stages of the campaign to prosecute MacLennan unfolded, John Griffiths was beginning to get a hint of the trouble that his drive to enforce the law on homosexuality would bring him. Difficulties had arisen as far back as August, when London began to take note of what he was doing, their interest aroused by complaints about the "witch-hunt" being conducted against homosexuals in Hong Kong. Norman St John Stevas, the leader of the House of Commons, had been contacted by both Elsie Elliott and Martin Potter, business partner of Gordon Huthart.[1] Howard Lindsay of the AG's own chambers, now on bail and awaiting trial, wrote to the AG on 30 August complaining about the way Quinn and Graham had investigated his case and about their intimidation of Michael Bunting, who had fled to Bangkok.[2] The same day, the governor received a telegram from the British ambassador in Bangkok saying that Bunting had come to see him to complain that Quinn and Graham were exceeding their authority to the extent of misconduct, and that Quinn was "mentally unstable", "alcoholic" and "unfit for his job".[3] Griffiths had already come across what he thought was Quinn's cavalier way of proceeding (but was actually probably Paddy Clancy's) when confronted with the unauthorized immunity letter given to Duffy. He now felt forced to speak to Peter Moor about moving Quinn out of the SIU, but the DC Operations resisted this suggestion and told the AG that he would have Clancy speak "sternly" to Quinn, whom he would ensure would behave thereafter. Clancy did not take such an action, which is unsurprising in the light of his own involvement in the offer of immunity to Duffy. The AG wrote to Moor on 31 August asking that someone more senior than Clancy, i.e. Moor, "direct more closely" the SIU's work.[4]

Until now, both the commissioner of police and his deputy had been able to keep the SIU's work at arm's length. There was a seeming reluctance on the part of both men to become involved, to the extent that Moor claimed he had even been unaware of the unit's existence until the end of July. From August, however, Moor could not avoid becoming the key player in police HQ in all matters regarding the SIU. Moor was an old Hong Kong hand who had joined the police force just after the war and was at the end of a career in which he had seen the commissioner's post to which he might have aspired go to Roy Henry (and later would see it go to another outsider, Ray Anning, when Henry retired). He had worked all his life with Illingworth, Blackburn, and Clancy. He was well liked in the force, although he had the appearance of a martinet[5] and was known to have a sharp temper when aroused. He was a married man but there were rumours circulating in the force that he had once been spotted in a bar in the Philippines surrounded by boys, rumours which were also current in Hong Kong society.[6]

Moor was therefore skating on ice dangerous to him, if not so dangerous as it was to Roy Henry, and he was not at all happy about getting involved in the SIU's work because he recognized that it was a "touchy area". "It was obvious" he later said, "that there was widespread homosexuality at all levels." He was to claim ignorance of much about the MacLennan case. Despite the fact that he had known MacLennan as a very junior officer in Kowloon, he claimed that he knew nothing of the Yuen Long incident until he decided to target MacLennan on the basis of the three prostitute statements of 16 October.[7] He contradicted himself in this on another occasion by stating that he had not known of the Yuen Long case until his approval of the creation of a court file on 16 November. This was despite the probability that he had been recipient of the tittle-tattle forwarded up the chain by the SIU since August, and the fact that he was briefed at the end of September about Dick Stanford's gossip about MacLennan. Clancy notably included Moor in the list of the senior police officers who resented MacLennan's reinstatement. On 4 September Moor wrote to the attorney general to tell him that both he and the DCI would from now on be personally involved in the SIU's work.[8]

The issue of Quinn's methods had by now reached the governor, who called Moor in after the AG showed him his letter of 4 September and himself decided that Quinn should be left where he was. He felt, as he usually did, that to move an officer would look like giving in to complaints from suspects and "as another investigation was going on at the time, it might be thought that something was being hushed up."[9] Griffiths wrote a misleading reply to the ambassador in Bangkok, telling him that Bunting was "unreliable by nature".[10]

Howard Lindsay, whom John Griffiths was by now probably coming to viscerally dislike, was the vector for the next bout of complaints about the SIU. These surfaced on 20 November. The previous month, Mike Fulton had contacted Lindsay while the latter was living in the Lee Garden Hotel awaiting trial. They had then met at Disco Disco, where Fulton related the SIU's instruction to set up MacLennan. He told Lindsay that Quinn was "peeved" due to MacLennan's involvement of the governor to gain reinstatement. Lindsay "was incandescent with rage" about Quinn, "both at this time and forever after", and told Fulton that Quinn could be accused of criminal intimidation as he was "attempting to pervert the course of justice". He advised Fulton to speak to his solicitor.[11]

Lindsay later asked Fulton to his hotel. When they met, he introduced a colleague from the Legal Department, barrister Clare-Marie Beeson, who, although taken by surprise by the meeting (Howard had telephoned her to invite her to the hotel without speaking of Fulton), listened as the inspector described the course of his relationship with the SIU and their demand to "frame-up" (as she remembered he put it) MacLennan. She had come across Fulton before when she had, as a crown counsel, advised him as inspector in charge of a case. She was unimpressed by him. He was, she thought, "a nervous sort of chap who had been made more nervous by the case." In her cool assessment, "he was not officer material." Beeson, and other friends of Lindsay in the Legal Department, who thought him "a bit of a drama queen", were concerned at his talking to the police when he was about to face his own trial. "We felt", she said, "he should have exercised his right to silence." She advised Fulton to take his case to CAPO, but he would not do so through fear and because he hoped that the interview he had been granted with Paddy Clancy "would keep Quinn off his back". She advised both men against contacting Elsie Elliott, who, she believed "in her self-appointed role as government gadfly was extraordinarily powerful" but "was not very balanced in her distrust of the police and authority." "Many chancers and opportunists," Beeson thought, "took advantage of her crusading zeal to push their less than worthy cases."[12]

Despite this, both Lindsay and Fulton then rang Elsie Elliott to ask her help, and Fulton gave her MacLennan's name. She advised, very sensibly, that Fulton should consult the attorney general, which he would not do, or a lawyer. She was mindful, it seems, of the harm she had done John MacLennan by her help the year before and was not about to repeat that.[13] Lindsay also telephoned Magistrate Henry Daniell, although by now Fulton was blowing cold, as he had already been interviewed by his boss, Senior Superintendent Merritt, who had persuaded Paddy Clancy to instruct Brooks to sever the SIU's connection with him. Fulton now hoped there would be no need for further complaint.[14]

Lindsay went for trial on 16 November, and four days after he had engineered his own acquittal, he went to see the attorney general, only to find that Griffiths wanted to interview him in order to force his resignation. Nevertheless, he brought out in the interview what Fulton had told him, said that the SIU had committed criminal offences and asked the attorney general to prosecute Brooks and Quinn. Griffiths refused, instead suggesting that Fulton report the case to CAPO (which Fulton had already set his mind against, as he still had hopes of maintaining his career in the force). Quinn, Griffiths mistakenly asserted, had been given a "last warning". Griffiths later claimed that he had no memory of MacLennan's name being raised by Lindsay, something which Lindsay could not later be sure he had done. This was immaterial, for by that stage Griffiths had known that Fulton had blown cover over a month before over his refusal to set up MacLennan. He could have been in no doubt about the man to whom Lindsay was referring.[15]

Two days later, Lindsay repeated in a letter to the AG what he had told him on 20 November and demanded the prosecution of Brooks and Quinn for false evidence, conspiracy, and intimidation. This time Griffiths thought it best to be seen to check what was happening and asked Warwick Reid, who was now back at work, whether there was any truth in the allegations. Reid said there was none, and Griffiths later stated: "I have no reason to doubt Reid's integrity and the truthfulness of his reply." So on 5 December, when Lindsay came once again to see the attorney general, it was to be told that he would only take action if a formal complaint were to be made.[16]

There was to be one more opportunity for an intervention to stop the impending tragedy. The attorney general invited Elsie Elliott to call on him on 20 December, an invitation that had nothing to do with the case, but rather was part of his "familiarization" programme of meeting Hong Kong's prominent figures. Griffiths gave Elsie an opening in the interview by asking her if she was aware of any law that needed changing in Hong Kong. So far, she had uncharacteristically kept her powder dry in the MacLennan case, but as she now had the opportunity, she determined to raise the issue and replied that the law on homosexuality needed amending due to the power it gave to triads and blackmailers. She added that she knew of a homosexual officer who had been asked to "frame" another. She refused to disclose any names in case the officers lost their jobs.

It may have come as something of a surprise to Griffiths that this old-fashioned looking, rather demure lady could raise the issue of homosexuality without seemingly suffering embarrassment. He was well aware, of course, that she meant Fulton, but once more he responded that the complaints should be referred to CAPO. Elsie explained why this would be impossible and later recalled that the "AG seemed impatient and would not discuss the matter." Her blood now up, she queried the dismissal of Howard Lindsay. Griffiths was not best pleased at being questioned in this way about decisions he had taken personally and replied that he had got rid of him "because I know he was guilty. I would bring about the dismissal of any public officer I knew to be guilty."

Elsie had by now taken some dislike to Griffiths, and shot back: "In that case, did you ever consider the Commissioner?" The AG could only reply lamely that "it's a matter of evidence."[17] Theirs was an inauspicious meeting and set the scene for later confrontation.

John Griffiths did not seek to halt, or to inquire further into, the ongoing process of prosecuting John MacLennan.[18] Elsie Elliott once more held her fire, thinking that there was no imminent danger to MacLennan as the SIU's set-up had failed. The case remained on her mind, however, and when she spoke to the Law School at Hong Kong University on 11 January, she mentioned the "frame-up" without giving names.[19]

Justice Yang was to criticize the attorney general for not listening to either Howard Lindsay or Elsie Elliott. He concluded that:

> In my view [the attorney general] should have at least asked Moor to ascertain the truthfulness of Fulton's allegations or alerted the Director of Public Prosecutions and/or the Senior Crown Counsel Mr Duffy with a view to ensuring that the evidence against MacLennan had been properly obtained. There is no evidence that the Attorney General did either.[20]

In coming to this conclusion, Yang had accepted the attorney general's assertions that he had ignored Lindsay because he was obsessed with revenge against the unit that had arrested him and Elsie Elliott because of her record of attacking the police. The record, however, suggests that Yang was not critical enough here of the attorney general. Griffiths had known since October about the SIU's failed attempt to make Fulton set up MacLennan. The police were being assiduous in following the instruction given them in the SIU charter to keep him informed. The attorney general had certainly been told of the Yuen Long incident by Moor on 30 November.

In addition, as the governor had earlier been told of the fact that Fulton had become an informer, it is probable that he would have been told that Fulton had ceased to be one along with at least a tailored version of why that had happened, which implies that the AG would have had to tell him. At the inquiry, it would not be established exactly when the attorney general had found out about the Fulton set up, although it would be made clear that the issue had in fact been discussed at the highest level around this time. Griffiths took care not to make this point explicitly in his testimony before the commission. Justice Yang's opinion would nevertheless be confident enough to be able to say:

> Did the Attorney General know at the time who the potential "victim" was? Apparently he did. The Attorney General said in evidence that at about that time, he had mentioned the Fulton matter to Mr Moor and the Chief Secretary, and he was made aware that the potential victim was John MacLennan.[21]

It is a fair assumption, therefore, that Griffiths had no reason to make inquiry about the issues raised to him by Lindsay and Elsie Elliott because he knew all about them already.

John Griffiths was the author of the policy of applying the law of Hong Kong to its homosexuals. He had drafted the SIU charter. The prosecution of John MacLennan, as of Colin Logan, and others of their ilk, was what he had intended to happen. He had directed that the prosecution of John MacLennan go forward *knowing* that the SIU had tried to set him up. To Griffiths, the failed set-up seemed an irrelevance, as in effect it was.[22]

There was an issue of government policy at stake here, too. The governor, and so the attorney general, had set the SIU in motion to demonstrate that something was being done in Hong Kong in response to the Duffy allegations. The prosecution of MacLennan was part of the proof that had to be offered to London. The sacrifice of a few selected junior officers of the government and police was necessary in order that the more serious security issues raised by Duffy's allegations could be made to disappear.

In retrospect, it can be seen that whatever Howard Lindsay and Elsie Elliott had said to John Griffiths about John MacLennan's case, he was not going to order a halt to his prosecution. It was a prosecution he both wanted and needed to succeed.

14

Suicide

In the first week of December 1979, John MacLennan learned that his world was about to fall apart. He was warned then on at least two separate occasions that the SIU was constructing a case against him. Two of the prostitutes who had been coerced into giving evidence felt bad enough about what they had done to contact him and tell him what was afoot. These were Bobby Po and Jimmy Cheung, both of whom liked MacLennan and wished to help him. One or other of them seems also to have got wind of the earlier attempt by the SIU to force Mike Fulton to set up MacLennan with a boy, and this information was also passed to MacLennan; perhaps Raymond Lam had been gossiping.

It had only been about three weeks since MacLennan last brought Bobby Po back to Ho Man Tin for sex (the final occasion when it is known that he paid for a prostitute).[1] Jimmy Cheung took the risk of visiting MacLennan in his flat in Ho Man Tin to warn him of the evidence he had been forced to give the SIU, but, unfortunately for him, he then told Peter Sung that he had done so. Sung relayed this snippet to Sergeant Leung in his next session, so Jimmy was brought into the SIU offices, and according to him beaten up and warned that he was making himself liable for "chopping". The SIU adopted an air of injured grievance, telling Jimmy that he had betrayed them when "we are protecting you so you can do business in Tsim Sha Tsui."[2] A report was to surface later that colleagues had also told MacLennan of the SIU's interest in him, although, if this was so, there is no record of it now.[3] The SIU became aware that MacLennan knew of their activities in early December. They did not, however, bother to speed up their planned arrest and search, and left their victim dangling in the wind over the Christmas and the New Year.

Detail about the trial of Colin Logan appeared in the press about the time that MacLennan was contacted by Bobby and Jimmy. Arrested on 5 December, Logan was charged with three counts of indecency with Peter Sung, Jimmy Cheung, and Eddie Chu. He pleaded guilty before Mr Paul Corfe at Western Court on 13 December and the next day was given an absolute discharge and ordered to pay HK$600 costs.[4] It was an insignificant sentence but one that ruined Logan's career. MacLennan could not have been unaware of the stark consequences that faced him now that he knew he was a target of the SIU.

The lurid details surrounding Logan's case were only later made public. During his interrogation, the SIU learned that he was being blackmailed by three of the men who had given evidence against him, Peter Sung, Jimmy Cheung, and Eddie Chu, so they set a trap at Logan's flat in McDonnell Road and placed Logan there as bait. When the prostitutes demanded HK$1,000 from him to enable them to disappear into China and avoid testifying, SIU officers emerged from an inner room and arrested them all. This put them out of circulation and made any testimony by them against John MacLennan impossible.[5] Had Logan not been shamed by the SIU into admitting his guilt, he would have had no case to answer.[6]

* * *

Despite all this activity, both private and public, and the fact that he must have been aware by then that he was likely to have been placed under surveillance, John MacLennan did not seem to be on his guard. There is no record that he hired any more prostitutes after the warnings he had received from Bobby and Jimmy, but he continued to see Slasher George and they slept together in the Ho Man Tin flat over the New Year of 1980.[7] For the rest, he carried on his duties and his social life as before. There was nothing else that he could have done, for to take up the matter officially in some way would have been to admit that he had been warned by the two prostitutes, and that in itself would have amounted to an admission of guilt. He continued to see his friends, to go out drinking and to visit his mistress, using her car to drive himself and others about.[8]

Some of his friends did note that at around that time he seemed to be behaving a little unusually. Inspector Matt Handley later reported that he had seen that MacLennan was troubled and recalled that he had missed some appointments to meals with him and his girlfriend.[9] Handley thought this was uncharacteristic and resolved to raise it with MacLennan, but in the event, never had the opportunity to do so. Others did not see any change in MacLennan. Mr and Mrs Alex Thomson, a couple who were friends of the MacLennan family in Scotland and whom John had known in Hong Kong for about a year, met up with him on 15 December. Margaret Thomson, who had a son of the same age as John and had come to consider him "like a son" to her, later recalled that she found him "in very good form", and when they last met she invited him to dinner for 17 January.[10]

On Christmas Eve, a Chinese contact of Elsie Elliott, presumably a police officer, had a drink with MacLennan and saw no sign of depression.[11] MacLennan spent Christmas Day with Nick Angell, Matt Handley, and Sally Haddon, who was an occupational therapist, an evangelical Christian and a platonic girlfriend of his, and none of them noticed anything amiss that day.[12] On New Year's Eve, he celebrated Hogmanay with other police officers at a small post in the New Territories, where he provided music for the occasion from the Andy Stewart tapes his family had sent him for Christmas. When he wrote a five-page letter to them on 2 January, he reported that "everything's back to normal now after the Christmas and New Year", added a good deal of news and concluded "I'm fine myself".[13] He was adept at disguising his true feelings from his family and his friends. Whatever ominous thoughts he was having at this time, he took care not to show them.

Only to Slasher George did MacLennan reveal anything of the strain under which he was living. They were together over both the Christmas and New Year; MacLennan must have come straight down from the New Territories on New Year's morning to meet George in Ho Man Tin, for they were sleeping together when "the phone rang at six that morning". George heard the caller say "Happy New Year you queen" then hang up. The phone rang again ten minutes later. He later related to Aileen

Bridgewater that "John was upset. We couldn't sleep. He took the phone off the hook, we got up and went swimming on New Year's day in Victoria Park, but it was closed so we went to South Bay, swam for three hours, then went back." MacLennan told George what was happening to him:

> At Christmas he told me he was being watched by the SIU pinning him for something. I knew about the Yuen Long case. It was true. The boy had sex with him but on the boy's will. John was a very, very easy-going person, quite emotional as well, when he had problems he would speak out, but because of his rank this was difficult. He spoke to me on many occasions and mentioned police names and the SIU. He told me he was on their list and mentioned a name like Quinton, not Quinn, John Quinton. He also said Henry, now I know he meant Roy Henry. He said he was being hassled. Some of his police colleagues called him queer and mocked him when he produced a girlfriend. He told me he was bi. [...]He was a very frank person. "It's my life, it's my private life. I can do what I like as long as I don't break the law."
>
> Alright, homosexuality is breaking the law, but they haven't done anything about it. In your own privacy — who knows? John had the same attitude. He's a very careful person. On one occasion he pointed to his lips and went into another room and he said he felt someone had been in his home. He's afraid someone is watching him or listening to him. That evening the phone rang, he said "Hallo" and got upset and took the earpiece off, saw nothing, banged it and dropped it on floor. He said "I'm very pissed off. I can't do anything in peace. Let's get the hell out of this damned place." [...]
>
> I told him I was leaving Hong Kong on 11 January. John asked for a forwarding address to write to me. I received two letters, one on the 13th, one on the 16th. I found out he died on the 17th. In one he wrote that he was mentally depressed and feeling very drowsy as he said a lot of people were trying to bug him. I didn't reply then the

> second letter came [...] He told me he had two enemies in the Police Force, one European, one Chinese. One quarrelled about money. The other called him a big queen, sissy and things like that. He knew quite a lot of triads but he wasn't mixed up in any.[14]

The phone calls are most likely to have come from some expatriate officer in the SIU. These unattractive attempts to harass and intimidate were to become something of a hallmark of their work over the next year.

As the New Year of 1980 opened, John MacLennan knew that it would not be long before he would be brought face to face with the SIU. He would have to decide then whether to fight, as he had in Yuen Long, or give up, as had Colin Logan. Fighting was not going to work this time, for he had paid for sex with at least some of those who he knew would be brought to testify against him. Pleading guilty would keep the detail of any charges out of court, but there was no way that such offences would be kept out of the press and it was inevitable that his family would hear of them. Whatever happened, this time he was going to lose his job. He could make no official complaint, and resigning now would probably not prevent action being taken against him. The possibility of suicide must have entered his mind about now, something put off perhaps but which may have seemed to offer a way out of an impossible situation. He must have been confused, anxious, living from day to day, hoping against hope that the worst would not happen, sure in the depths of his stomach that it would.

Little seems to have broken the surface of these very turgid waters for some days. Felix Muller called in to see MacLennan at his flat on the evening of 10 January and had Irish coffee with him and Sally Haddon. Muller thought he looked "happy and relaxed", something confirmed by Haddon, who reported that "he was in a very good mood in fact". They all had supper together in the Mexican Mess, a restaurant in Tsim Sha Tsui, then went back for a nightcap to MacLennan's flat, after which he took her home.[15]

The following day, however, MacLennan uncharacteristically drew a revolver from the armoury and, with Matt Handley, drove to the police range at Smugglers Ridge in the hills above Kowloon to fire some practice shots. It was well known in Ho Man Tin that he did not like firearms, to the extent that he was one of the few CID officers not to have one permanently out on signature, and Handley was surprised that he had done this.[16] Iain Grant, his immediate superior, confirmed this antipathy, recalling that, in the run up to an inspection by the divisional superintendent, he suggested to MacLennan that he draw a revolver. MacLennan told Grant that he knew what he was like, and that if he got drunk in Tsim Sha Tsui he'd lose it, and he'd rather not.[17]

On the way back from the range, MacLennan and Handley stopped off at the Urban Council Library in Waterloo Road, Kowloon. Handley noted that MacLennan withdrew no books, giving the reasons when asked that they were in a hurry and that there was a queue, neither of which was true. They then met a TV journalist named Ian Whitely, whom MacLennan had known since September of the year before. They all dined together at the Gaylord Restaurant in Chatham Road and ended the evening in the Waltzing Matilda, going home at about 1 a.m. Both Whitely and Handley thought that MacLennan seemed talkative, relaxed, and untroubled that night.[18] It was MacLennan's last visit to the bar.

As the days drew closer to the SIU's arrest, MacLennan carried on working his usual duty shifts and engaging in the lively social life he had built up in Ho Man Tin. He lunched with a girl he knew from Balintore, who was visiting Hong Kong (and was to be labelled "a girlfriend" in the Hong Kong press).[19] Late in the afternoon of 13 January, he and Sally Haddon spoke by phone and arranged to go out on the 17th; once more, to her he seemed completely normal. In this, however, he was not paying attention to his diary for the days ahead, as this was the day he had agreed to have dinner with the Thomsons.[20] Matt Handley and his girlfriend came round to have drinks at MacLennan's flat on the night of 13 January; MacLennan seemed anxious to return a couple of magazines he had borrowed earlier, something that Handley in retrospect once more found to have been out of character. Yet, as always, MacLennan was relaxed and the perfect host, plying them with drinks and making a fuss of Handley's girl. Nick Angell and his girlfriend visited later that night and also found MacLennan to be "quite normal". They overheard him make arrangements by telephone to meet Christopher Burns at Kai Tak Airport on his return to Hong Kong on 16 January. They stayed drinking till 3 a.m.[21]

Under the surface, however, John MacLennan was feeling far from at ease. On 11 or 12 January, he wrote the letter to Slasher George, who was now with his family in the Philippines. There are signs that he began to set about clearing the decks before whatever it was he faced. That week, he submitted an unusually large number of completed case work files to Iain Grant, who noted his unusual diligence, but put it down to the fact that the divisional superintendent's inspection was about to occur; at the time, it appeared to Grant that MacLennan was just getting his work up to date.[22] It seems that, at least in part of his mind, he had achieved a sort of clarity about what it was that he would have to do if the expected axe fell, an acceptance that led to calm.

* * *

On 14 January, MacLennan worked the shift from 8 a.m. to 8 p.m.; his next shift was scheduled to be the night shift starting at 8 p.m. the following day.[23] The blow that he had feared and partially expected for over a month now finally fell. Divisional Superintendent Jack Trotman had been told on 11 January to have MacLennan report to his office to be arrested by the SIU at 10.30 a.m. on the 15th. He had specifically been told not to inform MacLennan, but he found that he could not hand over one of his officers to the shame of arrest, interrogation, and probable charge without giving him the chance to prepare and to defend himself. He consulted with his assistant divisional superintendent, Marc Pelly, and they both came to the conclusion that they had to inform John MacLennan in advance.[24] So on the day before the arrest, Trotman told Iain Grant to send MacLennan in to see him, although without telling Grant why.

MacLennan arrived at Trotman's office at 12.45 p.m. and was told that the SIU would be coming the next day to interview him. The wind knocked out of him, he could only stutter in reply that "I thought all that nonsense was finished with ages ago."[25] Dazed, he went to the bar in the mess at the Ho Man Tin service flats and cashed a cheque for HK$200, with which he paid for a couple of double vodkas and orange (which the barman, Liu Tai-lun, thought unusual as it was MacLennan's habit to sign chits) and made some phone calls, it was never established to whom. He then went back to his office. Rather surprisingly, one of his reserve team members, Detective Constable Leung Kai-wong, who saw him then and occasionally for the rest of the afternoon, thought that he was "in a good mood with nothing troubling him".

At about 5 p.m. MacLennan went back to the Ho Man Tin bar, had another vodka and was in the mess kitchen when he bumped into ADS Marc Pelly, who saw that he was looking worried and of course was aware of why. Pelly was a decent and popular officer, who had come to Hong Kong from the Northern Rhodesian Police. He liked MacLennan. He had found him to be "distinctly extrovert, loyal, honest, a person who always appeared happy with life and was never afraid to speak his mind" and he wanted to help him now. He asked what was troubling him and MacLennan related that he was to be interviewed by the SIU in connection with the Yuen Long incident, something he had assumed was in the past, but which it now seemed was not. Pelly took him to the bar and bought him a vodka tonic.

MacLennan told Pelly that he was being persecuted for his time in Special Branch when he had been investigating "queer hawks" and had seen the name of a very senior officer on the list of suspects. The SIU, he believed, had assumed he was one of those, which he was not. Pelly told him to get legal advice and suggested Hampton, Winter & Glynn, where he knew a good solicitor named Stephen Llewellyn. The firm had been MacLennan's lawyers during the Yuen Long case, so this made sense. They telephoned Llewellyn, who agreed to be at the mess at 6.30 that evening. Pelly, who had heard rumours of John MacLennan's private life, advised him that he would need to think about finding money for bail, something that seemed to panic MacLennan, who had no savings. Pelly suggested he borrow from his friends.[26]

When Llewellyn arrived, Pelly put him with MacLennan in his own office and fetched Jack Trotman to see them both. Llewellyn had some time alone with MacLennan, who seems at that point (although this was never fully established) to have been open with his lawyer, at least to some degree, about his sexual orientation and his liaisons with prostitutes. He certainly gave Llewellyn the name of Peter Sung.[27] Llewellyn asked Trotman to get him Brooks on the phone and when they had tracked him down in the mess at police HQ, took Brooks aback by telling him that he was representing MacLennan. As he was to appear in court the next morning, Llewellyn requested that the interview with MacLennan be delayed so that he could attend. Brooks angrily refused and asked how he knew of the interview, to which Llewellyn replied that Trotman had told him. There then ensued an angry altercation on the phone between the two superintendents. Immediately off the phone with Trotman, Brooks rang Bill Ross, who told Paddy Clancy that MacLennan already knew he was to be interviewed. Llewellyn fell back on instructing a junior solicitor from his office, Paul Stevens, to be present the next day.[28]

MacLennan then headed back to his office, where Detective Constable Leung could see this time that something was wrong. In a hurry now, MacLennan picked up his personal typewriter and some files and left.[29] This was highly uncharacteristic — Iain Grant said that he was the sort of officer who never took work home.[30] At some time before 5 a.m. the next morning, he delivered the completed files back to Iain Grant's desk.

* * *

What John MacLennan did overnight will forever remain a mystery. There is a gap in the record of about three hours. The investigator Vincent Carratu later made clear to the press his own interpretation of events:

> That evening, he went out and tried to find out what evidence there was against him. We don't know who he saw or what he did that evening. We have never been able to establish that. He took the typewriter because he was ready to write a report defending himself. We know that he saw someone. He couldn't have done anything else as he was out for about three hours [...] None of his friends admitted seeing him and I accounted for all their whereabouts and their movements [...] The trouble was he was a very secret person. He was very wrapped up in himself. He did have friends which the average friend, if you like the "real" friend, never knew about. A sort of secret world, if you like.[31]

Carratu's is but one possible view, and there is no evidence that MacLennan wrote a report defending himself. He already knew the evidence against him. Carratu was not aware that John MacLennan had a mistress, so the possibility that MacLennan had visited her for comfort or succour would have passed him by. It is certain, though, that MacLennan did not go to the usual bars; he would have been spotted had he done so and it is unlikely in any case that he would have sought out the prostitutes who had already told him of the SIU's intentions. He may have sought help to raise his bail money, or may just have driven up into the hills to look down at the lights of the harbour spread below him. It will never be known where he went that night.

One thing he did do was to write and post a letter to Slasher George. In it he wrote that he would wait for George to come back and that he was thinking of going on holiday with him. He told George that the SIU had informed him that he was to be interviewed and wrote that he was very frightened about it. But he did not mention suicide and George was never to believe that he had taken that step.[32]

Between 1.30 and 2 a.m. on the morning of 15 January, WPC Poon Yuk-ling of Ho Man Tin received a telephone call from someone describing himself as Inspector MacLennan, whom she did not know, asking to speak to the duty officer, then adding "it doesn't matter, I only want you to call me up at 5.30 a.m." The caller gave the telephone number and asked her who she was, so she gave him her number. She wrote his message on the Availability Board in the Report Room and on the desk calendar pad. She thought the voice sounded tired but heard nothing in the background.

When, at between 5.32 and 5.35 a.m., PC Lam Mei-kuen made the call, he rang and asked "Is that Mr MacLennan?" A European answered, "Yes". Lam then said, "This phone is morning call". Lam thought the person on the other end of the line appeared confused and his voice sounded very tired and very quiet. There was a noise so Lam repeated his message, and the person at the other end said "Thank you".[33]

At 5.55 a.m., John MacLennan entered the station report room and showed Station Sergeant Li his warrant card.[34] Li knew him as a CID inspector at the station. MacLennan said to him, speaking rapidly, "I am Inspector MacLennan. I am going on a raid and I want a revolver. Raid R-A-I-D C.I.D. Raid." Li said "Oh Sir, I recognize you" and telephoned the armoury constable, PC Lee Hok-lun, to tell him that an officer was coming to draw a revolver and to give it to him.[35]

At about 6 a.m., MacLennan appeared at the armoury and said good morning in Cantonese. He showed his warrant card and Constable Lee, recognizing him as a CID inspector, issued the weapon and six rounds of ammunition. There were none of the short-barrelled .38 Smith and Wesson specials used by CID left in the armoury, so instead he issued what he thought was the long-barrelled type of .38 Smith and Wesson issued to uniformed police officers attached to the CID, but which was actually a Colt.[36] The weapon was numbered 4894. Lee then gave MacLennan the Beat Equipment Register to sign. MacLennan made two mistakes in his entries: he entered "0500" not "0600" (this was disputed later by a handwriting expert, Derek Davis, who thought he had first written "1800"); and he signed in the "Issuing/Rec.[eiving] Officer" signature column 8 (i.e. the column for the armoury constable to sign), instead of column 9, "Signature, Rank and Number" (the column for the recipient to sign).[37] Despite this evidence of confusion, P.C. Lee believed that MacLennan spoke clearly and normally, and when he pointed out the incorrect time to MacLennan, he amended it to "0600".[38]

These were not the only discrepancies in the register on Constable Lee's shift. Lee recorded in the "Remarks" column that MacLennan was "DDI/HMT CID", which of course he was not; Lee obviously did not know exactly who he was. The stamp marking the inspection of the armoury by the duty officers, completed at change of shift and timed between 6.40 and 7 a.m. was inserted immediately below MacLennan's entry and above an entry for a withdrawal timed at 6.30 a.m.[39] At the inquiry Lee would be unable to recall accurately what happened that morning. Some were to find all this suspicious, but it can equally be taken as an indication that PC Lee was not the brightest of officers and had been posted to the armoury for that reason.[40] One might also wonder if PC Lee had been on duty at all at the time and was covering up that he had already been relieved for some reason.

* * *

Sometime after 6 a.m., physiotherapist Sandra Hills, the resident of Number 610B, two floors above John MacLennan's flat, was awakened by a sharp bang, which she thought was something like the explosion of a fire cracker. It was followed by a number of further bangs. Thinking drowsily that this had maybe been the sound of a window closing below her, she drifted back to sleep.[41] There was no other sound heard by her, and none at all by John MacLennan's neighbours in the flats on either side, Inspectors Rod Colon and Colin Shaw, or by Felix Muller in the flat below, none of whom were awakened.[42]

At about 9.30 a.m., Madam Lai Kwai-ho, the cleaning amah for the fourth floor of the service apartments, tried to enter John MacLennan's room to clean it, but found it locked. Thirty minutes later, Madam Wong Kin-fun, the laundry amah, also tried the door to MacLennan's apartment, but discovered that her master key didn't work as the door had been locked from the inside.[43]

* * *

Senior Inspector Iain Grant was handling two jobs that morning, on duty as OC CID at the station and attending a case in court involving the theft of perfume from a duty free store. As he was leaving Ho Man Tin, the armoury constable came up to him and asked him if he knew that MacLennan had drawn a revolver, showing him the register with MacLennan's signature, a signature which Grant recognized. Grant then spent the day in court, only returning to Ho Man Tin at 4 p.m., at times during the day asking himself what John MacLennan was doing with a revolver and thinking to himself that "he must be doing some proactive work, which is surprising".[44]

At 9 a.m. on the other side of the harbour, Chief Inspector Mick Quinn gave Inspectors Loughrin and Tin orders to arrest

MacLennan in Senior Superintendent Trotman's office. Loughrin was told to search MacLennan's flat, and for this purpose Quinn instructed Sergeant Leung to bring with him the exhibits officer, DC Cheung Fat-yeung, and the photographer, DC Poon Ngok-ming. He also included two additional constables in the team, which now totalled nine. At 10 a.m., they left in two cars to cross over to Ho Man Tin.[45]

Paul Stevens, the solicitor arranged to represent John MacLennan, arrived first at Ho Man Tin Station and was told to wait in MacLennan's office. Trotman had detailed the division staff relations officer, Inspector Lee Siu-leung, to be present to ensure that MacLennan's rights were respected; this was on the instructions of the district commander Kowloon, Li Kwan-ha, whom Trotman had informed of the SIU's plans on 11 January. Quinn's party was late, as one of their cars broke down, so they arrived only at about 10.40 a.m. The atmosphere was frosty, Quinn having been made aware by Brooks that Trotman had told MacLennan he was to be interviewed. He showed Trotman their search warrant.

MacLennan should already have been there, but there was no sign of him, so Trotman began to telephone around the station to try to find him, ringing the officers' mess, the canteen, and several times to MacLennan's flat, where he got either no answer or an engaged tone. Alarmed now, Trotman went to MacLennan's office, where Stevens was sitting with Inspector Blake Hancock, who had also been phoning MacLennan's number. Loughrin showed Paul Stevens the search warrant. By now it was just before 11 a.m. and it was clear that something was very badly wrong. At Trotman's suggestion, they all piled into three vehicles and drove to the Ho Man Tin service quarters, where Trotman showed the search warrant to the manageress, Mrs Janet Gafoor.[46]

Together they took the lift to MacLennan's flat. Mrs Gafoor tried to open the door with her passkey, but failed, finding that the door was bolted. Trotman tried the door, too, and found the same. All the windows were closed. Trotman sent Inspector Lee to fetch a crow bar to break down the door.[47]

Ho Man Tin station, from where Lee needed to collect this, was about ten minutes away on foot, so Trotman made use of the time to go to the next-door flat to use its phone. As the two worried police officers conferred by telephone with their superiors, Detective Constable Cheung, one of Trotman's CID officers, took the initiative to find the odd-job labourer attached to the flats, but the man had no tools, so he too could not break in.

At 11.35, Inspector Lee returned with a constable carrying a crow bar, and two of the SIU police officers, Inspector Tin and Sergeant Leung, started to force an entry. They smashed the door's central panel to reveal that it had been bolted from the inside, top and bottom, as well as locked with two locks. The door was old fashioned and tough, and it took a full ten minutes for the two men to break off the door handle and smash their way in. Chief Inspector Quinn led the way into the darkened room, switching on the light as he entered. He was immediately followed by Trotman, Inspector Tin, Sergeant Leung, Mrs Gafoor and Paul Stevens. There was no one in the sitting room they entered. The door to the bedroom was locked.

As Trotman conducted a quick sweep of the adjacent kitchenette and shower room, Quinn scanned the room. On the desk at its centre was a cream-coloured sheet of lined A4 paper with a handwritten note, and next to it was a manila envelope, this with fewer lines of writing. Solicitor Stevens managed to read the longer note before Quinn placed it in a plastic bag and put it in his pocket. Although he saw it only briefly, for some ten to fifteen seconds, it was enough time for Stevens to see that the note had two paragraphs, the first protesting the innocence of the writer and the second explaining that he had been a good police officer. All told, Stevens saw some eight lines of closely written handwriting. It was clear to him that it was a suicide note, and he was so shaken that he left the flat. Sergeant Leung also noticed the A4 paper before Quinn took it in his charge.

So when Trotman joined Quinn at the desk, he could see only the manila envelope placed on its lower right-hand corner. Next to it was a ring of keys, which included some for a Volkswagen car. He drew the envelope to Quinn's attention. Written in Victoria blue biro ink, the note it bore read: "Please, please tell my family it was an accident and that I was a good Police Officer. JM. 0610 hours 15.1.80."

Quinn called in his photographer, Detective Constable Poon, to take photographs of the broken down door and of the room looking towards it. It was now 11.55, some seven minutes after the front door had been smashed open. Inspector Lee brought forward the constable with the crowbar to prise open the bedroom door. It was a weaker door and this time it did not take long to break the single lock and force entry. Quinn once again led the way into the room. Despite the fact that it was late morning, all was in darkness, for the windows were covered with blacking and the curtains had been drawn. Trotman switched on the light, enabling them to see a single bed, slightly in disarray but not slept in. Beyond it, on the floor to its side, protruded a leg. Quinn switched on the bedside light.

Sprawled on its back beside the bed was the body of John MacLennan. On the floor beside him lay a .38 service revolver. One of his hands clutched the legs of the bedside chair, as if for support in his final spasm. He was wearing a jersey that had four bullet holes ringed by powder burns in a small circle around his heart.

15

Investigation

John MacLennan had requested in his suicide note that his family be told that his death was an accident and that he was a good police officer. It was in the interests of all those now in control of events that the public be told exactly the opposite. Once MacLennan's body had been discovered, those in police HQ who were aware of the way he had been targeted and the reasons for it (and in the immediate chain of operational command that meant Peter Moor, Paddy Clancy, and Bill Ross, along with Eric Blackburn in Personnel and Training) realized that they had a potential public relations catastrophe opening up before them.

Their obvious course was to limit the information available to the public to conform to the picture they wished to be accepted, then to hope that the affair would blow over. The governor and his advisers had a different priority, one derived from the background to Operation Rockcorry, which was to demonstrate to London that the investigations mounted to follow up on the information given by Duffy were being effectively pursued. Whatever was to be released could not, of course, endanger the colony. One of these advisers, the attorney general, retained his own interest in continuing his policy of enforcing the law on homosexuality in Hong Kong.

For all these players, it was now important to maintain the line that the charges which John MacLennan had been about to face had been properly brought against a homosexual police officer who had broken the law and was unfit to serve in Hong Kong; that the investigation into his case had been properly conducted; and that, despite MacLennan's suicide, the SIU's work must continue. Other priorities would develop as the year progressed, but for the time being anything that deviated from this line was to be suppressed.

There were, however, two immediate problems with this approach. Influential and vocal members of the public (Elsie Elliott was only the most well known of these) were aware of some of the methods used to obtain evidence against MacLennan, of the allegations against homosexuals in high places, and of details of the Yuen Long affair. It was inevitable that their suspicions would be aroused by MacLennan's death. The second problem was that the investigations conducted into MacLennan's death and the attempts made to suppress evidence that conflicted with the government line were so ineptly conducted that they amplified the suspicions of those who had knowledge of the case.

* * *

Difficulties began as soon as the body was found. Both Jack Trotman and Mick Quinn made the immediate assumption that

MacLennan had killed himself. The existence of the note on the envelope in MacLennan's handwriting was enough to create a reasonable presumption of suicide. There were other indications that led to the same conclusion. The body was found behind two doors that had been locked and bolted from the inside. The windows were closed (they had no locks but were secured by catches). There was no sign that anyone other than MacLennan had been in the flat. There was no evidence of a struggle. The cause of death was most obviously the police revolver lying by the body.

Both Trotman and Quinn also knew of the pressure under which John MacLennan had been living and of the arrest which he had faced that morning. It is not surprising that neither had any doubt that they were looking at a suicide nor that, despite the four bullet wounds visible to the chest, they saw no reason to have the scene investigated as if it had been a crime.[1] So sure was Trotman in this conviction that he told all those who came later to the scene that it was a case of suicide, and this governed the actions of all those who subsequently joined the investigation.

There was, therefore, little attempt to control access to the scene of death. Before the body was removed to the mortuary, at least four officers from Ho Man Tin station, solicitor Paul Stevens, manageress Janet Gafoor, and up to nine officers of the SIU had gone in and out of the flat. As the day progressed, these were followed by: the station death enquiry constable, PC Wan For-hing;[2] the sub-divisional inspector (Kowloon City), Chief Inspector Kong Cheuk-hoi, accompanied by Inspector P. Peters;[3] police pathologists Dr Wong Kin-ming and Dr Yip Chi-pang accompanied by their assistant, Sergeant Szeto Mei-sheung;[4] police ballistics officers Alastair Cimino and Chief

Inspector Robert Nicholl;[5] officers from CID Kowloon: Senior Superintendent Toby Emmet, Superintendent Brooke, and Divisional Detective Inspector Kowloon City Lo Chu-hun,[6] who left after only fifteen minutes on site after learning of Trotman's assessment that the case was one of suicide;[7] Assistant Divisional Superintendent Marc Pelly;[8] and police photographer Lau Moon-chi and fingerprint officer, PC Cheng Lai-leung.[9]

There were thus at least twenty-nine people moving in and around the body whose movements were not controlled. No steps were taken to prevent items being picked up, examined, and moved, and it would later be spotted that the photographs taken by both photographers were to some extent "posed"; items and furniture had been rearranged before they were taken.[10] Some staging of the photographs is evident from a cursory view of them, for some have been taken in what seems to be a flat entirely empty of people, which could not have been the case at first. A photograph of the flat taken from the smashed front door and clearly showing the damaged wood lying around (which is not visible in other photographs) has a jacket slung over a chair by the desk. This is not shown in other photographs and the chair over which it is draped has been moved.[11]

Command and control exacerbated problems at the site from the start. The arrest was the SIU's, so initially the affair was managed by Quinn, but when it became clear that there was a death involved, responsibility passed to Trotman and Quinn left, taking his party with him. Both Trotman and Quinn were shaken by what they had found.[12] Unsettling as was the discovery of the body of a young officer who had seemingly killed himself, there was from the start more on their minds. Quinn was well aware that he was liable to an accusation that he had personally driven the dead man to his death. Trotman was already beginning to feel pangs of guilt, feelings that would remain with him, for having warned MacLennan of his arrest, thus giving him the motive and opportunity for suicide. Neither man could have been acting with a totally clear mind.

At 12.10 p.m., Trotman appointed one of his own officers, Chief Inspector Kong, to take over from him as investigating officer, but Kong did not arrive until sometime between 12.18 and 12.25 p.m. He in turn was superseded on the direct instructions of the deputy commissioner, Peter Moor, who ordered that Superintendent Marc Pelly be appointed, purportedly because the task required a more senior officer.[13] This in itself was suspicious; the death had already been classified a suicide and the investigation did not appear complicated.

What Moor could see to be a source of potential difficulty was the background to the MacLennan case, and to handle that he wanted a man he could rely upon to act as was required. Pelly was in the flat from around 1 p.m., but was not told he was to be in charge for another hour or more, meaning that Kong had to try to control the scene with his two superior officers present, one from the start, the second from within an hour of his appointment. Trotman remained on site for an hour or more after Pelly assumed control. As a result, no officer was fully in charge until after that point.

The lack of application of many forensic procedures that day was not surprising, for the force had no standing instructions for the forensic investigation of a suicide.[14] In addition, within the force there was no direction that an apparent suicide with multiple wounds should be treated as a potentially suspicious death. Suicides of police officers were something with which the force was used to dealing as they were not uncommon, linked as they often were to gambling debts or crime. At the scene of a suicide it was not thought necessary to employ what little forensic science was available, but even had the scene been considered potentially a murder, things might have gone little better. The forensic techniques available in Hong Kong in 1980 were limited.

In the case of John MacLennan, the forensics employed were very limited indeed. Fingerprints were not taken from the suicide note or from many of the areas of the flat, including the inside doors, locks, or windows (which would have helped to prove or disprove access by others), or from the empty cartridge cases. Those areas that were dusted included only the revolver and the back of the main door, and what was found there proved to be almost useless. Only one print from the door was good enough to lead to an identification, and that proved to belong to the cleaning amah, Madam Lai Kwai-ho.[15] The commander of the Identification Bureau, Senior Superintendent Bruce Ferguson, declined to attend the scene when he was told it was a suicide. He asked that the revolver and the suicide note be sent to him for examination but subsequently he received only the revolver.[16] MacLennan's hands were not examined for powder residue or bagged. Inspector Kong considered calling a government chemist, but decided it was unnecessary, although he did later send the suicide note to the chemist.[17]

All this made it subsequently impossible to prove that MacLennan had pulled the trigger to fire the rounds that killed him. There was no careful ballistic examination to trace the course of each bullet, and as the autopsy did not reveal the order of shots, it could not later be determined in what order the rounds had been fired, from what position, or in what direction.

It proved impossible to come to a firm conclusion, therefore, as to how MacLennan's body had come to be slumped in the position it took on the floor.

Only nine photographs in total were taken by the police photographer, PC Lau Moon-chi.[18] None were taken of the doors or windows, so there was nothing to support Trotman's statement that he had checked them and found that they were secured. The photographs of the windows that appeared later in the report of the Commission of Inquiry were taken only on 9 February.[19]

The time of death was never exactly determined. From his initial examination of the body, the police pathologist Dr Wong Kin-ming and his colleague Dr Yip Chi-pang estimated this as between 6.30 and 7.30 a.m.[20] They based this on the temperature of the room, which was twenty degrees centigrade, and that of the body, which was thirty-two degrees, and the fact that rigor mortis had set in.[21] This timing matched the recollection of the occupant of flat 610 above who had heard the shots, Sandra Hills, but after the autopsy, the unsigned, undated post-mortem report showed the time of death as 7.35 a.m., which did not match her account.[22]

The cause of death was not, however, in doubt; it was gunshot wounds to the chest with injuries to the heart, aorta, and spleen.[23] Dr Wong was informed by someone in the force that the officer whose body he examined was that of "John Richard MacLennan", and so he completed the autopsy report in that name. MacLennan did not have a middle name and this mistake was perpetuated for the next ten months until finally corrected at the inquiry. So on 25 April 1980, after an inquest had been held into the death of "John Richard MacLennan", the death certificate was issued for a man with that name.[24] The only John Richard in the whole affair was, of course, Duffy, who was clearly on police minds when MacLennan died.

Irregularities concerning the items found in John MacLennan's flat began almost immediately the police entered it. The pen with which he wrote the surviving suicide note was not listed among the three that were found there. The pen on the desk in the photographs shown in the inquiry report, a black Parker-type ballpoint pen which then disappeared, was not the one used to write the note. That had been written by a ballpoint pen containing Victoria blue ink. Such a pen seems to have been recovered at some stage, although how and from where was never established, but it was to be held by the clerk to the Commission of Inquiry, would not be produced in evidence, then vanished.

The wristwatch shown on the desk in the photographs had a leather strap and was not listed as MacLennan's; his Jaeger-LeCoultre and Mido watches both had metal bands. It was put there, perhaps, to indicate the time of the photograph, which was thus itself placed in doubt.[25] The Brother portable typewriter which MacLennan had used to type his final reports does not appear anywhere in the photographs of the room in the commission report; it is certainly not on or near the desk, yet it was listed among his effects and was recovered. When examined later, it was found that it had been cleaned and an unused ribbon had been inserted.[26]

Some of the personal documents that are known to have been in the flat did not surface subsequently. Pelly noted that he had seen papers kept by MacLennan relating to the Yuen Long affair, but these disappeared, as did the letters which Slasher George had seen in the flat and would later tell Aileen Bridgewater about. "He had two letters," he related, "one from a Chinese girl, one from a Chinese boy who went with his lover to Holland, the boy and John have had sex and liked each other very much."[27] Even more strange was the fact that John MacLennan's warrant card, which he had used literally minutes before his suicide to draw the revolver from the armoury, was never found. Nor, oddly, was the kilt of which he was so proud.

Trotman, Pelly, and Inspector Peters spent the rest of the day cataloguing MacLennan's property and boxing it up before having it removed for retention in police cell number eight in Ho Man Tin Police Station. Peters made a careful list of all the items, although Pelly took some that were, for some reason, considered important for the investigation and they were listed separately. These items were later held for the inquiry but they would not be so carefully handled. Amongst them, MacLennan's Jaeger-LeCoultre watch, his pocket book, gold cuff links, and four pens were all to go missing. At the end of the day the flat was stripped bare.[28]

Mystery surrounds the pens found in the flat. None of the three listed nor the one in the photograph were used to write the suicide note. Three of the pens were photographed and appeared in a plastic bag at the inquiry with a label inside the bag stating that this was exhibit C6: "All pens found amongst the deceased's personal effects." The fourth pen, the black, push-button biro-type pen with a pocket clip photographed by police photographer Poon lying next to the suicide note on the desk of MacLennan's room, supposedly at the time of the discovery of the body on 15 January, vanished immediately afterwards and was never mentioned again.[29] The property taken for the inquiry by Superintendent Pelly is listed in the Commission of Inquiry report, but contains only two pens, a "gold Parker pen" and a "gold enamel Montblanc pen". The silver pen, the third pen of exhibit C6, is not listed. So there are in effect three missing pens: the pen that wrote the suicide note; the black pen on the desk; and the silver pen in the exhibit bag. It is not possible to account for this now, although explanations can be proffered. One might account for the missing silver pen by guessing that once the inquiry realized that the pen that wrote the note had not been found, it was thought sensible to "lose" another pen to account for that. Rather like the watch with the leather strap in the photograph of the desk, the black biro-type pen may not have been John MacLennan's at all, just a pen placed next to the note for verisimilitude. Both losses were, perhaps, examples of the ways in which the evidence was "tidied up" for the inquiry. The missing pen that wrote the note, however, must have been absent for a real cause, perhaps, for example, because MacLennan wrote the note in his office and left the pen there before returning to his flat. It may just have been stolen.

Marc Pelly's investigation very swiftly established that MacLennan had parked the Volkswagen loaned him by his mistress in the car park of the service flats, and the car was impounded and then kept under a tarpaulin in the Ho Man Tin Station car park. However, neither the existence of the car nor of the mistress was to be revealed to the inquiry.

Whilst the actions of the police in the lead up to the death were examined in detail and published at the inquiry, those of the police who acted in the follow-up to the death were not.[30] Within hours of the discovery of the body, two plain-clothes officers, one an expatriate and one Chinese, visited the mistress and warned her not to talk about the incident to anyone, especially the press. Her existence would only come to light subsequently as she was a friend of broadcaster Aileen Bridgewater.[31]

16

Outcry

Any "management" of the investigation and of the information subsequently revealed at the inquest could only have been done by, or through, Superintendent Pelly. It was unfortunate, therefore, that he was a man who did not inspire public trust, one who was already known to those who would shortly lead the calls for an inquiry.[1] Elsie Elliott wrote to the governor on 29 January objecting to Pelly handling the case as he had, she said, been indicted for corruption in the Mong Kok conspiracy trial of 1978, although he had not been convicted.[2] She and others familiar with corruption in Mong Kok, she told MacLehose, felt that Pelly should have been removed then under Colonial Regulation 55. An investigation handled by Pelly was not one that was going to inspire confidence in a Hong Kong public by now skeptical of anything they were told by the police.[3] Even the attorney general was forced to accept that the choice of officer to lead the inquiry had been unfortunate. He reported to the governor:

> I confess I agree with Mrs Elliott that it is unfortunate that Mr Pelly, who was acquitted in the Mong Kok conspiracy, is in charge of the investigation into MacLennan's death. However, he will now be working under the direction of the Coroner's Officer so that in practice, despite what Mrs Elliott says, I do not think the investigation is likely to be inhibited.[4]

The coroner's officer was a lawyer appointed by him, so at best this was a little naive.

Rumours of the death seeped out in Hong Kong very quickly and it was already in the news the same day, although initially without detail.[5] By the next day, someone in the police force had let the media know that MacLennan had committed suicide, had shot himself five times with a service revolver, and had been about to be arrested on charges of gross indecency. This news was carried on Scottish radio that day and was repeated in the Scottish press on 17 January.[6]

Until then, all that MacLennan's family had received from Hong Kong was a message from the staff officer (inspectorate) in police HQ, Keith Radcliffe, who, on the day of MacLennan's death, telephoned Mr Angus MacDonald at the neighbouring farm and asked him to convey the contents of a telex to the MacLennans. It stated:

> Regret to report the death of John MacLennan who has died as a result of a shooting incident. Further details will follow.[7]

Radcliffe told MacDonald that MacLennan had died from five bullet wounds, that foul play was considered unlikely, and that suicide had not been ruled out. He gave them the telephone number in London of Dick Lidster, who was now the RHKP liaison officer there.[8] As the MacLennans later told Aileen Bridgewater, they were "grief stricken, taken aback, appalled."[9] They collected their family around them and began to mourn.

The following day, Lidster sent the MacLennans a telegram via the Northern Constabulary asking permission for an autopsy and seeking instructions for the disposal of the body.[10] Katie MacLennan telephoned Lidster, who tried to persuade her that her son should be cremated in Hong Kong. She was very reluctant to allow this, as the family's Christian faith and local custom all demanded burial, but Lidster made alternatives seem so difficult that she felt compelled to agree. Incredibly, he told her that a burial in Hong Kong was not advised as the body might have to be disinterred and moved, and that flying the body home was too difficult as it would need a metal coffin. The countries that the body would pass over would all have to be informed, he said, and some "objected to bodies being carried through their airspace". Airlines did not like to carry bodies, he added, "because it is considered unlucky."[11] He did not inform her that the body could be flown home by the RAF, as it could have been.

Mrs MacLennan was very upset and could not think straight, so she asked for time to consult the family and when she had, she rang Lidster back to agree to a cremation.[12] The MacLennans were the sort of family which did not make a fuss. They agreed to the autopsy by telephone two days later, on 18 January, but before that Lidster had already told Hong Kong that they had given this permission and the coroner had authorized it on the 17th.[13]

The police, it was clear, wanted the whole affair over and done with as soon as possible and with the least possible ceremony, whatever the consequences for the family. That day, Roy Henry wrote a letter of condolence, crassly addressed only to "Dear Mrs MacLennan", which expressed sympathy but gave no details of anything connected with the death or of subsequent events.[14] Save for a very similar letter from Martin Rowlands, secretary for the Civil Service, written on 31 January and also for some unexplained reason addressed to "Mrs MacLennan", that was all the MacLennan family ever heard from the Hong Kong Government.[15] They were never told when, where, or how their son had died.

A worse indignity was being inflicted on the body of their son back in Hong Kong, where on 17 and 18 January Dr Wong, the police pathologist, carried out the autopsy in the presence of Inspector Blake Hancock and Death Inquiry Constable Wan; Marc Pelly chose to be absent.[16] Contrary to later gossip, the government chemist, Y.Y. Cheng, found no drugs and very little alcohol in the sample of MacLennan's blood that Wong extracted and sent to him. At "fifty-two mgms. %", the alcohol in his blood stream was insufficient to "have any significant effect upon someone used to social drinking", Cheng stated.[17]

Someone in the force, and it was not Hancock, had ensured that Wong had been given specific instructions to prove that MacLennan had been a passive homosexual. A police photographer had been sent to take photographs of John MacLennan's anus.[18] Wong duly reported: "Anal opening (loss of puckering of skin) funnel shaped [...] Anal swab taken, no sperm."[19] Subsequently, Professor Keith Mant of Guy's Hospital was to destroy any significance in this finding, stating that "it would be most unwise to state that signs of buggery are present, both because dilation of the anus occurs naturally after rigor mortis wears off", and in this case because MacLennan's anus "was being stretched as shown in the album of photographs by two different people."[20]

* * *

Having leaked the detail of MacLennan's death, the police issued a short official statement on 16 January. It said little and included the words "no foul play was suspected".[21] If they thought that that was sufficient to allay public concern, they were sorely mistaken. Reaction began almost immediately. That day, Howard Lindsay, bitterly angry at what he saw was a death that could have been prevented, wrote to John Griffiths congratulating him on causing a death by his inactivity (Lindsay was not aware that the AG had been more complicit than this accusation of negligence implied).

Someone who was now feeling very guilty indeed was Mike Fulton, who went to the offices of Haldanes, his lawyers, to inform them that the dead man had been the intended victim of the set-up about which he had earlier told them.[22] He was becoming seriously disturbed and on 18 January, when he met Inspector Norrie MacKillop of the SIU at their old meeting place in the Wine and Cheese Bar, be blurted out that he believed that he was responsible for MacLennan's death as he had been asked to set him up. MacKillop denied that this was true and Fulton ended up apologizing for the trouble he had caused the SIU. Not the least amazing thing about this meeting was that, two months after the SIU had been warned not to make further use of him, Fulton had allowed it to take place at all.[23]

Elsie Elliott was appalled at the death, horribly aggrieved that her warnings had not been heeded and very angry with the attorney general. On 19 January, she wrote to Griffiths, linking the Yuen Long affair with what she described as "a deliberate plan by two Policemen named Brooks and Quinn to frame" MacLennan. This time she named Fulton as the officer who had refused to carry out that plan. "I see no reason why", she wrote, "if all I say is correct, this thug Quinn should continue to blight other people's lives and get off scot free himself."[24] She, like Lindsay, did not appreciate that Quinn was a mere agent of the attorney general's own policy.

She had already written to the *Sun* newspaper the day before (her timing was as always perfect), calling for an inquiry and alleging that MacLennan was the victim of a "high-powered Police frame-up" because he had investigated homosexual offences involving high-ranking policemen. She laid bare that the governor had saved him before and that she had informed the attorney general of the "frame-up" three weeks before MacLennan had died. To rub this in, she sent the paper a copy of her letter to Sir Murray MacLehose of 28 November 1978. The *Sun* printed both letters in full on 19 January, Elsie's letter on the front page under the headline "Suicide Cop Was Framed".[25]

This was incendiary and there was now no possibility that MacLennan's death could be swept quietly under the carpet. Pelly was instructed to widen the scope of the statements he was taking as part of his investigation, which was by then aimed at producing a report for the coroner to use at the inquest. He began to question those concerned in the Yuen Long affair and the set-up.

No one, it seems, thought it sensible to halt the cremation of MacLennan's body, and on 22 January, after a memorial service at the Union Church in Kennedy Road on Hong Kong Island, this went ahead at Cape Collinson Crematorium.[26] The pallbearers included at least one young police officer, a contemporary of John MacLennan, and the coffin they bore carried a plaque to "John Richard MacLennan". So little public notice was given to the ceremony that Alex and Margaret Thomson were unaware that it was happening and to their great sadness did not attend. Elsie Elliott was told that the minister, the Reverend Keith Anderson, had spoken in his address of "the death of a young man who took his own life", at which members of his congregation had taken immediate offence.[27]

The inquest now being planned continued to be delayed as Superintendent Pelly's investigation widened, and the public became impatient for an answer to Elsie Elliott's allegations. Pressure began to build. On 22 January, Dr L.K. Ding, the chairman of the Christian Industrial Committee and vice chairman of the Association for the Promotion of Public Justice, made a public statement seconding Elsie's call for inquiry.[28] The next day, Howard Lindsay wrote to the coroner's office giving details of the Fulton allegation and mentioning that Fulton had spoken to him of the set-up in front of Clare-Marie Beeson of the Legal Department. This was the second revelation to embarrass the attorney general inside a week, this time one of which he had not been aware, and he was not best pleased when he summoned Beeson and had her write a statement for the coroner.

Lindsay's letter was immediately passed to Peter Moor.[29] Elsie raised the stakes that day when she was featured on Ian Whitely's TVB *Open Line* programme and said that John MacLennan's death "may have been murder".[30] It is unlikely that she believed at this point that the death had been a murder, but she was skilled in arousing the public and knew the value of a lurid line.

John Griffiths now made an attempt to head off Elsie Elliott's criticisms by inviting her to his chambers. When they met on 24

January, her letter of the 19th had not yet reached him; he opened it just after she left. He thought perhaps to convince her that her fears were groundless using his undoubted charm and powers of persuasion. He made sure that Joe Duffy, the senior crown counsel who had advised on MacLennan's prosecution, was also present, and Duffy showed Elsie copies of the statements made against MacLennan by the eight prostitutes. She read, she was clear later, eight short statements, all by prostitutes who claimed to have been paid amounts of HK$50 or HK$100 by MacLennan.

She came away from the meeting believing that she had been told that Duffy himself had taken these statements (although this could not have been possible). She also recalled that she had commented to them both that it was better that Duffy had taken the statements rather than the police, and neither man had corrected her. These statements were to cause a great deal of woe later. The AG's attempt to reassure her that the prosecution had been properly brought was a failure.[31]

In a further attempt to pacify Elsie, Griffiths wrote the next day, telling her he would have Fulton's allegations investigated by an interviewer who was not a police officer.[32] He did make a half-hearted effort to do so, instructing his assistant, Ray Astin, to conduct the interview. Fulton would not play ball, however, having been advised by the head of his bureau, Chief Superintendent Clemence, not to see Astin.[33] He still had vain hopes of continuing his career in the force and he refused to be interviewed.[34]

Griffiths wrote to tell Elsie Elliott this on 2 February saying "Haldane tells me he won't talk to my staff. Instead, he provided in the same way a written statement he had made which denies that he was asked to frame anybody." This was of course true. Fulton, now trying to keep his career intact, was tacking. The

AG was also being clever with Elsie, starting here a denial he would make again in public that there had been no "frame-up" and ignoring the fact that Fulton had alleged a "set-up", legally a different phenomenon; a frame-up blames an innocent person for a crime, a set-up instigates a person to commit a crime. Elsie was not at this point clear about the difference.[35] Nevertheless, Griffiths told her, the coroner had asked the coroner's officer to interview Fulton.

Elsie Elliott made clear her refusal to accept the AG's assurances when she dictated a letter to him on her return home after their meeting of 24 January. In this, she queried the police version of events and questioned both the reasons for the targeting of John MacLennan and the quality of the witnesses against him. She asked why those who had sex in the privacy of their own homes were targets and why triad procurers or their customers were not. She recited a list (by post or profession, though not by name) of those she knew were homosexuals in high places. It was all too easy to entrap innocent men, she wrote. "What," she wondered, "is there to stop a group of men conspiring to give evidence of their own alleged relationship with the man they want to frame?" She regretted that she had not warned MacLennan when told of the Fulton allegations.

Hers was a worried, yet still very civil letter, evidence that her trust in the attorney general had not yet evaporated and that she still believed that through him justice might be done.[36]

Yet things had gone too far for Elsie Elliott simply to leave them in the hands of the attorney general. She was an old campaigner, adept at garnering public support, and she now began to muster her forces. She did not find this difficult. Although many of the expatriate public (unlike many ordinary

Chinese people) remained ambivalent, skeptical, or in denial about the veracity of the revelations in Elsie's campaigns, in this case there was a growing mistrust of what officialdom said due to the apparently mysterious circumstances of the death.

She began to send out letters, including one to Richard Duffy asking to visit him in Stanley Prison, and another to Edinburgh Police HQ, seeking information about MacLennan's Scottish police service.[37] After the appearance of both her article and broadcast, members of the public began to contact her to offer information and help. Mrs Margaret Thomson, for instance, contacted her to tell that she did not believe in the suicide. "John MacLennan is not gay," she said, he is "a very nice good young man."[38] Elsie received a letter on 31 January from a Michael King who was just emigrating to Canada and wanted to tell her that he had a friend in the ICAC who had told him that MacLennan was bisexual and that he only went after boys when drunk.[39]

Disregarding the fact that she had earlier leaked her correspondence to him to the *Sun*, Elsie wrote again to the governor on 29 January, stating that "all the evidence against MacLennan points to the possibility of a frame-up by triads brought forward possibly by the police." She objected again to the fact that Pelly, whom she believed to be corrupt, was handling the case.[40]

When the governor asked the AG for a report, Griffiths repeated what he had been told by Clare-Marie Beeson, writing: "Frankly, I am not happy about this, because I know now that Fulton in October 1979 repeated the allegations made to Mrs Elliott in front of Miss Beeson, one of my Crown Counsel." He did not inform the governor that he had known of the plan to set-up MacLennan before being told of it by either Elsie Elliott or

Howard Lindsay. He added rather provocatively (for it was the governor who had insisted on Quinn's retention) that

> I have always been unhappy about the employment of Quinn in this unit. He is the officer referred to in the telegram you received from the Ambassador in Bangkok. He is an officer covered by the ICAC amnesty. He, I believe, has an animus against homosexuals.[41]

In his reply to Elsie Elliott, the governor confined himself to stating that he was satisfied that "there are no grounds for intervening at present" but he did ask the AG what truth there was in Fulton's allegations. Whilst he had probably known for some months of the end of Fulton's time as an informer, it seems that the details of the Fulton set-up of MacLennan had been withheld from him, as they were now.[42] Griffiths replied that it was not possible to tell what truth there was in Fulton's account until Pelly and the Coroner's Office had completed their investigations:

> My guess is that the truth is likely to prove to be that Fulton undoubtedly told various people that he had been asked by Quinn and Brooks to frame MacLennan [...] I suspect that in fact Brooks/Quinn wanted to use Fulton as an agent provocateur rather than to frame; I expect it will be found that pressure was brought to bear on MacLennan because he learned that Quinn/Brooks were interviewing his boyfriends, and he was told by his superior he was to be arrested; I expect that it will be shown that Quinn behaved in an unsatisfactory fashion as a policeman during the Rockcorry investigation. I believe it will be demonstrated that MacLennan committed suicide, but that suspicion that he did not will remain with some people.[43]

These "expectations" of the attorney general were remarkably close to the truth, but then he was aware of the truth of them when he wrote them.

Howard Lindsay, now in Manila, where he had gone to recuperate and reassemble his life after his dismissal, also kept up the pressure, writing another letter to the coroner, this time of six pages, on 25 January.[44] The coroner did not respond. On 1 February, he finally ordered the inquest into John MacLennan's death.[45]

* * *

The allegations made by Elsie Elliott and Howard Lindsay and the accompanying calls for an inquiry altered the priorities of the governor, the attorney general, and the police. No longer could their actions be governed by the requirements of Operation Rockcorry alone. The recovery in the force and in its public reputation, which the governor's amnesty and subsequent reforms had achieved, was still in its early stages and was now threatened by the accusations arising in the MacLennan case. The police were being attacked for conducting a witch-hunt against homosexuals (the cause of which, it should be noted, could never be fully explained to the public), for setting up one of their own officers and even for having had him murdered. If the MacLennan affair was not handled carefully, the recently hard-won public trust in the police would evaporate, police morale would be jeopardized, and the bad times of 1977 would be with Hong Kong once more.

London, of course, would also be alarmed. Despite the revelations in the Duffy petition, the Foreign and Commonwealth Office had been growing more and more confident that the situation in Hong Kong had stabilized.[46] It was vital that none of this be endangered. It remained more than ever vital that no hint of the scandal latent in the Duffy revelations be allowed to reach the public.

The attorney general also had new reasons to ensure that the MacLennan case was handled as he had initially instructed. His credibility, if not culpability, was now in question and his position had to be defended. He had not, however, abandoned in any way his determination to see that the law on homosexuality was enforced in Hong Kong. His determination that the SIU carry on with its work was indicated by a snippet of information given by the Legal Department to the media on 26 January. The AG, it was stated, would offer immunity to any homosexual "who gave evidence against hustlers, procurers and extortionists."[47] He had yet, it seemed, to realize that MacLennan's death had made it impossible to conduct business in the "normal" fashion he had intended.

The police were similarly placed. They needed to defend themselves, for the allegations of murder that had begun to surface, although as yet unfocussed, could be aimed at two very vulnerable sets of officers: homosexual senior officers seeking to cover their tracks; and the SIU, which had at the very least bullied its way to the death of a police officer.

The governor, the attorney general and the police now needed to control information and the course of events, and this necessity would intensify rather than diminish, for the mistakes, failures, and lies of the past two years were about to come back to bite them all hard.

* * *

The teakwood casket containing John MacLennan's ashes and bearing a plaque naming "John Richard MacLennan" was flown to Scotland by commercial aircraft. The Hong Kong Government had arranged payment for transit only as far as Aberdeen, and, when it arrived there, staff at the airport telephoned the MacLennan's neighbour, Mr MacDonald, who had the only nearby telephone, to tell the MacLennans to collect it. It was by then over a month since John MacLennan had died and his parents and friends were distraught and angry that they had been given no information about his death.

MacDonald was furious at the parsimony of the Hong Kong Government, and when he got the phone call he exploded. Muttering to himself: "What do they think it is, groceries?" he did not tell the MacLennans about the call, but drove down to Aberdeen to collect the casket himself. When they received it, the family was dismayed to see the plaque, so they were forced to have a new one made by local undertakers. They had registered a plot for their son in Fodderty Cemetery on the other side of Dingwall. Their minister, the Reverend MacLeod, did not usually countenance cremations, but for the MacLennans he conducted a short ceremony to inter John's ashes.[48] They had the stone inscribed:

IN
FONDEST MEMORY OF
OUR LOVING SON
AND BROTHER
JOHN MACLENNAN
DIED 15TH JANUARY 1980
AGED 29 YEARS[49]

17

Inquest

Among the expatriate community, Aileen Bridgewater was one of the most popular chat show hostesses on Hong Kong's airwaves.[1] By 1980, her Commercial Radio show *Naturally Speaking* was well established as a platform for exposing injustice and creating public support for good causes. Aileen was a beautiful and stylish woman whose warm personality belied a very swift mind and a sharp tongue. A fighter for the underdog and renowned founder of several local charities, she was fearless when she believed a principle was at stake. Uncovering corruption and malfeasance in government was, for her, both a personal mission and good radio. The fact that her husband, Ken, was an engineer employed by the government and that they lived in a government flat made no difference at all, and it took all the skills and patience of her producer, Joe Delacy, to keep her on the air. Aileen's show was a natural vehicle for Elsie Elliott's campaigns, and by the time of John MacLennan's death they had known each other for years.[2]

On 24 January 1980, the day she went to see John Griffiths, Elsie Elliott rang in to Aileen's programme. Although neither could have been aware of it at the time, this was the start of a partnership that was to win an inquiry into John MacLennan's death. Only occasionally prompted by Aileen, Elsie related what detail she knew of the Yuen Long incident and her involvement with John MacLennan. She also outlined the content of her report to the attorney general of the Fulton "frame-up". She was aware, she went on, that "it was a Chinese running the [prostitution] racket" and added (ominously for the police, for she could only have meant Molo Tsui) "I can name him". MacLennan, she believed, had been "driven to suicide by persecution", but she was not sure there was not a more sinister aspect to the case:

> As soon as I heard he was dead I immediately thought "Oh no, not suicide, he wouldn't do that", and then I heard he had five shots in him. Very strange, five bullet wounds. Policemen are voicing doubts. I understand people who know him are scared to speak.

The rapid cremation of MacLennan's body as soon as she had demanded an inquiry was, she contended, suspicious.

After Elsie rang off, Aileen telephoned Terry Coombs, the Police Public Relations Bureau spokesman, who told her audience that MacLennan had been found in a locked flat with five bullet holes in his chest at a time when he had been about to be arrested on a charge of gross indecency, and that he had left a suicide note. This was the first time the police had formally given such detail to the public, although they had already leaked much of the information.

The two calls aroused an immediate reaction. An army officer rang in to dispute that it was possible to kill oneself by firing five bullets from a .38 revolver, as its recoil would have made this impossible. The founder of the Hong Kong Samaritans contributed the view that a man would have been psychologically incapable of firing five times into his own body. The programme rubbed a very raw nerve in the government and police officers called at the studio to demand the tape.[3] They also demanded from TVB the tape of Ian Whitely's show, which had caused even more of a buzz among the English speaking community than had Aileen's.[4]

Superintendent Pelly had so far been unable to complete his interviews, so the inquest, originally set for 20 February, was postponed, giving Elsie Elliott the opportunity to send a telegram through the Stirling Police to the MacLennans asking if they wanted to appoint a watching brief at the inquest or needed help with legal aid.[5] At much the same time, Dick Lidster also contacted the family with a similar question from the RHKP's London office.

Pelly's work was done by 22 February and he sent the Death File to the coroner, Mr J.W. Hansen.[6] His report was a workmanlike document, which laid out the chronology of events but did not delve into their causes or say anything to bring the police version of events into doubt. There was no mention of the mistress or her Volkswagen car, nor was there to be at the inquest, for she was visited again before it opened, informed she would not be called as a witness and told not to speak out.[7] She refused to take the car back, so it remained with the police.

Pelly's report included an examination of the attempted set-up of MacLennan, but sidestepped the issue as to whether there had been any misconduct by the SIU by stating that Fulton had never alleged a "frame-up" and was now not making a complaint.[8] In Pelly's report emerged the line earlier developed by the attorney general and to which the government and police would adhere, that there had been no "frame-up" of John MacLennan. This was of course true, for the SIU had wanted Fulton to "set up" MacLennan to commit a homosexual offence, not frame him for one that had already been committed. From now on, "set-up" was a phrase that the government and police would do their best to avoid.

Pelly did not query the veracity of any of the prostitutes' statements.[9] His report concluded:

> From the evidence it would appear that the deceased took his own life by shooting himself five times in the body with a police revolver some time between 0630 and 0730 on 15.1.80 [...] All available evidence would indicate that the possibility of foul play including homicide can be ruled iut [*sic*] [...] The evidence of those who knew him well and the criminal evidence against him show a man who probably led two completely separate lives, and, whereas he led a life of high personal values and principles in front of his friends and in the course of his constabulary duties, he also led a twilight life that was not only against the law as laid down in Hong Kong but also against the high moral code that he outwardly professed. It is likely that he knew that he was going to be arrested and he took his life not only to pre-empt the course of justice but also to avoid the adverse publicity that a case would bring.[10]

In the meantime, the government continued its attempts to persuade Elsie Elliott to give up her campaign for an inquiry. She was asked to visit the man the AG had appointed as coroner's officer.[11] This was a lawyer, Barry Moorfoot, QC, a senior crown counsel and the man whom Griffiths had asked to investigate the Fulton allegations.

Elsie called on Moorfoot in his office in the New World Centre on 24 February. He described to her his own view of the sequence of revolver shots that had killed MacLennan. She asked him how they knew that MacLennan was a homosexual, to which Moorfoot replied that he had seen pictures of his anus to prove it. Elsie was not convinced that she had been told anything that disproved what she suspected about foul play and she resented what she saw as an attempt to dissuade her from speaking out.[12] The visit was not a success.

On 29 February, the inquest into John MacLennan's death opened at North Kowloon Magistracy, to be immediately adjourned until 3 March at the request of Bernard Downey, the barrister appointed by the government to represent the family. He had not yet had, he told the inquest, any instructions from the MacLennans.[13] His appointment had been made late in the day and his services were paid for not by the government but by charitable funds held by the RHKP and provided through the assistance of General Purdon.[14] When the inquest resumed, he was to do rather a good job of uncovering the deficiencies in the police investigation.

The jury of three convened to serve in this case consisted of an Australian architect, Anthony B. Pannell, who was normally known as Tony, and two Chinese women, Madams Cheong Lai Wah and Ip Wai Ching.[15] By now, Hansen had been replaced as coroner by David Leonard, a short-tempered magistrate who would spend the seven days of the inquest scribbling notes in longhand and being curt with the witnesses who were getting ahead of him.[16] He was evidently unhappy about his role in the case but was not about to allow his inquest to be hijacked by either the government or the campaign of Elsie Elliott and her supporters.

It was in the official interest that the maximum detail of the charges against MacLennan be made public. The governor made this clear on 2 March in an explicit instruction to the attorney general, dictating the "wide approach" he wished to be taken by the legal department counsel.[17] Leonard would not play ball with this and ruled most of the Pelly report and its eighty-three statements inadmissible; they were, he declared, irrelevant to the death. In the event, only thirty-eight witnesses would take the stand. Ironically, this would be taken by Elsie Elliott and by Aileen Bridgewater, both of whom attended the inquest, as a deliberate attempt by the government to suppress information related to the case.

Proceedings resumed on 3 March and were again delayed, but this time for only a short interval, as one of the female Chinese jurors rose to request that she be excused; she was unwilling, she said, to hear details of a case involving a homosexual. The coroner told her to sit down and the inquest carried on in English, which at least one of the Chinese jurors seemed to have difficulty in understanding. The next morning, the juror who had asked to be excused was found to be absent, and there was further delay while the police went to the convent where she lived and brought her to the court. When the inquest resumed, Aileen, who was in the public gallery, noted that Leonard was writing in longhand and could not observe the witnesses; she was a journalist and picked up on that sort of thing.[18]

The senior crown counsel appearing for the police was Andrew Hodge, an Australian and a man brimming with the sort of self-confidence that could ride roughshod over men of weaker calibre, but he got nowhere in his attempt to persuade the coroner to widen the scope of the inquest.[19] Leonard was not to be browbeaten by anyone and specifically ruled out all mention of the Yuen Long incident, any allegation that John MacLennan was homosexual, and anything connected with Inspector Fulton.[20] It is difficult to see how any sense at all could have been made of the case with such restrictions imposed, and Hodge, who had the reputation of being a loose cannon and unafraid of either judges or magistrates, was reduced to slipping into the proceedings the allegation that MacLennan was homosexual. He did this when questioning the pathologist, Dr Wong, regarding the autopsy he had conducted, saying in a loud and clear voice: "I put it to you that in your examination of the deceased in the anus, does it confirm that he was a chronic bugger?" The coroner was not amused and disallowed the question, but the cat was out of the bag. Not that there could in any case have been any doubt in the minds of either jurors or onlookers that MacLennan had been about to be charged with gross indecency when he died. The police had already made sure that this was public knowledge, as the Chinese juror had made clear when she attempted to be excused.

There were several pieces of information revealed at the inquest that had not emerged before. Dr Wong's head of department, Dr Frederick Y.K. Ong, the government's consultant resident pathologist in charge and a pathologist of great experience, told the inquest that he was unable to speculate on the order in which the shots might have been fired. MacLennan's injuries, he considered, were consistent with self-inflicted wounds, although he was only able to base this view on the post mortem report and photographs, as he had not seen the body. He was supported in these views by Professor James Gibson of the Pathology Department of the University of Hong Kong, although Gibson differed in his account of the order of shots. Both pathologists were able to agree, however, that none of the shots would have been immediately fatal and that, despite four of them being in and around the heart, MacLennan could have remained conscious for long enough to squeeze the trigger five times.[21] By bringing the testimony to bear of three expert pathologist witnesses, the government was doing its best to override the common-sense view that that it would be impossible for a man to fire five times into his own body. The attempt did not succeed.

The government had greater success with the issue of the suicide note, for all but one witness agreed that it had been written by John MacLennan. However, solicitor Paul Stevens caused a small sensation when he claimed that the suicide note presented as an exhibit was not the one he had read at the scene of death.[22] His evidence was simply ignored.

More of a sensation, and for the government a disaster, came on 12 March at the close of the inquest. The coroner gave a "meticulous" three-and-a-half hour summing up, pointing out to the jury that in light of the evidence only two verdicts were possible, either suicide or an open verdict, and indicating clearly that it was his view that it had to be the former.[23] He was stunned and "most upset" when the jury, by two to one, returned an open verdict. He asked them to reconsider this but they refused, and jury foreman Tony Pannell stoutly requested more time to allow them to consider a number of riders which they wished to add to their finding. When these emerged, they were demands for a reform of the law on homosexuality and severe criticisms of the police handling of the case.[24]

The coroner was not the only one taken aback by this verdict. The government was embarrassed. The police were very sore indeed at the damage caused to their reputation by the jury's disbelief in the findings of their investigation and its criticism of their conduct of the case. Superintendent Marc Pelly had been made to look a fool and was visibly shaken. Worst of all, the MacLennan affair was now in the public mind and would not be easily forgotten; those campaigning for an inquiry had been given an unlooked for boost. John MacLennan was dead but his death had turned him into a *cause célèbre*. This was the last thing the government had wanted to see happen.

* * *

Why had the jury so roundly rejected the official version of the death? The governor demanded an immediate explanation, which Andrew Hodge provided for him in a written brief on 17 March. He reminded the governor that his advisers had recommended a narrow approach at the inquest but that the governor had decided otherwise, "due to clashing interests" and "your own position, personally and professionally." Hodge offered several disparate reasons why the jury's suspicions had been aroused: the delay in the arrest; the lack of attention by his superiors to MacLennan's access to a weapon; the "nervousness" of Chief Inspector Quinn when giving evidence and his confusion over factual evidence. Quinn had claimed no animus against MacLennan but had been forced to admit that he had called him "arrogant and brass-necked". Hodge added here that "one of my colleagues in Chambers [this was Warwick Reid] who has advised the SIU has said that Mr Quinn told him that they were out to 'get' MacLennan."

Procedures at the scene had been lacking, Hodge continued. The empty flat above had not been searched. Physical evidence had been lost; the lock on the bedroom door had not been produced as it had been repaired and refitted. The photographer had not been controlled and some of the photographs showed the same chair in different positions. Hodge attempted to make the best of a bad job by saying that "reading between the lines" the jury had accepted that the death was a suicide but had not wished to give the police "the 'gratification' of announcing the expected verdict"; he was to be shown wrong in this assumption. Hodge recommended that the inquest not be re-opened but that an internal police inquiry be held into the failure of procedures.[25] As a result, Assistant Commissioner Li Kwan-ha was tasked with investigating the measures adopted by the police investigation. He would report very swiftly on 25 March, but although he highlighted deficiencies in police procedures and criticized Trotman, he did not come to any conclusions about the death that were dissimilar to those reached by Pelly.[26] His report was not published.

18

Campaign

Elsie Elliott called for an inquiry immediately after the inquest. She rang in to Aileen Bridgewater's radio show to dispute the five bullet hole suicide and to complain about the inquest. Once again the police demanded a tape of the show.[1] This time, the *Hong Kong Standard* and the *South China Morning Post* supported Elsie with editorials, the former stating "Too many questions were left unanswered at the Inquest and the air must be cleared."[2]

Ominously for the government, the press in the United Kingdom now began to pick up on the story, with articles both in the *Spectator* and by investigative reporter Duncan Campbell in the *New Statesman*.[3] *Private Eye*, as usual, went even further and made a blunt allegation that MacLennan had been murdered.[4] The issue went international with coverage in *Newsweek*,[5] and interest in Scotland was fed by both the press and Radio Scotland.[6] The Scottish Homosexual Rights Group wrote to Lord Carrington, the foreign secretary, to ask for an inquiry.[7]

In another of what was by now a growing file of letters to the governor on this subject, Elsie Elliott wrote on 18 March asking for an independent inquiry:

> Whatever the cause of death, there was no justification for hounding a man on eight charges of the kind with consenting adults, male prostitutes with undoubtedly triad connection [...] Any further investigations by the police can only be intended as a second cover up. No honest witness will come forward now, if the police are in charge [...] The Inquest was quite shamelessly fixed up, and we can only be thankful that the jury dared to question the evidence by giving the verdict they did.[8]

The governor replied that he was satisfied that any further inquiry would reveal that MacLennan was a homosexual, the charges justified and the death suicide.[9] This simply prompted her to reach beyond him and she wrote to Scottish MPs Robin Cook and Robert Parry, both of whom raised the issue with Peter Blaker, the minister of state at the FCO.[10]

The attorney general began to feel the pressure to respond and issued a statement on 18 March, which gave no indication of any change of mind on the part of the government.[11] A much more sinister reaction arrived two days later in Aileen Bridgewater's mail, an anonymous typewritten note saying: "I strongly advise you not to proceed with seeking an independent inquiry on the MacLennan affair."

Aileen was not the type to buckle under this or any subsequent pressure. She hit back that day:

> Naturally, I read it out over the air. I added that in all my years on a talk show I had never had any pressure put on me by Government or anyone else to restrict me in any way until this last week when I had received quite a lot.[12]

Aileen was not alone in this. Elsie Elliott was also a victim of attempts to intimidate her. "I was getting strange phone calls during this time. Someone would whistle down the phone or breathe down it."[13] Was this the SIU? It seems possible, even likely, given the way intimidating calls had been made to MacLennan, and in the light of much that was to follow.

Undaunted, Elsie was back in Aileen Bridgewater's studio on 23 March to say that John MacLennan was on trial for murdering himself (this did not make much sense, but she was good at producing memorable turns of phrase). MacLennan's family, who were Presbyterians, were in "great distress" as their son had been publicly accused of committing "the unforgivable sin".[14]

Goaded by this, John Griffiths for the first, but not the last, time asked his staff to investigate whether Elsie's statements could open her to a prosecution for libel.[15] The same idea occurred to the police shortly afterwards and Peter Moor forwarded papers to the AG with a view to taking action against both Elsie Elliott and the media, stating that he was very concerned that the attacks were having an effect on morale, especially in the SIU.[16] Both the AG and Moor were told that a libel action would be possible but was not advisable, so they desisted.[17]

The police did what they could to deflect the deluge of questions and criticisms. Peter Moor, who was acting commissioner at the time (Roy Henry being on leave), issued a press release announcing the completion of Li Kwan-ha's report and stating that his recommendations on improvements in procedures would be acted upon. He took the opportunity to add that the original decision to treat MacLennan's death as a suicide had been correct.[18]

* * *

It is likely that events would have continued in this vein, Elsie writing frequently to the press until it lost interest and the issue gradually fading in the public consciousness, had not the governor accepted the advice of the attorney general to adopt a more proactive approach. On 22 April, he agreed to the AG's suggestion that he announce that there would be no further inquest and added:

> I also agree that we owe it to the police that the AG should restate the overwhelming weight of evidence indicating suicide [...] I agree that the best way of wrapping all this up would be by a statement by the AG at a press conference.[19]

This was to prove disastrously counterproductive, but at the time the governor did not believe that the issue was dying. Another Scottish MP, Dennis Canavan, had just submitted a written question on the case to the FCO, which Peter Blaker answered in May.[20] *Private Eye* had responded questioning Peter Blaker's motives, leading him later to issue them a writ, which itself served to keep the issue alive in London.[21] The *New Statesman* continued its reports on the case and *Gay News* chipped in with the headline "Hong Kong — M.P.s Act".[22] Hong Kong's English language press had also given no sign of abandoning their call for an inquiry.[23]

John Griffiths therefore held a press conference on 23 May, for which a press release was issued beforehand. With him that day was a bevy of minders to make sure all went well — David Ford, the secretary for information, Ray Astin, the AG's assistant, and the solicitor for the police — but it was nevertheless the attorney general's handling of this conference that subsequently made it impossible to avoid the institution of a public inquiry.[24] The release stated that:

> There was overwhelming evidence at the inquest into the death of Inspector MacLennan which shows that he committed suicide. Accordingly there is no reason to re-open the inquest and I would have no power to do so under the Coroner's Ordinance.

Griffiths used the conference to announce that he had asked the Law Reform Commission to conduct a review of the law on homosexuality.[25]

Had the AG stuck to his script, all would have been well for the government. The points he made seemed so straightforward to many (including Aileen Bridgewater, who suggested this to Elsie Elliott on air the next day), that it looked as though the call for an inquiry would have to be dropped.[26] Unfortunately for the attorney general, he did not so restrict himself. He went on to add that "There is no question of over-ruling the verdict. But the conclusion I have come to as a result of a long, cold look was not made in heat and drama", and he rubbed salt in the wound by attacking the "tittle-tattle" being circulated by those seeking an inquiry.

Griffiths also allowed himself to be drawn into a discussion of the detail of the evidence concerning bullets, windows, and locks, many of the issues, in fact, that had revealed at the inquest the shaky nature of the police investigation. Some of what he said was misinformed. He stated that the lock on the bedroom door could only be operated from the inside; some pointed out that unscrewing the plate on the outside would have enabled the door to be locked. He stated that the windows were locked when they were merely shut. He told the conference that Professor Gibson had seen the body; he hadn't, and when this was pointed out, the AG then suggested he had meant Dr Ong, who had not seen it either.[27] His excursions into the detail of the case served only to arouse further public doubts.

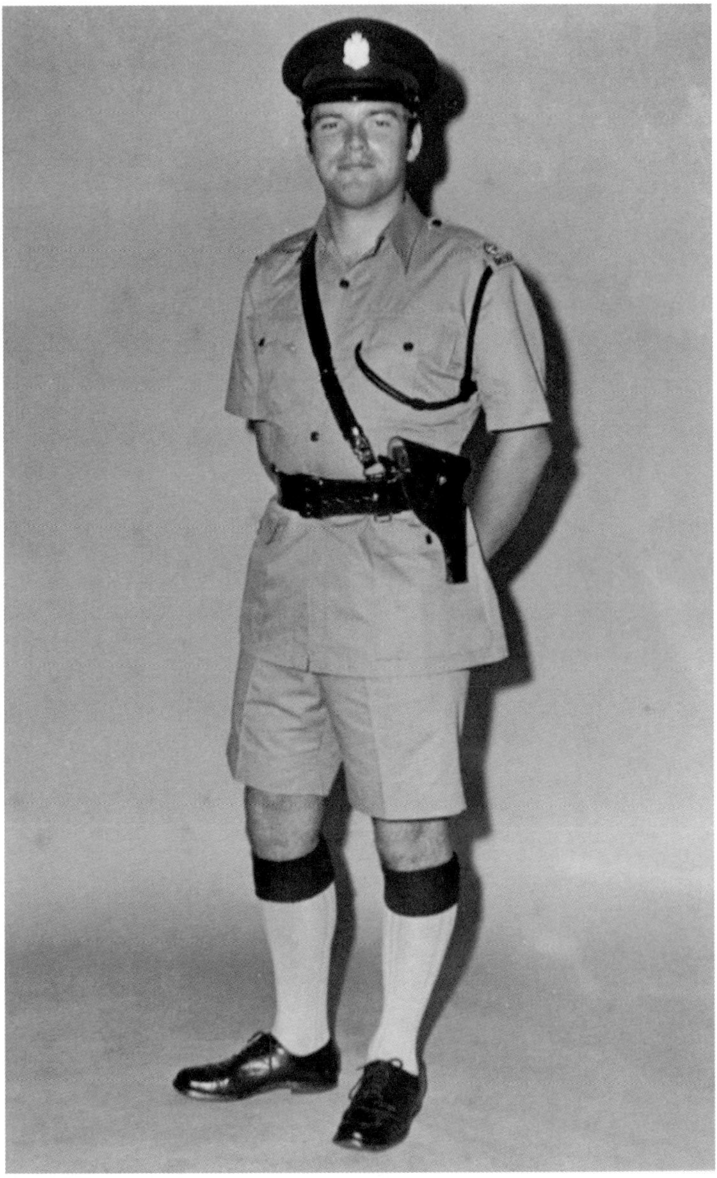

1. John MacLennan (Bridgewater Collection)

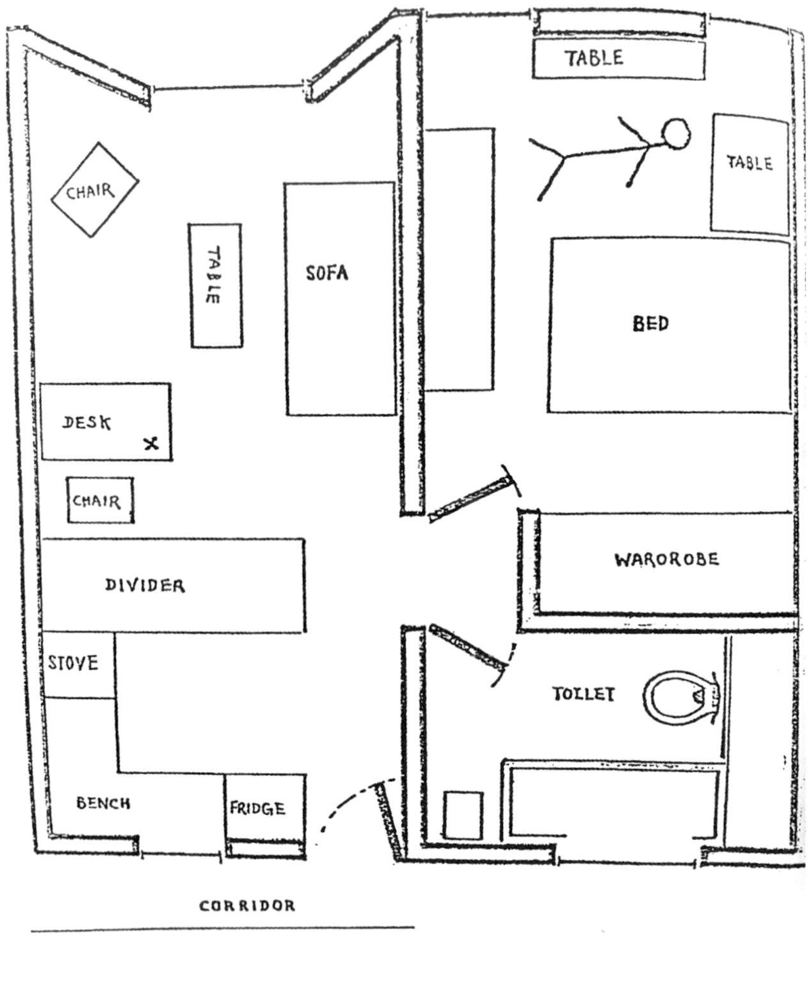

2. Floorplan of MacLennan's flat (National Archives)

3. Room rearranged (Bridgewater Collection)

4. MacLennan's flat (National Archives)

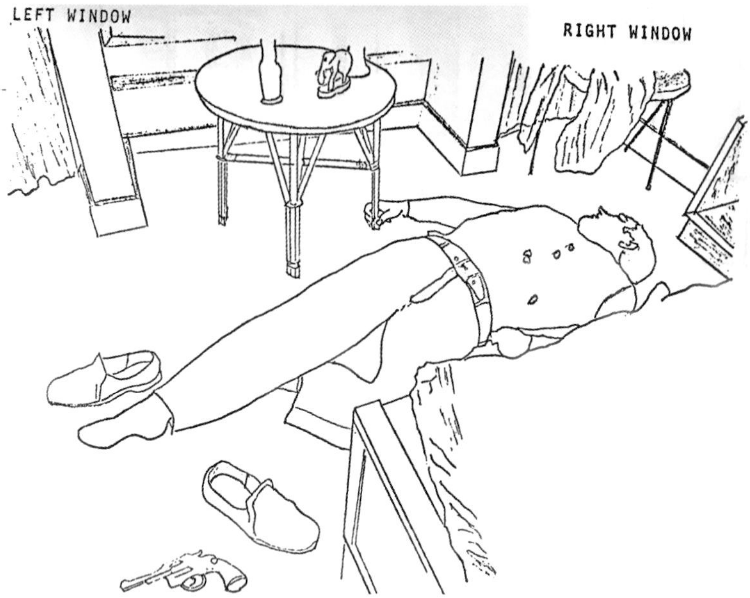

5. Crime scene: the body (National Archives)

6. John Richard Duffy (SCMP)

7. The revolver MacLennan used (National Archives)

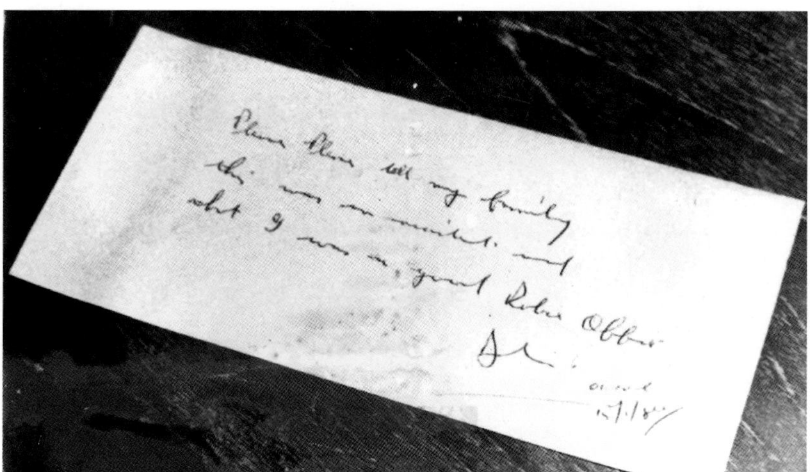

8. MacLennan's suicide note (Bridgewater Collection)

9. The Commissioner of Police, Roy Henry (SCMP)

10. Counsel for the Inquiry, John Beveridge (SCMP)

11. Assistant Commissioner of Police, Eric Blackburn (right) (SCMP)

12. Commissioner of the Inquiry, Justice Yang Ti-liang (SCMP)

17. Superintendent Bob Brooks (SCMP)

18. Superintendent Mark Pelly (SCMP)

11. Assistant Commissioner of Police, Eric Blackburn (right) (SCMP)

12. Commissioner of the Inquiry, Justice Yang Ti-liang (SCMP)

13. Counsel for the Commission, Michael Neligan (left) (SCMP)

14. Counsel for the MacLennan family, Conrad Seagroatt (SCMP)

15. Chief Inspector Michael Quinn (SCMP)

16. Inspector Michael Fulton (SCMP)

17. Superintendent Bob Brooks (SCMP)

18. Superintendent Mark Pelly (SCMP)

19. Counsel for the police, Andrew Hodge (SCMP)

20. Deputy Commissioner (Operations) Peter Moor (The Standard)

21. Attorney General John Griffiths (The Standard)

22. Elsie Elliot/Tu (Judith Mackay)

23. Aileen Bridgewater (The Standard)

24. Local antique dealer, Ian MacLean (SCMP)

25. David Lau, who alleged that John MacLennan made sexual advances to him in Yuen Long (SCMP)

26. Retired Metropolitan Police Constable John Conway (The Standard)

27. Senior Superintendent Jack Trotman (SCMP)

28. Sir Murray MacLehose, Governor of Hong Kong (National Archives)

The remarks made by John Griffiths about the jury and "tittle-tattle" infuriated Elsie Elliott, who from this time on ceased to credit him with behaving honourably. She took his remarks as a personal affront. On Aileen Bridgewater's show she threw the AG's words back at him, accusing him of using the "tittle-tattle" of the tainted evidence of male prostitutes to prosecute a man. "Now I think he is irresponsible," she declaimed, "provocative and prejudiced."[28] She let rip further the same day, telling the *Sun*:

> How dare he say the jury is wrong — what is the purpose of putting a jury there if he does not want to hear the result?[29] So far, I have always addressed my remarks to the Attorney-General personally, in letters or on the phone. He has seen fit to discredit me in public, so I owe him no courtesies, and will therefore address him in public.[30]

She was not alone in rejecting the AG's apparent attack on the jury. The most damaging condemnation came from Tony Pannell, the foreman of the jury, whose letter to the *South China Morning Post* appeared on 1 June and was widely reported in the English papers, and, for the first time, in the Chinese press. He publicly challenged the attorney general on six points concerning the detail that had arisen at his press conference, and ended his letter in capitals: "LONG LIVE THE JURY SYSTEM."[31]

Stung, John Griffiths issued another press release reiterating his view that the death had been a suicide, but not answering Pannell's challenges.[32] This was insufficient now to allay public disquiet.[33] Dr Denny Huang Mong-hwa, an urban councillor, took up the call for an inquiry, alleging that the public now doubted the attorney general.[34] Huang was a long-term critic of the colonial system who had earlier called for the legalization of homosexual acts. He had political links to Beijing and his intervention was not at all welcome to the government.[35]

Public criticism of the AG and calls for an inquiry were now occurring almost daily. The *Star* chipped in the next day with an editorial saying: "We don't pretend to understand the Attorney General's obviously esoteric thinking, but it does seem to us that even if Mr Griffiths somehow isn't over-ruling the jury, he would seem to be over-ruling the Coroner."[36]

The government had little with which to fight back, although it made a very feeble attempt to do so. On 4 June, the *Hong Kong Standard* was fed an unsubstantiated report that prostitutes in Tsim Sha Tsui had come forward to say that MacLennan was a regular customer of theirs, so regular that he was allowed to pay by cheque (there is no sign that he ever did so).[37] This story vanished without trace and was overshadowed by the much more striking TVB programme shown the next day in which Ian Whitely suggested that MacLennan's flat could have been entered through the closed, but not locked, bathroom window. Whitely demonstrated this feat himself and the programme caused a sensation.[38]

Others took a different tack. On 6 June, the *Star* published an article saying that there had been no evidence presented to prove that the suicide note had been written by John MacLennan. This stung Ronald Edgley, the chief chemist of the Government Laboratory Forensic Division and the police's chief handwriting expert, who had told the inquest that the note was certainly in MacLennan's handwriting, and he accused the *Star* of a "serious libel".[39] The attorney general was beginning to make similar threats of prosecution aimed at his detractors. On 5 June, the *Hong Kong Standard* quoted him hinting that Tony Pannell might be guilty of contempt of court. Griffiths demanded that the public trust him to do his job honestly and fairly.[40] They no longer did, and this distrust began to have a bad effect on the credibility of the government.

At least one junior police officer who was unsatisfied with the handling of the case spoke anonymously to the press at this time. He described MacLennan to the *Hong Kong Standard* as:

> a conscientious and hard-working Police Officer who enjoyed his job and was respected by those under him [...] John was a great mixer. The life and soul of a lot of parties. He lived life to the full, worked hard and played hard, but he was never careless about his work. He was certainly never lost for company.

The officer did not believe MacLennan was homosexual. He reported "an undercurrent of feelings among the junior officers that there is something not quite right in the background of the whole thing" and he expressed concern over the way evidence had been collected in the case.[41]

The Hong Kong Bar Association, whose views were usually taken great notice of by the government, issued a statement on 6 June that it was "unfortunate that the Attorney General gave the impression that he thought the jury had made the wrong verdict."[42] Aileen Bridgewater kept the kettle boiling by reading on air a short story entitled "The Inspector Who Knew Too Much", which had been sent to her by a member of the public calling himself "Simon Blake". This alleged that the police had murdered MacLennan. After the broadcast, the police seized the studio's copies of the script and threatened Aileen with a libel suit.[43]

The carefully planned campaign continued to ensure that the issue was not allowed to die. MP Dennis Canavan again raised the issue to Lord Privy Seal Peter Blaker in Parliament; Blaker responded on 10 June that the attorney general had studied the case and concluded that there was "overwhelming evidence at the inquest [...] which showed that [MacLennan] committed suicide" and that he had decided he had no legal powers to reopen the inquest.[44] For the first time the MacLennan family threw its weight into the demand for another investigation. Speaking to the *Hong Kong Standard*'s correspondent in Inverness, they said they wished to clear their son's name.[45]

The temperature was raised to a new level by Elsie Elliott on 17 June, when she held a press conference in the Fung Shui Room of the Hong Kong Hotel. She revealed that she had been told in October 1979 of the attempt to force Inspector Fulton (whom she still did not name) to set up John MacLennan, and that she had told John Griffiths of this in December. She demanded to know why the attorney general had not followed up her report. Was that, she asked, "gossip and tittle-tattle" — she was still sore about the remarks Griffiths had made the previous month. She questioned whether it was any longer possible to trust the AG and called for the disbandment of the SIU. Her remarks were covered in the British newspaper, the *Observer*.[46]

The government now felt obliged to reply once more. After a meeting between the governor and his closest officials, the attorney general issued a third statement on 19 June, this time one that ran to four densely packed pages.[47] In this, he reaffirmed that he would not re-open the case. Interestingly, he revealed for the first time that when Elsie Elliott had come to him on 20 December to warn him of the attempted set-up of MacLennan, he had already known of it and had discounted it:

> But before then, those and similar allegations had already been made and were known to the Government. They had been drawn to the attention of the Deputy Commissioner of Police and were dealt with.

Griffith's statement is at best incorrect, for the issues drawn to Peter Moor's attention in August 1979 involved Quinn's attempt to bully Magistrate Blue Wilson and counsel Michael Bunting, and they had not been "dealt with" as Paddy Clancy had not followed the instructions given to him to do so. He was muddling the issues here. The AG was, though, making it clear that he had known of the set-up and that he had not let on that he had been aware of it during the visits of either Howard Lindsay on 20 November or Elsie Elliott on 20 December.

Griffiths concluded the release by emphasizing the same point. He had made the decision to prosecute MacLennan on 30 November, he said, "knowing of Mrs Elliott's second-hand allegations and of the fact [...] that Inspector XYZ [Fulton's name had so far not been mentioned in public] had refused to do what was allegedly asked." Griffiths had, as has been noted, not told the governor of his knowledge in such stark detail and had merely stated to him that he had taken real notice of the Fulton allegations only when Miss Beeson's statement was before him *after* the death. The AG's revelation now must have undercut his position to some degree with Sir Murray.[48]

Griffiths then rubbed salt in the wound by making some personal remarks about Elsie Elliott. While his press release opened with the words: "I admire many things that Mrs Elliott has done, but she is not always right", he went on to complain of her

> unsubstantiated allegations of homosexuality based on gossip about a number of what, in her press statement, she describes as "frighteningly high-ranking members of the police and judiciary". Though I have asked her to do so, she has never once been able to substantiate these allegations [...] To mount a campaign of rumour and innuendo based on hearsay is in my opinion a wicked thing to do.[49]

Griffiths never seemed to know quite when to stop. In his release, he cited the letter he had sent Elsie Elliott on 2 February, in which he had referred to "European Inspector XYZ who had withdrawn his allegations of a 'frame up'". This statement had been untrue at the time, but it had been in a private letter. Now, the attorney general was foolish enough to repeat the obfuscation in a public document. Fulton had never alleged a "frame-up" and had *not* withdrawn his allegations of a "set-up".[50]

Elsie Elliott was, naturally, unimpressed at the attorney general's classification of her actions as "wicked". She retorted that she would fight to the end for an independent inquiry. It was the AG's duty to investigate crime, she said, and if he had reacted to her report MacLennan might not have died. She was not "being wicked" but was telling the truth.[51] She challenged the AG to produce the Inspector XYZ "even anonymously".[52] She then published open letters to the governor and Commissioner Henry, asking them to allow the inspector to speak out. Her letters were covered extensively in Hong Kong's Chinese press, which, ominously for the government, seemed at last to be catching up on a scandal it had so far largely ignored.

The governor still held firm, but the logjam began to break after 30 June, when Howard Lindsay wrote to all the English language papers revealing that Inspector XYZ was Mike Fulton and informing them that Fulton had told him of the SIU's attempt to force him to set up John MacLennan. Lindsay mentioned, too, that he had arranged for Fulton to repeat this to Elsie and in front of Claire-Marie Beeson, and that he had reported the issue to the attorney general.[53] This stimulated even more demands for an inquiry, and the first lengthy editorial appeared in the Hong Kong Chinese press, saying that: "There should be an exhaustive enquiry [...] the future administration of justice in Hong Kong is at stake".[54]

* * *

It had been over three months since the inquest, and still the government would not move, although the pressure had now grown to a level that was becoming increasingly dangerous to the orderly administration of the colony. Trust was being rapidly destroyed and the outside world was noticing. It was a bad time for this to be happening, as the scandal at Little Sai Wan was just then breaking in the English press. On 16 May, the *Daily Mirror* had revealed the inquiry ordered by Prime Minister James Callaghan.[55] The *Observer* and *New Statesman* had followed up with more in-depth articles, and the whistleblower who revealed the scandals, Jock Kane, was interviewed on the BBC's *Newsweek* programme. The uproar this coverage caused, including a protest by one hundred MPs when Granada's film on the subject was banned, continued through the summer months. The last thing Hong Kong needed now was a second issue whipping up contention in London. Peter Blaker had felt it advisable to make a statement in the Commons on 19 June giving full support to the attorney general, a move always reckoned to be the last before any drastic action.[56] London would not remain patient for much longer.

Rather than dying away, the campaign for an inquiry had grown and was revealing more and more damaging details in public. It must have appeared possible to the governor that the steady drip of information leaking into the press might eventually include some of the information that John Richard Duffy had given (they were aware of his correspondence with Elsie Elliott), and that had to be avoided. Police standing and morale were deteriorating.

Now, at last, the only man who had so far refrained from speaking out in public found the courage to do so. Mike Fulton's solicitors, Johnson Stokes and Master, issued a press release on their client's behalf on 2 July. This was endgame.

Fulton's solicitor, Ashley Burns, had taken the precaution of submitting a copy of his statement to police HQ for clearance before its release.[57] This the police gave to the AG, who advised them to submit a copy to the governor. Griffiths called in his assistant, Ray Astin, and together they pored over the office law books to establish their position. The AG then telephoned Burns directly. The young solicitor was taken aback to receive a call from the attorney general, and more so when the AG told him that it would be irresponsible of him to issue the press release. Had Burns considered, the AG asked, whether the release might constitute contempt of court? He added that in his view the statement was also a libel upon his person. Despite his disadvantage in age and rank experience, Burns was not prepared to be bullied in this fashion, and replied that he had considered but rejected both ideas.

Burns and his principal, Robin Pears, rapidly checked their own law books but could see no grounds for any case of contempt or libel. Nevertheless, they took no chances and consulted counsel, Charles Ching QC, who re-drafted but cleared the statement, saying that: "I find that the Attorney General was wrong in law in his view that the draft statement was capable of being a contempt of court as well as a libel upon him personally."

The press release was issued at a conference with Fulton present. It stated that Fulton had never claimed that anyone was being "framed" and had therefore never withdrawn such a charge.[58] It went on:

> At a recent press conference Mrs Elliott stated that an Inspector in the Royal Hong Kong Police Force had informed her that he had been instructed by the Special Investigation Unit of the Force ("SIU") to "set up" the late Inspector MacLennan. Our Client is that Inspector; we are instructed that he did receive such an instruction from certain members of the SIU and that he did so inform Mrs Elliott.[59]

This was *prima facie* evidence that the attorney general had deliberately misled the public.

Elsie Elliott was now joined in her campaign by Mr Ian MacCullum, chairman of the Hong Kong Branch of Justice, who called for a judicial inquiry into whether attempts had been made to set up MacLennan. Ray Chan, the senior assistant secretary general of UMELCO, said they would be looking very hard at the CAPO report into the Fulton case.[60]

Protests grew. The British newspaper the *Guardian* for the first time took an interest in the case and reported Fulton's statement.[61] On 5 July, the *South China Morning Post*, the *Hong Kong Standard*, and the *Sun* all published leaders demanding an inquiry, the *Post* saying "the half-truths and incomplete statements that have been published are causing deep public misgivings." The *Standard* was stronger, saying that the AG did not hold the trust of the public, had remained silent, and perhaps should resign; "A public inquiry into this alleged illegal activity of a law enforcement unit is vital to the wellbeing of our society."[62]

It seems that it was a gentle hint from London that finally made up the governor's mind. The FCO was coming under increasing pressure from MPs and the press calling for an independent inquiry. They were well aware, from advice from David Ford and the attorney general, that the administration in Hong Kong feared that launching an inquiry might open a Pandora's box. Ford had told Clift, head of the Hong Kong and General Desk, that the governor had consulted Sir Y. K. Kan, who had advised against an inquiry as the MacLennan affair was not "a matter of concern to the Chinese population". Griffiths had pointed out to Clift

> very forcibly, and has maintained the line that, given the amount of existing rumour and the overlapping of investigations concerning homosexuality, there would be a real danger that the enquiry would lead to revelations about senior members of the administration, including the Commissioner of Police [...] it would be politically very difficult to avoid acting on them without the Governor appearing to condone a cover up.

Despite this, on 4 July, when Minister Peter Blaker received a letter from MP Robin Cook asking for an inquiry, he sent a telegram to Sir Murray which informed him of that fact and concluded: "Parliamentary interest has increased [...] I need to expand a line in response. Appreciate the issue of the inquiry is yours to decide."[63]

Two days later, the governor finally buckled. He replied to Blaker that he had considered an inquiry when the coroner had said there were many questions unanswered, but had rejected the idea then as he had thought it only an expatriate issue and as he had not wanted to try a dead man. "Nevertheless in view of media reaction to the Fulton statement I can no longer accept the issue will soon die, and the longer it continues the more it acquires a spurious validity."[64]

Signs began to appear in the colony that the governor was preparing to yield. Press reports on 6 July indicated that a

Commission of Inquiry would be set up after the CAPO report into Fulton's allegations had reached UMELCO.[65] On 8 July, the police announced that the CAPO investigation had been filed.[66]

The next day, the attorney general made an announcement in the Legislative Council and issued a further press release. He stated that the Governor-in-Council had appointed a Commission of Inquiry into the death of Inspector MacLennan and that Justice Yang Ti-liang had been informed of his appointment as its commissioner.[67]

After three months, Elsie Elliott, Aileen Bridgewater, Tony Pannell, and their fellow campaigners had finally won their inquiry.

19

Commission of Inquiry

On 11 July 1980, Sir Murray MacLehose left Hong Kong to take four weeks' leave in the United Kingdom.[1] Before he flew, he held a press conference for which a statement was prepared about the MacLennan case. This addressed, head on, the question of the public's trust in the attorney general; "Should the AG be fired?" The reply was robust: "Of course not. He is a very brilliant lawyer and very highly thought of by legal circles here." The statement maintained that the governor had set up the Commission of Inquiry due to public confusion and the allegations made about the case. It also gave a specific answer to one of those allegations: "I have seen no list of senior officials who are homosexual, nor know if such a list exists."[2]

The governor told the press that the turning point had come for him when the Chinese papers had begun to take note of the issue.[3] This was true to some extent, but they had done so only as the decision to appoint the inquiry was being taken: four Chinese papers (*Sing Tao Wan Pao, The Express, Kung Sheung Daily News* and *Hong Kong Daily News*) had called for an inquiry on 8 July, and another, *Oriental Daily News*, had reported the case in a neutral fashion on the same day.[4] There was little local Chinese interest in the case.

The real reason for the governor's change of heart could not have been made public, for it was threefold: the loss of public trust, particularly in the person of the attorney general; the danger to police morale; and pressure from home. When he passed through London on his way to Scotland, the governor called on Peter Blaker at the FCO and discussed the MacLennan case. Blaker told him that he was sure that instituting a judicial inquiry had been the right thing to do, for it would relieve the pressure both in Hong Kong and in London.[5]

The establishment of the Commission of Inquiry also relieved the considerable pressure on those who had been campaigning for it. Each of them had felt very exposed by their opposition to the government; each had faced direct or indirect pressure to desist. Aileen Bridgewater, for instance, had been at supper one night at the United Services Recreation Club in Kowloon when she was button-holed by the AG, who took her to his table and sat alone with her until midnight to gently threaten her: "He said he could get me three months for libel, contempt or defamation."[6] Attempts had also been made to exert pressure at work on her husband, Ken, who was a government servant.[7]

On 7 July, Aileen invited Elsie Elliott, Tony Pannell, and other campaigners to a champagne supper for John Miller, the New Zealand lawyer at Hong Kong University who was advising her *pro bono* and had just been called to the bar. This was the only time the group had got together. "Everybody there had been speaking out and feeling alone. Tonight they found they weren't."[8] The announcement of the inquiry eased their very real fears.

The inquiry was welcomed widely. The president of the Law Society, Edmund Y.S. Cheung, said that "it will dispel the suspicions of a great many people". The chairman of the Hong Kong Bar Association, Martin Lee, was quoted as saying: "I personally would have preferred the announcement to have come a little earlier, but it's better late than never." Elsie Elliott, however, was not satisfied and, making public her fear that "it was yet another cover up", she continued to campaign for the appointment of a commissioner from London and an independent lawyer to represent the MacLennan family.[9] She made contact with the Labour Party peer, Lord Fenner Brockway, and over the next two months he continued to raise this issue and others connected with the inquiry in the House of Lords.[10]

The terms of reference given Justice Yang were wide. He was to examine:

a. Whether, in the light of all the evidence available and any additional enquiries you make, there are good grounds for a belief that the death of Inspector MacLennan was other than suicide and what conclusions you draw.
b. What official investigations immediately after the death of Inspector MacLennan were conducted, whether there were any shortcomings in them, and if so, what conclusions you draw as to the reasons for these shortcomings.
c. Whether the charges which were about to be preferred against him on the day of his death were properly brought, and whether on evidence properly obtained.

d. What investigations or enquiries (other than those resulting in the charges at (c)) were conducted regarding Inspector MacLennan, whether they were conducted with propriety, and what bearing, if any, they had on Inspector MacLennan's death.
e. Whether the investigations and enquiries under (b), (c) and (d) were properly motivated.[11]

Yang was a good choice for commissioner.[12] A High Court judge with a long record of service, he had presided over Godber's trial in 1975 and had already run several commissions of inquiry. He had been considered for the post of commissioner of the ICAC in 1978 but the governor had preferred to keep his talents in the judiciary.[13] He was steady, methodical, undemonstrative, and slow to anger, and had the deportment, appearance, and slightly detached air of an English gentleman. Conveniently, he had, since 5 July, chaired the subcommittee of the Law Reform Commission that had been tasked to examine the law on homosexuality in Hong Kong.[14] From the start, he was unhappy with the inquiry's terms of reference, which he felt "were almost unworkable" in their scope as they included the need to investigate the motivations behind what had occurred.[15]

On 14 July, Yang called for those with evidence to come forward and give their details to Norman Chan, the young civil servant appointed as secretary to the commission.[16] Yang's task was not made easier by an announcement from the AG's office three days later that no amnesty would be given to homosexuals coming forward to testify, a ruling that guaranteed that none would do so of their own volition.[17]

Two key figures remained to be appointed: the counsel and solicitor for the commission. It would be the task of the counsel to direct any investigation conducted into evidence for the inquiry, to bring to the commission both evidence and witnesses to be heard in public and to organize the hearings, a role as crucial as that of the commissioner. The solicitor for the commission was to assist him in handling all the legal matters connected with the inquiry's work. In addition, a barrister was to be appointed to represent the MacLennan family; a solicitor from the Legal Aid Department, Alan Harrison, had already been appointed in Hong Kong to instruct him.[18] It was decided that all those who might be affected by the findings of the commission would be represented, so at the start of the hearings there were seventeen barristers present and their numbers grew as the inquiry progressed. This was to be a feast of legal argument and of massive fees.

The Legal Department set about finding a counsel for the inquiry in the United Kingdom, using the firm of Charles Russell & Co., which often acted for them in London. Their nomination, Michael Neligan, QC, was appointed. A treasury counsel, he was one of a number of private practitioners who from time to time represented the British Government in the Old Bailey. He had been in Hong Kong in 1975, when he had assisted in the prosecution of Godber. The government could reckon that he was a man who knew when not to rock the boat.[19] A subordinate who came to know him well felt he was rather timid and described him as "not quite top of the range", a "senior junior criminal barrister".

Neligan was told that, apart from the open verdict at the inquest, the case was a straightforward one and would take only four weeks or so to complete. After he arrived in Hong Kong on 17 July, he was invited to meet the attorney general at the Hong Kong Club. The AG did so as a matter of courtesy and to reassure Neligan that the inquiry would be concluded in a matter of weeks, but the invitation was noted and laid Griffiths open to an accusation of trying to fix the inquiry.[20] Before it even opened, the inquiry began to show signs of growing beyond its intended size; in under two weeks of his arrival, Neligan had secured the appointment of an assistant, a further counsel for the commission, Anthony Neoh.[21]

It is likely that the government also viewed the solicitor appointed to the commission as a safe pair of hands. Murray Burton was a young and not very experienced Scottish lawyer of the firm of Zimmern & Co, which had been appointed solicitors for the commission. Zimmern's managing partner, Donald Cheung, was a friend of the attorney general and Burton was a family friend of the governor.[22] He had first come out to Hong Kong in 1976 with Sir Murray's personal help. He would not, however, prove to be anybody's poodle.

The commission opened in the Legislative Council Chamber on 2 July 1980, only to be immediately adjourned until 5 August at Alan Harrison's request to allow Conrad Seagroatt, the barrister he was to instruct for the MacLennan family, to arrive from London. Seagroatt was a junior barrister who had been a pupil at 2 Crown Office Row Chambers, in which the attorney general had practised.[23] Seagroatt himself came to believe that he had been appointed to represent the MacLennans because the attorney general "may have thought that he would seek a junior, keep it low profile, and have a man from 'our' chambers."[24]

Things would not work out in this fashion but this was exactly the sort of government behaviour which Elsie Elliott had expected, and she continued to campaign for the appointment of an independent barrister for the family. She secured a meeting with Neligan to browbeat him about it, but without success.[25]

She wanted her old friend Albert Sanguinetti to represent the MacLennans, but the government was having none of that idea and she was told that the family had requested that the government appoint a barrister on their behalf.[26] This, Elsie said, was just what they had said about the "request" for the cremation of John MacLennan's body. She publicly challenged the veracity of the government's line, causing Norman Chan (presumably acting for the commissioner) to threaten her with prosecution for contempt of court.[27] She wrote to the Scottish MP, Hamish Gray seeking his help to further her demand that the inquiry be held in England, and another Scottish Labour MP, Dennis Canavan, continued to raise the issue in the Commons.[28]

Some assistance for the campaigners did arrive from Britain, in the shape of a retired police officer named John Conway, an acquaintance of the MacLennan family. It did not emerge until later that he had taken it upon himself to persuade them that he should go to Hong Kong to conduct investigations on their behalf.[29] Conway had experience in forensics and ballistics in Northern Ireland and had been listed as a handwriting expert in the Law List of England and Wales.[30] He informed Elsie Elliott that he would reach Hong Kong on 3 August, telling her that he was the father of the Inspector Lloyd Conway who had been a pallbearer at John MacLennan's funeral. Elsie was ecstatic that help from an independent source was at last to hand.[31] However, Conway's involvement in the case began in a way that became typical; he claimed in his call to Elsie that his son Lloyd was MacLennan's "best friend", which was an exaggeration. Lloyd Conway was indeed a friend of John MacLennan, one of his drinking companions, but he was not his best friend. John Conway, it turned out, had a habit of insinuating himself into cases that for some reason interested him, then of putting the backs up of the people who trusted him. He could be cavalier in his adamant expositions of what he regarded as the truth.

However, when Elsie Elliott and Aileen Bridgewater went to meet him at Kai Tak Airport, it was with relief that at last an independent expert had come to their aid. In Aileen's words, they met an "ebullient, white-haired, sharp featured man of sixty-five who behaved like forty-five and claimed to feel that age [...] Elsie [was] so happy. John had lifted a great load off her shoulders."[32] Conway had flown at his own expense — the family had no resources to pay him — and was not on the payroll of the inquiry or accommodated at its expense with other witnesses in the Metropole Hotel. Instead, he was accommodated by the Bridgewaters in their government flat. Elsie Elliott later managed to persuade the inquiry to grant Conway a daily food allowance of HK$100, but for the rest he depended upon those who were hosting him. Aileen described him as "almost a caricature of a detective", a combative man whose "attitude was always that of an active rival. He belittled the rest."[33] At the start, they got on very well, and Conway would talk late into the night with Ken Bridgewater about what he had found in his investigations of the day.

Conway's first port of call was to meet the family's lawyer, Conrad Seagroatt, who was staying at the Hilton Hotel. They did not take to each other. Conway told the Bridgewaters that he believed "Seagroatt [was] already nobbled".[34] This proved to be a grossly mistaken assessment, but Seagroatt's appraisal of the other man was to prove more accurate; Conway was, he thought, "a charlatan who had climbed onto the bandwagon for his own purposes".[35]

* * *

The inquiry reconvened on 5 August with Michael Neligan making the opening remarks. In his preparation, he had made use only of the police reports and had not engaged any independent investigators.[36] Elsie Elliott and Aileen Bridgewater were so incensed at the way he seemed to accept the official line before the inquiry had even begun that they walked out in disgust.

Conway put in a short appearance, presenting Justice Yang with a letter accrediting him for the family, and Yang gave him permission to conduct investigations and forensic tests, although he made him sit in the public gallery. When not present at the sessions, Conway got on with conducting tests on the revolver and with examining the bullets and the suicide note. He found that the revolver was eighteen years old, leaked gas, and had a low muzzle velocity, features that would have reduced any recoil and made repeated single shots possible (features supported by the fact that of the five bullets fired at point blank range, only two had passed through MacLennan's body and one had been caught in his jersey).[37]

Throughout the inquiry, the commissioner and the lawyers for the police made strenuous efforts to keep secret the names of any alleged homosexuals listed in the documents submitted as exhibits. Yang's ruling that they were "irrelevant" to the case was true for most of them, and it was a sensible measure to protect the reputations of many men innocent of any offence. This meant continual dispute about what could or could not be seen by the lawyers or exposed to the public. The first days of the inquiry were devoted to these arguments, and when they were resolved, the inquiry adjourned to enable all those ruled entitled to do so to read the files. This gave Elsie Elliott time to write to Justice Yang to complain about Neligan's acceptance of all the "facts" from the police reports.[38] Yang had taken as much of Elsie's interference as he would put up with, and when the inquiry resumed for the fourth time on 11 August, he made a statement that the case was now *sub judice* and threatened with punishment anyone who in future attempted to influence him outside the hearings.[39] The English language reporters who were in attendance every day from the start of the inquiry (the Chinese press were usually not present, "continuing to adopt an attitude of 'what is all the fuss about' and considering it an expatriate affair"[40]) published Yang's warning. Elsie took the hint. For the time being, she desisted. The commission then at last began to hear evidence.[41]

Things progressed very slowly, partly because Neligan and Norman Chan had not ensured adequate support for the hearings. Murray Burton found his work greatly hampered by the "initial amateurishness".[42] There was no stenographer, despite the earlier public announcement, and instead the commission made use of a tape recorder. This was cumbersome to operate when it was necessary to read back witnesses' statements and meant that Burton had to take the tapes to his office after the close of the hearings and transcribe them manually for his secretary to type up, a proceeding that usually took until 3 a.m. the following morning and rapidly wore him out.

Expert witnesses and members of the SIU were the first to be called. The government had taken care to bolster the forensic evidence it had presented at the inquest and London experts were now on hand to support the views of the locals on ballistics and forensics. These new experts suffered the disadvantage, of course, of not having seen the body.

Dr Hugh Robert Molesworth Johnson, of the Department of Morbid Anatomy at London's St Thomas Hospital Medical

School, gave his opinion that "there is nothing inconsistent with the views expressed by the three pathologists that the wounds on MacLennan's body were self-inflicted."[43] Peter Prescott, who was principal scientific officer in the Firearms Department of the Home Office Forensic Science Service, had examined the revolver and found that it had a minimum trigger force of 3 lbs. per single action (meaning the pressure needed to fire the weapon when it had been cocked by hand), 10 lbs. per double action (the pressure needed to cock and fire the weapon by pulling the trigger only). He agreed with all the other experts that this was a case of suicide.[44]

Prescott was caught out in an embarrassing fashion when he stated that "I have examined the sweater and shirt [...] There are five bullet entry holes in the front of both garments." On the day of John MacLennan's death there had only been four entry holes in the clothing, as had been shown in the photographs taken then. The single shot into the abdomen seemed to have been taken with the muzzle of the revolver poked up inside the clothes. This is why both Trotman and Quinn had initially reported that there were only four gunshot wounds. John Conway spotted this error and prompted Seagroatt to point out that the clothing had four entry holes. When the sweater was examined in court, there were indeed four entry holes.

Yet by the time the drawing of the body and the photographs of the clothing appeared in the final inquiry report, there would be five entry holes in the jersey.[45] The evidence had been tidied up. There was no actual significance to this fraud, save that it further undermined confidence in the police investigation and went some way to discredit the expert witness called by the government.

Inspector Gus Graham and Chief Inspector Mick Quinn were the first police officers called to give their accounts of what had led up to the death. Graham confirmed that Mike Fulton was a "self-confessed homosexual and one of the SIU's principal informants [...] a voluble and willing informer."[46]

Quinn was on the stand over four days.[47] He blustered confidently at first under very gentle questioning by Michael Neligan. He lied about the origin of the investigation into MacLennan, producing an account that several police witnesses were subsequently to attempt to hide behind:

> Initially he was never a target, or subject of Special Investigation Unit enquiries, however whilst enquiring into other personalities engaged in the procuration of youths, the deceased's name frequently surfaced as being a customer of male prostitutes.[48]

Quinn denied that any attempt had been made to set up MacLennan and claimed that he was himself the victim of a "homosexual campaign to discredit" him, adding that

> I have for a number of years been conducting enquiries into homosexuals, and I am fully aware that they are fickle beings who are subject to changes of mood. It is completely out of character for me to raise my voice, ridicule or harass them.[49]

He complained that Elsie Elliott and Howard Lindsay had made remarks about him that were criminally libellous. In thirty years of police service, he claimed, he had never had a complaint made against him and he was distressed that he had now been the subject of two in this case.

The easy ride he was getting was not to last. When Neligan sat down, Conrad Seagroatt rose to cross-examine and showed for the first time the formidable mettle that gradually changed the minds of those who had hitherto doubted his independence. He put Quinn on the spot, had no truck with his outraged sensibilities, and courteously but steadily discredited the quality of the SIU's evidence.

Seagroatt made Quinn admit that the prostitute Jeff had identified MacLennan in only one of the photographs he had been shown and that both Eddie and Jeff had given the SIU non-existent addresses for the locations at which they had claimed to have engaged in sex with MacLennan. They had also, Quinn was compelled to admit, wrongly described MacLennan's flat and, in their different statements, had altered the dates on which they claimed to have met MacLennan. The earlier statements had not matched MacLennan's movements, the later ones conveniently had. Other details they had given the SIU, Quinn was forced to agree, were simply wrong. They had said that he was driving a white car, then altered the colour to blue, when MacLennan had no car at all (Seagroatt was not aware of the existence of the silver-grey Volkswagen).[50]

Perhaps because of his now apparent intent to do what he could to properly represent the MacLennan family, Conrad Seagroatt now found himself subject to adverse pressure. He was telephoned one evening at his hotel by a lawyer he recognized, who knew that he had been a pupil in the firm in which the attorney general had been a junior. The caller made the suggestion that, since there was a conflict of interest arising from this fact, Seagroatt should inform the MacLennan family and Elsie Elliott. Seagroatt did not see that there was any conflict and believed that an attempt was being made to have him withdraw from the inquiry. When the lawyer rang again the next day to ask whether he would take the suggested action, Seagroatt said that he would not. He did not inform the MacLennans or Elsie Elliott, and he did not withdraw.[51]

On Quinn's third day in the witness box, Andrew Hodge, who was once again representing the police force, caused a sensation by asking if it was true that in 1978 John MacLennan had told a police personnel officer that he had seen a Special Branch list of homosexuals, and that this had included the name of Commissioner Roy Henry. Justice Yang called an immediate halt to proceedings and withdrew into his chambers for ten minutes with the bevy of barristers. When they returned, Neligan made an announcement that "the allegation against Roy Henry was totally unsupported and that it was only a rumour." Yang made it impossible to raise the issue again at the inquiry, despite the fact that it was certainly of relevance to MacLennan's death. From now on, he refused to permit any questioning on the subject of the sexual orientation of the commissioner of police.

Hodge gave the unlikely explanation for his "outing" of the name of the commissioner of police that "there had been hints of vendettas in the past by the SIU against members of the homosexual community" and he wished to discount them by showing the even-handedness of the unit. It was more likely that the revelation was made to prevent it being made by one of the opposing barristers. Conrad Seagroatt had certainly considered using the issue, although he had decided separately not to do so as he understood that it was potentially damaging to the colony.[52] By seeming to show that Henry had nothing to hide, Hodge was seeking to forestall any accusation that the commissioner of police had a motive to harm John MacLennan. His question successfully cauterized the issue, which was a highly dangerous one for the government.[53]

Eric Blackburn entered the witness box on 20 August. He stated that MacLennan was regarded as being disloyal for getting outside help in 1978 and admitted that he had personally warned him to "weigh in the balance the possible damage he may have caused his future prospects."

After less than two weeks, it became evident that Michael Neligan was feeling the pressure of the inquiry. On 16 August, he appeared wearing a patch over one eye, claiming to be suffering from an infection. In his examination of the minor witnesses who followed Prescott to the stand, he seemed to observers to be painfully slow.[54] He lost his place during questioning one afternoon, started to speak nonsensically, repeating himself and rambling on and on without relevance to the matters in hand. To save him embarrassment, Conrad Seagroatt took the initiative and asked for an adjournment.[55] Yang feared that Neligan might have suffered a stroke and was glad to accede. On 20 August, it was announced that Neligan was too sick to go on and he immediately flew back to London. Few believed the reason given for his rapid departure. It was widely assumed that he had buckled under the pressure of the case and the workload it involved. Charitable observers felt he had suffered a sort of breakdown;[56] others suspected he had not wanted to carry on in a case which he had discovered, only when he arrived in Hong Kong, was burdened with such a fraught political background; he could see no "swift fix" and fled.[57]

Neligan's departure halted the inquiry in its tracks. It was a disaster for the government, which had been relying on Neligan to conclude the inquiry in a short time (the expectation had been that all would be wrapped up in sixty days).[58] Now it was open to charges of procrastination (charges which Elsie Elliott and Aileen Bridgewater immediately made in the media).[59] More important was the fact that the government had lost its malleable counsel.

The crown solicitor later briefed the governor that Justice Yang "would have been able to assert himself against Neligan" and that "had Neligan been able to see the Inquiry through, there is little doubt but that these proceedings would have concluded before Christmas 1980."[60] Things were not going as the government had intended.

There was now another delay while a search started for a fresh counsel for the inquiry. Justice Yang informed the governor that the inquiry would not be able to resume work until 10 September and that he estimated it would take six weeks after that to conclude. This was an estimate that would be exposed by events to be wildly optimistic.[61]

Yang now took Norman Chan with him to London to find a replacement for Neligan, once again making use of Charles Russell & Co., who had initial difficulties finding volunteers for the post as most of the barristers in London were out of town for the summer holidays. Shortly after Yang's arrival, they introduced him to one of the few volunteers they had been able to locate, and, after an initial interview, Yang was sufficiently impressed to appoint their candidate. This was John Beveridge, QC, a much more powerful advocate than Neligan and a man with a fine reputation. Yang clearly wished things to be handled better in future. Unfortunately for the government, Beveridge was also a man with a highly independent mind, a lawyer who would bend to no pressure and would do his utmost to ferret out the truth, wherever he suspected it led and however long it took. Sir Murray MacLehose's hopes of a swift and painless outcome to the inquiry were about to be further frustrated.[62]

Beveridge immediately saw the impossibility of conducting an inquiry into the actions of the police relying solely on the information they had supplied. He persuaded Justice Yang to agree that independent investigators be appointed to examine the evidence so that the inquiry had a base of facts from which to work. Yang also agreed to seek the advice of more forensic experts to allow a fuller examination of the evidence, and they set about recruiting these in London. From the beginning, John Beveridge made his mark on the inquiry and Justice Yang came to realize what sort of man he had appointed. To Yang, "he had seemed to be a man of good sense" when they met, but he soon came to feel that Beveridge was something of a "gung-ho character".[63]

20

The Carratu Investigation

Almost exactly at the time when the inquiry was grinding to a halt, Slasher George, who had by now returned to Hong Kong from Manila, contacted Aileen Bridgewater. He was intent on giving evidence at the inquiry on behalf of John MacLennan. He rang Aileen during her show on 22 August, calling himself Robin and asking to speak to her off air. When he explained who he was, Aileen agreed to meet him after the programme at a Chinese café in the industrial area of San Po Kong in Kowloon.[1] It was a place not usually frequented by expatriates, and when she got there by taxi, she dubiously poked her head around the door of the café and was called over to his table by George. She described him as a "nineteen year old Chinese-looking boy", an "insignificant but neatly dressed and groomed Eurasian [who] spoke good English with a slight American accent." He introduced himself as Robert, not Robin.[2]

The restaurant was noisy and packed. They sat near the door and had been talking for a while when three Europeans dressed in Hawaiian shirts came in. One of them, a tall, craggy man with short hair, came over to them, stared at them, then walked away.[3] George was terrified; "they are SIU, and that's their uniform", he told Aileen.[4] Nevertheless, they stayed put and Aileen managed to record an interview in which George told her of his relationship with MacLennan. He had two letters from John, he said, which he would bring to show Aileen at their next meeting. He wanted to testify.[5]

What George told her disturbed Aileen very much. He related that, after he had arrived back in Hong Kong, he had been met at the airport by two gay friends, who told him that "some people were trying to stop the MacLennan case from being disclosed to the public." Since he returned, he had been stopped twice in the street, the first time about 11.30 p.m. by a European and a Chinese who claimed to be off-duty police officers.[6] They told him that he should "stay out of the MacLennan case or you had better be very careful where you walk," said "remember, we're not joking", and pushed him against a wall. On the second occasion, about a week later, late at night at about 1.30 a.m., he had been set upon behind the Park Theatre by three eighteen- or nineteen-year-old boys, who he thought were triads.

> When I came out of the restaurant, they pushed me against a wall. They searched me. Didn't show me a warrant card or anything. They took HK$500 bill from me plus two US$50 bills and HK$60 cash. They also took my travellers cheques which I had from my parents. Also some personal belongings, a gold chain and a ring. "This is what's going to happen to you if you get involved in the MacLennan case." [They] hit me in the face and I had a bruise for three days.

When I got home, I was just opening the door and collapsed. I guess it was the shock. I woke up about two hours later. I was so frightened. I was close to suicide [...] I took razor blades and tried to slash myself. Now I'm broke.[7]

Slasher George also gave Aileen a good deal of information about the gay scene in Hong Kong, including a lot about Gordon Huthart, whom he knew well, and who, he said, was one of the men who took advantage of boys and gave them Mandrax to make them incapable of resisting his sexual advances. Another of these men was named Ian McLean, someone of whom Aileen had not so far heard, and who, George said, was:

Very, very, very wicked, evil and exactly the same as Gordon Huthart [...] He's the owner of the antique shop in front of Victoria Police Station in Central. He's a very fat European, he lives up the Peak. Also called McLean Mansion. A lot of Chinese boys know him. They call him *Dai Yee Ma*. Translated it means "big second mother", which is like a *mama san*, because he looks like one and so feminine in how he speaks and dresses. Huge and fat and ugly. Something like bald but curly and all [...] He's not a *mama san* but he gets all sorts of kids, little kids. I for one know he carries grass on him twenty-four hours a day on his body. I've actually been with him and he carries it in his handbag, in his car, in his home [...] He even grows it. In his home. Just a little flowerpot.[8]

Three days later, George called Aileen again, this time in much distress.[9] He said he had been beaten up and had gone to the Queen Mary Hospital with facial and abdominal bruises but had not been kept in.[10] Aileen arranged to meet George the next day at the café in which they had met before, but this time whisked him away in a taxi to the safety of the United Services Recreation Club, where he told her what had happened.

George told Aileen that on Sunday 24 August he had been "approached by three Chinese guys. I was beaten. They took everything from me, my wallet, my watch, my ring." He recognized one of them as one of those who had first met him on his return to Hong Kong and had warned him to stay out of the case, and two of them were those who had beaten him on the second occasion. He gave Aileen two conflicting stories as to how he had been set upon. Firstly, on the telephone, he told her that three Chinese boys claiming to be police had ambushed him in Central having lured him there supposedly to attend a job interview, which seemed to Aileen unlikely as it had been a Sunday. They said, according to George: "We told you not to speak to anyone" then beat him up.[11] At the USRC, he told her that he had gone out on Sunday morning for a newspaper: "I had breakfast out. I was approached by three Chinese. One I had seen before. They said 'Stay out of the case or you've had it.' Punched me five or six times in the stomach." He told Aileen:

> I think the police are in this. I am being hassled by the police, not triad members, but policemen [...] I have had everything taken from me. I am going to send a telegram to my father in Hawaii for more money, then I will leave, then I will come back with my own attorney and I will find you and we will go to Justice Yang.[12]

George was unable to give Aileen MacLennan's two letters because his flat had been ransacked while he was out and the letters had gone. He was scared stiff, far too frightened now to testify. He was never to do so. Instead, he made a half-hearted attempt to commit suicide, and the next time Aileen spoke to him he was in the Queen Elizabeth Hospital where he was recovering.[13] By then, however, Aileen had tapes of the two interviews.

The story related by Slasher George indicated that the SIU was not about to allow any version of events that was different from the one they had compiled to emerge into the light of day. It was also around this time that two police officers once again visited John MacLennan's mistress and told her she was not being called to testify at the inquiry. She was warned that "it would not be in the interests of herself or her husband or of his business if she did not keep well out of the case." Evidence that MacLennan had been bisexual, and that he had been fully capable of carrying on an affair with a woman of a reputable class, was not to be allowed to cloud the picture that they wished the inquiry to accept.[14]

* * *

On 4 September 1980, John Beveridge arrived in Hong Kong.[15] His initial remarks to Justice Yang worried the judge, as they might well have done in the light of what was to follow. "Now," said Beveridge, "we can uncover all the dirt in Hong Kong."[16] Six days later the inquiry reopened, only to be adjourned yet again for four weeks to allow the commission's own investigation to be completed.[17] This, it was announced, was to be run by a man the *Post* called the "legendary Vincent Carratu", a former Metropolitan Police Fraud Squad expert who now ran his own private investigation company.[18] He brought with him to Hong Kong a retired English detective chief inspector, Terry Reeder, whose police service had included seven years in a murder squad. They were to lead a team of ten investigators recruited locally by Anthony Gurka, a Yugoslav who was boss of Asian Inspection Services, one of Hong Kong's investigating and security firms.[19] Unfortunately, Gurka drew his men from former Tsim Sha Tsui policemen and ex-detectives from various branches including Special Branch, and this immediately made the team he assembled suspect in the eyes of many who viewed all recently retired policemen as corrupt. Gurka's company did indeed have a poor reputation in some quarters[20] and in less than two weeks the local ex-policemen he had employed were weeded out. The *Post* carried a story that they had been sacked because of their "dubious connections", a story perhaps once again deliberately leaked to the press.[21] This meant that the activities of the team were somewhat circumscribed. Thereafter, Carratu was assisted only by two Chinese language staff supplied by the Home Affairs Bureau.

The Carratu investigation was to receive few plaudits in Hong Kong. John Beveridge told Conrad Seagroatt that the team did not impress him, a view also held by other lawyers at the inquiry.[22] The team's work was hampered not only by having to rely on untrustworthy local investigators but also by the fact that the police, particularly the SIU, regarded them as interlopers and as a threat. Immediately they began work, they found that witnesses were being taken out of circulation. Between 16 and 18 September, the police conducted a series of raids and arrested thirty people, including the masseur Sunny Chan Chi-fong, whose advertisement stating "New Way Massage, Sunny Chan, Perfectly Relax, 5-7908408" had appeared in the *Sun* for the last four years.

Chan was charged with procuring an act of gross indecency and living on earnings of prostitution. The police took the opportunity of smearing MacLennan in connection with him, leaking to reporter Kevin Sinclair (who duly published the information) that "the name of a dead police inspector appeared in a document seized in a raid on Tuesday night." This story was baseless and deservedly never resurfaced.[23] Charges against

Sunny Chan were increased later to include seven more counts of procuring an act of gross indecency, incitement to commit buggery, and committing an act of gross indecency and he was kept out of the way as his case proceeded to trial.[24]

Throughout the two years following John MacLennan's death, both Elsie Elliott and Aileen Bridgewater were fed information from anonymous sources inside police and government, people who supported what they were doing. Elsie managed in this way to collect both a large selection of classified government documents and gossip that gave her a very good idea of what was going on inside the administration. Aileen had many listeners who would phone in, some to ask her to ring them back off air. One such was a CID officer whom she knew but nicknamed Raven. On 18 September, this source spoke to her about the arrest of Sunny Chan, which, he alleged, had been carried out not by the SIU but by the CID. Chan had been hitherto protected by the SIU, Raven alleged, and had now been lifted to keep him out of Carratu's way.[25]

The gay community in Hong Kong made Carratu's task harder as they "pulled the shutters" down on his team, having been refused guarantees of immunity if they talked to the inquiry.[26] Despite these setbacks, Carratu and his men set about interviewing all the witnesses they could get their hands on, including most of the prostitutes who had been about to give evidence against John MacLennan. In all, they took a total of sixty statements, to which lawyers for the inquiry added another thirty.[27]

Under this questioning, many of the prostitutes changed their tune and recanted their incrimination of MacLennan. Justice Yang was so disturbed by this that he requested a written confirmation from the commissioner of police that the SIU not be allowed to have any further contact with the prostitutes.[28] He was being naïve, perhaps, to believe that such an undertaking would be honestly observed, but the undertaking was given. Nor was Yang happy with the conduct of investigations by Vincent Carratu and his team, which he felt were being directed into areas not connected with John MacLennan. On one occasion, Carratu rang Justice Yang and told him that he was about to investigate the chief justice, Sir Denys Roberts, on the orders of John Beveridge. Yang had neither been asked about nor informed of this and stopped it immediately. He did not, he said "believe that the Inquiry should be extended to all the homosexuals in Hong Kong."[29]

Carratu was by now the butt of what became a distressingly wearisome series of threats against himself and his team. "Threats and warnings to leave Hong Kong 'if he knew what was good for him' were commonplace," he later told the press, and he calculated that by the end of his inquiries he had been threatened thirty-four times and had lost four witnesses who "had gone for a swim in the harbour".[30] Intimidation, clearly, was not to be confined to MacLennan's mistress and Slasher George. The day Carratu arrived in Hong Kong, the tyres of the Bridgewaters' car were spiked outside their flat.[31] TV reporter Ian Whitely was assaulted in the toilet of a bar by an expatriate he believed to have been a police officer, who thrust a revolver into his face and told him to stop broadcasting about the MacLennan case. He was so unnerved by this that not long afterwards he left Hong Kong for good.[32]

* * *

Two events now occurred which served to indicate that the inquiries of the Carratu team were coming dangerously close to the truth. The first of these seems sadly to have been the result of an act of public spiritedness on the part of Aileen Bridgewater, who, on 29 September, finally allowed her conscience to overcome her fears for the safety of Slasher George and played a copy of the tapes of her interviews with him to Murray Burton.[33] Burton telephoned Ian McLean and arranged to interview him on 3 October. When they spoke, McLean expressed himself willing to talk. The day before the interview, McLean was murdered by two Chinese boys whom he had taken to his flat.[34]

The Hong Kong press, covering the story in some detail, reported that the fifty-year old bachelor businessman had been found dead in his home in Mountain View Mansion at 23 Plantation Road. He was naked, had been gagged, his arms and legs had been tied with cords, and he had been suffocated. An attempt had been made, it seemed to some, to make the scene look like a death by sexual bondage that had gone wrong.[35] The flat had been ransacked but seemingly after the death, as the only signs of struggle were on the bed.

McLean was an Australian who had come to Hong Kong twenty-one years before to take a post as a physics lecturer at the University of Hong Kong, but for the last nine years he had been running a highly successful business as an antiques dealer and decorator. It was reported that he had been the first person to go to China to advise the Chinese Government on how to market replica antiques and he had been licensed in Shanghai and Peking to make copies for export worldwide. He had a shop on Fifth Avenue in New York. His success, however, was surface deep, for after his death he was found to be massively in debt.

McLean's death had occurred between midnight and 6 a.m. on the day before he was to be interviewed by Carratu. The police established that he had gone to Disco Disco on the previous evening, where he had been seen later getting into his Volvo with a couple of young Chinese men. His car was found the next morning outside number 18, Ventris Road in Happy Valley, having been abandoned after being involved in a traffic accident at about 6.30 a.m. The first press reports were suspicious in that they made an immediate linkage with the MacLennan inquiry; the news of the Carratu interview had been leaked, presumably by the police, and the press reported: "underworld sources say he was about to be interviewed by Carratu, who would not comment."[36]

The two youths were swiftly arrested. It seemed that it was intended that the murderers be found. The fact that McLean's car had been driven away and abandoned so publicly was revealing, as was the fact that one of the men was about to serve a prison sentence. On 1 November 1980, an eighteen-year-old Chinese dance hall captain named Wong Chee-keung was charged with the murder of Ian McLean, with stealing his car and driving without licence or insurance, and, with his companion Ma Chun-fat, of stealing HK$80 from the flat.[37]

When their cases came to two separate trials in May the next year, they were heard in person by the chief justice. Wong would claim at his trial that McLean had taken the sixteen-year-old Ma into the bedroom to have sex while he himself stayed outside. Hearing fighting, he had burst into the bedroom and found them naked and struggling. He had helped his friend, they had overpowered McLean and tied him up, then suffocated him with a pillow, gagged him with socks, and left. Forensics revealed that McLean had been the victim of a vicious assault. His body was extensively injured on the neck, right arm, chest, and thighs, and bruised on the right temple. An attempt had been made to strangle him, but he had died from asphyxiation caused by the pillow.[38]

Ma Chun-fat, who had just started serving three years for another robbery when charged, admitted that McLean had picked him and Wong up at Disco Disco and taken them home. There, he said, he had engaged "in certain acts" with McLean, but when he objected to performing other acts, McLean had slapped his face. Wong rushed in, McLean shouted for help, they put a pillow over his face to quieten him, then tied him up and put socks in his mouth. His counsel, Patrick Yu, said that McLean had "asked for trouble and got it". Chief Justice Roberts accepted this "gay defence". No other evidence of McLean's sexual orientation was adduced, so in this Roberts was accepting the word of two killers, one of whom was already a convicted felon. He accepted a reduced plea of manslaughter and sentenced both to three years, nine months in prison.[39] Roberts was himself a man accused of being a homosexual who preyed on young boys. He was on Duffy's list.

It will never be known who really killed Ian McLean and it is not recorded why he had been considered important to the inquiry. There was no apparent connection with MacLennan. The two men had never met. The few dots left to connect, however, give some indication as to why McLean was murdered. He was undoubtedly involved in a good range of unsavoury activities, including drug trafficking and procuring.[40] Perhaps trailing a red herring he had been given, reporter Kevin Sinclair speculated in the *Post* that McLean had been connected with a gay blackmail circle, a gang of twenty or so men that were known to target rich gay men by placing a prostitute in their home as bait.[41] It is unlikely, however, that such low-level criminality would have featured in McLean's more highly priced activities.

Slasher George had informed Aileen Bridgewater that McLean was a procurer of small boys for rich and important men. This role of intermediary was one that businessman Ka Sze Chow had earlier performed for Sir Geoffrey Briggs and his friends. McLean, too, had powerful contacts. His neighbours told the press that he "was very generous and good hearted and frequently entertained influential bankers and members of the diplomatic corps at his home."[42] Someone of this type was needed as an intermediary by the rich or prominent. If you were, say, the chief justice of Hong Kong or the chairman of a large and highly respectable banking corporation, and you wanted to offer the guests at a party in your house on the Peak the opportunity to make use of the little boys who, stark naked, were serving them canapés, you could not go down yourself to the streets of Tsuen Wan or to Disco Disco to find those boys. You needed an intermediary to do that for you, and that had been the beauty of John Richard Duffy's activities, for he did it for free for those he liked. Others had to pay for such a service. The people being paid by the intermediary, either in money or favours or both, would have been triads. Ian McLean was a procurer of little boys for rich clients and the prospect of his squealing about the sources of his supply would have been a sufficient motive for his murder. His triad suppliers would not have been beyond killing him to protect themselves and the clients who were important to them. In return, they might have expected something back, something that included, perhaps, two paltry three year, nine month sentences for the murderers they had provided.

This, of course, is speculation. Yet it is unlikely that Ian McLean just happened to be murdered on the morning before his interview by Carratu. The suspicion that he was killed to prevent his talking is strong. It would have been impossible to realize this at the time, but the murder was the closest that Carratu or anyone involved in the inquiry would get to probing the scandal that underlay it, the scandal Duffy had revealed of the procurement of children and youths. It was a scandal the revelation of which both government and perpetrators were desperate to prevent.

Whatever the real story behind the murder, McLean's death left the Carratu team without their witness and their investigation looking like a leaky sieve.

Two days later, a second incident occurred which halted the Carratu investigations completely. On 4 October, Terry Reeder and interpreter Leung Bo-san picked up the prostitute Jeff Tso in the car park of the RTHK studios, where he worked in the canteen. Under questioning, Tso alleged that Inspector Tin of the SIU had made him sign a fabricated statement against MacLennan. Tso was naturally frightened of retribution and agreed to stay under guard for a couple of days in the Lee Garden Hotel.[43] In the early hours of his second day there, he absconded, taking from his sleeping guards HK$2,300 in cash, a wristwatch, a lighter, a gold finger ring, keys, and even some of their shoes. When arrested by the police a few days later, he made the allegation that he had been held against his will.[44] Terry Reeder rightly called the incident "a fiasco".[45] It utterly destroyed the credibility of the Carratu team and resulted in Justice Yang calling for their immediate removal from the inquiry. John Beveridge was said to have had to threaten to resign if they were not allowed to complete their report. Somehow, all this was leaked to the press; once more it was Kevin Sinclair who reported on 13 October that the Carratu investigation had been brought to a halt before it had been able to conduct its appointments with senior police officers. The team, he wrote, had not even interviewed either the procurers or their boys.[46]

The timing and consequences of this incident were alone enough to make them suspicious. When it is remembered that Jeff Tso was a prostitute with a criminal record whose partner, Dick Stanford, was a police informer, and who was a man who had been persuaded, under threat of a prison sentence, to give false witness against John MacLennan, it becomes difficult to avoid the conclusion that his escape had been a successful attempt to discredit the Carratu team; an attempt made, one has to assume, by the SIU. Whoever it was that looked after Tso in recompense, they did so successfully. When he appeared in court on 17 November, charged with the thefts from the hotel, he was given only a suspended sentenced of twelve months and ordered to pay back what he had stolen.

Despite all this, Beveridge managed to ensure that Carratu was given until 29 October to submit his report. It was a document that was never published and it was not seen by the barristers representing individuals at the inquiry. Beveridge stated at the opening hearing that it contained irrelevant confidential material that would later be destroyed, and that it had "no evidential value".[47] All that can be said of it with confidence is that it concluded that MacLennan had committed suicide. It was never read by Justice Yang, who took the view that for reasons of impartiality he needed to remain free from its influence. Nevertheless, the Carratu report had some crucial consequences. It gave John Beveridge an independent framework from which to develop lines of questioning at the inquiry. More importantly, it alerted him and thus the public to the weakness of the SIU's case against MacLennan as well as to the methods they had employed.

The events involving the Carratu team, and the intimidation that occurred throughout the summer months of 1980, reinforced the suspicions of those who believed that John MacLennan had been murdered. Those now believing this included John Conway and, largely guided by Conway's speculations, Aileen Bridgewater and Elsie Elliott. The SIU and other parts of the police had done their best to prevent new evidence coming to light. They had failed, but in so doing they had further undermined the trust of the public in themselves, in the Legal Department, and in the government.

* * *

On 29 October 1980, John Beveridge rose to make his opening address in the Legislative Council Chamber. The MacLennan inquiry had at last resumed.

21

Opening Moves

The hearings of the Commission of Inquiry were to last for a little over seven months, and were to be open to the public and press throughout. The commission's remit was clear, but beneath the surface participants had aims not limited to a mere disclosure of the facts. Conrad Seagroatt, among others, believed that the government wanted to achieve three things: to show that John MacLennan was a disloyal hypocrite; to protect the attorney general; and to discredit Elsie Elliott.

As John Beveridge stated in his opening address, any person who was likely to be adversely affected by evidence presented at the hearings had the right to be represented by a lawyer.[1] There were many likely to be so affected and by the end of the proceedings sixteen lawyers had appeared to represent such persons.[2] Audrey Eu joined Beveridge and Neoh as an assistant counsel for the commission when it reopened on 29 October.[3] Of the twenty-six witnesses who had been called by Neligan, it was planned to re-examine five,[4] and in total 110 witnesses would be examined during the hearings.[5] Proceedings were therefore slow, and there was much tedious repetition and legal wrangling. The paperwork produced for the inquiry was voluminous, and included 142 statements, of which fifty-seven were read out in full during the hearings.[6]

The issues involved in the commission's work were serious in themselves, but the atmosphere was worsened by the animosities that the hearings laid bare, not only among witnesses, whose opposing views and personal antagonisms were given full opportunity for exposure, but also between the lawyers involved in the case. There were too many strong characters present and proceedings were soured from the start. A division soon appeared between, on one side, the London barristers Beveridge and Conrad Seagroatt, the counsel for the MacLennan family, and the group of Hong Kong barristers who represented the police (Andrew Hodge), the SIU (Kemal Bokhary), and in later stages the Legal Department (Barrie Barlow and Max Lucas). Charles Ingham, also of the Legal Department and representing Chief Superintendent Trotman, was part of the latter group when matters affected his client. The hostility between these two sets became as much personal as it was professional.

The character of John Beveridge was at the centre of much of the personal antagonisms that developed. He was a man of wealth, joint master of the Westmeath Foxhounds and a member of Brooks's, the Turf, and the Travellers clubs. He had been a recorder (a part-time circuit judge) in England since 1975.[7] Beveridge had an incisive, highly organized, analytical mind and proved to be a master of the vast amount of information generated by the commission. He wrote and spoke a precise, elegant English. Most came to admire his abilities but none grew to like him; few found him easy to deal with, many could not stand him at all. He was not a man who suffered fools gladly and as he thought himself (and as he probably was) more intelligent and a better courtroom operator than anyone else at the commission, he treated many with disdain. He was particularly arrogant and contemptuous towards the local group of lawyers, all of whom soon came to loathe him. Conrad Seagroatt, who got on with Beveridge better than anyone, described him as a man who was "extremely able, missed nothing and could be an abrasive personality."[8] Solicitor Murray Burton, who worked directly for Beveridge for ten months and strongly believed that he had driven the inquiry in the right direction, nevertheless found him very hard to cope with and described him as "incredibly competent, but the most arrogant, self-centred man you could meet." He had peccadillos that he expected all to humour, such as making his staff wear gloves so that he would not be exposed to germs.[9] Nevertheless, as soon as proceedings opened, he demonstrated that he was the force behind the inquiry and what it uncovered was to a great degree owed to his thoroughness.

Barrie Barlow, who represented the Legal Department along with his colleague Max Lucas, and whose remit was to protect the attorney general, was one of those who suffered from Beveridge's tongue lashings. Barlow had a very harsh opinion of Beveridge, who, he thought,

> conducted a McCarthy style inquiry, which he dragged on far too long [...] seemingly enjoying the lifestyle of his rooms in the Mandarin, his car and his fees, which he renegotiated upwards during the Inquiry. He manipulated the weaker Justice T.L. Yang, to whom, as Counsel to the Inquiry, he should have been answerable [...] he was not really answerable to anyone.

Barlow accused the commission (meaning Beveridge) of "an abominable disregard for the reputations of witnesses".[10] He and his fellows believed that Beveridge was seeking to use the stage of the inquiry for personal advancement and wished to bring down the commissioner of police and the attorney general as trophies.[11] Barlow, a tough and no-nonsense Australian, was so angry with Beveridge on one occasion that, when the commissioner withdrew into chambers, he told Justice Yang that he and his fellow barristers "were concerned at some of John Beveridge's McCarthyite tendencies, which could, if unchecked, lead to Judicial Review proceedings being brought on behalf of one or more of my client colleagues."[12]

Kemal Bokhary, representing the SIU, had a more charitable explanation of the conflicts at the inquiry:

> As it seemed to me, Mr John Beveridge, QC adopted the line of ensuring at just about any cost that the Inquiry would not be seen as a cover-up. And as it seemed to me, part of the cost which he was prepared to incur was extremely abrasive questioning by him of the SIU officers who gave evidence. Socially he and I got on well enough, but the atmosphere at the Inquiry was often strained by reason of what he felt it was his duty to do and what I felt it was my duty to counter.[13]

Bokhary, who had the year before unsuccessfully prosecuted Howard Lindsay, was by habit an elaborately courteous attorney, but his task was to clear the SIU of any wrongdoing and he was moved at times to complain that Beveridge was biased against the SIU and in favour of John MacLennan.[14]

Andrew Hodge, who had been representing the RHKP since the inquest, and was the man who had named Roy Henry as a suspected homosexual, also had an abrasive personality, at least in court. Another Australian, he was very much the AG's man, having first worked with him on the Ma brothers narcotics case. Hodge could be "a charming loose cannon",[15] but he was not a man who respected authority or procedures (as he had shown at the inquest), and at times he was breathtakingly rude to Justice Yang, who was usually too good-natured to object. When prevented by the commissioner from following a line of questioning on one occasion, Hodge retorted:

> Very good, my Lord. Thank you very much for indicating your attitude to me. No doubt at some stage you'll enlighten me about why — with the greatest of respect — that was regarded as being an improper remark.[16]

Only very occasionally did Yang rouse himself to ask Hodge to be more civil.

Hodge, too, was accused of using the inquiry for his own purposes; Conrad Seagroatt considered that "Andrew Hodge believed the Inquiry was a stage to display his egotism; on a good day, he was a nice bloke, but he could be a viper if you weren't careful."[17] Beveridge treated him like "some naughty schoolboy disobeying the rules of the game".[18] He clearly disliked him intensely; Bokhary described their clash of personalities as "titanic".[19]

Beveridge was not alone in displaying open contempt for Hodge and the group of barristers on his side of the room; Albert Sanguinetti, representing Elsie Elliott, was of similar mind. When Hodge and Ingham suggested something to him during one of his examinations, he said in a loud voice: "When I want advice from you two I will ask for it."[20]

It must have unnerved those representing the government side that John Beveridge had, through his reading of the Carratu report, a better grasp of the failings of their clients than they had themselves. It was more than ever necessary for them, therefore, to discredit Carratu and his team. Kemal Bokhary did his best to do so at the start of the hearings, alleging that the team had illegally detained Jeff Tso. Vincent Carratu flew back to England on 10 November.[21] He left with a very nasty taste in his mouth and a very jaundiced view of what he'd found in Hong Kong. He wrote to Elsie Elliott two weeks later about the falsity of the case constructed by the SIU against John MacLennan:

> The discrepancies and lies being told at the hearing are exactly what we expected and automatically make one wonder how any sensible, experienced Police Officer could possibly suggest a prosecution based on the evidence of these witnesses. It merely confirms what I felt from the beginning.[22]

The following year, Carratu was called back to Hong Kong by John Beveridge to clear up some details of the case and he reappeared at the inquiry in February.[23] He had supper with Aileen Bridgewater on that occasion and was indiscreet in some of the things he told her. The inquiry, he believed, would have to result in a clean-out of the government's stables: "A lot will go after the Commission of Inquiry, AG, CP, not the Chief Justice, but mid levels too. Moor will have to go."[24] Carratu also told her that he had been under police surveillance and that the police had files on both of them; Aileen's, he added, describes her "as having lesbian tendencies." The "police are panicking — they are like wounded rats. Really dangerous," he told her.[25] Later that year, he wrote in similar vein to Elsie Elliott: "Hong Kong is a fantastic place, and I have enjoyed all my time there, regardless of my popularity, with certain people, but I have never met such a corrupt and devious crowd in all my life."[26]

One of the pieces of information that Carratu passed on to Aileen concerned John Conway, who, Carratu had discovered, had more of a chequered background than he had revealed. He had been dismissed from the Nottingham Police.[27] Aileen Bridgewater had begun to find him "almost unpleasant" and at some point he moved out of the Bridgewaters' flat to stay in the YMCA.[28] Solicitor Alan Harrison indicated to Conway on 6 October that the commission was finding his presence embarrassing — partly, no doubt, caused by his continual exposure of flaws in the investigation. That month Conway informed the commission that MacLennan's death certificate was invalid as it had been issued in the name of "John Richard MacLennan".[29]

Beveridge had no time for Conway and very early on called him to testify so that he could be removed from the inquiry. In questioning on 30 October, he made Conway admit that he had failed to survive a two-year probation at the Northern Ireland Forensic Laboratory. Beveridge cruelly revealed that Conway had a criminal record — he had once been prosecuted for a minor theft — and forced him to deny that he had ever claimed to be an "expert".[30] In terms of the inquiry, this was true, for he had not been appointed as an "expert witness" but this ignored Conway's undoubtedly recognized status as a handwriting expert in London. Most damagingly, and highly embarrassingly, Conway was also made to confess that "I was not requested by the MacLennan family". He had, it was now evident, inserted himself into affairs of his own volition. Justice Yang was led to state that he believed that he, the public, and Conrad Seagroatt had been misled by Conway. He also raised the issue of an old charge of perjury, of which Conway had been found innocent, and withdrew the food subsidy he was being paid.[31] Conway went back to Scotland with his tail, for the time being, between his legs, taking with him some of the items that the MacLennan family had requested from their son's property, which was still in Ho Man Tin Police Station.

* * *

One other figure who departed Hong Kong during this time, and on this occasion not to the inquiry's advantage, was John Richard Duffy, who was finally released from prison on 21 October.[32] He had served his full sentence, having lost all remission when found smuggling letters out of the prison. He flew immediately out of the colony and remained in Taiwan for some time before making a swift return to Hong Kong in the new year. The commission had statements taken earlier from him by Neoh and Burton (which Yang would reject *in toto* at the inquiry), but dearly wanted him to testify. Duffy had other ideas and on 5 January left Kai Tak with his Chinese man-of-the-moment, this time for Bangkok. Tipped off too late, Murray Burton hastened to the airport, only to see Duffy disappear through immigration. He followed Duffy onto the plane and tried to give him a summons to the inquiry. Duffy refused to accept it and said he was not coming back to Hong Kong. As the pilot would not have him taken off the flight because the subpoena was not a criminal one, Burton had no alternative but to give up, and his quarry flew away.[33]

Efforts continued to get Duffy to return to Hong Kong, using his local lawyers as intermediaries, but he amused himself by setting conditions for his return that he knew were impossible to fulfil. He demanded immunity from prosecution were he to return. The inquiry was reduced ultimately to requesting a magistrate to issue an arrest warrant, one that was never to be enforced.[34]

Duffy was playing with the commission whilst at the same time trying to make money out of information he was leaking to the press. On 27 March, TVB newsreader and sub-editor Richard Belford told the commission that Duffy had been passing the commission's communications to the media. He had done rather worse than that, as the governor reported to London on 15 January, for he had been attempting to sell his list of paedophile and homosexual Hong Kong figures to the London press. The list had, the governor told David Ford in London, been in the hands of the Hong Kong press for some months, but "so far editors have treated it with total discretion". The list was published nowhere, an indication of the power of the colonial authorities in Hong Kong at the time.[35]

22

The SIU Case Collapses

The lack of solid forensics in the case had been one of the reasons for public disquiet ever since the inquest, and the commission now did its best to fill the gap. Those who had testified earlier were recalled to repeat their earlier evidence. Ray Cimino and Murray Burton were dispatched to MacLennan's flat to conduct tests of the sound of firing five revolver rounds. They found that the sound carried two floors upwards to be heard in Sandra Hill's flat, as she had testified, but not downwards to the flat below.[1]

Three experts from London also testified. Derek Davis, an independent handwriting expert, testified that the handwriting on the suicide note and in the beat register was that of John MacLennan, and added that the time and date had been added to the note while MacLennan had been standing, a position different from that he had adopted when he wrote the note itself.

He testified that the time and date had not been written on the spot on the desk where the note was shown on the photograph.[2] Professor A. Keith Mant, head of the Department of Forensic Medicine at Guy's Hospital, London, testified that he had no doubt that "this was clearly a death by suicide".[3] Major Peter Mead, a serving army officer, who had worked at the Forensic Science Laboratory in Northern Ireland, conducted in front of the press a test of the power of the revolver and its recoil, using a block of gelatin suspended from a wire. He demonstrated that the revolver did not kick back after a shot, meaning that subsequent shots were not thrown off aim. He also demonstrated how the bullets fired by the revolver lacked the force to move the gelatin more than slightly, making it unlikely that they would have knocked over the person being shot.[4] "Even children," he stated, could have withstood the impact from bullets fired from that revolver. He told the inquiry that there was insufficient space in the bedroom for another person to have fired at close range. MacLennan's body had moved between the shots, and had there been another person present, MacLennan would have had to cooperate to enable the firing to take place at all. Mead concluded that the death had been a suicide.[5]

The testimony of the new experts differed scarcely at all from that adduced from earlier witnesses. The forensics, in sum, left no doubt that John MacLennan had committed suicide. Of the terms of reference, question (a) — "whether, in the light of all the evidence available and any additional enquiries you make, there are good grounds for a belief that the death of Inspector MacLennan was other than suicide and what conclusions you draw" — had been answered in the negative.

* * *

Early to take the stand were the youths scheduled to be cited in the case against MacLennan, that is all those who could be found to testify. Beveridge clearly wished to establish whether the SIU had properly brought charges. By the end of the testimony of those who had been scheduled to appear in court against MacLennan, it was evident that they had not.

The first to appear was Peter Sung, who acknowledged that he had been charged with, although not convicted of, blackmailing Colin Logan and claimed to have been beaten by Inspector MacKillop of the SIU, in Sergeant Leung's presence, for telling John MacLennan that he had given evidence against him. He acknowledged that he had been a paid informer, but testified that he felt guilty about MacLennan's death, as it had been his fault for giving the SIU his name. He said he believed that the SIU "tried to nail John", whom "they wanted to get because he had got off before."[6]

Alan, the boy whom Peter Sung had introduced as a potential boyfriend to John MacLennan, continued to deny that he and MacLennan had had sex. He also denied that he had told Inspector Tin of the SIU that MacLennan had patted his thigh and shoulder. He admitted to being effeminate and wearing make-up at discos but would go no further. Even Kemal Bokhary, a skilled and dangerous counsel in cross-examination, whose verbal stiletto was sheathed in a gloss of courtesy, was unable to shift Alan into any admission that he was gay.[7]

The third to appear was Lula, Sun Kam-hung, who spent an unconvincing week on the stand. There were, as both Seagroatt and Beveridge pointed out, many discrepancies between his different statements. He told the hearing that he hated the SIU and thought they wanted to "get at" MacLennan. On 14

November, he retracted his statement that he had had an affair with MacLennan in its entirety, then retracted his retraction. He drew a picture of MacLennan's flat that resembled only Fulton's and said he was frightened of Inspector Tin. By the end of all this he had no credibility left at all.[8]

Next to take the stand was Michael Tsang, whose performance was no better than Lula's.[9] On his first day of testimony, he drew a sketch of MacLennan's flat, but on the second day, having met Lula overnight despite a strict warning by the commissioner, he drew a different one. When Beveridge said that he believed that Michael Tsang had conspired with Lula, Andrew Hodge objected, to which Beveridge replied that if Hodge did not stop interrupting, he would make an application to have him removed. The dates which Tsang gave of the supposed liaisons he had with MacLennan had altered in each statement he had given and his notebook was a fraud. He failed to identify MacLennan's photograph and failed to describe his flat; his description was "not even approximately correct". When this became evident, he burst into tears, told the commission that he hated himself for being gay and would kill himself if convicted of a homosexual offence. He was now in such evident distress that Justice Yang adjourned the session. Michael Tsang had removed any possibility that his evidence could have been relied on in a court, and he was not recalled.

Ironically in the light of what now transpired, the best witness that the SIU had been able to bring against MacLennan was Jimmy Cheung, the man who had warned him of the SIU's pursuit. He appeared before the commission over three days and seemed to enjoy the experience, evidently relishing the chance to show off in public. He was the exact opposite to Michael and shocked the inquiry by explaining that he was a prostitute because

"I like sex". He had no hesitation in describing being flagellated with a feather duster by Colin Logan and the three sexual acts he had performed with John MacLennan. When Jimmy had warned MacLennan that the boys had given statements against him, he said, he had been taken to the SIU offices, where Inspector Tin hit him and threatened him "with chopping".[10]

The press lionized Jimmy Cheung in their daily reports, particularly when he cheeked Conrad Seagroatt. He was lightening the reporters' by then very tedious days: "Slim, handsome, bisexual Jimmy [...] made the room laugh." Cheung explained the discrepancies between his statements by the fact that Inspector Tin had not written down what he said. His statement to the SIU had been false. He claimed that the SIU protected prostitutes in Tsim Sha Tsui in return for information. John MacLennan was more like a friend than a customer and Jimmy liked him, he said.

The inquiry was still wading through this sort of nonsense by early December, when Bobby Po, "Big Mouth Woman", appeared in the witness box. Here was a third witness who could have been really useful in the case against John MacLennan, but Po's evidence in the inquiry showed that he, too, would not have come through a court case with his testimony unscathed. He related the occasions on which he had sex with MacLennan and described the appendix scar on MacLennan's abdomen. He correctly identified MacLennan's photograph, which he had initially refused to do in the SIU's office, until, that is, he was hit by Sergeant Leung and threatened by Inspector Tin with a charge of blackmail and intimidation.[11]

The press reported that "curly haired Bobby said Jimmy lied about the date he first had sex with John MacLennan" and had cast doubts concerning the authenticity of Jimmy's telephone list.

Bokhary made the best of all this evidence damning his client by pointing out that Bobby had not spoken to investigators of any assault or threat by the SIU. Bobby said at the close of his testimony that he had been too frightened to warn John MacLennan, but that he had been "very close" to him.

Jeff Tso was the next to be examined. It was less than a month since he had been sentenced to twelve months suspended imprisonment for theft of the Carratu team's belongings at the Lee Garden Hotel, and counsel did not bother to pay him much attention. In the fourth statement he had given, he had admitted that all his earlier statements had been false and that he had made them because Inspector Tin had threatened him with prosecution for being a triad member. At the inquiry, he consistently failed to identify John MacLennan's photograph and described a totally different man. He claimed that he had lied to assist the SIU and to throw them off the scent of his real client at Ho Man Tin Police Station, who was also called John.[12]

Ricky Kwok (who had certainly sold sex to MacLennan) and Eddie Chu (who hadn't) had by now made themselves scarce, so their statements were read to the inquiry in their absence.[13] In the new year, a prostitute called Ah Tung was produced. He got as short shrift as had Jeff Tso, for it soon became clear that he had been supplied by procurer Molo Tsui to add testimony to bolster the SIU's case.[14] At the age of sixteen, Tung had been taken into Molo Tsui's home in Westland Garden, Quarry Bay, and sold to clients there and in the Carnarvon Road bathhouse. He claimed that John MacLennan had become his regular customer in 1976, paying him HK$250 a time and spending on him up to HK$2,000 a month. At one point, he claimed, MacLennan had said that he wanted Tung to live with him. Tung was, however, forced to admit that Molo Tsui had telephoned him and told him to give evidence. The sums of money he mentioned were beyond any possible basis in reality and there was no evidence that he had even met John MacLennan.[15]

Ah Tung's evidence was further discredited when his procurer, Molo Tsui, described as a "jewellery broker", put in an appearance in the hearings on 27 January. Since his arrest in 1979, Tsui had been kept out of the way. He had spent eight months in jail before his trial, when he had been sentenced to eighteen months on eight charges of procuring and gross indecency. He had been found not guilty of three counts of buggery and seven of committing and procuring gross indecency, as the crown had offered no evidence on the last ten charges.[16] Having served his remaining ten months, he was now once again a free man. He told the inquiry that he was not a procurer and that he had not told Ah Tung to lie.

Justice Yang made evident his distaste for Molo Tsui and got him out of his commission inside the day, dismissing him for lying in his statements. "I have also observed his demeanour while giving evidence," Yang said, adding that Tsui's unreliability was "fundamental". As Tsui was unable to distinguish lies from fiction, Yang informed the hearing, he would disregard all his evidence.[17] Justice Yang's unusually energetic intervention was convenient for the government, of course, in that Molo Tsui was one of the few persons to appear at the inquiry who had been named by Duffy. It is possible that Beveridge engineered his appearance as a witness for that reason. Tsui's swift removal meant that he was prevented from making any embarrassing statements in open session.

The examination of the evidence that would have been brought against John MacLennan, had he lived to face a trial, had made it plain that much of it was manufactured and that almost all the witnesses were unreliable. An effective barrister such as, for instance, Kemal Bokhary, would have easily destroyed such a case. Of the terms of reference, it seemed that question (c) — "whether the charges which were about to be preferred against him on the day of his death were properly brought, and whether on evidence properly obtained" — had been answered in the negative.

* * *

The commission had been tasked to examine deficiencies in the investigation into MacLennan's death, and to assist them in this they had to hand the report of Acting Assistant Commissioner Li Kwan-ha into Pelly's handling of the case, as well as Pelly's own report for the coroner.[18] Beveridge was therefore already well aware that the police had admitted to shortcomings in the investigation, especially in the area of forensics, shortcomings borne out by the evidence of the scientific experts. He was also already aware that Li had criticized Trotman for informing MacLennan of his impending arrest, saying in his report that: "Such a specific disclosure was unnecessary and unwise. Mr Trotman could have been more circumspect."[19] All the evidence heard at the inquiry in this area matched what had been disclosed before. Li, by then the deputy director criminal investigations, repeated verbally the conclusions of his report, stating that Trotman had been wrong to inform MacLennan and that the handling of the scene of death had been confused by too many officers who had been giving orders; that suicide had been too readily accepted as the cause of death; and that, as a result, full procedures had not been followed. He also criticized the SIU's very sketchy filing system and gave his personal view that, after the death, the services of an independent pathologist should have been offered to the family.[20]

Chief Superintendent Trotman was called shortly after this and confirmed the detail of the events at the scene of death. He told the inquiry that he had not checked the walk-in wardrobe in MacLennan's bedroom, but that he was satisfied that no one was there, although he could not say how he could be so satisfied, as the wardrobe had been opened first only in the afternoon by Inspector Peters. Trotman added to the mysteries of the pens; he stated that the gold Parker pen in the photograph had gone missing (it was listed in the inquiry report as among the effects kept by the inquiry, so it must have been the silver pen that had gone missing). This issue was never to be resolved as eventually all the pens went missing.[21]

The officer who had been designated by Trotman to take charge of the scene of death, only to be superseded by Pelly, had been Chief Inspector Billy Kong, who had left the force by the time the inquiry called him as a witness and had taken advantage of a government training scheme to become a barrister. He stated that he had decided within ten minutes of arrival at the scene that the death had been a suicide. He clarified that what had been thought to be a missing telescope had been found to be actually an ornamental bottle of Old Spice.[22] Inspector Blake Hancock gave testimony that he had attended the post mortem. He had known John MacLennan for only six months, and thought him a quiet officer and a hardworking colleague. Their offices had been adjacent.[23] Senior Inspector Iain Grant's two statements were read to the commission.[24]

On 13 April, Superintendent Marc Pelly told the inquiry that he had heard rumours in the mess that John MacLennan was gay. The body had been removed by the time he took over the case. He reported that the pen that wrote the suicide note had been found to be missing, as had MacLennan's kilt (which was never found). He added that he had not shown photographs of MacLennan's anus to his solicitors or to the inquest, and MacLennan's parents had not told been told of the detail of the death "for humanitarian reasons".[25]

The testimony heard at the inquiry made it possible to answer question (b) of the terms of reference — "what official investigations immediately after the death of Inspector MacLennan were conducted, whether there were any shortcomings in them, and if so, what conclusions you draw as to the reasons for these shortcomings?" No one had contested that there had been major deficiencies in the investigation, so the only answer that could have been returned to the question seemed very clear indeed.

From the evidence heard so far, however, there had been no indication of any conspiracy, merely of a series of mistakes, misjudgments, and failures, compounded by belated attempts to tidy up the evidence to cover all these up.

23

Discrediting the Police

The evidence presented at the inquiry by, and about, officers of the SIU related both to the impropriety of the charges brought against MacLennan and to the motivation for his targeting by the police. These officers were called after the inquiry had heard the testimony of the prostitutes whose evidence was to have been used to charge MacLennan, testimony which had been damning about the way the SIU had created a false case by intimidation. To a man, the officers of the SIU denied the allegations made against them by their own witnesses, but they were not able to shake off the mud that had already been thrown at them.

John Beveridge managed to ensure that the less significant witnesses, for instance subordinates of the more important figures, would appear early. This enabled a lot of the factual detail to be clarified and established tripwires over which unsuspecting more senior witnesses could fall when giving their testimony later. Catching out the bigger fish was not the only reason for keeping them till last. Beveridge had a good sense that what he was conducting had many of the elements of public theatre. Interest had to be maintained, and expanded, as the hearings progressed, until the climax of the appearance of those upon whom he wished to focus his final attention: the commissioner of police and the attorney general.

Starting at the bottom, Beveridge called DC Liu Man on 9 February 1981. Liu was nervous and upset at being labelled a homosexual. He claimed to be a happily married man with two children and denied his affair with Peter Sung, saying that Sung was lying to harm him because he had refused to give him bail money. Sung, he alleged, had also resented being passed on to Inspector Tin as an informer.[1]

Inspector Stephen Tin followed Liu Man into the box and remained there for four days from 10 February. He was perhaps the most effective officer in the SIU, the man who had pressured Liu Man into handing over Peter Sung and so had given the unit the means to create a legitimate case against John MacLennan. He was also the only officer in the unit who had followed regular procedures and kept a record in his police notebook of what he had been doing (not one of the others had done so), although suspiciously he had not done so from 22 September to 5 November 1979, the period which covered the start of Peter Sung's work as an informer and the creation of the case against MacLennan. Unfortunately, his evidence was not all truthful. He stated that, as he didn't think the information Sung could give was worth paying for, he had rejected his request for cash (this was exactly the opposite of what his subordinate, Sergeant Leung, was to tell the commission). When Beveridge indicated that he did not believe this account, Tin stalled by asking for an interpreter.

The next day, with an interpreter slowing things down, Tin claimed to have completely forgotten that they had investigated Liu Man, despite the fact that it was only two weeks after he had personally interviewed him that Liu had arranged the meeting with Peter Sung. He acknowledged that MacLennan's details and photograph had been in the target card index when he arrived in the SIU in August 1979. He admitted that Sergeant Leung had paid Peter Sung HK$20–30 "travelling expenses" and that Liu Man had been targeted as a homosexual in his card index. Beveridge concluded his cross-examination of Tin by asking why the prostitutes had incriminated themselves by giving evidence of homosexual acts "solely out of a desire to help the Police". Tin had no ready answer. His was a very unimpressive performance.[2]

Tin was followed by his fellow inspector, Norrie MacKillop, whose testimony was equally revealing. He sought to turn the tables on Fulton by alleging that the SIU had turned down an offer from him to set up MacLennan; Fulton, he alleged, was willing to offer first his boyfriend, then himself, to MacLennan. However, when pressed, MacKillop admitted that he was the only one to say this and that he had not said so in his earlier statements. When he joined the SIU on 14 September 1979, MacLennan's name had been top of their list, even though the unit knew then of three other homosexual inspectors. At the time that MacLennan was being investigated, half the SIU was chasing him and Logan, but MacKillop did not know why they were targeted. He was also revealing of his personal attitude; he admitted that he had been offended by MacLennan's mention of Roy Henry and the way he had gone outside the force to get reinstated.[3]

Inspector Gus Graham's evidence had at least the saving grace of amusing his audience.[4] He was outrageous in his replies to counsel, for instance telling Conrad Seagroatt he was talking "rubbish", and was impervious to most attacks, although he bridled when Beveridge threw at him the unflattering remarks that he was alleged by Fulton's friend, Inspector McDaid, to have made about Quinn. McDaid was "a liar and a queer and was on the SIU list", Graham countered, adding gratuitously that "anyone sympathetic to homosexuals is a member of the homosexual community." McDaid had to be brought back later to the inquiry to state that he was solidly heterosexual.

Interestingly, Graham did not appear to lie to the inquiry. He even admitted that the SIU had tapped the phones of those in whom they were interested, thus confirming the suspicions of Aileen Bridgewater, who had been to see the head of Hong Kong's telephone company to complain that her phone was tapped. His short temper made Gus Graham an easy man to rile, and Beveridge made use of this neatly. To Beveridge's accusation that he had a paranoia about homosexuals, Graham responded: "Not paranoia, but some people might consider my views extreme." Fulton, he added for good measure, deserved discrediting because he was a self-confessed homosexual and a liar. Graham thought that Hong Kong had always been a haven for homosexuals and it was the job of the SIU "to purge them out". Homosexuals were everywhere, Graham told the inquiry, and he believed Michael Fulton that almost everyone was gay. Turning to Justice Yang, Graham said in his broad Scottish accent that Fulton had suggested that "even you, My Lord, might be homosexual". The assembled barristers had to stifle guffaws and the next day were highly amused to see Yang walking into the court like John

Wayne.[5] Yang let the remark stand and it passed into police legend.[6]

The last of the SIU's junior ranks to appear before the commission was Sergeant Leung, who tied himself in knots. He said that he had paid Peter Sung for information but that he had not had to intimidate the prostitutes to whom Sung introduced him, as "they liked gossiping and regarded themselves as women". He was then forced to admit that the prostitutes had been threatened with prosecution if they didn't cooperate. A member of the arrest party on the day of the death, he had seen "a piece of creamy white or yellow paper on top of a desk", thus confirming solicitor Paul Stevens's account of the suicide note that he had seen, yet he still identified the note on the manila envelope that was produced to him as the note that he had seen in MacLennan's room.[7]

All these testimonies prepared the ground for the re-examination of the two key SIU witnesses, Superintendent Brooks and Chief Inspector Quinn, who had both appeared at the first sessions of the inquiry. Quinn was examined first on 3 March, and this time was questioned over eleven days. He restated his personal view of MacLennan as "brass-necked" and his own belief that MacLennan had escaped dismissal because he knew of top homosexuals, whom Quinn indicated were untouchable by the police. He had found the same in 1966, he said, when Taffy Hunt, for whom he was working, had got too close to important people and had been transferred overnight; "it was said he had been too good."

It had been DPP MacDougall's direction in July 1979 that had made "even consenting adults vulnerable to prosecution". He recalled that he had told MacDougall then that "there's quite a lot of top people mentioned in this," and MacDougall had said "Go ahead — everybody." Quinn confirmed that he had seen the names of eighteen police officers who were suspected to be homosexual listed in a loose minute from the commissioner of police, but before he could add the number of names of lawyers in the Legal Department who were also on this list, he was stopped by Justice Yang.

Beveridge forced Quinn to admit that he would not have been surprised if the prostitute witnesses had not been cautioned when questioned, if they had been told that they might be prosecuted if they refused to talk, or if they had been threatened that their families might be told what they were doing. Quinn would not, however, go so far as to admit that the SIU might not have been above administering the occasional slap.

Quinn related that he had given Duffy immunity in return for a copy of his petition on the direct orders of Paddy Clancy, and that he had been flabbergasted when Clancy had denied this. His superiors had been motivated by the obscene photographs of boys in Duffy's house; these showed, he alleged, that Duffy had been buggering little boys and forcing beer bottles up their anuses. They were astounded when they saw from Duffy's statements "that homosexuality was so rife in Hong Kong". Some of those superiors also had strong feelings about MacLennan's reinstatement and Quinn confessed that he felt that "it was very wrong of him to use the tactics he did." The SIU as a whole did not want MacLennan "to get away with it twice." However, Quinn lied in order to deny that the SIU had targeted MacLennan, telling Conrad Seagroatt at one point that Duffy "put the finger on MacLennan".[8] Beveridge asked "Which of the criteria for the SIU matched John MacLennan?" "None, Sir!" was the reply.[9]

Fulton, Quinn said, had been "confused by his instructions" and had not been directed to set up MacLennan (there was no whisper here of MacKillop's idea that Fulton had offered himself or his boyfriend for the set-up). Beveridge's questioning, however, gradually exposed the falsehood in this account, using, as he customarily did, no more than common sense:

> Beveridge: Mr Fulton was a timorous kind of person, wasn't he?
> Quinn: Very timorous.
> Beveridge: Would not asking Mr Fulton to arrange a friend to "chat up" John MacLennan mean making a homosexual approach, like you might chat up a girl?
> Quinn: Yes.
> Beveridge: Don't you feel now that Mr Fulton might well have taken all that to mean that he was being asked to set up Mr MacLennan?
> Quinn: He could be, yes. Looking back now, yes. Yes. He may have thought. I agree with you.[10]

Quinn nevertheless gave a good performance in the witness box and provided a credible, if at times revealing, account. He scarcely fumbled in his responses or tripped up over his own feet, which was creditable, given the number of statements he had been called upon to make over the previous fifteen months. He even elicited some sympathy. The barrister appearing for his unit, Kemal Bokhary, was quite touched when Quinn related that he had suffered from the accusation that his pursuit had driven MacLennan to his death. Some had called him a murderer. His daughter had come home tearful from school, crying that the other children had told her that her father had killed somebody.[11] He could not say so at the inquiry, but it must have been gut-wrenching for Quinn that he had pursued John MacLennan on the orders of superiors who were now busily running for cover and leaving him to carry the can. He let his frustration slip once only while giving testimony: "Why would I frame a person?" he exclaimed, "What am I getting out of it? Do I get feathers in my cap — medals, or promotion — no! Just a lot of hard stick from everybody!"[12]

Although Quinn was later to be called back for a third session of questioning, Bob Brooks was the last of the unit to appear in Beveridge's scheme of things. He kept things much closer to his chest, but he was, however, quite strident in some of the views he expressed. He thought Fulton's attempt to get assistance from his lawyer, Warwick Haldane, in October 1979 had been "a conspiracy to pervert the course of justice." He "had disapproved of MacLennan because of the Yuen Long incident [...] most loyal officers had taken the same view of the incident."

Denying that he had noticed that Gus Graham had "strong feelings" about homosexuality, Brooks contradicted himself by saying that his own views were "a little less stringent" than Graham's. He was forced to defend his unit's record system and to admit that a file on John MacLennan was missing. He had been "given advice by superiors that notebooks should be used very sparingly — even though this contradicted police general orders." He had made a mistake in saying on oath at the inquest that the SIU had received information before 16 October 1979 that MacLennan had used a prostitute, and admitted that the three reports he had written since MacLennan's death had also given this impression; this was a mistake, not an attempt to misrepresent the truth, he said.

Beveridge did not care for Superintendent Brooks at all; he called the fact that Brooks had not ensured there was an intelligence sheet on MacLennan "a shining example of unfairness or rank stupidity."[13] Brooks's testimony served to confirm that he had failed to ensure that proper procedures were followed in his unit and that he had lied about why MacLennan was targeted. Taken together, the evidence of the SIU officers had confirmed that whoever had told them to target MacLennan was not motivated by evidence which they had themselves uncovered and that the case they had constructed against MacLennan had not been properly brought. This should have enabled the commissioner to confirm a negative answer to Question (d), what investigations or inquiries were conducted regarding Inspector MacLennan, whether they were conducted with propriety, and what bearing, if any, they had on Inspector MacLennan's death. It also went some way to answering Question (e), whether the inquiries had been properly motivated.

* * *

The commission's attention then turned to more senior officers in police headquarters. Their evidence, attempts to exonerate themselves of any action arising from their ill will towards John MacLennan, whilst at the same time shifting all blame onto the shoulders of their subordinates, made for depressing listening. Eric Blackburn, in the first of what were to be two reappearances before the commission, said that Roy Henry's decision to dismiss MacLennan had been unjust.[14] He was brought back to testify again after the SIU officers' testimony had made it clear that they were following orders in targeting MacLennan. On the second occasion, Blackburn did admit that he thought MacLennan had been very disloyal to the force and to Roy Henry, but he would not admit ordering the SIU to target MacLennan. Contradicting the testimony of his subordinate, Mansell, who had been trying to protect him, he denied that he had instructed the SIU to vet

MacLennan for homosexuality. He also denied meeting Ross to brief him on this request. Blackburn told the commission that it would have been vindictive to vet MacLennan after his reinstatement and the reassurances he had been given. That, he said, was not his way. The other evidence the inquiry heard did not support Blackburn's denials.[15]

Even Bill Ross, otherwise a truthful and straightforward witness, found himself in the position of needing to cover up the tracks of his superiors. Beveridge asked him why the SIU, which was under his direct command, targeted MacLennan when there were better targets in the SIU files. Without naming names, Beveridge mentioned three examples of these: a transvestite policeman; a senior officer who was promiscuous and who used a procurer regularly to obtain young boys; and an officer of "medium to senior rank" whose sporting association gave him charge of young boys, and who had been found in bed with some of them by his amah. Ross could only reply that the evidence was stale, in one case over thirteen years old, and that the third officer had already resigned. "All these names had to be kept in view," he added. "We had to clear the tables first, then take care of other matters — which we are now doing." MacLennan's name, and in this Ross lied directly to the commission, was "the only policeman's name to surface during an investigation into an active ring of procurers."[16]

Next up from Ross in the chain of command was Paddy Clancy, at the time of the MacLennan affair the director of criminal investigations. Clancy gave the lie to Blackburn's testimony straight away by stating that the police Personnel Department had asked Ross to have MacLennan investigated by the SIU in February 1979. He repeated Ross's lie that

MacLennan's name had surfaced "as a result of an investigation during August to September 1979 into a ring of procurers and male prostitutes in the Tsim Sha Tsui area." However, he was forced by Beveridge to agree that record of no such investigation existed in SIU files. There had been, of course, no such investigation. MacLennan, in his view, had been disloyal for mentioning the name of at least one senior officer when fighting the Yuen Long case. Clancy left Chief Inspector Quinn to twist in the wind by denying that he had ever approved the attempt to give Duffy immunity in return for a copy of his petition. Beveridge's response to all this was to suggest that Clancy was subject to "deliberate forgetfulness", that he was being "deliberately evasive", and that his explanations were "manifestly absurd".[17]

On 30 April, Deputy Commissioner Peter Moor entered the witness box. He rather unbelievably claimed that the first time he had heard of MacLennan's name in connection with homosexuality was in August 1979 and that he had not known of the Yuen Long incident when he had ordered the investigation into MacLennan. At the meeting where that had been decided, which had lasted no more than ten minutes, he had not read the file but merely followed the advice of Superintendent Brooks. The furthest he would go to disclose any animus against MacLennan was to say that the tidbits of information first fed to him in August 1979 might have been shown him due to MacLennan's unpopularity in the force arising from the Yuen Long incident, as the SIU had not given him such information about any other officer. Pressed by Beveridge, he finally admitted that he must have been told of the Yuen Long incident when he agreed to target John MacLennan. Save for that, Moor managed to avoid any other mud sticking to him.[18]

Last of all came Commissioner Roy Henry, who having made a very lengthy written statement on 1 May, appeared before the commission on the 11th.[19] It was an appearance to which he could not have been looking forward. Andrew Hodge's gambit of bringing the issue of his sexual orientation into the open in the hearings had perhaps been a successful one in deflecting a similar public airing at the hands of a more hostile counsel. It had not, however, stopped widespread press speculation. Henry and the government could not be sure that the issue would not arise again at the commission, so, to forestall that eventuality, another cursory investigation into the matter had secretly been instigated by the government the previous September (this was perhaps the investigation to which Quinn had referred in his testimony). Then, the attorney general had declared himself satisfied and the investigation had been closed.[20] The stress, though, seems to have been telling on Henry and in April, a month before his appearance at the commission, he spent five days in the Queen Mary Hospital being treated for hypertension.[21]

In his written statement, Henry had done his best to exculpate himself for dismissing John MacLennan after the Yuen Long incident. He had believed MacLennan's dismissal to be in the force's, and MacLennan's, best interest. He had not been consulted on MacLennan's reinstatement and when he next heard MacLennan's name raised in the latter part of 1979, when Moor had told him he was to be targeted by the SIU, he had not recalled it. He had then been unaware that MacLennan was even still in the force. At the inquiry, Henry attempted to maintain this line but would fail to do so before Beveridge's relentless questioning.

Justice Yang felt himself constrained to repeat his earlier prohibition of allowing mention of the allegations that Roy Henry was homosexual. He commented on the:

> Reports of allegations of a homosexual character about the Commissioner of Police, Mr Henry, which have not been substantiated in evidence but which have been publicly reported. Whenever these matters have been raised I have indicated that I consider them to be outside my terms of reference and therefore not a matter for investigation. [...] I am quite satisfied no cross-examination of Mr Henry as to those matters would be sufficiently relevant for me to permit it.[22]

John Beveridge and Murray Burton were incensed that one of the motivations for action against MacLennan should have been placed beyond examination in such a fashion. They demanded that at least a confidential investigation be carried out into Roy Henry's sexual orientation.[23] Yang was forced to accept the logic of this and asked Deputy Commissioner Peter Moor to have such an investigation conducted. Asking a senior police officer to make such an inquiry about his immediate superior was not an ideal way of handling the issue, but Yang had perhaps no other recourse. Moor tasked the SIU, which duly carried out a perfunctory investigation, partly by questioning sources that had no possible knowledge of the matter.

Peter Crush recalls being awakened at about 6.30 a.m. on 18 March 1981 by Superintendent Bob Brooks and another officer banging on the door of his flat. This was some years after Crush had resigned, but the atmosphere in the gay community was by now very apprehensive, and Crush feared he was being raided. His boyfriend was at that very moment in his bed. Crush took the police officers to the TV room at the rear of his kitchen while his boyfriend got out of the flat. Brooks was, however, surprisingly affable and said that he had an embarrassing question to ask about the sexual orientation of the commissioner of police. Crush knew nothing of that, although he had heard that a rumour had gone around the force that Roy Henry had been found at a party in his flat. When Brooks heard that Crush had never met Roy Henry, that none of his circle had and that nobody Crush knew had ever mentioned him, he said he was pleased with the answer, which was "helpful", and left.[24] Unsurprisingly, Moor reported to Justice Yang that Roy Henry had a clean bill of health.

Counsel all observed Justice Yang's strictures to avoid any reference to the sexual orientation of the commissioner of police, so in his testimony Henry was allowed to get away with saying that, despite the fact that there had been no policy on the employment of homosexuals in the force, "a proven, practising homosexual places himself in a position whereby it is highly undesirable for him to continue in the police service." He also made every effort to disassociate himself from both the SIU (about the establishment of which in 1978 he claimed he had no recollection)[25] and the MacLennan case. He had, he said, only been told of the intended arrest on the night before it was due to occur.[26] He had "weak or no memory of the follow up to the Duffy case."[27] None of this was very believable.

Beveridge called Henry on the issue of why MacLennan, and MacLennan alone, had been targeted by the SIU, pointing out that the Special Branch had thirty-five names in the Black Book, but that no action had been taken against any of those listed in them. Henry had initialled them all. Some entries said "confirmed", some indicated "admission", one named Fulton, one was for another inspector known to the Inquiry and yet another for the "manager of a football team of little boys". Yang objected to the word "football", as it no doubt identified to many the officer who had been found in bed with a boy. Beveridge, who must have done this deliberately, apologized for forgetting they were not using specific terms and then asked Henry: "Why did you not take action?" Henry lamely replied that he "thought the initiation of cases would have been dealt with at lower level."[28]

Finally, Beveridge cornered Roy Henry into agreeing that the dismissal of MacLennan was, "looking at it purely from an analytical point of view, unfair."[29] Beveridge twisted the knife a little by adding that Henry would therefore "be consoled to know that Mr Illingworth agrees with me it was unfair." Beveridge was not content to let the matter rest there and dangled Roy Henry on the hook for just a little longer, making him admit that there was a fifty-fifty chance of MacLennan having been innocent of the Yuen Long accusation, meaning that there had been a fifty-fifty chance of doing an injustice by terminating his service. Henry was forced to state that "it didn't justify termination [...] in itself." Beveridge went on: "Not one person, sitting in that chair, or writing a report, has supported the decision you took, Mr Henry." Henry weakly responded that he had thought to take into account the good of the force and "indeed [...] of the good of the young man himself."

"Even though that step involved a fifty-fifty chance of terminating the contract of a man who was innocent of everything?"

"Yes."[30]

Roy Henry stepped down from the box with his reputation for decency in shreds. He had rested much of his defence of his failure to prevent the tragedy on vagueness and on having been uninformed, but this had left him appearing as a commissioner of police who either had no grip on his force or had been deliberately excluded by senior officers from the decision-making process.

* * *

The commission's examination of those involved in the Yuen Long incident and the senior officers of the force had enabled it to answer two of the questions set by its terms of reference. To question (d) — "what investigations or enquiries (other than those resulting in the charges at (c)) were conducted regarding Inspector MacLennan, whether they were conducted with propriety, and what bearing, if any, they had on Inspector MacLennan's death" — the commissioner had heard evidence indicating that the investigations into the Yuen Long case had not been conducted with propriety and that the reinstatement of MacLennan after that case had had a direct bearing on his death. To question (e) — "whether the investigations and enquiries under (b), (c) and (d) were properly motivated" — the commissioner should have been drawn to conclude that none of the investigations had been properly motivated.

24

Hostile Witnesses

There were three people who were called to give evidence at the inquiry who were witnesses regarded as hostile by the counsel representing the government side. These were Howard Lindsay, Inspector Michael Fulton, and Elsie Elliott.

Lindsay appeared between 9 and 11 December 1980. His testimony was of value in two ways: it served, as hearsay, to validate Fulton's allegations of a set-up; and it assisted in an assessment of the attorney general's actions. Counsel for the AG (Barlow and Lucas), for the police (Hodge), and for the SIU (Bokhary) needed to discredit his account. They were partially successful in doing so. The techniques they jointly applied proved effective in catching Lindsay out and wearing him down. They would repeat, seemingly endlessly, the same questions, then pounce on any differences in his replies. They would ask questions on issues upon which they knew there would be difficulty in answering (particularly, for both Lindsay and Fulton, any issue surrounding their homosexuality), then make use of any reticence or attempt to avoid a direct reply to indicate the untrustworthiness of the witness. They would make blatant use of any homosexual's predicament in Hong Kong, which was that his very survival there depended upon his living a lie, to show that the witness was ill-intentioned, criminal, deviant, and deceitful. The examinations of both Lindsay and Fulton were painful affairs.

Lindsay had flown back to Hong Kong from Gibraltar, where he had begun to rescue his life and had found work. He told what he knew of Quinn's history as a sort of gay "witch-finder general" and of his own attempts to warn the AG. He admitted to being bisexual and to having had sex with men in Hong Kong. He believed that "injustice had been done to MacLennan, to himself and to innocuous homosexuals in Hong Kong."[1]

Andrew Hodge sharpened his tongue for his attack on Lindsay by once again being rude to Justice Yang; "My Lord, I notice that you didn't appear to be listening to the evidence." Having got away with that, he then turned on Lindsay, questioning him about a "breakdown" which Lindsay had told his colleagues in the Legal Department was severe depression caused by the breakup of a relationship with a woman in the United States. Lindsay had to admit that it was really due to the breakup of his homosexual relationship in Hong Kong, to which Hodge riposted that in his view Lindsay had shown himself "prepared to mislead your colleagues for our own ends [...] Mr Lindsay, you were living a lie, were you not?"

"I was a homosexual." Hodge then accused Lindsay of making use of Clare-Marie Beeson by inviting her to listen to Fulton without her knowledge.[2]

Hodge's approach was scrappy and nasty, but Bokhary's was more subtle and effective. He took Lindsay through the detail of his trial, something which he was easily able to do as he had been the prosecutor. As the Commission of Inquiry was not a trial, Bokhary had wider scope to blacken Lindsay as a promiscuous homosexual, a user of prostitutes, and a man who had laid himself open to blackmail. He could also lay bare the fact that Lindsay had not been convicted due to weakness in the evidence, not because of the falsity of the charges. How, Bokhary pressed Lindsay, could he hope to be a crown counsel prosecuting homosexuals given his admissions?[3]

Despite this battering to his character and reputation, Lindsay nevertheless managed to get across the point that he had believed Fulton's allegations of an intended set-up and that the attorney general had not taken any notice of him.

* * *

The second of these witnesses was Inspector Michael Fulton, who occupied the witness box from 15 to 26 January 1981. His testimony lasted a gruelling eleven days, and, because of his more central role, he was subjected to a much more severe attack than that inflicted on Lindsay, and by more of the barristers present. His testimony was important in establishing the motivations of the police and the SIU and in illustrating the methods which they were prepared to use. The inquiry had worsened his habitual nervous disposition. His superior, Senior Superintendent Merritt, told the inquiry two days after Fulton stepped down from the witness box that he had thought Fulton close to suicide at times. He had seen him six weeks before, "grey, ashen, red-eyed and shaking."[4] This all made Fulton a bad witness, a man, as it turned out, whom hostile barristers might get to say almost anything they wished.

Fulton took the inquiry through the course of his work as an informer for the SIU, described their instruction to him to set up MacLennan, and related what he had done to raise the alarm.[5] He admitted that he had provided a list of 122 homosexuals to the SIU; this was handed to the commission, but not published. "It was names of friends and associates that I knew. A lot of them were Chinese names but not full Chinese names."[6] He had given the SIU the list only because he had been told that there would be no witch-hunt. He had not, he said, enjoyed being an informer; it had ruined his career. He regarded himself as too soft to have resisted the SIU, "I am too nice. I forgive people too easily, therefore it is easy for people to get me to do what they want." His phone had been tapped. The press release his solicitors had issued had been incorrect in that he had not, as it claimed, been prevented from seeing the commissioner of police, rather the request had been intercepted and instead he had been interviewed by a junior officer, which he had accepted.

Under pressure in the last few days of his testimony, Fulton began to change his tune, swinging wildly to follow each of the counsel questioning him. He was persuaded to agree that both Howard Lindsay and Elsie Elliott had used the information he had given them for their own ends, their own "public vendettas [...] In that way, I suppose they misused it."

Naturally, the hostile counsel focused on Fulton's homosexuality and his relationship with Raymond Lam, whom they labelled a prostitute. Kemal Bokhary attempted to intervene in questioning at one point, giving another instance of the friction always crackling like electricity in the air of the inquiry. Beveridge jumped in:

Beveridge: Well my Lord that in respect is improper.

Bokhary: My Lord I resent that observation. There's nothing

> improper about it.
>
> Bokhary: Well my Lord I claim the protection of the tribunal that is an improper observation by my learned friend. Your Lordship has my protest.[7]

Bokhary did manage to skewer Fulton neatly on his treachery. "Was it not you who told the SIU that MacLennan had tried to chat up your boyfriend?" Fulton denied this, despite the fact that his denial made no sense. "What you did do is shop about one hundred of your friends." Which, of course, was exactly what Fulton had done.[8]

Andrew Hodge accused Fulton of being one of a "group determined to prevent the police enforcing the law against homosexual offences towards minors." Charles Ingham, for Superintendent Trotman, sneered that Fulton was "gay", which he informed the inquiry, was "a much-abused word, which I understand means homosexual."[9] Barrie Barlow accused Fulton of "blackmailing" Roy Henry (without explaining how), and, evidently trying to be clever, asked Fulton's view of a line from American playwright Mart Crowley's depressing play *The Boys in the Band*, "You show me a happy homosexual and I'll show you a gay corpse."

There was, of course, no polite answer to such a question, but Fulton was past the point by of being able to give a sensible answer to anything. Some of those in the court were appalled to observe his "slurring speech, stutter and stumble." Justice Yang saw this too, and ineffectually tried to bring the examination to a close, but Barlow would have none of it and did not desist for another full day. That gave him time to talk Fulton into agreeing that the attorney general's press release, denying that there had been an attempted "frame-up", to which Fulton's own press statement had objected, was in fact correct.

And yet, pressed as he was, Fulton would not alter the one point in his testimony that was really important. He would agree that he had not been asked to "frame" anyone, but he was adamant that he had been told to set up John MacLennan, and he would not go back on that. On his last day in the box, he revived;

> I was to introduce someone to test MacLennan and if he took the bait, that person should report back to me or the SIU. They were trying to assess from the reaction of MacLennan towards him and what subsequently happened whether MacLennan was a homosexual.[10]

When Fulton's ordeal was finally over, Beveridge remarked to Justice Yang that:

> I am concerned with the question of the pliancy of this witness in the answers he has given. It may be that on some matters he has made concessions that he simply shouldn't have given [...] He says or emphasises different things in statements to different people.

Yang replied: "Well, actually, the point is not lost on me."[11] Indeed, Beveridge need not have worried. The mauling that Fulton had endured from hostile counsel had revealed him to be a weak and foolish man, precisely not the sort of man who would have taken it into his head to invent, then go public with, a story of a set-up against a fellow police officer, a story that would have (as it did) upset his handlers sufficiently to ruin his already tattered career. The only conceivable reason for his sticking to his account was that he had at last decided to act on principle.

* * *

Elsie Elliott was the third witness whom the government side considered hostile. The problem for the swarm of barristers intending to assail her was that, as far as anyone knew, Elsie had no weak spots and was unshakeable on points of principle. There was to be no crack in Elsie Elliott's evidence into which counsel might insert a chisel. In fact, the only weak spot visible in the course of her testimony was that she infuriated most of those on the official side to the point of distraction, and that, of course, put them, not her, at a disadvantage.

That is not to say that Elsie was in any way immune to the pressures exerted by the case, far from it. She had suffered intimidation, and knew more than most that in Hong Kong threats could all too easily turn into actual attempts to harm. She had been as frightened as Aileen Bridgewater before the inquiry started. On 10 February, she had collapsed, suffering from the severe emotional stress caused by the strain of the case.[12] In April, she developed a case of shingles.[13] But by 8 May when she appeared before the commission she had recovered and was prepared.

In the event, she had to endure only two days in the witness box. She let rip immediately, telling the commission that the case had been a "cover up". She was not surprised, she said, that Moorfoot, the coroner's officer whose interview she had so disliked, had been involved in such a cover-up (she did not explain her disdain for Moorfoot, but she seems to have come across him in her past).

Elsie gave a clear description of her involvement with MacLennan and her warning to the AG about the Fulton allegations. She explained why she had fought for an inquiry after MacLennan's death. She was still, she said, unsure whether John MacLennan had been homosexual or whether he had been murdered. What mattered was the way he had been hounded. There had been, she said, an "unholy haste" to have MacLennan's body cremated. The prostitutes' statements shown to her in the inquiry were not those that had been shown to her by the AG. "Anyone who says that is the same file is lying." She attacked the attorney general's prejudice against homosexuals. He had, she said, told her that "as long as I am Attorney-General that law will never be changed", giving the excuse that the Chinese would not like it.

Aileen Bridgewater watched Elsie give evidence and thought "she was super. She had such a sweet, charming way of calling the AG a liar." When asked whether she was conducting a vendetta against Quinn, she had replied: "Oh no."

"But you said he was a thug."

"Oh, well, he is a thug."

"What do you mean by that?"

"A thug is a bully, that's what Quinn is — a thug." Elsie and Albert Sanguinetti, her counsel, reminded Aileen of "Hercule Poirot and Miss Marples".[14]

No one moved Elsie Elliott one jot from her account of the Yuen Long affair or the Fulton allegation. The attempts made to brand her a confused fanatic bent on destroying Chief Inspector Quinn backfired and seemed merely silly. It was her accounts that had proved publicly acceptable. The government was forced to fall back on other witnesses in their attempt to discredit her.

The two magistrates who had initiated MacLennan's reinstatement after the Yuen Long incident were to prove sadly malleable to government influence. By the time they appeared at the inquiry it had become well known in legal circles that both Daniell and Rattigan had been summoned to see the chief justice, who had then made a statement to the press downplaying their part in the affair.[15] Elsie Elliott for one was convinced that the backtracking that both then indulged in was due to the pressure exerted upon them; both were newly made judges and susceptible to influence.[16]

At the inquiry, backtrack they did. Rattigan got away with it by claiming that he had hardly been involved with MacLennan at all. He had not, he asserted, questioned MacLennan in 1978 and his knowledge about MacLennan's dismissal had come from Elsie Elliott and Daniell.[17] Daniell let him get away with this nonsense, but his own new line was stomach-turning. He now blamed Elsie for exaggerating the MacLennan and Fulton issues out of a sense of grievance.

Daniell was a man hitherto well respected for his defence of the underdog, but he now forced himself to say that "the affair had been made highly embarrassing" because his comments in defence of MacLennan had been "exaggerated beyond the truth" by Elsie Elliott. He had been further embarrassed that Elsie had used his name to the governor and the press. She was "a very good and very honest woman, but confused." He said he had never had the impression that MacLennan had been set up or framed (this was despite Father McGovern's testimony that Daniell had used the words "frame up", an account Justice Yang was to believe).[18]

Under cross-examination by Beveridge, Daniell began to sweat. He tried but failed to deflect the blame to Father McGovern for involving Elsie Elliott. He became flustered when Beveridge asked him why he had not pointed out errors in Elsie Elliott's letters to the press and why he had not denied Elsie's account until led to do so by Andrew Hodge. Beveridge inveigled Daniell into admitting that he had encouraged Lindsay with at least "sympathetic noises" that he would take a formal complaint in his court from Fulton against the SIU.[19]

It was a pathetic exhibition of turning one's coat by a man who had a real reputation to lose, and who now did so. Elsie Elliott never forgave the judge. She wrote to Howard Lindsay in sorrow, saying she could not excuse Daniell; "he really did lie in the box. A bit of male chauvinism, to think he can get himself off the hook by blasting a confused woman."[20]

Another of the lawyers involved in the case was destined to become a judge. This was Joe Duffy, who had shown Elsie Elliott the eight prostitutes' statements in the attorney general's office. Since the inquest, Elsie had maintained stoutly that the statements she had seen that day were not those produced subsequently by the police. Duffy had assured her back in March 1980 that they were, and he was brought to the inquiry to do so again, seemingly for the sole purpose of discrediting her. He supported his boss, the attorney general, in telling the inquiry that Elsie was mistaken, and so became another of those whom Elsie would never forgive. Like a Fury, she would pursue him throughout his subsequent career. She wrote to him immediately after he had given testimony:

> I was surprised and aggrieved at the MacLennan Enquiry that you supported the Attorney-General's statement that I saw those long statements against John MacLennan, when I visited the Attorney-General's office on 24th January 1980. You know as well as I do that those were not the statements I was shown, but that in fact the statements I was shown were read through in a few minutes [...] Only you can know why you are willing to support a statement which you know to be untrue. I did not expect you to do that, and even now it is not too late for you to admit that it was untrue. I expected to find more sense of honour, having myself been brought up to play a fair game.[21]

Justice Yang believed that Joe Duffy had discredited Elsie, and printed this letter in his inquiry report to indicate how extreme she could be. At this distance, and given the fuller state of knowledge we now possess about the way the affair was handled, we can form our own opinion as to who was discredited.

Elsie could be implacable when aroused. In 1987, she wrote again to Duffy on the occasion of his being made a judge:

> Before you take up your new post, I think you have a matter to clear up with me, concerning the case of John MacLennan [...] You and Mr Griffiths both said on oath in court that the long statements were the same as those you had shown me. (I happen to know that the long statements were made at a much later date and under police (SIU) violent interrogations). A great injustice was therefore committed [...] I am prepared to believe that you acted on the instructions of your superior [...] But I feel that you need to clear this matter up [...] because [...] you will go down in my memory as a person who is not qualified to judge others.[22]

Even then she did not leave him in peace. When he retired in 1996, she wrote again to say that "I have never sought to discredit you publicly" and to ask him to "please admit the truth now."[23] Duffy never shifted from the reply he gave her in 1987: "I have nothing to add save to say that I do not agree with your recollection of the events to which you refer in your letter."[24]

* * *

The three "hostile" witnesses had survived their ordeals at the inquiry with different degrees of success. They had, however, provided enough evidence to enable the commissioner to understand that the Yuen Long incident had been badly handled, that the SIU had been tasked to pursue John MacLennan and had been prepared to do so by illegal means, and that the attempts to alert the attorney general to the SIU's conduct had been rebuffed.

25

Intervention

The spectre of government interference had hung over the inquiry from the first. It had been for that reason that Elsie Elliott had demanded that the inquiry be held in England, chaired by an independent commissioner, with a lawyer appointed directly by the MacLennan family to represent them. She and many others had never lost the fear that the commission would be a whitewash. They were convinced that Justice Yang would do what he was told by the government. The initial composition of the inquiry under Michael Neligan, and the line he had begun to take before he withdrew, had served to confirm their suspicions.

Rumours of government interference circulated in the small goldfish bowl that was Hong Kong's expatriate society. In 1980, Elsie heard gossip that Yang had been promised promotion to chief justice if he handled the inquiry well.[1]

Government interference was, in truth, always a possibility. There was too much at stake for the colony to allow the commission a free hand to destroy the reputations of its principal officials. The governor had real concerns that the MacLennan affair would serve to undo the repairs that he had initiated to the morale of the RHKP and to its public reputation. He had set up the inquiry in order to deflect the possible damage that reaction to MacLennan's death had caused. It was unlikely that he would be content to see the commission worsen a situation it had been established to ameliorate.

MacLehose showed his continuing anxiety about the state of the police force in September 1980, when Lord Carrington, the secretary of state for foreign affairs, visited Hong Kong. Sir Murray cancelled a dinner at which Carrington had been intended to meet senior police officers, and for the first time in nearly two years he was forced to place the issue of police morale, effectiveness, and public status on the agenda for discussions with his guest.[2]

That the Hong Kong Government was extraordinarily sensitive at this time about any form of public criticism was shown in December 1980 by journalist Duncan Campbell's revelation in the *New Statesman* of the existence of a secret government committee, the Standing Committee on Pressure Groups (SCOPG), a body the press began to called "a conspiracy to inhibit free expression in Hong Kong".[3] This committee had been set up in 1978, according to the government to monitor public opinion in order to understand it and provide better policy responses. The press saw things very differently, and alleged that the body had been set up to control those holding views adverse to the government. In January 1981, the local press revealed government plans for the infiltration of groups such as school and college associations, including the Hong Kong Professional Teachers' Union, the Hong Kong Federation of Students, and the Government School Non-Graduate Teachers Union.[4] The exposure of the existence and activities of the SCOPG had such an adverse effect on public opinion that the committee was wound up, at least officially, in 1983. The revelation of its existence at the time of the MacLennan case served only to increase public fear of government interference.

* * *

By the end of 1980, the government had severe concerns about the course being taken by the commission. The inquiry seemed to be stretching endlessly into the future and costing far more than had been budgeted. In early December, they were told that hearings would last until the end of January and cost between HK$5 and HK$10 million, but a few days later the estimated end date had been pushed back to the end of March. In February, the commission sought to reserve the Legislative Council Chamber, where hearings were being held, until the end of June.[5] The Financial Committee of the Legislative Council began to grumble about having to authorize further expenditure. The government was also alarmed when it emerged that the commission intended to issue Salmon letters (notifications to a person of accusations that they would face at the inquiry) to the commissioner of police and the attorney general.

The Legal Department and the judiciary now perceived that the attorney general was not the only law officer who was being put at risk by the inquiry. Investigators for the commission had questioned Howard Lindsay and Chief Inspector Quinn about what they knew of the sexual orientation of the chief justice.

Similar questions had been raised about DPP MacDougall, and in his case, and in that of Joe Duffy, lines of inquiry had been followed indicating an attack on their part in the targeting and investigation of MacLennan.[6] The Legal Department began to fight back against what they had come to view as an assault upon them by the counsel for the commission.

A whispering campaign began in December 1980 aimed at discrediting the commission, initially by portraying Justice Yang as improperly controlling the proceedings, later by making him out to be weak and in the pocket of his counsel. John Beveridge was to be portrayed as hostile to the government and a threat to the colony and the governor. The campaign started in London, while the attorney general took Christmas leave. He called in at the FCO and personally briefed both Dick Clift, head of the Hong Kong Desk, and the secretary of state. He did this *before* he formally raised the issue of Yang's control of the commission with the governor in Hong Kong (he was not to do this for another two months), although it does appear that the governor had instructed him to brief the Foreign Office on the current state of play.

Griffiths told the Hong Kong Desk that he was "particularly exercised by the antics of Mr Beveridge the Counsel for the Commission." He and others he listed (Martin Rowlands, Sir Jack Cater and Sir Philip Haddon-Cave) had been asked if "there is a conspiracy in Hong Kong to keep homosexuals out of civil service appointments." The AG added that Beveridge had asked to see the file on the "alleged homosexual activities" of Roy Henry and that the governor had been asked why he had interviewed Roy Henry on that subject (this last statement does not appear to have been true. The governor received a set of questions only in the following year and they did not include this one. Perhaps that question had been asked of others).[7]

Griffiths told Clift that he believed Yang to be sincere and not completely under the thumb of his counsel. Yang had, however, the wrong idea of how to conduct an inquiry. The commissioner of police was to appear shortly and it was likely that his private life would come under scrutiny (Yang's robust ruling that this was not to be discussed was not mentioned). Beveridge, according to Griffiths, had been pursuing the line that there was a conspiracy to protect senior officials from prosecution for homosexual offences "while allowing smaller fry to go to the wall". The attorney general felt that he was himself the immediate object of attack, but that the chief secretary and the governor could come under fire (this was pure speculation, and misplaced speculation at that, but it was the first appearance of a line that had the power to worry the administration). He left the FCO with the impression, which they duly recorded, that "the MacLennan Inquiry has clearly misfired" and that "a good deal of damage is being done." Griffiths had meant to plant a seed of anxiety in the minds of the civil servants on the Hong Kong Desk and he had succeeded. Clift advised his minister of state, Peter Blaker, that ministers could not be criticized in any of this but "this does not mean that if there is a row in Hong Kong some of the criticism will not brush off on HMG."[8]

Other than the Hong Kong Government, the FCO had no source of information on what was happening at the commission, and so took these comments at face value. The deputy under secretary summed up their understanding of the situation in a note: "The main risk is that the Counsel of the Commission, Mr Beveridge, has possibly sufficient material in his hands to make a case of 'conspiracy' to protect senior officials", and that "the Chief Secretary and the Governor may have to defend themselves." Griffiths had also told the Hong Kong Desk that confidence in Yang had been shaken at the start of the inquiry when he had decided to show the whole of the dossier the AG had given him on the SIU and Roy Henry to *all* the counsel on the commission.[9]

From London, the AG sent a telex to the governor advising him that John Beveridge was their real problem and that some change of course was needed at the commission. He suggested that crown counsels Max Lucas and Barrie Barlow enter the inquiry to represent government servants (in effect, mainly to represent himself). He advised the governor: "Do not, repeat not, enter with all guns blazing or criticize Justice Yang" but concentrate on excluding irrelevant evidence. Government, he believed, should be

> very slow to hinder investigative role of Commission save on security grounds or by persuasion [...] The aim must be to motivate Mr Justice Yang to regain personal control of direction of tribunal and not continue to believe that he must just sit quietly and judge the evidence presented to him.[10]

The Legal Department formulated the opinion that Yang had deviated from the rules of inquiry established by the Royal Commission chaired by Lord Justice Salmon. This was a dubious view, probably an excuse, as Yang and Beveridge were adhering to the six Salmon principles, which made quite clear the adversarial element that they required.[11]

Barlow and Lucas duly joined the inquiry as counsel "for the Attorney General and Members of the Legal Department" on

5 and 26 January respectively. The governor also took steps to ensure that his personal interest was protected by having Peter Allen of the Legal Department appointed "For His Excellency in the Right of the Crown."[12] Barrie Barlow, in a somewhat bumptious opening remark to the inquiry, made plain the government's feelings to Justice Yang, who by now would very likely have caught wind of what was afoot in the Legal Department. Barlow said:

> I formed the impression from the reading which I have done of the papers in this case, that your Lordship is more or less following the procedure suggested in the Salmon report, and with great necessity my Lord, I would ask if you are able to indicate whether or not that impression is well founded.

"Yes," was the only reply Justice Yang felt called upon to reply to that barb.[13]

* * *

Behind the scenes, the antagonisms that were being played out at the commission were being replicated in the personal relationships of some of the key players. It had become apparent by 1981 that John Griffiths and John Beveridge had developed a strong dislike for each other. The attorney general resented the way Beveridge seemed to be extending the inquiry and focusing its attention on his actions. The evidence he had heard at the inquiry had led Beveridge to lose all respect for the principal law officer of the crown in Hong Kong. Their mutual antipathy broke into the public domain one night when Beveridge and Conrad Seagroatt were dining at the Hong Kong Club. Griffiths and a few of his lawyers, including Andrew Hodge, were at a nearby table. Initially, things seemed to be going amicably, and one or other party sent the other a glass of port. At this, Griffiths' party came over and an altercation began, Griffiths needling Beveridge about the inquiry and asking him how far he wanted to go up the chain with his conspiracy theories — was he aiming as high as the governor? Beveridge decided to withdraw, and was accompanied by Seagroatt, who had become most uncomfortable and so declined an invitation by Griffiths to remain with his party. Soon afterwards, Seagroatt learned that Griffiths wished him to know that he had once regarded him as a friend, but was now disappointed in him. The following morning, news of the argument had circulated widely around the town and Justice Yang called all the barristers into his chambers in an attempt to defuse the hostility. He was not successful.[14]

* * *

Soon after hearings resumed after the Christmas and New Year recess, an incident occurred that gave the Legal Department an opening to attack Beveridge. On 15 January, the *South China Morning Post*, commenting on the length of time the inquiry was taking, quoted Beveridge on his view that the wide terms of reference made lengthy hearings inevitable. The reporter added that "an agent of the commission" had said that the range of the inquiry had "crept from the gutters to Government House". The context of the piece made it clear that it was not Beveridge who had said this, but Andrew Hodge rose at the start of that day's hearings to insinuate that it had indeed been a remark made by the counsel for the commission. "I take it M'lord, of course, that that was a statement made without your authority [...] and which you would deprecate." The quotation from the *Post* would reappear, at a later date, to the commission's detriment.[15]

In early February, the commission sent the governor and the chief secretary a set of questions concerning their roles in the MacLennan affair. The questions were straightforward and were to be the only ones put to either man during the inquiry. There is no documentary evidence that the commission intended to send either governor or chief secretary a Salmon letter or a subpoena to appear at the hearings. The questions were enough, however, to alarm Sir Murray, who objected to being questioned and felt there was a sinister intent behind the inquiries. He telexed the Foreign Office that it seemed to him that the commission was seeking "to ascertain whether there may have been a conspiracy among very senior members of Government to select and set up MacLennan for prosecution. Needless to say there was not."[16]

Worries about the revelations that might be forthcoming in the final stages of the hearings continued to exercise minds both in Government House and the Legal Department. In February, the governor told London that "the original claim made by the SIU to the effect that MacLennan's name came to their notice as the result of a spontaneous remark by an informer is likely to be discredited." Sir James Crane, the FCO's police adviser, was at that stage in Hong Kong, and the governor asked him privately to suggest the name of a senior British police officer who might be appointed DC (Ops) "fairly soon, with the idea that this person might step into the Commissioner's shoes if Mr Henry had to go at short notice." The Foreign Office was alarmed by this and the head of the Hong Kong Desk briefed minister of state Blaker that:

> The MacLennan Inquiry has clearly misfired. The side issues have overtaken the inquiry into MacLennan's death. The risks to the Hong Kong Government should not be exaggerated [...] Mr

> Beveridge is quite likely to ensure that the "conspiracy" theory gets a considerable airing and some criticism of the Governor is not to be ruled out. Mr Henry's position remains very much in the balance. I am sure that the Governor remains very unwilling to get rid of him. But his position may yet become untenable.[17]

The governor began to fear that he would be called to the commission to give evidence. There is no indication that the commission actually contemplated this, and it seems that this fear was one played upon successfully by those seeking to rein in the inquiry. His position as the inviolable representative of the crown in Hong Kong was of supreme importance to MacLehose and the idea of being dragged into a courtroom to be questioned by his inferiors was anathema to him. He asked London if he could be compelled to appear. The secretary of state personally replied that: "You cannot legally refuse to appear although you may refuse to disclose particular documents if you so judge." [18]

Two days later, the attorney general received the Salmon letter issued to him by the commission, making it clear that he was to be challenged not only on his actions in the MacLennan case, but also on those in the Howard Lindsay case as well.[19] Griffiths was so concerned by the allegations put to him in the letter that he asked the governor whether they would affect the discharge of his duties. The governor replied: "Certainly not".[20]

By now, the Legal Department was making sure the governor was aware of their misgivings about the threats that the commission posed. The governor did not need much prompting. On 26 February, he wrote a minute to the attorney general about what he was being told. "Many verbal complaints about the conduct of this Inquiry emanating from your chambers have come to me either directly or indirectly." Word had come from

Max Lucas that the recent revelation by Gus Graham that Justice Yang had been mentioned as a suspected homosexual was an opportunity to do something about the way the commission was operating (perhaps Lucas felt that Yang might at that stage have been more inclined to yield to an attempt to restrict the scope of the questioning — to his credit he was not). The governor suggested to the AG that they must either "bite the bullet" or "make a recommendation to me for action."[21] This was the opportunity that the Legal Department had been seeking and they took it.

Before the AG could reply, however, Justice Yang took a step which forced the governor's hand. Although he had adopted a passive, supervisory stance at the inquiry, Yang was far from the cipher that he was portrayed as by the Legal Department. By the end of February 1981, he had become so appalled by what he had heard of the tales of misconduct by the SIU that he resolved to add an annex to his final report outlining their failings in detail. This was beyond his terms of reference, so on 4 March he applied to the governor through Sir Jack Cater, the chief secretary, for an extension of those terms.[22] This brought the issue to boiling point in Government House, where three days later the governor personally chaired a meeting to discuss, not whether there should be an extension of terms granted, for that was assumed by all present to be off the table, but instead how to rein in the inquiry.[23] Among those at the meeting that day were Sir Jack Cater, the chief secretary; MacDougall, the director of public prosecutions; the crown solicitor; and Barrie Barlow.

The timing was perfect for the AG's reply to the governor's minute to be used as a brief for the meeting. Claiming to wish the governor to have a brief from someone not affected by the inquiry, but also, he admitted, to avoid being questioned at the commission upon it were it to come to light, the AG directed Tom Jones, a crown counsel then acting as crown solicitor, to write a brief for the governor recommending that the commission be made to sit *in camera* and that it be given a date by which it had to complete its hearings.[24]

To make sure there was no doubt in the governor's mind, Griffiths covered the brief by Jones with a minute of his own, in which he made recommendations similar to those made by Jones and gave his personal views of the counsel to the commission. Beveridge, he wrote, is

> an obstinate though forceful man who is obsessed with the opinion that he is, as he says, "conducting a case of minor constitutional importance" which he believes will prove his pre-conceptions as to Colonial government to be correct — "We are moving from the gutter up to Government House"; "you have a corrupt Governor", etc.

These were gross misrepresentations. John Beveridge is not recorded as having uttered either of these remarks. Griffiths went on, seeking to add to the governor's concern, by suggesting that the commission "may cause some to resign — CP, DC (Ops), AG, maybe CJ in view of the enquiries made to potential witnesses as to whether he has homosexual proclivities."[25]

The crown solicitor's paper was similarly cavalier in its use of emotive language and more expansive in its citation of issues calculated to worry or arouse the governor. It was to prove all too successful in this. Jones wrote that there was likely to be a public airing of allegations against Roy Henry and that this would have "a most adverse effect on Police morale." He feared an investigation into Mr Justice MacDougall personally, and into the Legal Department generally, aimed at revealing bias in their approach to homosexual prosecutions. He expected attacks on senior police officers, especially Moor, and an attack on the CJ, including his earlier conduct as AG, relating to the allegations in the Duffy petition. "MacDougall J.," Jones wrote, "seems destined for similar treatment for being unfortunate enough to have been involved on the periphery of various events and for being middle-aged and unmarried." With no evidence for this cited, he concluded that he expected an "attack on Y.E.'s office and perhaps you personally."

The reason all this might happen, Jones postulated, was "the abrogation by the Commissioner of his powers to Mr Beveridge, QC" and "a bias on the part of Mr Beveridge [...] to demonstrate his pre-conceived views of colonial administration." Yang, according to Jones, had "adopted a completely subdued role." "Beveridge, QC", Jones went on,

> seems wholly pre-occupied with the upper echelons of our 'colonial administration'. His conduct has betrayed a curiosity, almost amounting to fixation, with the question of possible misconduct by senior officials — and if such misconduct might relate to sexual aberration, so much the better.

Jones then repeated the canard that Beveridge had told the press that the inquiry "has gone from the gutters to the corridors of Government House." Hong Kong's security, Jones alleged, was being imperilled.

Jones then turned from this rambling and intemperate tirade to address the recommendation he wished to make to hold the inquiry *in camera*. "It is not necessary," he wrote, "for the public to review the spectacle, only the results." Forcing the commission to hold its hearings *in camera*, would, Jones stated, be beneficial because:

> It is likely that if the limelight is removed this Inquiry will proceed far more swiftly towards its conclusion since the Commissioner and his Counsel can be expected to get on with the job instead of dollying at length on sensational but irrelevant material in order to supply the media with its daily diet of titillation [...] Probably the root cause of the inordinate length of time this Inquiry is taking is the combination of an ineffectual Commissioner and an aggressive and strong-willed Counsel to the Commission.

Jones recommended that the governor-in-council direct that the commission proceed *in camera* and produce a report by a set date. He concluded with the vain hope, but one the Legal Department evidently cherished, that the governor consider one other course "that may be well be considered justifiable", that was "to stop the enquiry."[26]

The governor reserved his position at the meeting's close, but was heard to remark as an aside: "A pity about T.L.; I used to think he would be the first Chinese C.J."[27]

Sir Murray then flew immediately to London on what had already been planned as a visit to the FCO and, when he met Minister Peter Blaker and his staff there on 10 March, he informed them that problems had arisen at the inquiry due to the fact that "the Commissioner had allowed it to drag on and to cover a much wider field than had been originally intended." John Beveridge, he went on, "had undue influence over Mr Justice Yang". It had been, MacLehose said, his "clear understanding that the Commissioner had intended to hold most of the proceedings *in camera*" (something that had never been mentioned as an intention before and which would certainly not have survived the public outcry had it been essayed). That had not happened and the open hearings "had caused undesirable publicity and subjected individual witnesses to unfair pressure." Yang had now asked to expand his terms of reference. He had already been given access "to any files". "Beveridge, however, wanted more than that."

Blaker was not at all happy about the idea of holding the inquiry *in camera*, but the governor said that most people in Hong Kong had expected it (this was simply untrue) and he ignored Blaker's objections. Sir Murray concluded discussion of the topic by saying that he would speak confidentially to the commissioner in an attempt to get Mr Yang himself to ask that proceedings should be held *in camera* and to get him to work in future within his original terms of reference. This would obviously be preferable to a directive from the governor, but if Mr Yang refused he would have to be instructed immediately in this sense.[28] The minister reluctantly accepted this line, but took the precaution of seeking advice from the FCO's legal adviser, Sir Ian Sinclair, who, using only the papers supplied by Hong Kong, and principally among those the crown solicitor's inflammatory report to the governor, supported MacLehose's line. On 13 March, Morrice of the Hong Kong & General Department minuted R.D. Clift, his superior, what Sinclair had said:

> Given the manner in which the inquiry was being handled, and particularly the failure on the part of Mr Justice Yang to ensure that all the evidence given was relevant to the terms of reference of the inquiry, there seemed to be ample justification for the proposed action.[29]

Morrice also reported that the treasury solicitor "fully shared his views." The minute was copied to Hong Kong. The governor returned there that day prepared to implement this policy.

No record has so far come to light of what then transpired. What is certain from what occurred is that, despite the governor's intentions and his seemingly awesome power in Hong Kong,

Yang resisted, and did so for about a month. This must have enraged the governor, who put the issue to his Executive Council on 25 March and persuaded them to pass a resolution backing his demands. The minutes record that the Governor-in-Council resolved "that the Commissioner should be directed to conduct all further proceedings of the Inquiry *in camera*; the timing of this direction and the terms in which it was conveyed to be left to the Governor." The council also

> expressed the view that while the evident disadvantages of directing the Commissioner [...] were serious, they were outweighed by the probable disadvantages of permitting the proceedings to continue in open session, if the Commissioner continued to conduct the Inquiry in the way he had been doing.

They turned down Justice Yang's request for an extension of his terms of reference.[30]

The decision of the Governor-in-Council, the colony's highest organ of government, should have ended the issue as the governor wished, but Yang would not yield and the governor held back from implementing his policy, fearful, no doubt, of the public outcry that would have ensued had he done so. There is no public record of the negotiations that must have gone on at this time. They must have included Beveridge. It was he, rather than Justice Yang, who held the most powerful card, perhaps the only one available to the two of them, which was his own resignation. He had used the threat of it once already, over the Carratu report. Yang was a Hong Kong judge with, if things went well, prospects of greater things, but if he resigned, no prospects at all. Beveridge could go home, to be met by headlines that one can imagine: "British Barrister Resigns from Hong Kong Inquiry in Protest at Government Interference", or worse. Neither the FCO nor Sir

Murray would have wanted to countenance that.

Nothing moved until April, and Peter Blaker was moved to ask the governor what was going on. Had he told the commissioner "that he must sit in secret?" The governor replied by telex on the 13th that he had not, and that although his Executive Council had approved this, he still wished "to use persuasion".[31] Two days later, the governor followed this up with a letter to London indicating that he would insist on his new policy. He told the FCO that Andrew Leggatt, QC, had been instructed to give independent advice as to whether crown privilege exempted the governor from being called as a witness (it didn't).[32] MacLehose was still considering whether to order the commissioner to proceed with senior officials "including Henry" *in camera*. He had been baulked so far, but had not given up. He added that if Leggatt could conclude "a more satisfactory agreement with the Commissioner about what is and is not relevant [...] it may still be possible to avoid a direction into *camera*."[33]

Once again the record falls silent. No account has come to light to explain the fact that the inquiry proceeded in public, with no alteration of its terms of reference and no time limit set for its completion. The governor's design had been completely frustrated, something unique in MacLehose's long tenure of office. To compound the mystery, Sir Ti-Liang Yang (as he is at the time of writing) categorically denies that any pressure was brought to bear upon him by the government, or that any negotiations through Andrew Leggatt ever took place.[34] Yet Yang must somehow have been informed that his request for an extension of terms of reference to allow him to include an annex to his report criticizing the SIU had been turned down, for he was to write no such annex.

In the event, too, there was to be a noticeable attempt to reduce the time span of the inquiry. The final witnesses were reduced in number and their examination speeded up, Elsie Elliott, for instance, having to endure only two days in the witness box, Aileen Bridgewater just a few hours. On 29 April, when whatever had been settled had already occurred, Andrew Leggatt joined the commission "for the Governor in the Right of the Crown", presumably to report directly to MacLehose on the proceedings.[35]

26

Endgame

That left only the evidence of the attorney general to be heard, which still had the potential to damage the government, and of course John Griffiths personally. The AG had not done well so far in his public appearances. It had been his seeming dismissal of the inquest jury's verdict, his statements about the Fulton affair, and his handling of the press that had been largely responsible for bringing about the inquiry. The government and its legal team must have had doubts about what would happen when the AG came to testify. It seems they took steps to ensure that the worst did not occur.

Griffiths was, in any case, a highly experienced and effective lawyer, and a courtroom was his métier. In the event, he did not disappoint his side. On the contrary, when he emerged from the witness box on 15 May, after just over three days of giving evidence, he did so remarkably unscathed, so much so that the question arises as to why. John Beveridge had been preparing for so long to grapple with the man who he by now clearly felt was at the centre of the MacLennan affair, that one would have expected him to succeed in nailing the attorney general to the wall. Yet he did not.

There were, indeed, issues which the attorney general could not avoid. His own words and actions had laid him open to attack. His clumsy attempt to intimidate Fulton's lawyers before the release of his press statement had already been branded by solicitor Ashley Burns as a misuse of his government office in an attempt to suppress the statement.[1] His remarks about the inquest verdict had drawn outside criticism from the Bar Council and others. These matters could not be ignored. They had to be allowed to speak for themselves and to be commented upon, as indeed Yang did in his final report.

Other issues, however, could be dealt with more subtly. The AG was vulnerable on two more serious counts that had not been noticed publicly and that Beveridge now uncharacteristically allowed to slip by. In his cross-examination, he permitted Griffiths to be vague about what had caused him to initiate the enforcement of the law on homosexuality when he had first arrived in Hong Kong. He let the AG claim that his reasoning for this policy had included the Duffy petition. This was not the case; the SIU's leash had been let slip before Duffy's last bombshell exploded. The policy was the AG's own, and it was this policy that had enabled the police to bring about the tragedy of John MacLennan's death.

Secondly, Beveridge allowed John Griffiths to get away with a defence of his actions over the Fulton allegation of a set-up, a defence in which he justified his refusal to listen to Howard Lindsay and Elsie Elliott on the grounds that he trusted neither.

He had, however, already given away in one of his earlier press releases that he had known of the allegations before he met either of them. Beveridge allowed him to place a cloud around just what and when he knew about the pursuit of John MacLennan by the SIU. At worst, Griffiths was as complicit as they and the police were, but the point was never driven home, and when Justice Yang came to write his report, he criticized only the fact that Griffiths had failed to take notice of Lindsay and Elsie Elliott.

John Beveridge, it seems, held his fire. His seemingly lacklustre performance was commented on by Aileen Bridgewater, who watched Griffiths giving testimony. She noted that on 13 May Conrad Seagroatt, who kept up his assault over nearly two days, got deep under the AG's skin when pressing him about his failure to act on the Fulton allegations. Griffiths "became nervous and apprehensive," she recorded, "during the afternoon instead of the battle of the tigers it became the lion against the frightened fawn [...] Towards the end he started crumbling [...] he was losing concentration."[2]

Beveridge, however, devoted only the afternoon of 15 May to his cross-examination. "Within ten minutes," Aileen noted,

> the AG's voice became tense. But he was on marvellous form, had clearly foreseen all the points on which he was vulnerable and had prepared a marvellous case for the defence. Beveridge fell in line and became the prosecutor and it was a fascinating tussle. Nobody won.

The AG was even allowed to repeat his earlier threats against those who had criticized his misleading the public, alleging that prosecution for libel and contempt were possible.[3]

The transcript covering Beveridge's cross-examination on the issue of the enforcement of the law on homosexuality gives the flavour of their rather flat encounter:

> Beveridge: Why were you interested in homosexuality in Hong Kong?
> Griffiths: It was the Duffy petition which arose after I became Attorney General, but also in terms of a previous discussion in London before I came here, which was itself preceded by the meeting to which I referred, or the lunch to which I referred, where Mr Derek Davies, the Editor of the *Far Eastern Economic Review*, and other journalists were present.
> Beveridge: So the first time that your mind turned to the question of prosecution policy for homosexuals in Hong Kong was at that luncheon table?
> Griffiths: Yes.
> Beveridge: And the second time was when you were briefed before coming out here?
> Griffiths: Yes.
> Beveridge: And so the Duffy petition represented the third link in that chain?
> Griffiths: Yes.[4]

It is possible that John Beveridge was just having an off day. A more persuasive explanation for this damp squib is that he was giving the attorney general an easy ride. Destroying the credibility of the AG might have damaged the government so protecting him was a government priority. Perhaps it was to save the attorney general that the inquiry had been allowed to proceed without the imposition of the restrictions for which the governor had so firmly called.

Beveridge gave Aileen his private view of John Griffiths at a party she threw on the night of his cross-examination of the AG: "He said that the AG was a crook. He said Elsie and I had accepted objective judgement without complaint but that the higher you go in government the less that was so."[5] John Beveridge's view was by now held to some degree by Conrad Seagroatt. When the inquiry opened, Seagroatt had come to Hong Kong believing in the AG's high reputation. By the end of the inquiry, he had lost his admiration for the man; he had come to believe that events were getting to Griffiths and that he had lost his self-control.[6]

* * *

It was fitting, perhaps, that the last question to be posed at the inquiry was put by a homosexual barrister on the topic of homosexuality. Albert Sanguinetti, representing Elsie Elliott, attacked Joe Duffy on the subject of the disputed prostitute witness statements. It was an exchange that revealed Duffy's own prejudices. The transcript is redolent with the tone of contempt in Sanguinetti's voice:

> Sanguinetti: No, I'm asking you whether these statements contain certain practices.
> Duffy: They contain descriptions of sexual perversions. Yes.
> Sanguinetti: Perversions ...
> Duffy: Yes.
> Beveridge: My Lord, I think it's fallen to my learned friend, Mr Sanguinetti, to ask the last question at these hearings, because this is the last witness. May he be released?[7]

The inquiry was to produce one more surprise. On 20 May, Andrew Leggatt rose to transmit to the commissioner a statement by the governor. Sir Murray, he declaimed, called for a "cogent, compelling and conclusive report" and had let it be said that he "did not expect [...] gratuitous criticism" of the attorney general and others in it. The final report, for the benefit of the man in the street, should be "concise and intelligible." It should show, Leggatt went on, oblivious to the hackles rising around him, what was central and what peripheral. His Excellency had originally wanted the report by 18 September 1980, but had decided not to foreshorten the Commission of Inquiry. He had been satisfied by the inquest and "did not want to see a trial of a dead man or to cause distress to his family." He was also satisfied that his own role had been made clear at the commission and he was not going to "enter down into the arena". He was graciously refraining from proposing to Justice Yang that the commission make any specific findings of fact.[8]

This statement was very much in Sir Murray's autocratic style, but it was a tremendous mistake. Apart from belittling and offending Justice Yang, the statement was widely seen, and as widely resented, as an attack on judicial liberty. The immediate outcry from the public and the legal profession forced a change of heart and the governor sent another counsel, Andrew Morritt, QC, scurrying down to the commission to repair the damage Leggatt had done. The governor, Morritt said, rather unconvincingly, "did not intend to influence the final report" and the chief secretary had instructed him to say that "the governor's address does not warrant the construction that it is a warning, direction or interference."[9] Justice Yang had been so taken aback by Leggatt's peremptory speech that he had distrusted his own initial negative reaction to it. As Leggatt spoke, he had watched the faces of his legal team, but none had given anything away in their expressions, so he gave himself time to reflect before responding. Overnight, he concluded that he had to rebut the gist of what Leggatt had said and he did so firmly the next day by robustly defending in open session "the sanctity of judicial independence which brooks no interference from any quarter."[10] The press had a field day, their comments ranging from: "Some people are asking also if the Governor's words might be construed as 'a direction for a whitewash'," to "We still find it regrettable that the Governor's name was invoked in this way."

Summing up by all the counsel present took another week. Those appearing for the government side did their best to maintain that the inquiry had proved their clients innocent of any wrongdoing and that black really was white. Kemal Bokhary stated with a straight face that the SIU had done nothing wrong. "They stand exonerated," he said, and the accusation that MacLennan had been hounded to death was "utterly without foundation".[11] Charles Ingham maintained that Trotman had been right to tell MacLennan of his impending arrest.[12]

Max Lucas and Barrie Barlow jointly summed up for the AG. No one, they stated flatly, had contested that the charges against MacLennan had been properly brought. The AG had not acted on the Fulton allegation because the complainants were "unreliable and manipulators," Lindsay was "embittered" and Elsie Elliott was "clumsy and careless about the facts." Max Lucas lost his place at one stage and managed to read one page of his submission twice, then had the cheek to say that what bothered him was that no one had noticed; it maybe did not occur to him that no one present had any interest in what he was saying.[13]

Andrew Hodge characterized critics of the police as "misguided pyromaniacs" and repeatedly attacked Elsie Elliott, whom he termed a "publicist" and her behaviour "a gross abuse of her responsibilities as a public figure." Her role had involved only a furthering of "her own public vendettas at the expense of the memory of MacLennan." "She saw in this issue," he said, "an opportunity to exploit her grievances against this Police Force." Her letter to the governor was "an epistle of shameless deception." She had "a mentality warped beyond reason by her own Messianic vision." He gave his own warped vision of events when he said that all the evidence against MacLennan had been properly obtained; that there had been no attempt to cover anything up; that proper use had been made of Inspector Fulton; that MacLennan, who was "no victim save to his own tastes, had not been hounded to death"; that Blackburn had always acted "properly, fairly and in good faith"; that Ross "would not have permitted any improper pursuit"; and that Roy Henry had "acted rightly."[14]

On the other side of the argument, Albert Sanguinetti called the SIU charter "a discrimination charter. It has a sinister and dangerous smell about it." It had been partly to blame for hounding John MacLennan to his death.[15] Conrad Seagroatt accepted that MacLennan had been bisexual and had committed suicide, but said that the police had produced "a deliberate smoke screen" to hide an unfair and inordinate interest in him. He laid the blame at Eric Blackburn's door for sparking the SIU's interest MacLennan.[16]

Last of all to sum up was John Beveridge, and despite what he had said in his opening address about not giving his views to the commissioner, by now he clearly considered that he had to. First, he very neatly addressed the issue of the governor's attempt through Andrew Leggatt to interfere with the inquiry.

> No further Order having been made by the Governor-in-Council under the Ordinance, your Lordship cannot receive assistance by any indication of what His Excellency, or anyone else, may think about the matter [...] Amongst the most important of the procedural

> decisions which your Lordship has had to take is that relating to the power to hold hearings of the evidence in camera [...] The Salmon Report suggests that this course should be taken only when an exceptional need arises [...] Subject only to certain powers of the Governor-in-Council, exercisable by public order made under the Ordinance (and no such orders have been made in relation to this Commission) neither the Governor nor any lesser authority in the Colony has any right or power to influence the way in which this Commission carries out its functions. I respectfully indicate that the submissions of learned Counsel for the Governor are entitled to just the same considerations as the submissions of other Counsel, but insofar as they may be thought to disclose any views of the Governor, they can be of no assistance to your Lordship.[17]

It would be difficult to conceive of a better or more withering put down of a governor of a crown colony.

He then moved on to answering the questions posed by the inquiry's terms of reference. The cause of John MacLennan's death had been, he said, established

> with an absolute and compelling authority rarely to be found with regard to any area of fact in any case [...] No single item of evidence has been unearthed by any of your Lordship's advisers or investigators which indicates murder, or identifies a murderer, or provides a motive for murder.

He went very light on the SIU; their failings, he said, "were not serious". There was evidence, however, that the Yuen Long case had given impetus to the SIU's taking up MacLennan's case. Surprisingly, he dealt similarly lightly with the Fulton evidence: "It seems clear that Senior Inspector Fulton's evidence at no stage went so far as to indicate an allegation of attempted frame up and it is doubtful that it went as far as to suggest an allegation of set-up in any criminal sense."

He was not prepared to let all the senior officers escape so lightly. He went on to say:

> Your Lordship may feel the need to determine the reasons why snippets of insubstantial information in relation to Inspector MacLennan were passed up through the chain of command as far as Deputy Commissioner Moor, when no other information as to homosexual activity was being passed to him. You may wish to determine the process of targeting Inspector MacLennan and in particular, the way in which Deputy Commissioner Moor made the decision to do so.

Beveridge specifically rejected Andrew Leggatt's call for the inquiry to exempt the attorney general from attack. So moved had he been by that interference, that he listed for the commissioner the criticisms that were possible:

> a. Failure to act on the Fulton complaint.
> b. Unduly pressing his views on the inquest privately to the coroner's officer, a junior member of his own department.
> c. Conducting a public relations exercise suggesting that the Coroner's jury was wrong.
> d. Publishing a statement on 19 June 1980 misrepresenting facts to answer Elsie Elliott's criticisms.
> e. Telephoning a solicitor using the weight of his office to attempt to pressurise him.[18]

He did not, notably, make mention of the two serious issues over which he had glossed in his cross-examination. They were, it seemed, to remain off limits.

As John Beveridge finally sat down, the hearings ended. The proceedings had lasted 134 days, 110 witnesses and fifty-seven statements had been heard, and 13,000 pages of transcript had been created, all at a cost, it was estimated, somewhere in the region of HK$20 million.[19]

27

The Commission Report

Justice Yang, assisted by Murray Burton, who was delegated the compilation of the factual elements of the final report, worked swiftly through the following two months.[1] He signed the report on 30 July 1981 and submitted it to Sir Jack Cater (then acting governor, as Sir Murray was away) on 1 August.[2] On his return to the colony, the governor presented the report to the Executive Council on 22 August and it was published on the 29th.[3]

Justice Yang's report is perplexing. At a number of points throughout its dense text, Yang makes clear his criticisms of the actions of the principal characters in the case before him. Yet his findings do not match the evidence he cites, being mild and seemingly calculated to ensure that no consequences should befall those he has criticized. He was an experienced judge, and was not unaware of what negligence, improper conduct, and ill will looked like. He seems to have concluded that in the MacLennan case no one was guilty of those things, despite having recorded the evidence that they had occurred. This was not due to any failure on the part of the judge to apply his mind to a complex problem. With one or two exceptions, Justice Yang got the detail of the case right. The contrast between the evidence of failures, mistakes, poorly conceived and executed policies, ill will, illegalities, and the lies told to cover these up, most of which he detailed in his report, and the gentle criticisms which he made of those at fault is stark.

The final paragraph of his report makes it plain what Justice Yang set out to show throughout its contents:

> The conclusions in this Report reveal a number of defects, more in the nature of human frailty and errors than a defective system. We have spent a year looking into a microscope. Instead of cancer, we have found eczema.[4]

In excusing the causes of this "eczema" by attributing it to "human frailty and errors", Yang passed over the culpable motivations and actions laid bare by the inquiry he had chaired. When this book was being written, and when questioned on this point, Sir Ti-Liang Yang acknowledged that his criticisms were "gentle"; he is, he says, "a gentle man and his criticisms of others are always gentle."

Justice Yang did not arrange his findings according to his terms of reference, but answered them throughout his 411 pages of closely typed text.

In answer to question (a), the mode of death, Yang stated that "I am compelled to record that MacLennan committed suicide with revolver 4894." There could not, he judged, have been another person in the flat. He concluded that the motive for suicide was the imminent disclosure of the offences MacLennan had committed with Peter Sung and others, the shame of which he had been unable to face.[5]

Question (b) of the terms of reference asked whether there had been deficiencies in the investigation of the death. Yang gave the police a cleaner bill of health than had Li Kwan-ha in his report on the subject. He refused to criticize poor control at the site, believed that to expect Pelly to have attended the post mortem was a "counsel of perfection", and complimented Pelly on his report. Trotman alone was singled out here for criticism, and then only for his "error of judgement" in warning MacLennan of his arrest. He did not, Yang stated, commit an error in his investigation. Chief Inspector Kong was also not at fault.[6]

In answer to question (c) of the terms of reference, whether the charges had been properly brought and the evidence properly obtained, Yang denied that MacLennan had been "chosen" from a pool of subjects but believed he had been targeted only because his name had been given to Constable Liu Man in the course of intelligence gathering. He credited the evidence of the prostitutes even though they were blackmailers and took scant note of the false witnesses brought against John MacLennan. He did criticize Superintendent Brooks and Chief Inspector Quinn for suggesting that Fulton approach MacLennan, saying that they were "improperly motivated by their resentment" of him, but went so far as to praise Quinn as "a very experienced detective inspector".[7] "The police investigation which followed," Yang concluded, "was properly conducted except for some improprieties in the handling of the male prostitutes."[8]

Yang reported that he believed that the SIU had only wanted Fulton to introduce a homosexual friend to MacLennan to see what happened. "I do not accept the suggestion that Fulton was asked to introduce his homosexual friends to incite or entice MacLennan into committing any homosexual act."[9] And further: "I find no evidence of Quinn or any member of the SIU having harassed, or in the popular term used by the press in 1980 and by Mrs Elliott, 'hounded', MacLennan to death. I reject such a claim."[10]

Nevertheless, there is some trace left in the report of the annex in which he had planned to analyze in full what he had seen were the SIU's failing, but which he had not been permitted to write. He accepted that some of the male prostitutes had been subject to pressure and made specific mention of the failure to use police notebooks.[11] He went so far as to state: "Having given very careful consideration to the matter, I find that the evidence against MacLennan was credible but improperly obtained."[12] Yet in sum, he stated, "I find that the charges to be preferred against MacLennan were properly brought."[13]

The Yuen Long affair was the subject of question (d) of the terms of reference. Yang found that there had been no frame-up at Yuen Long and that the case had not influenced high ranking officers to get rid of MacLennan. "I accept the DCI Mr Clancy's evidence that the Yuen Long incident did not play any particular part in the subsequent decision to target MacLennan though the incident had been discussed. The officers read the Yuen Long file purely for the purpose of information. I am satisfied that there was no ulterior or sinister motive in the reading of the file."[14]

Yang made similar mild criticism of Mike Illingworth for the "strong view and prejudice" he had shown in his remarks about

MacLennan but refrained from any criticism of him further than to say he was "ill-advised and careless". Roy Henry, Yang found, was at fault in dismissing MacLennan, but again his criticism was mild: "My final opinion of Mr Henry's decision is that whilst properly motivated, he committed an administrative error, an error of judgment."[15]

The final question set by the terms, question (e), related to the motivation of the investigations. Yang reported that in his view "Mr Moor's handling of this matter was in no way unacceptable. He had done all that he was required to do." He added that the elevation of this matter to Moor's level showed how sensitive the police were in the case. He believed the version of events given by Ross (that Blackburn told Ross to have MacLennan checked by the SIU) in preference to the denial sworn by Blackburn, but cleared both of any impropriety in asking for the information, which was "in the normal course of their duties". "There was in my view nothing sinister in Blackburn and Mansell asking Ross to 'vet' MacLennan."[16]

Despite all this faint censure, Yang did make it clear that he understood senior levels of the force were "interested in MacLennan" before Peter Sung's information made him a target, and stated: "The only plausible explanation for such interest at the very senior level was the Yuen Long incident which was widely discussed among Police Officers."[17] He held his fire here, despite being aware of what was motivating the pursuit of MacLennan. Had he found an improperly motivated investigation, those senior police officers would have been liable for punishment. That, it seemed, was not something that the government could permit.

There were only two figures who received lengthy criticism in the report. The first of these was the attorney general. Justice Yang clearly thought that he had much to answer for in the MacLennan affair, that the AG was guilty of more than errors of judgement and that he could be accused of misusing his power. He spent fourteen pages of his report bringing Griffiths to account.[18] He did so, however, in a way that avoided any subsequent necessity for the AG to resign or be removed.

The commissioner brought himself to criticize the attorney general on four major points. The first was his failure to rein in the SIU when its method of operation, and in particular its attempt to set up MacLennan, had become clear to him. Yang criticized the attorney general for failing to react to the warnings of Fulton, Lindsay, and Elsie Elliott and to check the behaviour of the SIU; "I do not accept the Attorney General's stance that he was satisfied that Quinn would not behave improperly simply because Moor took a tighter control of the Unit." Having said that, he was persuaded to soften his remarks by stating: "The Attorney General's omission was not improperly motivated."[19]

The second concerned the attorney general's press release and conference of 23 May 1980, when he had told the public that "There was overwhelming evidence at the Inquest into the death of Inspector MacLennan which shows that he committed suicide." Yang concluded that "he failed to appreciate that in so doing he would in fact be seen by the majority of reasonable people as using the weight of his high office to challenge the finality of the jury's verdict. The Attorney General has, therefore, made an error of judgement."[20]

The third related to the press release of 19 June 1980, which had used the term "frame up" while ignoring the "set-up" which had been alleged. Although he stated that "I would make it clear that I do not question the Attorney General's proper motive",

Yang found himself "constrained to criticize the Attorney General for this material omission in his public statement."[21]

The fourth was the AG's attempt to intimidate Fulton's solicitor. Yang stated "I cannot help but feel that in the then prevailing climate he was unwise in personally phoning a junior solicitor in a matter such as this." Yet he concluded "I have no reason to criticize his motivation."[22]

It is a feature of the report of the commission that at every stage that Yang stated that he had found an error of judgement, he specifically pulled his punches by adding that he did not criticize the motivation of the person making the error. There can be two reasons for this. The first, and an observer of the events would have to be naïve to accept it, is that no one in the MacLennan affair had any ill will towards anyone else, and that all were working solely for the public good. The second is that Justice Yang was unable to lay blame as he thought appropriate because he had agreed that his report would not do so. Yet he could not hide what had been done. Perhaps he hoped that readers would read between the lines. His attack on the attorney general was so detailed and irrefutable that, despite Yang's softening of his blows by declining to criticize Griffith's motivation, it was evident, by reading between those lines, that Justice Yang did not think the attorney general fit for office.

Justice Yang spent a surprising amount of time and space, four pages of his report, discussing one issue that was not in his terms of reference, this one being a matter on which he had no need to seek government approval to extend his remit.[23] This was a person rather than an issue, the person of Elsie Elliott. Yang turned his attention towards the disputed witness statements in a separate section of the report headed "Credibility of Mrs Elsie Elliott". He said that Joe Duffy had given his evidence in a most convincing manner. He had been calm and collected and answered all questions dispassionately and in a straightforward manner. "His high integrity, competence and honesty are obvious. I accept his evidence in full." Yang took the exact opposite view of Elsie Elliott. He specifically mentioned the letter Elsie had written to Duffy after his testimony. "In my opinion, this letter was grossly improper and completely unjustifiable. Such obstinate and unreasoning suspicion in a person of her public standing is deprecated."

A casual reader of Justice Yang's report could well draw the conclusion that the only person who had been badly at fault in the entire MacLennan affair was Elsie Elliott. Regarding her view of the cause of death, Yang said

> She had in fact a closed mind on the question. She has the tendency to draw conclusions or express opinions too readily [...] to resort to extravagant and emotive language [...] to make accusations without hearing all interested parties [...] to make serious allegations without having regard or sufficient regard to her prominent status as a public figure [...] She has the propensity to interpret simple and straightforward facts in the most sinister light.[24]

Yang gave Elsie Elliott no credit for her almost single-handed fight to ensure the establishment of his commission and no credit for her selfless pursuit of justice for a dead man. In writing this assessment, he was for once far from his customary gentle self. What he wrote was rude, cruel even, and largely untrue. In publishing it, he damaged no one's reputation but his own.

* * *

Justice Yang's Commission of Inquiry report remains the most authoritative document concerning the MacLennan case left in the public domain. It is beautifully produced and meticulously documented. It is, however, far from being a comprehensive account of what had led to John MacLennan's death, and Yang's refusal to apply the harsh criticisms deserved by those who had taken a hand in that death was to allow all of them to escape any retribution for what they had done.

28

Justice T.L. Yang

The application of Occam's razor to the evidence heard by Justice Yang at the inquiry, as well as to the information that never reached his ears, leads to the simplest interpretation of the events surrounding John MacLennan's death. MacLennan was set up in Yuen Long in 1978 for reporting to the ICAC the corrupt arrangements still lingering there. Mike Illingworth, either for corrupt reasons or because he had earlier been made aware of MacLennan's sexual orientation, wanted rid of him. Roy Henry was caught at just the wrong moment to oppose Illingworth, in whose hands was information given by Duffy that possibly incriminated him. Henry was about to be promoted commissioner, so he complied with Illingworth's wishes and committed the injustice of dismissing MacLennan. With no superior left to turn to, MacLennan appealed for help to the magistrates for whom he worked. They raised a hue and cry that, without MacLennan's intention, brought Elsie Elliott to his aid. She involved the governor. MacLennan was reinstated, but was now a marked man.

Eric Blackburn did not forgive this and instructed the SIU to find evidence to get rid of MacLennan, which they set about doing in 1979. The unit was led by incompetent, corrupt, and homophobic officers who tried to set up a case against MacLennan, but only succeeded when Peter Sung gave them real information of MacLennan's sexual orientation. Even then, unnecessarily, the SIU built a case on false witnesses gathered through intimidation. This leaked to John MacLennan before his arrest in January 1980, and rather than face trial, he killed himself.

The death was so obviously a case of suicide that investigating officers did not use forensic methods at the scene. The evidence they presented to the inquest was therefore deficient, leading to the return of an open verdict. The police were then faced with a Commission of Inquiry, for which they tidied up some evidence and suppressed more. Critics and potentially hostile witnesses were intimidated. Obstacles were put in the way of the Carratu team, which was eventually set up and discredited. The evidence presented before Justice Yang at the inquiry was partial, both because it did not cover everything connected with the death, and because it was biased towards the case which the police had presented before.

Whilst none of the principal players in the events that led to MacLennan's death committed acts that could have been considered illegal, some of them committed heinous errors of judgement and took courses of action motivated by selfishness and malevolence, failures sufficient to cause them to face administrative penalties and even the end of their careers. Police officers of the SIU broke both the law and police regulations and had made themselves liable to both administrative and criminal sanction. Both sets of those involved lied, and in the case of the SIU, intimidated others in order to protect themselves.

Behind the case lay the scandal of the abuse of underage boys by circles including senior members of the Hong Kong establishment, linked to triad procurers. The partial uncovering of this scandal had led to the establishment of the SIU and avoidance of any revelation of it at the inquiry was an issue of continual concern to the government. It was the triad associates of the paedophile rings that were most likely the originators of the more illegal attempts to intimidate that were experienced during the case, and probably led to the murder of Ian McClean, killed to silence him before his interview with the Carratu team.

Which leaves the question to be answered: why, in his report, did Justice Yang hold back from fully apportioning blame and from rigorously criticizing those he believed to be at fault? It is possible, of course, that Yang did not interpret the evidence as has been done here, but that seems unlikely, given the criticisms he did feel able to make in his report and as it is clear from his application for an extension of his terms of reference that he wished to make more severe criticisms of the SIU than he eventually did. With the SIU at the very least, he pulled his punches.

Any attempt to answer this must account not only for the gentleness of Justice Yang's findings, but also for the fact that the governor did not succeed in hamstringing the inquiry as he so carefully planned to do.

It is possible to point to three possible explanations for these two outcomes. The first is that, as Sir Ti-Liang Yang maintains to this day, he wrote his report in his customary mild fashion, preferring in this case not to be the cause of punishment of anyone in his purview, and that he was, and remains, unaware of any attempt by the governor to influence or hobble the inquiry. This would require that the governor did not, between 13 March and late April, even approach him or cause him to be approached by another (for instance Andrew Leggatt). Given the evidence that has so far come to light, it is difficult to accept either element of this explanation. That Justice Yang did wish to produce a more astringent report was shown by his attempt to expand the inquiry's terms of reference to allow him to list the failings of the SIU. He certainly had no qualms about acerbically attacking Elsie Elliott. And why would the governor simply change his mind? He had committed himself, to both the FCO and the Executive Council, to a policy of bringing the inquiry to heel. To fail to do so simply because he changed his mind would have shown him to be indecisive and weak, and Sir Murray was neither of those things. We are left here postulating some unknown influence that persuaded him to alter course, but there is no evidence of any such and it is difficult even to imagine what such could be.

The second explanation is that both Justice Yang and the governor were both independently but simultaneously influenced by some factor or factors unknown to us. Again, there is no evidence at all of any such factor and it is difficult even to imagine what such could be.

The third explanation is that Sir Ti-Liang Yang's unchanging rejection of the truth of any allegations that he had been put under pressure by the governor or his agents, that there had been any negotiations or even any contact, is an exercise in the perpetual discretion that one would hope to expect from an honourable judge whose duty would always be to maintaining the confidentiality of the matters with which he has dealt. This is the explanation preferred by this writer, who has been led by the evidence to the supposition (and admittedly it remains just that) that Justice Yang was forced, after a brave rearguard action of over a month, to shorten the inquiry, to reduce the number of witnesses, to persuade John Beveridge to go easy in his examination of the attorney general, and above all to soften the criticisms in his report.

If this explanation is the right one, and it is quite possible that further evidence may later undermine it, what reason could there have been for Justice Yang to yield? Again, it is possible to suggest that there are three solutions to this problem. Firstly, cynics could point to the fact that it was to Yang's benefit to go easy on those whom the government wished to protect. His subsequent career was to be a glittering one: justice of appeal in 1981; vice president of the court of appeal in 1987; a knighthood and the first Chinese chief justice of Hong Kong in 1988; candidate for the post of Hong Kong's chief executive in 1996; a member of the Executive Council in 1997. Were there to have been a reward for any conforming with the governor's wishes, he certainly received it.

Such a view, however, ignores both the character of the man and the circumstances in which he found himself at the time. It also flies in the face of the fact that Yang's handling of the inquiry and the criticisms he made in his report of the AG and Roy Henry made him so unpopular with the governor that he lost all favour and his career was stalled. Sir Murray made it clear to London that he blamed Justice Yang for what he regarded as the damage done by the inquiry. Indeed, it was only under MacLehose's successors that Yang's career would resume its upward path. Sir

Murray did not take kindly to being opposed by his own officials, and Yang had circumvented somehow a policy that he had sold personally to the minister and the Executive Council. If Justice Yang made a pact with the devil, it was not a very good one.

The second solution as to why Justice Yang would yield to the governor's wishes has more of a ring of truth. Justice Yang was perhaps brought face to face with the question of just what the inquiry had been for. Sir Murray MacLehose, who faced similar issues throughout his governorship, would have been especially adept in persuading Justice Yang that the inquiry had been meant for the good of Hong Kong, and that were it to end with recommendations that left him no other option but to dismiss the commissioner of police, many senior police officers and the attorney general, the damage to the colony would have been severe. The governor would have pointed out, rightly, that a report which honestly singled out for blame key persons in the administration would have set back the progress he had made in rebuilding the police force and its relations with the people of Hong Kong. The public would have seen, once again, an administration mired in corruption and ineptitude at the highest level.

Reinforcing this argument was the issue of relations with China. Increasingly, events in Hong Kong were being seen in terms of the way they would affect relations with the Mainland. In 1981, it was only sixteen years from the date when the lease on the New Territories would expire. A decision would need to be made very soon, and with Chinese concurrence, on the future of the colony (and in the event, this would occur after only two more years, when in 1983 Margaret Thatcher would be forced by Chinese intransigence to accept that Hong Kong would have to be returned to the Mainland). MacLehose believed that, were Hong

Kong to be made into a rich, model society, the Chinese would be unable to absorb it. It was not to work out that way, but in his mind nothing which showed that the colony's administration was weak or corrupt was to be made public and no opportunity was to be given the Chinese to take propaganda advantage of anything, for instance the procurement of boys for officials, that showed the British to be exploiting Hong Kong's population. In the light of all these compelling pressures, what public good could arise from any grant of justice to a man who was already dead?

Similar arguments had certainly been deployed at the highest levels. On 25 March 1981, the governor briefed the Executive Council on his plans to rein in the inquiry. The brief prepared for him before by the crown solicitor, which he seems to have used that day, said:

> There is also a theory of a "high level conspiracy to protect the Commissioner of Police". That, of course, is nonsense but [...] the potential damage to the territory if this catches the public mind is inestimable [...] Whilst the Commission has from time to time elicited some startling but nonetheless valuable evidence, scant regard has been paid to the reputations of individuals some of which have been or may be unjustly but immeasurably damaged by unsupported conjecture in public.[1]

The arguments for moderation were powerful, and would have been especially so for Justice Yang, who had devoted his life to the service of Hong Kong.

London would have concurred. Henry McQuade, an assistant secretary in the FCO, visited Hong Kong between 14 and 29 October 1981 and reported back that:

> As before, staffing of the police at senior and middle levels remains a major worry [...] The lack of really good people at the Deputy and Assistant Commissioner level is the chief headache. Morale in the police has certainly been affected by the MacLennan inquiry and also by the recent I.C.A.C. report on increased corruption in the Force [...] Police confidence has certainly been shaken.[2]

It is the third solution, however, which seems to offer the fullest explanation of Justice Yang's possible motivation. This was the fact that the governor's campaign to rein in the inquiry had boxed its commissioner into a corner. Yang had clearly intended to lay bare the failings of those he felt were responsible for the death of John MacLennan and the handling of its aftermath. Sir Murray was going to have none of this, intent as he was on damage limitation and the protection of British interest. Had the policy which he directed — the curtailment of the inquiry, the placing of it *in camera* and the restriction of its terms of reference — been implemented, it would have severely limited Justice Yang's ability to issue the report that he envisaged. He could, perhaps, have lived with accepting an end date laid down by the governor, for the inquiry was in any case drawing to a close. Holding sessions in secret would have caused the governor problems rather than Yang, as the inevitable political fallout from such a move would have been directed at the government, not the commission. What would have been totally unacceptable was a change in the terms of reference, for any change that was likely to be drafted by the government at that stage would have almost certainly ensured that no revelations would be permitted of misconduct by the commissioner of police, the attorney general, or the SIU.

There had to be a price for Justice Yang's brave obstruction of the governor, and it seems that the governor exacted one. The inquiry was speeded up, witnesses were reduced in number and treated more easily. It had, it seems, always been important to the government that Elsie Elliott be condemned by the inquiry, and she duly was, in language that was far more intemperate than that customary to Justice Yang, another small indication, perhaps, that her humiliation was on the price list. Most important of all, the inquiry report was drafted to avoid the necessity for anyone to be fully brought to account for what they had done. Justice Yang was to be allowed to reveal the story of John MacLennan's death, but not to attach blame to those who had had a hand in it.

29

Aftermath

Few could be content with Justice Yang's report when it was published. The governor resented the criticisms, mild though they had been, of the AG and the commissioner of police and instructed the government to reject them outright. On 25 August, he met Nicholas Ridley, the new minister of state at the Foreign Office and Lord Privy Seal and explained to him that the report contained criticisms of Roy Henry, John Griffiths, and, revealingly, also of Elsie Elliott. Ridley was relieved by the content of the report, which he said "was not alarming".[1] Its inclusion of a condemnation of Elsie Elliott was clearly important in London's eyes; she was regarded as a dangerous critic of the colonial administration and an unwarranted influence on public opinion, not to mention an irritation closer to home, for the questions submitted by her contacts in parliament kept the FCO busy drafting replies. The Hong Kong Desk was pleased that, as they imagined, she had been brought down more than a peg or two, and the inclusion of attacks on her in the report seemed to them to balance the fallout from its strictures on the attorney general.[2]

One aspect of the report did not please London at all, and that was the attacks it made upon John Griffiths. The deputy legal adviser to the FCO, Tony Rushford, refuted every one of the lines of Yang's criticisms, which he characterized as "gratuitous". His conclusion was extreme even for a department that had never shown any interest in John MacLennan personally and had only really ever been interested in avoiding the difficulties the case might have presented ministers:

> Mr John Griffiths, QC is an able and honourable man who has behaved well during the whole tedious business of the MacLennan case [...] (I gather their [Yang & Beveridge's] conduct has been questionable in other ways — certainly their censure of Mr Henry for trying to get rid of MacLennan seems unjustified — how much better it would have been if MacLennan had got the sack as a result of Mr Henry's perspicacity!) [...] I now feel sufficiently self-assured to say without hesitation that in my view we and the Governor can maintain our full confidence in Mr Griffiths and back him up to the hilt![3]

The governor was also unable to express himself as pleased with the report. He was forced on the day the report was published to issue a statement of "fullest confidence" in the attorney general and the commissioner of police, a confidence that it is unlikely he now fully felt.[4] However, he was not about to let Griffiths fall on his sword, as he told London:

> It would be a tragedy if John Griffiths allowed these ill-judged comments to make him think seriously of resignation. First and foremost we need him here where he is highly thought of. But

> secondly, as Rushford points out, resignation could be taken to imply that he had fallen short. I am afraid the report reflects badly on Justice Yang [...] we have to face the fact that on this occasion the Counsel for the Commission ran away with him, carried the Commission's enquiries outside the areas intended by the Governor-in-Council and in the process made damaging comments on persons and actions irrelevant to the grave central allegations the Commission was set up to investigate.[5]

This was to ignore the fact that the terms of reference of the inquiry had been drawn so widely as to include the motivation for both the Yuen Long incident and John MacLennan's death, which meant, as John Beveridge had explained on numerous occasions, that its investigations had to be extensive and had to follow the leads that appeared as the evidence opened up. The governor, however, was incensed that the inquiry had gone beyond what he personally had envisaged, and he cast about for legal measures to limit future inquiries. His letter to the Hong Kong Desk went on: "How to stop future commissions running away if a Commission of Enquiry runs amok? [...] Roberts suggests compulsory referring back by the Commissioner to the Governor." The Foreign Office and the British attorney general's staff toyed with this idea but turned it down as impractical.[6]

The chief secretary's note for the Executive Council on the day of the report's publication advised that:

> Care will be taken to avoid any impression that government "accepts" the report, because although the general conclusions (as to suicide, improperly motivated investigations, conspiracy, etc.) are indeed acceptable, the criticisms of for example the Attorney General and the Commissioner of Police are not.

Unsurprisingly, the Executive Council let it be known that it backed the governor's support for both Griffiths and Henry.[7]

In the public statement that it published that day, the government pointed out that the report had made no specific recommendations. This was largely true, for Yang had indicated only a few practical measures he thought necessary at the scenes of deaths that were potentially suicides, ideas taken from the Li Kwan-ha report. The government also noted that the parts of the report that required some form of action concerning individuals it named had been referred to the "appropriate authorities".[8] This was mere window dressing. The Legal Department made a very minor show of considering such action, letting it be known on 11 October that it was considering proceeding against some of the police officers named in the report.[9] It proceeded against none. Three police officers named in the report were referred by the police to the Complaints Against the Police Office, which exonerated them.[10] There the matter died.

This was normal practice for British administrations cleaning up in the wake of an inquiry. To refer items thought to require action against individuals to "the appropriate authorities" was usually, and in this case definitely was, a way to finally end an affair. Those "authorities" were often the very persons criticized in a report or were other officials of their departments. Whether any disciplinary action was taken or not was hardly ever released to the public. In this case, there would be no information to release, for there was to be no disciplinary action taken at all.

* * *

Critics of the government were appalled by the report, which was widely characterized as a whitewash. The *South China Morning Post* editorial on 30 September gave the immediate reaction of a paper that had followed the inquiry from day to day. "Regrettably there is little good or worthwhile to be learned from it," it opined.

Elsie Elliott had most reason to feel aggrieved. She had been attacked personally. After a day spent reading it, she told the press that she intended to issue her own report, and attacked Justice Yang for what she claimed were his mistakes and ill manners.[11] This raised alarm bells and the governor informed London of it immediately.[12] Elsie had her material ready by 5 October, when she published a fourteen-page document entitled "The MacLennan Affair", which she sent to the governor, government offices in Hong Kong and London, the London press, and her political contacts, including MP Dennis Canavan. She placed copies in Hong Kong's university libraries.[13]

The account she gave was a chronological narrative of her involvement in the case and a refutation of the attack on her in the Yang report. She called the attorney general and Duffy liars over the witness statements they had shown her: "I am willing to say on oath that they both lied. And take the consequences if they sue me for libel." Wisely, they did not. She concluded by sympathizing with those whose characters the lawyers, "merciless counsel", had "torn to shreds", acknowledging that she had been lucky "that they could find nothing against me morally." She despaired of the way British justice had been done — "that is what lawyers are for under the British judicial system which is not justice but merely legal skirmishing" — and that now there was "little chance of knowing the truth in the end."[14] "The MacLennan Affair" did not, however, add anything new to the issue and did little or no damage to the government.

Now that the case was no longer *sub judice*, Elsie was free to resume writing letters. She had already written in June to the AG over the issue of the witness statements, telling him then: "I hope you will restore a little of my fast-fading confidence by admitting the facts. Have the days all gone when people would rather resign than blemish their honour?"[15] Now, on 2 October, she wrote to Justice Yang:

> There are many points in your report where you indicate your prejudices, but I wish to mention one in particular where you did not do your homework [...] The papers they showed me on 24th January had no physical resemblance to the police files shown me six months later by Mr Carratu. But you conclude that Mr Duffy is a man of integrity — which means that I am a liar. Your mistake, unfortunately. If you threatened me with imprisonment for what I am writing, I would still say it, because it is the truth.[16]

She carried on writing similar letters until late in 1982.[17] In October that year, she wrote to John Griffiths to ask him why it had been necessary to falsify prostitutes' statements against MacLennan. "Apart from the evidence of my own eyes, I have been told that the prostitute 'witnesses' were at a later date beaten up and forced by the SIU to write statements." Where is the pen that wrote the suicide note, she went on, and why has MacLennan's property not been returned to his family?[18] In November that year, she was still attacking John Griffiths for attempting to fob her off with a reply from Max Lucas, a lawyer for whom she had no time at all:

> It does not help matters when a person like Mr Max Lucas answers your letters [...] Quite a lot of people, including you and me, are clear about these untruths [...] Anyhow, I just want you to know that I will not ever forget the two sets of statements. They indicate that there was a mighty cover-up and a gross deception.[19]

She also went public locally, condemning the "easy ride" given to the AG and Roy Henry, and the attacks on her in the report. So angry was she, that for the first time she mentioned the information that had arisen from the Duffy case. Given what she had known all along, for Duffy had sent her much of the evidence and many of the names he had given the police, she had actually been very discreet so far in her public statements, although the government never credited her for it. Now she alleged that none of the men on Duffy's list had become targets of the SIU, "because the convicted lawyer has named mainly very senior officials." Turning to MacLennan, she said that "the words of liars, pimps and prostitutes [were] believed, that of his decent friends disregarded." "The establishment," she went on, "stood together, bound by their own and mutual interests, not by their duty to 'the fourth estate' as the Attorney-General feudalistically and disparagingly terms the public." The public inquiry had scared away witnesses. "The case is concluded. The conclusion remains beclouded." She declared that she would not let the slurs on her credibility stand in case government servants would now say that they no longer needed to listen to her.[20]

That did not happen, and few believed what Yang had been led to say about her in his report. She carried on her "gadfly" attacks on the government, but she alone could not keep the MacLennan affair alive. The public had long since tired of it; the major interest in the expatriate community had been whether MacLennan had been murdered, and the inquiry had answered that. There was, in any case, no further recourse. Occasional calls to re-institute the inquiry would surface over the years but could be safely ignored.

* * *

Some years later, Vincent Carratu spoke to Aileen Bridgewater about his reactions on first reading the report. Aileen made notes of what he told her:

> Most disgusting thing I have ever seen in my life. John Beveridge and I got drunk over it. Lying cover up. Blaggard John Griffiths — highest legal authority in the land — lied in court. I believe he [MacLennan] committed suicide but what was covered up was why. They tried to make him out as a weak character. He wasn't weak he was very strong. Tremendously strong character. Even then, with their bullying and blackmail and framing, they murdered him by forcing a strong character to commit suicide [...] They didn't want the truth. What fools we were to think they did.[21]

Many in the legal profession had not been impressed by what had occurred and there was wide disquiet, particularly at what was seen as attempts by the governor and attorney general to use the position of their offices to influence the process of the law. In 1982, the *Hong Kong Law Journal* carried a damning assessment of the government's handling of the case by sociologist and historian Henry James Lethbridge, who was well known as a writer on legal and police issues in Hong Kong and was reader in sociology at Hong Kong University. Entitled "Pandora's Box: The Inspector MacLennan Enigma", Lethbridge's article attacked the SIU charter as discriminatory against junior officers, pointed to the inappropriate actions of the SIU, particularly their use of violence, and highlighted the government's inaction after the issue of the report. Many lawyers held views similar to Lethbridge's and considered the governor's closing address through Leggatt indefensible.[22] Unusually, Lethbridge's article was widely publicized when it came out on 5 February 1982 and it caused much comment.[23]

Albert Sanguinetti never forgave Justice Yang for his report. They had hitherto been friends, but years later, when Yang retired as chief justice, Sanguinetti told him to his face at his farewell party that he was glad he was going.[24]

* * *

Aside from the minor adjustments to police procedures recommended by the inquiry report, there was one change to government policy to which it gave impetus. On 5 January 1982, the Hong Kong Government finally instituted a policy on the vexed issue of whether, in the light of Hong Kong's continued criminalization of homosexuality, they should be employing homosexuals at all. This was a result of internal consultations which Martin Rowlands, secretary for the Civil Service, had been holding since the trial of Colin Logan in 1979.[25] His department now issued Secretariat Confidential Circular No. 106/82 "Employment of Homosexuals in the Civil Service", a document that was not intended to be seen by the public, but was guidance meant only for heads of government departments. Rowlands laid out procedures which he hoped such "may find helpful". It said:

> A "known homosexual" is someone (of either sex) who has been convicted of a homosexual offence or who has formally acknowledged being a practising homosexual.
>
> No known homosexual should be appointed to the Hong Kong Civil Service, irrespective of rank or grade. Where a candidate for appointment is a suspected homosexual, the case should be referred to Secretary for the Civil Service.
>
> Where a serving officer has been convicted of a homosexual offence, consideration should be given by his Head of Department to terminating his service in accordance with established Civil Service practice.
>
> Where it comes to the notice of a Head of Department that a serving officer is a known or suspected homosexual, the case should be referred automatically to the Secretary for the Civil Service for advice.[26]

The document leaked, of course. Elsie Elliott took up pen to Martin Rowlands as early as 29 January.[27] "I find it difficult," she wrote, "to square up this discrimination with human rights." She made sure that the press picked up the issue, telling them that the circular was "unbelievable" and a "giant jump backwards". She had told Rowlands, she said, that what people did in private "is none of his business." The press published all this with gusto, pointing out gleefully that the circular included lesbians, even though lesbianism was not illegal in Hong Kong. Civil service staff unions objected to the policy.[28] They were all very much aware that it was impossible to square such a policy with UK Government practice, for Hong Kong was now way behind London on this issue. The British press took up the news and on 27 February the *Guardian*, in an article headed "Going Straight", attacked the circular.[29]

Whether because of earlier actions by individual departments or because of compliance with the Rowlands circular, a number of government servants lost their jobs after the MacLennan inquiry. There is no public record of who these were or of how many were affected. Those homosexual junior police officers whose names had come to the attention of the Commission of Inquiry all lost their careers. It is clear, however, that not all known homosexuals were singled out for dismissal. Even some of those on the Duffy lists survived. The process seems to have been random, men being forced out of the police force, and to much smaller degree the legal and other departments, if their face did not fit, or if they had offended in other ways, with their sexual orientation used as an excuse. Others were protected by the many in government service who resisted the witch-hunt. Yet it is true, very sadly, that some fine young police officers, some of whom had been betrayed by

Inspector Michael Fulton, were lost to the service and had their lives blighted.

Otherwise innocuous government servants could still be at risk of arrest and dismissal. At the start of 1983, a treasury accountant working in the Economic Services Branch named Peter Winder was accused of homosexuality and investigated. Winder lived with his Chinese boyfriend, and was summoned to see the financial secretary. However, as they had with Brian Jenney, the department refused to get rid of him and he served out his career. People in senior levels in the government refused to yield to paranoia about gays in their ranks.[30]

The Rowlands circular only gradually became a dead letter after the Law Reform Commission published its report in June 1983. The commission recommended the decriminalization of "consensual sex" between males in Hong Kong, but with an age of consent set at twenty-one (higher by three years than for heterosexual sex), "to protect young males", as the report put it. The commission also recommended a ban on offensive conduct in public and the criminalization of soliciting by male prostitutes.[31]

The Law Reform Commission Subcommittee which considered this subject and authored the report had brought together some of the characters from the MacLennan case.[32] Its chairman was Justice Yang, John Griffiths was a member until November 1981, and Andrew Hodge was its secretary. Whether this was a comfortable gathering can be doubted, but it is probable that it would not have been possible to assemble a group of senior lawyers more experienced in the subject. Their work took a while to come to fruition and when their report was published it aroused a storm of opposition from conservative and religious groups. Within the month, 130 organizations had written to UMELCO to object to decriminalization, and many of these soon came together to form the Joint Committee on Homosexual Law to fight reform.[33]

Supporters of decriminalization were slower to organize, for the obvious reason that most were still keeping their heads well below the parapet. Only in 1989 did the Reverend Fung Chi-wood form the first campaigning group, the Association for the Welfare of Gays and Lesbians, which lobbied to implement the white paper "Homosexual Offences: Should the Law Be Changed?" which the government had finally published the year before. It was not until 1991 that the Hong Kong Government felt confident enough to enact a law legalizing homosexuality.[34] By then, it had taken Hong Kong twenty-four years to follow Britain in removing the "blackmailer's charter" from its statute book. In England, it had needed cases like the scandal surrounding the imprisonment in 1954 of Lord Montagu of Beaulieu to finally open the establishment's eyes to the counter-productivity of prohibitions of homosexuality.[35] In Hong Kong, it had taken the death of a young police officer.

* * *

Throughout the eighties, almost until the time when the law finally changed, the SIU carried on its work of ferreting out gay men in the public service. Their techniques became subtler. Perhaps as a direct result of the MacLennan case they now abided by the law, and they targeted procurers and men who, for other reasons, it was considered undesirable to retain in government service. They remained hated. A posting to the SIU was not a popular one in the police force. In late 1981, the police give evidence to the Law Reform Commission and stated that:

> During the past three years the Special Investigation Unit has been involved exclusively in the investigation of homosexual activities

> in Hong Kong [...] Their investigations indicate clearly that homosexuality is wide-spread [*sic*] in Hong Kong and involves personalities of many different nationalities from every strata of our society. Information gathered from interviews suggests that no less than 1,000 male prostitutes are operating full or part time, serving both resident and transient homosexuals [...] 1,352 offences against public morality were reported in 1981, of which only sixty-three were of a homosexual nature; similarly 692 persons were prosecuted for the former class of offence, but only fifty-four cases were for homosexual offences.[36]

By the time Norman MacKillop took over the unit in 1982, the SIU had notched up sixteen cases encompassing sixty-five charges.[37] Later in the decade, a highly respected police officer, Superintendent Steve Vickers, was brought in to command the unit. He came to notice in the press in 1985 when it was reported that the SIU was investigating men who had knowingly infected others with HIV.[38] By then, the SIU's work tended to be low key, more akin to the type of intelligence work conducted by Special Branch, and they avoided the public eye unless it was to advertise their more palatable successes. In June 1982, for instance, they announced the arrest of ten people selling boys and girls to tourists and local businessmen.[39] In their later days, they were used to investigate allegations of paedophilia.[40]

Whatever respectability the SIU slowly achieved did not serve to dissipate the dark cloud with which they and the MacLennan case had covered homosexuals in Hong Kong. Aside from the wealthiest levels of expatriate gay society and in the big *hongs*, where life could go on behind closed doors as though little had changed and where the police could intrude only at their peril, gay society shut down. The incipient shoots of community that gay men had managed to achieve before the Duffy case were mostly snuffed out. Especially in the immediate aftermath of the MacLennan case, sources recall "much flushing of paper down toilets" for fear of a witch-hunt, and although such did not actually happen, it would be many years before even the small degree of freedom that homosexuals had achieved by 1978 could be recovered.[41]

These were very dark years. No one could be sure any more that a blind eye would be turned. The price of exposure was prosecution, loss of employment, and ostracism, and men lived in a pervasive atmosphere of fear that seeped through gay society and dampened everything. People no longer gathered in the old ways at bars like Dateline, which was continually raided by the police. When they came, they turned on the lights, locked the doors, asked for identities and demanded proof of address and even of employer.[42] Dateline eventually closed.[43] The trade at Disco Disco survived, but only because the glamorous of every sexual persuasion carried on dancing there. It lingered on in slow decline and was sold by Gordon Huthart in 1986, closing in the same year. Most gay men avoided going anywhere that they feared would be subject to surveillance and the big private parties died; people were too afraid to be shown on the invitation lists.[44] The flavour of what was going on was revealed to the public by one brave gay man who called in to RTHK's "Open Line" programme to tell the public how he had been sacked for his sexual orientation. There was no legal remedy.[45]

This oppression was picked up in mid-1981 by John Thornton, a writer for *Gay News*, who visited Hong Kong and reported in his paper that he had found the clubs closed down and people too nervous to speak or identify themselves. He had been admitted to the last hearings of the Commission of Inquiry, but had been identified, and as a result had been warned (he did not say by whom) "not to abuse Hong Kong's hospitality". He had been followed during his visit. Neil Duncan, who had until the crackdown headed Hong Kong's very small Movement for Homosexual Law Reform, told Thornton that he had been instructed by the government (which was his employer; he was General Manager of the Hong Kong Arts Centre) to stop making waves. He refused to speak to Thornton and his movement evaporated.[46]

The prostitutes suffered, too, as their trade withered away. A reporter from the *Star* found some of the characters from the MacLennan affair still at the Waltzing Matilda in the middle of 1982. They told him that they had hit hard times, as tourists had been scared away by the MacLennan case. "Handsome" Jimmy Cheung, who told the reporter he was a waiter moonlighting as a prostitute, and Lulu (who must have been Lula, Sun Kam-hung) said that even the locals were avoiding them for fear of blackmail.[47]

The rent boys' trade also fell off steadily in the second half of the decade for another reason. As Hong Kong gradually became richer and as attitudes began to shift, albeit glacially slowly, men who had hitherto resorted to prostitutes found that they could find a partner without the need for a financial transaction.[48] Towards the end of the eighties, gay society began to re-emerge and shake off the pall that the Duffy case and the MacLennan affair had cast. In 1985, a new bar and disco, the Yin Yang Club, opened in Central and the following year activists formed the first gay social group, the Ten Percent Club. In 1989 the Hong Kong Lesbian and Gay Film Festival showed its first film.[49]

Slasher George did not live long enough to enjoy the freedoms that were eventually won. Suffering from AIDS, he became a social worker for others with the condition and had died by the nineties. Gordon Huthart, proprietor of Disco Disco, went back to jail for a year in 1989 when he was found guilty of assaulting his housekeeper and chauffeur, twenty-six year old Chan Kam-suen, with a fencing foil. He died of cancer of the oesophagus in 1996.[50]

No official or police officer was dismissed, or was in any way officially sanctioned or punished, for his role in the MacLennan affair. The governor would have had no illusions about some of those named in the report, but it was not MacLehose's way to hang his officials out to dry. That would have indicated that a mistake had been made. Instead, promotion, end of contract and time were allowed to winnow out the chaff.

Not only was no action taken against anyone in the MacLennan case, but there also was no real investigation of any of the prominent persons named by John Richard Duffy. Exploiters of young boys in Hong Kong were not sought, and so were not found, among the upper echelons of colonial society. When Duffy left the colony in 1981, he took his secrets and his allegations with him. No prosecutions were ever brought.

Sir Denys Roberts remained chief justice of Hong Kong until he handed over to Sir Ti-liang Yang in 1988. Roberts was aware of, and managed to live with, the rumours and allegations that he was a paedophile. On one occasion, he sidled up to Aileen Bridgewater at a party and said: "You know I don't like little boys, only little girls." Sickening as that remark sounded to her, she had no conviction of its truth.[51]

This was very much on a par with what was happening in Britain at the time. In the House of Commons in March 1981, the Conservative MP Geoffrey Dickinson named diplomat Sir Peter Hayman as a paedophile, but Hayman was not prosecuted and was left in peaceful retirement. It was not for another three decades that the crimes of the politicians involved in the abuse of children would be exposed, let alone prosecuted, and this was despite the fact that Cyril Smith, for one, was found by police in 1981 engaged in an act of abuse with a sixteen-year-old in the Elm Guest House, a place frequented by paedophiles in Barnes. A few of the many cases of the exploitation of children that were then taking place in boys' homes across the country, for instance in North Wales, were beginning to come to light, but official action would not be taken in any of them for many years.[52] In one case only was action taken to deal with a case of the sexual abuse and trafficking of boys; in April 1980, prosecutions were brought successfully against three of the staff at the Kincora Boys' Home in Belfast. It was only in the next millennium, however, that allegations would be made public that MI5 had known of the abuse there for some years and allowed it to continue in order that they could blackmail the Unionist extremists involved.[53]

Although Tom O'Carroll, the surviving leader of PIE, was convicted on conspiracy charges in 1981, his organization did not shut down until 1984, and Conservative Home Secretary Leon Brittan did not ban it. While in that post, Brittan, or his office, somehow mislaid a dossier given him by MP Geoffrey Dickinson detailing cases of abuse by politicians. It is alleged that Brittan's own name appears on a list of politicians who stayed at the Elm Guest House.[54]

* * *

In comparison with all of this, Sir Murray MacLehose had been faced with issues of smaller proportions, but ones that, in the small world of Hong Kong, had they been made public, would truly have "blown the lid off the Colony". Partly by luck, he had managed to suppress what could have been two very damaging scandals. So when he finally left Hong Kong in May 1982, he could count this as one of the many successes in his tenure of office. The day he reached London, his barony was gazetted, and as a life peer, Baron MacLehose of Beoch, of Maybole in the District of Kyle and Carrick, and of Victoria in Hong Kong, he remained an influential voice until his death in 2000. He was still a man very widely admired.[55] For Elsie Elliott, however, he had long before lost his shine. She wrote to him in 1980 (about John Richard Duffy's loss of remission):

> My greatest disappointment lies in what appears — forgive me for saying so — to be your apparent change of attitude since the amnesty of 1977. Many others have remarked that your former zeal for human rights seems to have waned. I hope I am wrong in this. It has not been easy to say, and it has been said with sorrow. It hurts the people, and it hurts your image as the best ever Governor of Hong Kong. I hope you are not angry at my saying these things.[56]

It would not have been surprising had he been angry, which might account for his allowing publication of the vitriol in the inquiry report. Her opinion of the governor hardened throughout the hearings of the commission, and, at its end, she wrote to Gordon Huthart: "My respect for the Governor is dead."[57] She was feeling kinder in 2004, when she wrote her account of those years.

> When at a Legislative Council meeting attended by Lord MacLehose after his retirement, I praised him for all he had done for Hong Kong, he replied, "But you pushed my elbow." Yes, I had pushed every governor's elbow, but he was the first colonial governor who

had been willing to be pushed into action.[58]

The attorney general did not leave office with a reputation enhanced by his time in Hong Kong. Whilst many took a hand in the oppression of homosexuals in the colony in the early eighties, John Griffiths, as its principal law officer, bears a large responsibility for the misery his policy caused. Despite all that had happened in the MacLennan affair, he stuck stubbornly to his policy of enforcing the law on homosexuality. What was surprising in this was that it seems, and he said so at times, that he believed that the law should be reformed.[59]

Aileen Bridgewater had dinner with Griffiths at the USRC in June 1981, and found that he "was very bitter about it all and had aged. He called it [the Commission] a waste of money and a set back to the law on homosexuality".[60] Perhaps due to what had happened during the case, Griffiths did not find himself in the closest circle of advisers, the men whom MacLehose really trusted. Nor did the staff in the FCO in London come to care for him. His visit to their offices in July 1981 was recorded in a minute from R.D. Clift, head of the Hong Kong Desk, who indicated that he did not think much of the string of complaints about almost everyone else in Hong Kong to which he had been forced to listen by the attorney general. Griffiths moaned at him about the poor quality of police officers, especially the junior ranks "many of whom," he generalized, "were simply incompetent." He commented on the poor quality of the judiciary, and singled out those at the district court and magistrate level for particular scorn. He advocated sacking those who had committed offences that couldn't be proved. He ended by finally antagonizing his host with the allegation (for which he gave no reason that was recorded) that people were becoming increasingly fed up with the interference of the FCO in Hong Kong's affairs. Clift thought that Griffiths underestimated the seriousness with which the governor regarded the position of the police. His visit clearly left a bad taste.[61]

When his first contract as attorney general came to an end in 1983, it was not renewed by the next governor, Sir Edward Youde.[62] Griffiths was left to go home with the award, not of a knighthood, but of a CMG, which, as they say in the army, at his rank was the sort of award they hand out with the rations.[63] Elsie Elliott had been given the CBE in 1977, an award of almost exactly the same prestige.[64]

The feud between John Griffiths and John Beveridge came to public attention in 1981 when the latter applied to join the Hong Kong Bar. Beveridge had suggested to Conrad Seagroatt that he apply at the same time, but Seagroatt had not wished to do so.[65] Neither of them was able to comply with all the requirements to practise in Hong Kong and such an application was something that fell within the AG's ability to influence. When the application was predictably turned down, Beveridge took the issue to court and lost, as was reported in the press.[66] Ultimately it was to be Griffiths, not Beveridge, who came back to practise law in Hong Kong, and he remained doing so there until he passed the age of eighty and finally retired to his farm in Wales.

Of the other lawyers in the story, Howard Lindsay found happiness with a partner and settled in Luton in England, where he died of a stroke.[67] Conrad Seagroatt, Clare-Marie Beeson, Joe Duffy, Kemal Bokhary, Neil MacDougall, and Albert Sanguinetti all succeeded in becoming Hong Kong judges. In May 1981, Sanguinetti won an action in the High Court and was awarded $60,000 damages, costs, and an apology from *Tin Tin Daily*

News, which had published an article alleging that he was homosexual.[68] He died in 2009, much loved by the Hong Kong Bar and hugely missed by the Bokhary family, with whom he had been close friends for many years. He had never taken silk, and told his old sparring partner Max Lucas when the latter became a QC: "I myself am thinking of taking mink."[69]

Sir Murray MacLehose was proved right at the conclusion of the MacLennan affair in his support of Roy Henry, whom he retained as commissioner of police and who was extended twice in post until he finally retired in 1985. Henry became a respected and well-liked commander. He was widely credited with leading the force out of the morass in which it had floundered in the 1970s. He put the MacLennan affair behind him and committed himself to reform and improve almost every aspect of police organization, operations, and terms of service. It is greatly to his credit that by the time he left post, the RHKP had at last earned the right to proudly bear the title "Asia's Finest." Having accomplished that, Henry retired and spent the rest of his life enjoying himself. He lived and travelled in Malaysia and many other countries and he lived with the boyfriends whom he had never before been able to acknowledge, although he seems not to have had a permanent partner before his death in 1998.[70]

When he went, none of Roy Henry's subordinates had proved themselves fit to succeed him, and the next commissioner of police, Ray Anning, had to be brought in from England. In 1989, he in turn handed over to Li Kwan-ha, who became the first Chinese commissioner. Peter Moor stayed in post as deputy commissioner (operations) until he retired in 1983. His parting words to the press indicated that he was still refusing to face the reality of what the SIU had done under his direction. He said that any change of the law would not remove the need for the SIU to target procurers; "We have never concentrated our actions against consenting homosexuals in private *per se*."[71] He died in 2012 while serving as president of the Royal Hong Kong Police Association. The police magazine reported in 2002 that he had attended the funeral of Henry Heath, the commissioner of police from the days of the deepest corruption, along with ex-commissioner Ted Eates and Richard Smallshaw, who retired as an assistant commissioner in 1994.

Eric Blackburn was promoted to deputy commissioner (management) in 1982 and served for another six years in that powerful post. When he retired, he worked for a time as security controller for Stanley Ho at the Macau Jockey Club.[72] Lower down the chain, Superintendent Bob Brooks handed over the SIU to Norman MacKillop and retired in 1982. He left Hong Kong in his habitually unobtrusive fashion, and no notice of his departure seems to have been taken, nor any of his subsequent death. As had been intended back in 1978, his old second-in-command, Chief Inspector Mick Quinn, was moved to the Hong Kong Interpol office during the Commission of Inquiry and in 1983 was given a two-year extension of service beyond his thirty years. His friend Kevin Sinclair of the *South China Morning Post* gave him a write up when he retired and he died in Liverpool in 1987.[73]

Of those who had served in Ho Man Tin, Superintendent Marc Pelly became divisional superintendent of Hong Kong's outlying islands in 1980, and after retirement died in England. Senior Inspector Iain Grant retired at the handover of the colony to Mainland China and emigrated to Australia. Chief Superintendent Jack Trotman, whose career was blighted by the MacLennan case and the censure he received for informing

MacLennan of his impending arrest, retired in 1982. He was appointed security manager for the Hong Kong and Shanghai Bank, after which he finally retired.[74]

Senior Inspector Michael Fulton did not survive long in the force. He was forced out even before the inquiry ended in 1981. He told the press at the time that Eric Blackburn had given him the choice of resigning or facing disciplinary proceedings. He chose the former, then had a nervous breakdown. He eked out a life in various types of civilian employment in Hong Kong, where he remains.[75]

The involvement of John Conway in the MacLennan family's affairs did not end when he was sent packing from the inquiry. The family gave him power of attorney to handle the return to them of their son's effects, and this was to be an issue that would involve him for another two years.[76] The property stored in Ho Man Tin Police Station was handed by Superintendent Pelly *in toto* to MacLennan's solicitors, Hampton, Winter & Glynn, sometime in late 1981. Those items held by the commission were handed to the solicitors separately, and by the time that happened, some of the valuable items had already disappeared, including MacLennan's Mido watch, his camera, his gold and silver cufflinks, and his pens.[77] The solicitors were unwilling for legal reasons to hand over the property to Conway, and a tussle ensued that lasted throughout 1982, with Conway at one stage even writing to the governor on the issue and the press reporting about it periodically.[78] Eventually, the MacLennans cancelled the power of attorney they had given Conway and authorized Aileen Bridgewater to collect the property, which she did in April 1983. By then, for reasons that remain unexplained, the several hundred items that had been stored in the cell had all been disposed of.

This, the solicitors claimed, had been done on the authority which Mrs MacLennan given to John Conway. Aileen was left to seek compensation in an amount equivalent to their value, so that the money could be given to the Salvation Army, as the MacLennans had wished all along. There was very little left to give to the family. It was a sorry story.[79]

Conway could not let the MacLennan saga go. He was convinced that MacLennan had been murdered, by, according to his theory, two police constables who were triad members and had been assigned to tail MacLennan on the night of his death. He based this idea on the last information given to Aileen by her source, Raven, and believed that the two constables had come upon MacLennan when he had shot himself in the abdomen, and that they had then fired the four shots into his chest which killed him. One of the constables, Conway believed, had remained in the flat, locking the door and staying in the wardrobe until he could exit and merge with the crowd of investigators. Aileen Bridgewater went so far as to start to investigate the two constables, and Conway's suspicions increased when both of them were murdered. The first, Constable Ma Sun-yuen, was found dead in the doorway of a building in Yuen Long the day before Aileen was due to meet him. The other, Detective Constable Cheng Tung-sing, was found strangled in a farm building at Pak Sha Tsuen, near Yuen Long. Police stated that he had been a triad member and had been lured to the farm to rent his police revolver to a gang to use in a gold robbery.[80]

In March 1983, spurred on by his belief in this theory, Conway took up the issue with the next governor of Hong Kong, Sir Edward Youde, seeking a review of the inquiry.[81] On that occasion, he claimed to have the support of MP Hamish Gray. Sir

Edward took no notice. It was reported a little later in the Hong Kong press that Conway was in the process of writing a book on the MacLennan case, which he intended to call *Death of a Bong Ban (Inspector) in Hong Kong*.[82] He never got around to doing this, but instead, in 1987, he produced what he called the "Conway Report", which he sent to both the governor (by then Sir David Wilson) and Prime Minister Margaret Thatcher. In this, he urged again that the case be reopened.[83] Still ignored, Conway continued throughout the following year to call for a new inquest and in 1994 he published his version of the story, including the names of the two constables, as a chapter in his book *To Speak for the Dead*.[84] By then, Aileen Bridgewater had also gone to print with her version of the Slasher George story in a chapter of her memoir, *Talk of Hong Kong*, which came out in 1985.[85] No one in the administration affected to notice any of these.

Long before this, in fact by 1983, the MacLennans had lost sympathy with Conway and had severed ties with him. He had, they felt, complicated everything. The last straw was an incident in which he distressed their daughter Anne at the bank where she was working. She was reduced to tears. The manager threw him out and threatened to call the police if he harassed her further.[86]

Conway was to come to a strange and gruesome end, found with his face burned away by the electric fire into which he was alleged to have fallen.[87] Another whose end was also unusual and unexpected was Anson Che Tak-ying, the ICAC officer to whom MacLennan had passed the envelopes from Yuen Long. Che was found dead in February 1981 in an Edinburgh guesthouse. He was on a four-week attachment and training course, and seemingly died of carbon monoxide poisoning when he closed the windows of his room and left his gas heater on as he slept.[88] A few months later in Hong Kong, the Chinese language *Oriental*

Daily reported that John MacLennan's ghost was driving away new tenants from the flat in which he had died.[89]

Both Elsie Elliott and Aileen Bridgewater never lost their belief that John MacLennan had been murdered. Elsie mentioned the MacLennan case in both her books, *An Autobiography*[90] and *Shouting at the Mountain*.[91] She married Andrew Tu in 1985. She remained a member of the Urban Council till 1995, and was a member of the Legislative Council from 1988–95. She lost her seats in that year due to what many perceived as a pro-Beijing stance in the run up to the handover of 1997, but was appointed by Beijing to be a member of the Provisional Legislative Council from 1997 to 1998. She was awarded the Grand Bauhinia Medal, Hong Kong's highest award, in 1997. Almost until her death in 2015 at the age of 102, she continued to write letters to the press and doubtless to government officials.

* * *

Aileen Bridgewater continued her career as a radio chat show hostess for many years and became well known in Hong Kong for her charity work, particularly for rescuing old people left to die in wire cages housed inside warehouses, and in providing Christmas toys for poor children. In her later years, she lectured in the summer months on cruise liners around the world. She was a pillar of Kong Kong's Foreign Correspondents Club until she died of heart failure in 2014. Just before she died, her husband Ken published *Open Verdict*, a novel based on the MacLennan case.[92]

Aileen and Ken Bridgewater travelled to Scotland in August 1983 to take the MacLennans the few surviving items of their son's effects: his typewriter, his address book and his photographs. They spent two days with the family at Torgorm Farm and found that they had been almost destroyed by the tragedy.

Joe and Katie MacLennan had been able to talk to nobody about their son's death, and were conflicted about asking the Bridgewaters for details. They had refused to accept the inquiry report when it had been sent to them in 1981, and for a time had considered trying to fight its conclusions. They had sought the help of their local Procurator Fiscal and of MP Charles Kennedy, both of whom had been sympathetic. At that, the government's London lawyers, Charles Russell & Co., had sent someone to see them and persuaded them to discontinue their calls for a further inquiry. It would, the lawyer said, change nothing.[93]

Katie MacLennan had been faced with the harrowing task of reading aloud all the documents and letters to her husband, whose eyesight had by then failed totally. She was still in grief when the Bridgewaters visited. John's brother Ron had taken the news of the death very badly and had never mentioned it to anyone since. His sister Anne had suffered a nervous breakdown, although she had since been helped back to health by the kindness of many, including the manager of the bank in which she was employed. Her husband, Graeme, told the Bridgewaters that he was unable to put into words what he called "the horror experienced by the family."

On the second day of the visit, the MacLennans opened up to Aileen and Ken. They poured their hearts out, telling them about John's childhood and his life in the Stirling Police. They told of how good he had been to them and said how proud of him they still were.

There was little comfort Aileen and Ken could find to give. Before they left, Aileen said to them both:

"If he had been killed in an operation against criminals and had been awarded a medal, would you have felt differently?"

"Yes, definitely," they were very sure of this.

"Well, that's what it was, only in this case the criminals were in the police, and there are no medals for that."[94]

Endnotes

1 Scotland

1 Birth Certificate no. 4, dated 7 October 1950, issued by Mary A. MacKenzie at Nigg, copy in the Bridgewater Collection.

2 Unless otherwise specified, information in this Chapter comes from notes made by Aileen and Ken Bridgewater in interviews with the MacLennan family and Robin Sutherland on 31.8.83 and 1.9.83, in the Bridgewater Collection, which is currently in the private possession of Mr Ken Bridgewater in Hong Kong.

3 *The Falkirk Herald*, 7.9.2013.

4 Inspector Peter B. Whyte; *South China Morning Post*, *Hong Kong Standard & Star* 8.1.81; *South China Morning Post*, 9.1.81. Whyte claimed they had met in 1967, which would have meant that they were at the Falkirk Technical College together.

5 *Report of the Commission of Inquiry into Inspector MacLennan's Case*, p. 29.

6 Letter from Strathclyde Police HQ, 30.1.80, to Elsie Elliott, in the Elsie Tu Collection, Hong Kong Baptist University Library, MSS 13 Manuscripts 1978–1987 12 4. Kate Whitehead, *Hong Kong Murders*, p. 19.

7 *Report of the Commission of Inquiry into Inspector MacLennan's Case*, p. 29, and Pelly Report, p. 353.

2 Hong Kong

1 The Hong Harbour Tunnel had opened the year before, but government vehicles still used the ferry as it was cheaper than the tunnel toll; Peter Mann, *Sheriff of Wanchai* (Hong Kong: Blacksmith Books, 2016), p. 28.

2 In 1976, the RHKP had an establishment of 16,234. *Hong Kong Annual Review 1977*; CO 1071/183.

3 Interview with Peter Hunt, 15.1.15.

4 See Chris Emmett, *Hong Kong Police Man* (Hong Kong: Earnshaw Books, 2014), p. 141.

5 Interview with Peter Hunt, 15.1.15.

6 Comment from Interviewee F, 27.7.15.

7 Interview with Peter Hunt, 15.1.15.

8 Comment from Interviewee F, 27.7.15.

9 Charles Payne Sutcliffe, CBE (1916–2005), Commissioner of Police, 1969–1974.

10 The Treaty of Nanking in 1842 and the Convention of Peking of 1860, which respectively ended the First and Second Opium Wars.

11 In the Second Convention of Peking in 1898.

12 There had been 400,000 people in Hong Kong at the end of the war. By 1971, there were about 3,000,000.

13 Crawford Murray MacLehose, Baron MacLehose of Beoch, KT, GBE, KCMG, KCVO, DL (1917–2000), governor of Hong Kong, 1971–982.

14 *The Times* obituary,1.6.00.

15 Information from Interviewee I, 22.1.15.

16 Information from Interviewee H, 21.1.15.

17 Or, more indelicately, a reference to a condom.

18 Peter Moss, *No Babylon, A Hong Kong Scrapbook* (Lincoln, N.E.: iUniverse, 2006), p. 175.

19 CPG — Central People's Government.

20 *Hong Kong Annual Review 1980*; CO 1071/186.

3 Corruption

1 See, for instance, *Private Eye*, "I-Spy; Letter from Hong Kong", 25.4.80, and "Business News: The Yang Bang", 18.6.81; also Chris Emmett, *Hong Kong Police Man* (Hong Kong: Earnshaw Books, 2014), p. 161.

2 Typescript of speech made by Mr. C. J. R. Dawson, 20.11.73, in the Bridgewater Collection. Dawson was one of those rightly able to resent the label of "corrupt", as he had fought corruption during his service and retired to become a much-loved Anglican non-stipendiary priest in Sevenoaks. Deputy Commissioner Christopher John Roland Dawson, OBE, QPM, CPM (1926–2011).

3 Annual Report by the Commissioner of the Independent Commission Against Corruption, 1975, p. 2, http://www.icac.org.hk/filemanager/en/Content_1238/1975.pdf. Sir Jack Cater, KBE, JP (1922–2006), Commissioner of the ICAC, 1974–1978; Chief Secretary, 1978–1981, knighted 1979.

4 The Chinese characters and the tones for their pronunciation differ, but they are close enough to make a typical Cantonese play on words.

5 Elsie Elliott (Tu), GBM, CBE (1913–2015). Arrived in Hong Kong in 1951; Urban

Councillor, 1963–1995; member of the Legislative Council, 1988–1995; member of the Provisional Legislative Assembly, 1996–1998; winner of the Magsaysay Prize for Government in 1975.

6 Andrew & Elsie Tu, *Shouting at the Mountain* (Hong Kong: Chameleon Press, 1994), pp. 131–132.

7 See Elsie Elliott, *The Avarice, Bureaucracy and Corruption of Hong Kong* (Hong Kong: Friends Commercial Printing Factory, 1971) and *Crusade for Justice: An Autobiography* (Hong Kong: Heinemann Asia, 1981).

8 FCO 40/827 Allegations of Corruption and Bribery in Hong Kong, 15.2.77. The speech was inflammatory because until then it had been widely believed that corruption had almost been eradicated in the previous four years; Cater worryingly spoke of the present.

9 H.J. Lethbridge, *Hard Graft in Hong Kong; Scandal, Corruption, the I.C.A.C.* (Oxford: Oxford University Press, 1985), pp. 119–121.

10 Kevin Sinclair, *Asia's Finest: An Illustrated Account of the Royal Hong Kong Police* (Hong Kong: Unicorn, 1983), p. 87. Kevin Sinclair, MBE (1942–2007).

11 Kevin Sinclair and Nelson Ng Kwok-cheung, *Asia's Finest Marches On: Policing Hong Kong into the 21st Century* (Hong Kong: Kevin Sinclair, 1997).

12 The system is described similarly by Chris Emmett, *Hong Kong Police Man* (Hong Kong: Earnshaw Books, 2014), pp. 89–91.

13 Interview with Peter Hunt, 15.1.15.

14 Chief Superintendent Peter Fitzroy Godber, QPM, CPM (born 1922).

15 Aileen Bridgewater Diary, 8.9.80, in the Bridgewater Collection.

16 Interview with Peter Crush, 18–19.3.15.

17 Henry Wylde Edwards Heath, CMG, QPM (1912–2002), Commissioner of Police, 1959–1966.

18 H.J. Lethbridge, *Hard Graft in Hong Kong; Scandal, Corruption, the I.C.A.C.* (Oxford: Oxford University Press, 1985), pp. 59–65.

19 H.J. Lethbridge, *Hard Graft in Hong Kong; Scandal, Corruption, the I.C.A.C.* (Oxford: Oxford University Press, 1985), pp. 88–98.

20 H.J. Lethbridge, *Hard Graft in Hong Kong; Scandal, Corruption, the I.C.A.C.* (Oxford: Oxford University Press, 1985), p. 71.

21 Superintendent Ernest-Percival Max "Taffy" Hunt, CPM (born 1930).

22 Deputy Commissioner James Joseph Edward Morrin, OBE, QPM, CPM (1933–2005); Superintendent Harry Norman Whitely, CPM, Assistant Director of the ICAC in 1975.

23 Robert (Roy) Thomas Mitchell Henry, CBE, LVO, QPM, CPM (1927–1998), Commissioner of Police, 1979–1985. He was made a Datuk for his service in Malaya and Malaysia, 1948–1967.

24 *South China Morning Post*, 9.2.14.

25 *First Report of the Commission of Inquiry under Sir Alastair Blair-Kerr* (Hong Kong: Hong Kong Government, July 1973), http://online.fliphtml5.com/afnb/hpuu/#p=1; H.J. Lethbridge, *Hard Graft in Hong Kong; Scandal, Corruption, the I.C.A.C.* (Oxford: Oxford University Press, 1985), pp. 91–99; Sally Baxter, *China Mail*, "In a Corrupt Town the Dirty Cop is King — Remembering Peter Godber", 20.8.14.

26 Sir Alastair Blair-Kerr, Kt. (1911–1992), Senior Puisne Judge, 1971–1973.

27 *Second Report of the Commission of Inquiry under Sir Alastair Blair-Kerr* (Hong Kong: Hong Kong Government, September 1973), http://online.fliphtml5.com/afnb/dzcv/#p=1, p. 25.

28 H.J. Lethbridge, *Hard Graft in Hong Kong; Scandal, Corruption, the I.C.A.C.* (Oxford: Oxford University Press, 1985), p. 75.

29 *South China Morning Post*, 9.1.83. Sir John Vincent Prendergast, KBE, CMG, GM, QPM, CPM (1902–1993), Head of Special Branch, 1960–1966; Director Operations, ICAC in 1973.

30 *South China Morning Post*, 9.1.83.

4 Amnesty

1 Transcript of the Commission of Inquiry, record read out by Conrad Seagroatt, in Hong Kong University Library, Pt. I, pp. 11,461–11,462.

2 Inspector Felix Muller; Commission of Inquiry Report, p. 366. Inspector Christopher Burns; Commission of Inquiry Report, p. 31. Burns left the police force soon after 1980. He did not respond to a request for an interview.

3 Senior Inspector Angus "Gus" Graham; Transcript of the Commission of Inquiry, Testimony of Chief Inspector Quinn, Hong Kong University Library, Pt. I, p. Q6.

4 Interview with Iain Grant 4.6.15; Detective Chief Superintendent Iain Charles Grant, CPM. Peter Mann describes the elaborate deception routinely inflicted on new recruits in his *Sheriff of Wanchai* (Hong Kong: Blacksmith Books, 2016), pp. 29–31, as does Chris Emmett in *Hong Kong Policeman* (Hong Kong: Earnshaw Books, 2014), pp. 10–14.

5 Pelly Report, Commission of Inquiry Report, p. 355.

6 Commission of Inquiry Report, p. 29.

7 International Police Association membership card in the Bridgewater Collection.

8 Chief Inspector Mathew Ratcliff "Jock" Atkinson, CPM (born 1932), joined Hong Kong Police 1958. There is a photograph of MacLennan with Atkinson and Christopher Burns in the Bridgewater Collection.

9 Transcript of the Commission of Inquiry, in Hong Kong University Library, Pt. VI, pp. 11, 461–11, 462; Pelly Report, Commission of Inquiry Report, p. 355.

10 Kate Whitehead, *Hong Kong Murders*, p. 19; Pelly Report, Commission of Inquiry Report, p. 355. Commission of Inquiry Summary.

11 Commission of Inquiry Report, p. 30.

12 Kate Whitehead, *Hong Kong Murders*, pp. 20–21.

13 Aileen and Ken Bridgewater interview with the MacLennan family, 1.9.83, in the Bridgewater Collection.

14 Commission of Inquiry Report, p. 83.

15 Aileen Bridgewater called him Sam in her published accounts of the meetings she had with him; at other times she called him Robin or Robert. See her *Talk of the Town*, pp. 281–289. His nickname is the real one but his family or second name is unknown.

16 Aileen Bridgewater Diary, 23.8.80 and 26.8.80, and transcripts of interview with Sam, 23.8.80 and 26.8.80, in the Bridgewater Collection.

17 Also known as the Lee Gardens Hotel.

18 Commission of Inquiry Report, p. 83; *Star, South China Morning Post & Hong Kong Standard*, 1.11.80.

19 HO 306/143, Extradition Case: Peter Fitzroy Godber, Former Chief Superintendent in the Hong Kong Police; Application of "Double Criminality Rule"; UK Relations with Hong Kong. Godber settled in Spain in a house close to Sir Douglas Clague, the head of the Hong Kong firm of Hutchison.

20 Brian Francis Patrick Slevin, CMG, OBE, QPM, CPM (1926–1995), Director of Special Branch, 1966–1969; Commissioner of Police, 1974–1979.

21 *South China Morning Post*, 10.6.06; *Vancouver Sun*, 20 May 2010. Lui Lok died untouched in Vancouver in May 2010.

22 ICAC Annual Report 1975, paras. 1.2–1.7, pp. 1–2; para 1.34, p. 7; paras. 3.11–3.20, pp. 17–21.

23 H.J. Lethbridge, *Hard Graft in Hong Kong*, p. 127; Commission of Inquiry Report, p. 29. English shot himself in the head: *Straits Times*, 6.7.76.

24 Driving licence in the Bridgewater Collection; Commission of Inquiry Report, p. 39, and Pelly Report, p. 355.

25 Deputy Commissioner Peter Thomas Moor, OBE, QPM, CPM, FCMI (1926–2012),

joined Hong Kong Police in 1947; Commander Kowloon District, 1975–1978; retired in 1983.

26 Commission of Inquiry Report, p.29, and Pelly Report, p. 355. There were two levels of vetting applied to the force; negative vetting was the simplest and allowed access to information up to "Confidential" level.

27 Letter from Inspector Christopher Burns to Brigadier Silvan, 20.9.76, in the Bridgewater Collection.

28 Aileen and Ken Bridgewater interview with the MacLennan family, 1.9.83, in the Bridgewater Collection.

29 Bank of Scotland account passbook, 1973–1978, in the Bridgewater Collection.

30 FCO 40/827 Allegations of Corruption and Bribery in Hong Kong, telex Governor to FCO, in answer to Parliamentary Question by Mrs Pryor, MP.

31 John Conway, "Conway Report", p. 12; Aileen and Ken Bridgewater interview with the MacLennan family, 1.9.83, in the Bridgewater Collection.

32 Commission of Inquiry Report, p. 29.

33 Commission of Inquiry Report, p.29, and Pelly Report, p. 355. Assistant Commissioner Geoffrey William Roper, QPM, CPM (1937–2012).

34 Roper statement to Pelly in the Elsie Elliott Papers in the Hong Kong Baptist University Library, MSS13 Death of John MacLennan. Documents 1980 13.3, 25.1.80; *Hong Kong Standard & South China Morning Post*, 22.8.80.

35 Commission of Inquiry Report, p.30, and Pelly Report, p. 356.

36 Roper statement to Pelly in the Elsie Elliott Papers in the Hong Kong Baptist University Library, MSS13 Death of John MacLennan. Documents 1980 13.3, 25.1.80. At the Inquiry, Roper lied that MacLennan had seen only Roy Henry's name, presumably to protect Redpath. *Hong Kong Standard & South China Morning Post*, 19.12.80. Chief Superintendent Ronald "Ron" Lorraine Redpath, C.P.M.

37 Read out at the Inquiry by Conrad Seagroatt, Transcript in Hong Kong University, Pt. VI, p. 11,468.

38 Commission of Inquiry Report, p. 29, and Pelly Report, p. 356.

39 Read out at the Inquiry by Conrad Seagroatt, Transcript in Hong Kong University, Pt. VI, p. 11,467. Chief Superintendent Brian Haigh, CPM.

40 Telegram in John MacLennan's papers, the Bridgewater Collection. MacLennan was struck off RHKP strength on 17.7.77; Commission of Inquiry Report, p. 30.

41 See Dominic Sandbrook, *Seasons in the Sun: The Battle for Britain 1974–1979* (London: Penguin, 2013), Chapter 27, pp. 643 et ff.

42 The only relic left from his time at Hendon is a St John's Ambulance first aid certificate issued in September 1977, in the Bridgewater Collection.

43 Lidster said of John MacLennan: "In my personal knowledge of this officer I consider that he is good material" — Transcript of the Commission of Inquiry in Hong Kong University, Part VI, p. 11,470. Senior Superintendent Richard "Dick" Charles Lidster, C.P.M.

44 H.J. Lethbridge, *Hard Graft in Hong Kong*, pp. 134–141; FCO 40/837 Disturbances by Police in Hong Kong. FCO 40/940 Local Intelligence Committee Assessment of Political Situation in Hong Kong, report for 23.1.78 shows that 14 officers were charged of whom 4 were dismissed; 6 were fined and given suspended sentences of dismissal; and 4 were acquitted.

45 Deputy Commissioner Richard "Richy" Arthur Joseph Richardson, OBE, QPM, CPM, Director Special Branch, 1971–1978.

46 There is dispute among ex-police officers serving at the time as to whether there had been a demand made for an amnesty. However, there is acknowledgement that there had been a request to halt prosecution for crimes prior to 1977, which amounts to much the same thing — information from Interviewee F, 27.7.15. H.J. Lethbridge records the suggestion that the commissioner and his senior subordinates supported an amnesty in order to prevent the leaking of information on homosexual senior officers — H.J. Lethbridge, *Hard Graft in Hong Kong*, p. 146.

47 H.J. Lethbridge, *Hard Graft in Hong Kong*, pp. 142–146.

48 Governor to Mr John Stewart, FCO 19.11.77, FCO 40/837 Disturbances by Police in Hong Kong.

49 Commission of Inquiry Summary; Commission of Inquiry Report, p.43, Pelly Report, p. 356, 367. MacLennan's Expatriate Inspector's Association membership card M52 was issued on 26 March 1978; Bridgewater Collection.

50 Commission of Inquiry Summary; Commission of Inquiry Report, p.43, Pelly Report, p. 356, 367.

5 Homosexuality

1 *Report on Laws Governing Homosexual Conduct* (Hong Kong: the Law Reform Commission, 1983), pp. 54–55, 58. Ordinances that covered homosexuality were (source HKRS70-8- 1870 Homosexuality 1976–1979):

Cap 200 S.146 (1) — Indecent conduct towards a child under 14.
Cap 212 S.49 — Sodomy and bestiality.
Cap 212 S.50 — Attempt to commit an unnatural offence.

Cap 212 S.51 — Act of gross indecency by a male with a male.
Cap 212 S.52 — Consent.

2 Robert Aldrich, *Colonialism and Homosexuality* (London: Routledge, 2003), p. 10.

3 There are, of course, no statistics on this, so the supposition is based on anecdotal evidence alone. If the usual proportion of gay men to the general population is taken at around 5%, there does seem to have been a rather greater percentage of homosexuals among officials in the colony, or at least among those involved in this tale.

4 Ronald Hyam, *Empire and Sexuality* (Manchester: Manchester University Press), p. 141.

5 *Report on Laws Governing Homosexual Conduct* (Hong Kong: the Law Reform Commission, 1983), p.54; Annexes 23 and 24, pp. A192–A197; H.J. Lethbridge, *Hong Kong Law Journal*, 1976, vol. 6, no. 3.

6 Interview with Stuart Wolfendale, 20.9.16.

7 Email "Cambus" to the author, 30.6.16. There was, for instance, a covert study made of the Firecracker Bar in the basement of the President Hotel, where the target was not to identify those in the homosexual community but to obtain information on a syndicate blackmailing, amongst others, government servants.

8 Commission of Inquiry Transcript in Hong Kong University, Part V, p. 6,764.

9 H.J. Lethbridge, *Hard Graft in Hong Kong* (Oxford: Oxford University Press, 1985), pp. 61–62. It has also been suggested that Hunt was seeking evidence against the campaigner, lawyer and politician Brook Bernacchi, who was known to be attracted to young boys.

10 *South China Morning Post & Hong Kong Standard*, 6.3.81.

11 *South China Morning Post*, 8.1.74.

12 Chief Inspector Quinn's evidence to the Commission of Inquiry, Transcript in Hong Kong University, Part V, pp. 7,585-6: "Illingworth had daily contact with Brooks about the Duffy case [...] I think he was disgusted!"

13 H.J. Lethbridge, *Hong Kong Law Journal*, 1976, vol. 6, no. 3.

14 HKRS70-8- 1870 Homosexuality 1976–1979, 5.7.75.

15 Email from "Cambus" to the author, 30.6.16.

16 *Hong Kong Standard*, 8.10.77 & Star, 7.10.77.

17 HKRS70-8- 1870 Homosexuality 1976–1979. The figures given here differ from those in the *Report on Laws Governing Homosexual Conduct* (Hong Kong: the Law Reform Commission, 1983), Annexes 23 and 24, pp. A192–A197, as the former relate to cases involving homosexuality, the latter to cases involving

"unnatural offences".

18 *China Mail*, 22.3.74.

19 *Hong Kong Standard*, 18.5.76; *Far Eastern Economic Review*, 4.6.76; HKRS 70-9-548 Homosexuality 1976–1979; HKRS70-8- 1870 Homosexuality 1976–1979. Brian George Jenney, OBE, Director of Audit, Audit Commission, 1992–1995.

20 *Star*, 24.5.76.

21 Email "Cambus" to the author, 30.6.16.

22 Interview with Stuart Wolfendale, 20.9.16.

23 Elsie Tu (Elliott) Papers in Hong Kong Baptist University Library, MSS 13 11.7 Cases of Homosexual Charges 1975–1981, 23.8.79 and 3.9.79. Sir Yuet-keung Kan, GBE, JP (1913–2012), a lawyer and Chairman of the Bank of East Asia for 20 years.

24 *Star*, 4.8.77.

25 Email "Cambus" to the author, 30.6.16.

26 Conversations between the author and Peter Moss, who was a government information officer at the time.

27 Information from Peter Moss, email to the author, 28.7.15, and htto://www.hkpsoc.com/articles/cd_trophy.html.

28 Interview with Graham Elsom, 27.7.15.

29 J.R. Duffy to Elsie Elliott 2.2.79 & 14.12.79, Elsie Tu (Elliott) Papers in the Hong Kong Baptist University Library, MSS 13 11.7 Cases of Homosexual Charges 1975–1981.

30 Information from Interviewee J, 21.1.15.

31 Email "Cambus" to the author, 30.6.16. Interview with Stuart Wolfendale, 20.9.16.

32 Email "Cambus" to the author, 30.6.16. Interview with Stuart Wolfendale, 20.9.16.

33 J.R. Duffy statement to the police, covered by letter, 2.2.79, J.R. Duffy to Elsie Elliott, Elsie Tu (Elliott) Papers in the Hong Kong Baptist University Library, MSS 13 11.7 Cases of Homosexual Charges 1975–1981.

34 Interview with Stuart Wolfendale, 20.9.16.

35 Nigel Collett, *Firelight of a Different Colour* (Hong Kong: Signal 8, 2014), pp. 56–57.

36 Interview with Danny Wong, 14.5.15 and Danny Wong, *Waltzing Matilda Memoirs*, p. ix.

37 Email from "Cambus" to the author, 30.6.16.

38 Interview with Geoffrey Charles Emerson, 23.4.15.

39 Interview with Stuart Wolfendale, 20.9.16. Wolfendale related the story in the

Channel 4 documentary film *When Steptoe Met Son*, 2002. Pixton was regarded by the police as a prominent member of Hong Kong's homosexual community and occasionally consulted by them on gay issues; email from "Cambus" to the author 30.6.16.

6 John Richard Duffy

1 Interview with Murray Burton, 9.2.15.

2 Statement of John Richard Duffy to the Commission of Inquiry, read out by Ms Audrey Eu, 12.5.81, transcript of the Commission of Inquiry in Hong Kong University, Part VII, p. 8.

3 Interview with Danny Wong, 14.5.15.

4 The cases were: Cheung Pik Yiu, accused of triad membership and of having an empty cartridge case; Lee Fu Wing, accused of triad membership and of possessing a stolen cheque; and Siu Kam Wai, accused of triad membership and drug possession, set up by a drug dealer for the police. Undated (?1978) note on the Duffy case; Elsie Tu (Elliott) Papers in the Hong Kong Baptist University Library, MSS 13 11.7 Cases of Homosexual Charges 1975–1981.

5 For instance, Duffy wrote to the Secretary of the Law Society on 13.9.76 about "the deplorable manner in which Mr Paul Choi conducts his court at San Po Kong magistracy"; on 30.5.77 he wrote to the attorney general to complain about the Police Prosecutor, Inspector Yeung Kam Leung. Elsie Tu (Elliott) Papers in the Hong Kong Baptist University Library, MSS 13 11.7 Cases of Homosexual Charges 1975–1981.

6 Hongs — business houses. Sir Geoffrey Gould Briggs, Kt., (1914–1993), Chief Justice of Hong Kong, 1973–1978.

7 Information from Interviewee C, 25.3.15.

8 Interviews with Barrie Barlow, 31.1.15, and Murray Burton, 9.2.15.

9 Chief Inspector Quinn stated: "One of Duffy's claims was that he stated that he was not part of the general homosexual set-up; therefore, he was expendable. He ran his own string, his own stable of boys – putting it this way, to use the word loosely – and did not use the services of the procurers, and he claimed that the procurers were providing boys for very senior people in town"; Transcript of the Commission of Inquiry in Hong Kong University, Part V, p. 6,791.

10 Transcript of the Commission of Inquiry in Hong Kong University, Part V, pp. 6,754, 6,785–6,786.

11 Information from Interviewee C, 25.3.15.

12 Assistant Commissioner Michael "Mike" Clafton Illingworth, QPM, CPM, District

Commander New Territories in 1972; FCO 40/1258 Reports On Leading Personalities in Hong Kong; Transcript of the Commission of Inquiry in Hong Kong University, Part V, pp. 6,756, 7,585–7,587.

13 Commission of Inquiry Report, p, 57. Commissioner of Police Li Kwan-Ha, CBE, QPM, CPM. A good portrait of Li is at Chris Emmett, *Hong Kong Police Man* (Hong Kong: Earnshaw Books, 2014), pp. 236–237. He did not respond to a request for an interview.

14 Information from Interviewee K, 14.9.12.

15 Commission of Inquiry Report, p. 57.

16 Unsigned, undated typed extract in the Elsie Tu (Elliott) Collection, Bridgewater Collection.

17 *South China Morning Post*, 24.8.78.

18 Duffy to Elsie Elliott, 9.10.78, Elsie Tu (Elliott) Papers in the Hong Kong Baptist University Library, MSS 13 11.7 Cases of Homosexual Charges 1975–1981.

19 Duffy to Elsie Elliott, 3.2.79, Elsie Tu (Elliott) Papers in the Hong Kong Baptist University Library, MSS 13 11.7 Cases of Homosexual Charges 1975–1981.

20 Senior Assistant Commissioner John "Jack" Ronaldson Johnston, QPM, CPM.

21 Roy Henry made it clear at the inquiry that he had been kept out of the loop. He stated that he had no recollection of playing any part in setting up the SIU, although he recalled receiving written advice shortly after it was set up and spoke to the DCI about it then. He stated that later (he could not recall when) he was "informed" that the SIU had been formed to interview complainants against Duffy and that as a result of the Duffy case the need for a general investigation into homosexuality became apparent, that the same team assumed this role and that this team was transferred to Police Headquarters in Hong Kong on 4.9.78. He stated that Illingworth and Li Kwan-ha were in overall charge of directing the investigation immediately after Duffy's arrest and that both officers would have had the authority to set up a special unit to deal with the case. He claimed to have a "weak or no memory of the follow up to the Duffy case" although he was passed the file by Slevin, then by Johnston, and was later also briefed by the latter verbally. He added that he had "no part in directing the investigations of the SIU." All of this is quite extraordinary given the explosive nature of the allegations; Transcript of the Commission of Inquiry in Hong Kong University, Part VI, pp. 11,394–11,402.

22 The only evidence we have concerning the superintendent and one of the inspectors is Duffy's statements. The other inspectors are known to have had gay associates; information from Interviewee J, 21.1.15. The chief justice and named members of the judiciary are all reported by other Interviewees to have been

homosexual. The administrative officer was said by colleagues to be homosexual and was known to have spoken of taking holidays in Thailand and to have had sex with young boys there; information from Interviewee I, 22.1.15. There is no evidence about the lawyer, whom Duffy did not name to Elsie Elliott.

23 Duffy to Elsie Elliott, 2.2.79, Elsie Tu (Elliott) Papers in the Hong Kong Baptist University Library, MSS 13 11.7 Cases Of Homosexual Charges 1975–1981.

24 Molo Tsui was variously known as Stephen Mo Lo Tsui, Choi Kwok-Wa, and Hak Choi.

25 Duffy to Elsie Elliott, 2.2.79, Elsie Tu (Elliott) Papers in the Hong Kong Baptist University Library, MSS 13 11.7 Cases of Homosexual Charges 1975–1981.

26 14.12.79 Duffy letter to Elsie Elliott, Elsie Tu (Elliott) Papers in the Hong Kong Baptist University Library, MSS 13 11.7 Cases of Homosexual Charges 1975–1981. Kazi Chow was variously known as Kazi, Kasi, or Ka Sze Chow, or K.C. Chow; he was said to run a funeral parlour in North Point with his brother.

27 Unsigned, undated typed extract in the Elsie Tu (Elliott) Collection, Bridgewater Collection.

28 Duffy to Elsie Elliott, 1.2.80, Elsie Tu (Elliott) Papers in the Hong Kong Baptist University Library, MSS 13 11.7 Cases of Homosexual Charges 1975–1981.

29 Duffy listed these by name in a letter to Elsie Elliott, 2.2.79, Elsie Tu (Elliott) Papers in the Hong Kong Baptist University Library, MSS 13 11.7 Cases of Homosexual Charges 1975–1981.

30 Slevin was widely rumoured to be homosexual but no specific evidence has come to light. Civil servants understood at the time that marriage had been made a condition for his appointment as commissioner and that police were sometimes called to domestic disturbances at his home — information from Interviewee I, 22.1.15.

31 Chief Superintendent Ronald "Ron" Lorraine Redpath, CPM, head of the Police Public Relations Wing. His name was seen by John MacLennan during his time in Special Branch listed as a suspected homosexual. Some in the force thought Redpath gay, others did not; interview with Peter Hunt, 15.1.15.

32 For eight of these, there is only Duffy's evidence that the officers were homosexual. There is anecdotal evidence that the four other officers were indeed gay — information from Interviewee J, 21.1.15.

33 A man who died in 1980; he was said to have had a private income and to have been interned in Shanghai during the war, where he acted as a camp prostitute; letter of Howard Lindsay to "Mother" — Mike Fulton? — 9.6.80, Elsie Tu (Elliott) Papers in the Hong Kong Baptist University Library, MSS 13 11.7 Cases of

Homosexual Charges 1975–1981.

34 This man was a friend of the administrative officer named by Duffy and was widely known to be gay; information from Interviewees G, 13.4.16, and C, 25.3.15.

35 A man known in gay circles as "Lady Napkins", one time senior official of the Royal Hong Kong Jockey Club and an art connoisseur, who died in Portugal, where he had been living with his boyfriend; information from Interviewee H, 21.1.15.

36 There is no other evidence about this person.

37 There is no other evidence about this person.

38 A man prominent in a Hong Kong youth group and later principal of a school, a mentor to many young men in Hong Kong and involved in Scouting.

39 There is no other information about the sexual orientation of this businessman.

40 H.J. Lethbridge, *Hard Graft in Hong Kong* (Oxford: Oxford University Press, 1985), p. 80.

41 Commission of Inquiry Report, p.58.

7 Yuen Long

1 Senior Inspector Matthew (Matt) Handley. The Fanling magistracy is described by Chris Emmett, *Hong Kong Police Man* (Hong Kong: Earnshaw Books, 2014), p. 175.

2 Commission of Inquiry Report, p. 43, and Pelly Report, pp. 356, 367.

3 Anson Che Tak-ying (1951–1982). Interviews with Aileen and Ken Bridgewater, 15.5.13.

4 Email "Cambus" to the author, 30.6.16.

5 Illingworth statement to Pelly, 18.2.80, in the Papers of Elsie Tu (Elliott) in Hong Kong Baptist University Library, MSS.13 Death of John MacLennan. Documents 1980 13.3. *South China Morning Post & Hong Kong Standard*, 16.12.80

6 Commission of Inquiry Report, pp. 40–41, and Pelly Report, p. 357. Superintendent Ernest "Ernie" Common. The words used were "keep him in view".

7 Email "Cambus" to the author, 30.6.16.

8 Commission of Inquiry Report, pp. 11, 37, 39, 220, 223. Chief Inspector Robert (Bob) Moffat Wilkinson, CPM (1943–2004), Hong Kong Police, 1964–1998. Chief Inspector Rab Nawaz, CPM.

9 Rich's report 7.9.78, p. 2, in the Papers of Elsie Tu (Elliott) in Hong Kong Baptist University Library, MSS.13 Death of John MacLennan. Documents 1980 13.3.

David Lau Wai-tong (born 1960). Kate Whitehead, *Hong Kong Murders* (Oxford: Oxford University Press, 2001), p.21. "Ah" is a term of endearment or familiarity.

10 Kate Whitehead, *Hong Kong Murders* (Oxford: Oxford University Press, 2001), p.22, gives his age.

11 Commission of Inquiry Report, pp. 4–16, 37–38.

12 Assistant Commissioner Peter George Else, PMSM, who had only joined the force the year before. He did not respond to a request for an interview.

13 Commission of Inquiry Report, p. 37, and Pelly Report, p. 357.

14 Chief Superintendent Peter Chan Yick-Sheung, CPM.

15 Commission of Inquiry Report, p. 38. Illingworth statement to Pelly, 18.2.80, in the Papers of Elsie Tu (Elliott) in Hong Kong Baptist University Library, MSS.13 Death of John MacLennan. Documents 1980 13.3.

16 Commission of Inquiry Report, p. 39, and Pelly Report, p. 357. Senior Assistant Commissioner Richard Edgar Quine, OBE, QPM, CPM. Chief Inspector Norman Rich.

17 Interview with Peter Hunt, 15.1.15.

18 Commission of Inquiry Report, p. 39, and Pelly Report, p. 357.

19 Commission of Inquiry Report, p. 38.

20 Tsang statement to Rich, 24.8.78, Papers of Elsie Tu (Elliott) in Hong Kong Baptist University Library, MSS.13 Death of John MacLennan. Documents 1980 13.3. H.J. Lethbridge, *Hard Graft in Hong Kong* (Oxford: Oxford University Press, 1985), p. 127.

21 Justice Yang made these criticisms in his Commission of Inquiry Report, p. 48.

22 13.3.80 Duffy note to Elsie Tu from Taipei through Addinell Investment, F.J. Kirkland. Papers of Elsie Tu (Elliott) in the Hong Kong Baptist University Library, MSS 13 11.7 Cases of Homosexual Charges 1975–1981; 3.5.81 MSS 13 Correspondence and Press Statements 1979–1981 13 1.

23 Conrad Seagroatt, Counsel for the MacLennan family, dissected Lau's evidence at the Inquiry; *South China Morning Post & Hong Kong Standard*, 26.11.80.

24 Hong Kong Standard & South China Morning Post, 7.1.81.

25 The Elsie Tu (Elliott) Papers in the Bridgewater Collection.

26 Kevin Sinclair's obituary of Bob Wilkinson is at *South China Morning Post*, 28.1.04. Wilkinson was a personal friend of the author.

27 Information from Interviewee E, 7.16. The Frontier Closed Area ran along the border with China and only residents and others with permits were allowed inside it. The Frontier was porous, with many routes from which smugglers and traffickers ("snakeheads") of illegal immigrants ("I.I.s") could profit, so a permit was

a licence to make money.

28 Interview 29.4.15 with Justice Conrad Seagroatt, who believed that MacLennan "had at least been indiscreet".

29 Commission of Inquiry Report, pp. 39–40, and Pelly Report, p. 357. Rich report 9.9.78, Papers of Elsie Tu (Elliott) in Hong Kong Baptist University Library, MSS.13 Death of John MacLennan. Documents 1980 13.3.

30 Commission of Inquiry Report, p. 40.

31 Transcripts of the Commission of Inquiry in Hong Kong University, Part VI, p. 11,419. Duffy and MacLennan did not know each other.

32 Commission of Inquiry Report, p. 40 and Pelly Report, p. 357. Ernest Raymond "Ray" Astin LL.B. (born 1937), Solicitor General, 1981–1984; Acting Attorney General in 1982; Securities Commissioner and Chairman Securities & Futures Commission Takeovers and Mergers Panel in 2013.

33 Commission of Inquiry Report, p. 71. *Hong Kong Standard & South China Morning Post*, 20.2.81.

34 Commission of Inquiry Report, p. 40 and Pelly Report, p. 357; Commission of Inquiry Summary.

35 Chief Superintendent Alistair Bain McNutt, CPM (1932–2005), Hong Kong Police, 1952–1980.

36 Commission of Inquiry Report, p. 78. Assistant Commissioner Richard Courtney Smallshaw, QPM, CPM, retired 1994. *Hong Kong Standard*, 18.12.80; *South China Morning Post*, 21.12.80. Illingworth minuted on the file that he was "surprised that Smallshaw was surprised at any suggestion that MacLennan could have homosexual tendencies", Transcript of the Commission of Inquiry in Hong Kong University, Part VI, p. 11,430.

37 Commission of Inquiry Report, p. 40 and Pelly Report, p. 357. Both officers were on three-year contracts, 1978–1981. Senior Assistant Commissioner John E. Over. Major-General Corran William Brooke Purdon, CBE, MC CPM (born 1921), Deputy Commissioner of Police for Administration, retired from the British Army 1976. *Sun* 13.2.81; *Private Eye*, "Business Secretary", 18.6.81.

38 *South China Morning Post*, 9.9.80.

39 Elsie Tu (Elliott) Papers in the Hong Kong Baptist University Library, MSS 13 11.7 Cases of Homosexual Charges 1975–1981, 20.10.78. Henry Lethbridge, "Pandora's Box: The Inspector MacLennan Enigma", *Hong Kong Law Journal*, 4, 1982, p. 9.

40 Commission of Inquiry Report, p. 57; Transcript of the Commission of Inquiry in Hong Kong University, Part VI, p. 11,415; Roy Henry statement 1.5.81 to the

Commission, Elsie Tu (Elliott) Papers in Hong Kong Baptist University Library, MSS.13 Death of John MacLennan. Inquest & Inquiry: Statements, Reports, Correspondence and Papers, 1978–1979 13.5

41 Roy Henry read this on 28.10.78. Transcripts of the Commission of Inquiry in Hong Kong University, Part VI, p. 11,373; Commission of Inquiry Report, pp. 40–41 and Pelly Report, p. 357. Illingworth minute in Elsie Tu (Elliott) Papers in Hong Kong Baptist University Library, MSS 13 Documents 1978–1981 13 2.

42 Commission of Inquiry Report, p. 41 and Pelly Report, pp. 357, 359. John Martin Rowlands, CBE (1925–2004), Secretary for the Civil Service, 1978–1985.

43 Transcripts of the Commission of Inquiry in Hong Kong University, Part VI, p. 11,482.

44 Roy Henry statement to the Commission, 1.5.81, Elsie Tu (Elliott) Papers in Hong Kong Baptist University Library, MSS.13 Death of John MacLennan. Inquest & Inquiry: Statements, Reports, Correspondence and Papers, 1978–1979 13.5.

45 Transcripts of the Commission of Inquiry in Hong Kong University, Part VI, p. 11,389.

46 Interview with Peter Hunt, 15.1.15.

47 Interview with Iain Grant, 4.6.15; Grant knew Roy Henry well; when posted to London as RHKP Liaison Officer, 1988–1990, he would meet Henry in the office. They often socialized. Grant says: "Roy Henry was a great guy for whom I had the maximum respect."

48 Interview with Peter Crush, 18–19.3.15.

49 Interview with Geoffrey Emerson, 23.4.15.

50 Interview with Stuart Wolfendale, 20.9.16.

51 Information from Peter Moss, 19.5.11.

52 Governor to Donald Murray, 3.7.78, FCO 40/1021 Visit of Police Advisers to Hong Kong.

53 Minute McLaren to Murray, 11.8.78, FCO 40/1021 Visit of Police Advisers to Hong Kong.

54 D.F. Murray to Cortazzi, 21.7.78, FCO 40/1021 Visit of Police Advisers to Hong Kong.

55 Minute by W.E. Chantill, 24.10.78, FCO 40/1021 Visit of Police Advisers to Hong Kong.

56 The FCO brief of 26.9.80 for Lord Carrington's visit to Hong Kong included the line: "allegations that the C.P. is a homosexual were investigated in 1978 and are

again being investigated", FCO papers released under the Freedom of Information Act in the Bridgewater Collection.

8 Appeal

1 Commission of Inquiry Report, pp. 41–42.

2 Senior Superintendent John Gillean Mansell, CPM. His medals were sold by internet auction on 17.2.16.

3 Commission of Inquiry Report, pp. 42, 228 and Pelly Report p. 357; manuscript notes and notes of John Beveridge's opening statement at the Commission of Inquiry in the Elsie Elliott Papers in the Bridgewater Collection.

4 Information from Interviewee I, 22.1.15, who said that Rattigan was a good man, and with Justice Conrad Seagroatt, 29.4.15, who said that Daniell had "a strong sense of justice for the underdog".

5 Judge Henry Stanislaus Daniell (born 1934), Army Legal Services, in 1965; Magistrate in Hong Kong; became Judge in 1979. Judge Patrick Michael Rattigan (born 1930), Magistrate in Hong Kong; became Judge in 1981. Neither responded to a request for an interview.

6 Commission of Inquiry Report, Pelly Report, p. 362. Transcript of the Commission of Inquiry in Hong Kong University, Part II, pp. 3,043–3,097.

7 Transcript of the Commission of Inquiry in Hong Kong University, Part II, pp. 3,018–3,033.

8 *Hong Kong Standard & South China Morning Post*, 20.12.80.

9 Commission of Inquiry Report, Pelly Report, p. 45 and Pelly Report, p. 362. UMELCO — the Office of the Unofficial Members of the Executive and Legislative Councils.

10 *South China Morning Post & Hong Kong Standard*, 6.1.81.

11 Commission of Inquiry Report, p. 43. Deputy Commissioner Eric Blackburn, QPM, CPM (born 1933), joined Hong Kong Police in 1954, and as a Divisional Commander in 1967 won the Governor's High Commendation for Bravery. In 1978, he was Assistant Commissioner, Personnel and Training and was promoted to Senior Assistant Commissioner by 1980 and Deputy Commissioner in 1981. He retired to join the Hopewell Group in 1989 and in 1993 became Security Controller, Macau Jockey Club at the invitation of Stanley Ho, *South China Morning Post*, 7.10.82 & 11.7.93. He was Director of Administration in that Club 2003–2009 and has been Chairman of the Standards Committee of Horsham District Council since 2005. He returned to Hong Kong from leave on 3.11.78.

12 Daniell stated that: "The impression I had was that Purdon was being shielded and that HQ were anxious I should not speak to the General"; Daniell statement to Pelly, 25.1.80, in the Elsie Tu (Elliott) Papers in Hong Kong Baptist University Library, MSS.13 Death of John MacLennan. Documents 1980 13.3.

13 Commission of Inquiry Report, Pelly Report, pp. 359, 362.

14 *Hong Kong Standard*, 12.3.80. Commission of Inquiry Report, p. 43.

15 Interview with Peter Hunt, 15.1.15; email "Cambus" to the author, 30.6.16, who adds that more derogatorily Blackburn was known as "Blackbum".

16 Email "Cambus" to the author, 30.6.16.

17 Commission of Inquiry Report, p. 43.

18 Commission of Inquiry Report, pp. 43–44, 222 and Pelly Report, p. 358. Copy of John MacLennan's appeal, 24.11.78 in Elsie Elliott Papers in Hong Kong Baptist University Library, MSS.13 Death of John MacLennan. Documents 1980 13.3.

19 Commission of Inquiry Report, Pelly Report, p. 360. This was on 25.11.78.

20 Slevin was, of course, in the same homosexual bind as Roy Henry.

21 Commission of Inquiry Report, p. 43, and Pelly Report, p. 359.

22 *Hong Kong Standard*, 8.1.81.

23 Commission of Inquiry Report, p. 44, and Pelly Report, p. 360.

24 There was considerable confusion later as to who had informed whom; McGovern stated at the Inquiry that Daniell had told Elsie Elliott, but Daniell claimed that McGovern had told her. This was not so; McGovern was right and Daniell was trying to evade responsibility. Transcript of the Commission of Inquiry in Hong Kong University, Part II, pp. 2,990–2,999; Elsie Elliott's statement of 3.5.81 to the Commission taken by Neoh and Burton says that Daniell called her at 10.10 am on 28.11.78 to inform her about MacLennan. Elsie Tu (Elliott) Papers in the Hong Kong Baptist University Library, MSS.13 Death of John MacLennan. Inquest and Notes 13.4.

25 *Hong Kong Standard & South China Morning Post*, 19.12.80. Transcript of the Commission of Inquiry in Hong Kong University, Part II, pp. 2,990–2,999.

26 Commission of Inquiry Report, p. 45 and Pelly Report, p. 361. Elsie Elliott must have gone straight to Fanling having received Daniell's phone call. Commission of Inquiry Report, Pelly Report, p. 363.

27 Elsie Elliott, "The MacLennan Affair", p. 1.

28 Elsie Tu, *Autobiography*, p. 289; "The MacLennan Affair", p.1. Pelly stated that MacLennan did not allege a frame up and that the idea of it came only from the magistrates, which is incorrect. Commission of Inquiry Report, Pelly Report, p. 63.

Elsie Elliott's notes on the Commission of Inquiry Report, ? October 1981, in Elsie Tu (Elliott) Papers in Hong Kong Baptist University Library, MSS.13 Death of John MacLennan. Report of the Commission of Inquiry. 14.1.

29 Elsie Elliott to the Governor, 28.11.78, in the Bridgewater Collection; Commission of Inquiry Report, pp. 45, 232 and Pelly Report, p. 361.

30 Elsie Elliott, "The MacLennan Affair", p. 2. Commission of Inquiry Report, p. 45, and Pelly Report, p. 362.

31 Commission of Inquiry Report, pp. 42–43.

32 Commission of Inquiry Report, p. 45, and Pelly Report, p. 361. Governor's letter to Elsie Elliott, 29.11.78, in Elsie Tu (Elliott) Papers, Hong Kong Baptist University Library, MSS 13 Manuscripts 1978–1987 12 4.

33 Commission of Inquiry Report, p. 44 and Pelly Report, pp. 360. Blackburn's notes in Elsie Tu (Elliott) Papers, Hong Kong Baptist University Library, MSS 13 Documents 1978–1981 13 2.

34 Commission of Inquiry Report, p. 234.

35 Commission of Inquiry Report, pp. 44, 46 and Pelly Report, pp. 360, 361. In so much of a hurry had the Civil Service Branch been to notify MacLennan of his reinstatement that they were still going through the process of writing to the police to inform them of the decision the day after. On 30.11.78, the Civil Service Branch wrote to Blackburn telling him to reinstate MacLennan and sent the letter cancelling his termination, Commission of Inquiry Report, p. 44 and Pelly Report, p. 360.

36 Commission of Inquiry Report, p. 46 and Pelly Report, pp. 360, 362.

37 A copy of the Governor's letter was found in MacLennan's papers after his death, something that MacLehose resented and commented on.

38 Commission of Inquiry Report, Pelly Report, p. 361. Elsie Tu, *Autobiography*, p. 290; "The MacLennan Affair", p.2.

39 *South China Morning Post & Hong Kong Standard*, 2.12.80. Commission of Inquiry Report, p. 84 and Pelly Report, pp. 364, 366.

9 The SIU

1 FCO 40/1351 Hong Kong Laws On Homosexuality.

2 Transcript of the Commission of Inquiry, Hong Kong University, Part V, p. 6,757.

3 Transcript of the Commission of Inquiry, Hong Kong University, Part V, p. 6,758–6,788. Interview with Justice Kemal Bokhary, 18.3.15. Interview with Peter Hunt, 15.1.15. Interview with Iain Grant, 4 .6.15. Superintendent Robert (Bob) L. Brooks (now dead).

4 Aileen Bridgewater Diary, 12.8.80, in the Bridgewater Collection.

5 Interview with Murray Burton, 9.2.15.

6 Transcript of the Commission of Inquiry, Hong Kong University, Part V, p. 7,333.

7 Transcript of the Commission of Inquiry, Hong Kong University, Part V, pp. 6,751, 6,753, 6,763.

8 Kate Whitehead, *Hong Kong Murders* (Oxford; Oxford University Press, 2001), p. 23. The *Sunday Times*, 7.9.80, gave his weight as 16 stone.

9 Interview with Iain Grant, 4.6.15.

10 Interview with Peter Hunt, 15.1.15.

11 Aileen Bridgewater Diary, 12.5.81, in the Bridgewater Collection.

12 Interview with Murray Burton, 9.2.15.

13 Aileen Bridgewater Diary, 12.8.80, in the Bridgewater Collection.

14 Elsie Tu (Elliott) Papers in Hong Kong Baptist University Library, 'The Vendetta against Quinn', MSS 13 Manuscripts 1978-1987 12 4, ?.9.81.

15 Interview with Peter Crush, 18.3.15.

16 Transcript of the Commission of Inquiry, Hong Kong University, Part V, p. 6,753. Inspector Stephen Tin Chat–man.

17 Transcript of the Commission of Inquiry in Hong Kong University, Part V, p. 6,758. This was an Inspector Melon; *Hong Kong Standard & South China Morning Post*, 24.2.81; *Hong Kong Standard*, 26.2.81.

18 Statement of Inspector McDaid at the Inquiry, 8.1.81, *South China Morning Post & Hong Kong Standard*, 9.1.81. Inspector Michael K. McDaid.

19 *South China Morning Post, Star & Hong Kong Standard*, 21.2.81.

20 Interview Peter Hunt, 15.1.15.

21 *Hong Kong Standard & South China Morning Post*, 24.2.81; *Hong Kong Standard*; 26.2.81.

22 *South China Morning Post & Hong Kong Standard*, 18.3.81.

23 Transcript of the Commission of Inquiry in Hong Kong University, Part V, p. 6,816.

24 Transcript of the Commission of Inquiry in Hong Kong University, Part VI, p. 11,396; Commission of Inquiry Report, p. 57. Ross took command of the SIU on 6.9.78. Chief Superintendent William "Big Bill" McIntyre Ross, QPM, CPM (1932–2003), joined the Hong Kong Police in 1954, retired in 1988.

25 Interview with Peter Hunt, 15.1.15.

26 Commission of Inquiry Report, p. 59; Transcript of the Commission of Inquiry in Hong Kong University, Part V, p. 6,759. Neil MacDougall (born Australia 1932),

Crown Counsel Hong Kong in 1965; Principal Crown Counsel in 1977; Acting Director of Public Prosecutions/Crown Prosecutor; Judge of the High Court in 1980; Justice of Appeal in 1989; Non-Permanent Judge of the Court of Final Appeal, 1997–2003. He did not respond to a request for an interview.

27 *South China Morning Post, Star & Hong Kong Standard*, 21.2.81.

28 Transcript of the Commission of Inquiry in Hong Kong University, Part V, p. 6,760.

29 Transcript of the Commission of Inquiry in Hong Kong University, Part V, p. 6,792. Justice Yang listed what he believed were the SIU's first tasks in the Commission of Inquiry Report, p. 57, but the formalization of this list seems to have been his own work, his inferences from what had been said, rather than any firm directive to the SIU. His list was: a) Who are procurers? b) Exploitation of youths. c) Homosexuals who might be security risks. d) Blackmailers. e) Homosexual fraternity (this last is actually what the SIU targeted, but does not seem to have been a task they were ordered to perform).

30 Transcript of the Commission of Inquiry in Hong Kong University, Part V, p. 7,075.

31 Evidence of Chief Inspector Quinn, Transcript of the Commission of Inquiry in Hong Kong University, Part V, p. 6,775.

32 Transcript of the Commission of Inquiry in Hong Kong University, Part V, p. 6,770.

33 Inspector Mia Thomas was posted into the unit in January 1979; Transcript of the Commission of Inquiry in Hong Kong University, Part V, p. 6,855.

34 Evidence of Chief Inspector Quinn, Transcript of the Commission of Inquiry in Hong Kong University, Part V, p. 6,763.

35 Evidence of Chief Inspector Quinn, Transcript of the Commission of Inquiry in Hong Kong University, Part V, p. 6,793.

36 Evidence of Chief Inspector Quinn, Transcript of the Commission of Inquiry in Hong Kong University, Part V, pp. 7,335–7,338.

37 Transcript of the Commission of Inquiry in Hong Kong University, Part V, p. 6,834.

38 Senior Inspector Peter Michael "Mike" Fulton (born Kenya, 1950), joined RHKP in 1975. He did not respond to a request for an interview.

39 *South China Morning Post*, 30.6.80.

40 Commission of Inquiry Report, p. 73. The flat was 403A, Government Service Flats, 19 Ho Man Tin Hill Road; Transcript of the Commission of Inquiry in Hong Kong University, Part III, p. 3,603.

41 Transcript of the Commission of Inquiry in Hong Kong University, Part III, pp. 3,746–3,758.

42 Commission of Inquiry Report, pp. 239–240.

43 Transcript of the Commission of Inquiry in Hong Kong University, Part V, p. 7,548.

44 Transcript of the Commission of Inquiry in Hong Kong University, Part V, p. 6,812.

45 This occurred in a meeting at the Kowloon Bowling Club, in December 1978 or January 1979; Commission of Inquiry Report, p. 237

46 Transcript of the Commission of Inquiry in Hong Kong University, Part III, pp. 3,628–3,630.

47 Superintendent David H. Hodson, QPM, CPM, joined RHKP in 1962, retired in 1997, founding Director and Vice Chairman of Oxfam Hong Kong.

48 Commission of Inquiry Report, pp. 236–237, and Pelly Report, p. 384; *South China Morning Post*, 30.6.80.

49 Senior Superintendent "Jolly" Jack Trotman, CPM. He declined to be interviewed.

50 Transcript of the Commission of Inquiry in Hong Kong University, Part III, pp. 3,613–3,616.

51 This list was handed to Justice Yang at the inquiry, but was not shown to all the counsel and has not been located.

52 Transcript of the Commission of Inquiry in Hong Kong University, Part V, pp. 6,801–6,815. Officers with live-in partners did not actually pay the government additional rent, but they did pay the accommodation management an additional charge for laundry, cleaning, and messing – interview with Peter Crush, 19.3.15.

53 Transcript of the Commission of Inquiry in Hong Kong University, Part V, pp. 6,801–6,815.

54 Quinn told the inquiry that Fulton had mentioned Roy Henry was gay at the end of 1978, and that they had checked this and found that "there was 'no substance' in the allegations". *Hong Kong Standard, Star & South China Morning Post*, 16.8.80. There is no indication that the SIU was allowed to conduct an independent inquiry into Roy Henry, but he was checked out again that year for his impending promotion, so they may have been asked whether they had anything on their files. This was the second time that Henry was investigated, the first having been his vetting in 1973.

55 Commission of Inquiry Report, p. 58.

56 Transcript of the Commission of Inquiry in Hong Kong University, Part V, pp. 6,840–6,843.

57 Transcript of the Commission of Inquiry in Hong Kong University, Part V, p. 6,772.

58 *Hong Kong Standard & South China Morning Post*, 6.12.80. Assistant Commissioner John Charles Clemence, QPM, BSc Econ (London) (born 1937); first Secretary General of the Association of the Commonwealth Realms; Chairman and later International President of the Royal Society of St. George. Chief Superintendent Brian Leonard "Bash" Merritt, QPM, author of "How Hong Kong Fights the Triads", *Police Review*, 19.7.91, and "Beyond the Triad Myth",

Police Review, 26.7.91.

59 Commission of Inquiry Report, p. 236.

60 Commission of Inquiry Report, p. 58; *Hong Kong Standard*, 14.3.80.

61 Commission of Inquiry Report, p. 61.

62 Transcript of the Commission of Inquiry in Hong Kong University, Part V, p. 6,865.

63 McLaren, Head of the Hong Kong Desk at the FCO, wrote on 14.6.78 to Murray, his superior that "Crane [an FCO police advser] felt Slevin was remote and unpopular and not a single Police Officer to whom Mr. Crane had spoken had been prepared to speak in his favour". M.J. Macoun, Overseas Police Adviser, told McLaren of the FCO on 17.8.78 that despite ten months' elapse of time since "the patently obvious failure of the command of the Force" no decision had been taken to replace Slevin; FCO 40/1021 Visit Of Police Advisers To Hong Kong.

64 Slevin died in Australia in September 1995 — *South China Morning Post*, 14 September 1995. His wife had committed suicide in 1980 — Aileen Bridgewater Diary in the Bridgewater Collection, 13.8.80. Briggs remained President of the Brunei Court of Appeal to 1988, was Justice of the Court of Appeal in Gibraltar, 1983–1988 and simultaneously was President of the Pensions Appeal Tribunal for England, 1980–1987. He died at Bath in 1993, leaving an estate valued at over 800,000 pounds.

65 Annual Review for 1978, 25.1.79, FCO 40/1047 — Hong Kong Annual Review 1978.

10 Pursuit

1 Transcript of the Commission of Inquiry in Hong Kong University, Part V, p. 7,087.

2 *South China Morning Post*, 17.12.80.

3 Commission of Inquiry Report, p. 71; *Hong Kong Standard & South China Morning Post*, 20.2.81.

4 Commission of Inquiry Report, pp. 71–72.

5 Commission of Inquiry Report, pp. 71–73.

6 *Hong Kong Standard & South China Morning Post*, 19. & 21.3.81.

7 Transcript of the Commission of Inquiry in Hong Kong University, Part III, pp. 3,631–3,640.

8 Commission of Inquiry Report, p. 58.

9 *Hong Kong Standard & South China Morning Post*, 27.3.81. At the inquiry, it was claimed that this too was connected with vetting of those being considered for promotion, despite the fact that John MacLennan was not being considered for

promotion; transcript of the Commission of Inquiry in Hong Kong University, Part V, p. 6852.

10 Commission of Inquiry Report, p. 72; statement by Inspector MacKillop to the inquiry reported in *Hong Kong Standard & South China Morning Post*, 20.2.81 & 4.3.81. Duffy had the information from an Inspector Greaves, who was serving a prison sentence alongside him, and the information is unsupported by any evidence.

11 He was transferred on 4 December to Kowloon District and accommodated in Room 410B, Ho Man Tin Government Service Flats, 19 Ho Man Tin Hill Road, Kowloon. Commission of Inquiry Report, p. 30 and Pelly Report, p. 369.

12 Interview with Iain Grant, 4.6.15.

13 Information from Interviewee A, 5.2.15.

14 Information from Interviewee J, 21.1.15.

15 *Hong Kong Standard & South China Morning Post*, 8.4.81.

16 Interview with Iain Grant, 4.6.15.

17 Interview with Iain Grant, 4.6.15.

18 John Conway, "Conway Report", 1987, p. 20.

19 John Conway, "Conway Report", 1987, p. 21.

20 Interview with Danny Wong, 14.5.15.

21 *Hong Kong Standard & South China Morning Post*, 12.3.81.

22 *Hong Kong Standard & South China Morning Post*, 2.12.80; Commission of Inquiry Report, p. 84.

23 Commission of Inquiry Report, p. 83; *South China Morning Post*, 5 & 6.12.80; *Hong Kong Standard & South China Morning Post*, 22.11.80, 28.11.80, 3.12.80.

24 *Hong Kong Standard & South China Morning Post*, 2.12.80.

25 Commission of Inquiry Report, p. 83; *South China Morning Post*, 5 & 6.12.80; *Hong Kong Standard, Star & South China Morning Post*, 1.11.80.

26 *Hong Kong Standard & South China Morning Post*, 8.11.80, 11.11.80.

11 The Honourable John Griffiths

1 FCO 40/854 and FCO 40/855, Appointment of Attorney General and Solicitor General — Hong Kong.

2 30.6.79 — Brief 11 — for Secretary of State's visit to Hong Kong June–July — Personality notes; The Attorney General is "something of an experiment; previous Attorneys have all been chosen from the Colonial legal service" — FCO 40/1053 Visits by Secretary of State for Foreign Affairs to Hong Kong.

3 John Calvert Griffiths, SC, CMG, QC (born 1931), called to the bar of the Middle Temple in 1956; QC in 1972; Recorder, 1972–1990; SC in 1979; Attorney General, 1979–1983; Master of the Bench of the Middle Temple in 1983. He did not respond to a request for an interview.

4 The Ma Brothers case had political and diplomatic ramifications as the narcotics empire they operated doubled as an intelligence network for the Taiwanese Kuomintang; see Martin Booth, *Opium: A History* (New York: St. Martin's Griffin, 1996), p. 282. I am grateful to Jason Wordie for the reference. Griffiths was clearly regarded as reliable enough to handle the information in the case.

5 He fascinated Aileen Bridgewater, despite the fact that they were opponents; Aileen Bridgewater Diary, 11.6.80, in the Bridgewater Collection. Griffiths married three times.

6 Sir Denys Roberts, *Another Disaster* (London: Radcliffe Press, 2006), p. 263.

7 Transcript of the Commission of Inquiry in Hong Kong University, Part VII, pp. 11,585–11,931; undated notes by Elsie Elliott in the Bridgewater Collection; "Conway Report", p. 25.

8 Christian Wolmar, "Looking Back to the Great British Paedophile Infiltration Campaign of the 1970s", the *Independent*, 27.2.14.

9 "Why Sir Peter Hayman Was Not Named", *The Times*, 7.4.81.

10 Derek Gwyn Davies (1931–2002), journalist and editor of the *Far Eastern Economic Review*, 1958–1989.

11 Information from Interviewee H, 21.1.15.

12 Commission of Inquiry Report, p. 59.

13 Transcript of the Commission of Inquiry in Hong Kong University, Part V p. 6,866. Other accounts place the collection of files on 20 July, but this is mistaken as the Attorney General informed the Governor of the results of the file search on 12 July — Commission of Inquiry Report, pp. 60–61. Gary Alderdice, QC (1946–1994) was a New Zealander, the Crown Counsel who had prosecuted Duffy and a colourful character who, when he went into private practice in Hong Kong, became known as "Never Plead Guilty Gary". In 1994, he took a Russian female prostitute to Vladivostok, some suggested in order to buy her out of prostitution, and was found shot dead through the eye in a flat alongside her tortured body; both had been killed by Russian criminals.

14 Evidence of Inspector Mike Fulton, Commission of Inquiry Report, p. 237; Transcript of the Commission of Inquiry in Hong Kong University, Part III, pp. 3,642–3,643.

15 *Hong Kong Standard & South China Morning Post*, 21.3.81; Commission of

Inquiry Report, p. 67. Roy Henry claimed in his statement to the Inquiry that he didn't know of Duffy's petition until 12 July, but he was being economical with the truth, and it was only its contents of which he was unaware; Roy Henry's statement to the Inquiry, 1.5.81, Elsie Tu (Elliott) Papers in Hong Kong Baptist University Library, MSS.13 Death of John MacLennan. Inquest & Inquiry: Statements, Reports, Correspondence and Papers, 1978–1979 13.5.

16 Commission of Inquiry Report, p. 68.

17 Commission of Inquiry Report, p. 59.

18 The allegation against this officer remains unsubstantiated.

19 Brief by the Crown Solicitor for the Governor, FCO 40/1351 Hong Kong Laws on Homosexuality. Howard Lindsay, whom he knew well, speculated that MacDougall was gay. MacDougall was not amused by this and told Barrie Barlow: "Damned Howard. How could he imply this of me, one of the biggest stick-men in Asia" — Barrie Barlow interview, 31.1.15.

20 Commission of Inquiry Report, p. 59 merely mentions Molo Tsui and not who was protecting him. All the proceedings of the Inquiry were very careful to prevent any leak of what it was that Duffy had alleged. The allegation that Henry protected Molo Tsui was made in a letter from Duffy to Elsie Elliott on 14.2.79, in which he discusses the content of his draft petition — Elsie Tu (Elliott) Papers in Hong Kong Baptist University Library, MSS 13 11.7 Cases of Homosexual Charges 1975–1981. Aileen Bridgewater's Diary for 28.8.80 includes uncorroborated information that the Governor did not want Roberts or Henry exposed in the Inquiry; Aileen Bridgewater Diary in the Bridgewater Collection.

21 The offence for which Greaves was imprisoned involved a break in to the home of a woman police constable whom it was alleged he intended to rape — information Interviewee J, 21.1.15.

22 Letter from Duffy to Elsie Elliott on 14.2.79, in which he discusses the content of his draft petition — Elsie Tu (Elliott) Papers in Hong Kong Baptist University Library, MSS 13 11.7 Cases of Homosexual Charges 1975–1981.

23 HKRS545-1-176-2 Public Order and Security 1971–1983, *Daily Mirror*, 16.5.80.

24 *Observer*, 22.6.80, reporting a Granada *World in Action* film on Little Sai Wan that was banned by the British Government.

25 On 25.5.80.

26 Minute from Roy Henry to Sir Jack Cater 24.7.79, in Elsie Tu (Elliott) Papers in Hong Kong Baptist University Library, MSS.13 Death of John MacLennan. Inquest & Inquiry: Statements, Reports, Correspondence and Papers, 1978–1979 13.5

27 The embargoed files are: FCO 40/853 Appointment of Chief Justice Hong Kong

1978, Temporarily Retained; FCO 40/932 Appointment of New Commissioner for the Royal Hong Kong Police, Closed for 60 Years; FCO 40/958 Threat to Hong Kong 1978, Retained by the Department; FCO 40/1017 Allegations of Bribery and Corruption in Hong Kong 1978, Closed for 40 Years; FCO 40/1018 Allegations of Bribery and Corruption in Hong Kong 1978, Closed for 40 Years; FCO 40/1022 Police Corruption: ICAC in Hong Kong 1978, Closed for 40 Years; FCO 40/1023 Police Corruption: ICAC in Hong Kong 1978, Closed for 40 Years; FCO 40/1046 Local Intelligence Committee Assessments of Political Situation in Hong Kong, Closed for 40 Years to 2020; FCO 40/1150 Hong Kong Annual Review 1979, Retained; FCO 40/1165 Local Intelligence Committee Assessments of Political Situation in Hong Kong 1979, Closed to 2021; PREM 19/787 Records of the Prime Minister's Office Correspondence and Papers 1979–1997: Hong Kong Intelligence Operations, Retained by the Department. The Hong Kong file is HKRS1054-1 Case Files Relating to MacLennan Inquiry.

28 Commission of Inquiry Report, p. 59.

29 Commission of Inquiry Report, p. 61.

30 *South China Morning Post & Hong Kong Standard*, 6.3.81.

31 Transcript of the Commission of Inquiry in Hong Kong University, Part I, p. Q 30, Part V, pp. 6,866–6,874; Annex to Commissioner of Police letter to the Governor, 20.8.79, p.2, para 5, in the Bridgewater Collection. Joseph "Joe" Michael Duffy, QC (born 1936), Senior Crown Counsel. A Scot, he joined the Legal Department in 1972; Director of Public Prosecutions in 1984; Judge, 1987–1996. He did not respond to a request for an interview.

32 Senior Inspector Frederick Craig Loughrin, a New Zealander. He did not respond to a request for an interview.

33 Transcript of the Commission of Inquiry in Hong Kong University, Part V, p. 6,868.

34 The Eastern District Court has a plaque commemorating Wilson's long service in the Causeway Bay Magistrates Court — information from Interviewee H, 21.1.15. He was a well-respected defender of the underdog, who, for instance, dismissed the charges against 1,661 people in 6 months for not carrying ID Cards; he objected to the law enacted in October 1980 obliging all in the Colony to carry one, because of the power he believed it gave to the police to abuse its enforcement — *Sarasota Herald Tribune*, 26.11.81.

35 Transcript of the Commission of Inquiry in Hong Kong University, Part I, p. Q 30, Part II, pp. 2,286–2,294, and hand written note by Professor D.M.E. Evans, p. 2,348. Manuscript in the Bridgewater Collection, 26.8.79.

36 Michael Robert Daniel Bunting, SC (born 1948), admitted to the Hong Kong Bar in 1974. Member of the Court of Final Appeal Rules Committee, the High Court Rules Committee, the Barristers Disciplinary Tribunal and the Inland Revenue

Board of Review; retired 2000. He was known in legal circles to be gay — interview with Barrie Barlow, 31.1.15.

37 Note in the Elsie Tu (Elliott) Collection, Hong Kong Baptist University Library, 26.8.79, MSS 13 Documents 1978–1981 13 2.

38 Commission of Inquiry Report, p. 60; *South China Morning Post* & *Hong Kong Standard*, 15.5.81.

39 FCO 40/1351 Hong Kong Laws On Homosexuality, ?7/8.79; Transcript of the Commission of Inquiry in Hong Kong University, Part V, p. 11,405.

40 Commission of Inquiry Report, p. 60.

41 Commission of Inquiry Report, p. 60.

42 Annex to Roy Henry's report to the Governor on Operation Rockcorry, 20.8.79, in the Bridgewater Collection.

43 *Hong Kong Standard* & *South China Morning Post*, 20.2.81. Gordon Richard Huthart (1951–1996), son of Robert Steer Huthart, Managing Director of Lane Crawford department stores. Howard Graham Lindsay, died from a stroke in Luton while living with his male partner; information from Interviewee H, 21.1.15.

44 Transcript of the Commission of Inquiry in Hong Kong University, Part III, pp. 3,644–3,646; Part V, p. 6878; *Hong Kong Standard & South China Morning Post*, 13.8.80.

45 Interview Justice Kemal Bokhary, 18.3.15; *South China Morning Post*, 17.11.79 & 18.6.80; Commission of Inquiry Report, pp. 89, 239.

46 *Hong Kong Standard, Sun, Star* & *South China Morning Post*, 10.12.80; Commission of Inquiry Report, p. 247; Interview with Howard Lindsay, notes by Aileen Bridgewater, undated, p.3, in the Bridgewater Collection.

47 Letter from Zimmern & Co, Solicitors for the Commission, to AG., 18.2.81, FCO papers released through the Freedom of Information Act in the Bridgewater Collection. Colin White also went under the aliases of Husain, Thomas (and perhaps Albert, although Albert is more likely to have been a prostitute friend of White).

48 Annex to Roy Henry's report to the Governor on Operation Rockcorry, 20.8.79 & Elsie Elliott notes in the Bridgewater Collection.

49 Note in the Elsie Tu (Elliott) Collection, Hong Kong Baptist University Library, ?.9.79, MSS 13 Manuscripts 1978–1987 12 4.

50 *South China Morning Post*, 22.9.96.

51 Gordon Huthart interview in *Hong Kong Standard* by Gilly Forge, 25.7.80.

52 Transcript of the Commission of Inquiry in Hong Kong University, Part II, pp. 2,297–2,298.

53 Annex to Roy Henry's report to the Governor on Operation Rockcorry, 20.8.79 in the Bridgewater Collection.

54 Annex to Roy Henry's report to the Governor on Operation Rockcorry, 20.8.79 in the Bridgewater Collection.

55 *Hong Kong Standard* & *South China Morning Post*, 28.1.81.

56 Aileen Bridgewater undated manuscript notes in the Bridgewater Collection.

57 Charles Warwick Reid, New Zealander, joined the Legal Department in 1974; arrested by the ICAC in 1989 when a Principal Crown Counsel but skipped bail through Macau and China. Extradited from the Philippines, he was jailed for eight years for having assets of HK$16 million, three-and-a-half times his emoluments.

58 *South China Morning Post*, 4.3.80.

59 Letter from Duffy written from Taipei on 13.3.80 to Elsie Elliott, Elsie Tu (Elliott) Collection, Hong Kong Baptist University Library, MSS 13 11.7 Cases of Homosexual Charges 1975–1981.

60 Roy Henry's report to the Governor on Operation Rockcorry, 20.8.79 in the Bridgewater Collection.

61 Commission of Inquiry Report, p. 67. The certificate of immunity from prosecution that Quinn gave Duffy is in the Elsie Tu (Elliott) Collection, Hong Kong Baptist University Library, MSS 13 Correspondence and Press Statements 1979–1981 13 1, dated 15.8.79.

62 Roy Henry's report to the Governor on Operation Rockcorry, 20.8.79 in the Bridgewater Collection.

63 Commission of Inquiry Report, p. 62.

64 Attorney General letter to Roy Henry entitled Operation Rockcorry, 31.8.79, in the Bridgewater Collection and at Commission of Inquiry Report, pp. 62-63.

12 Set-Up

1 Commission of Inquiry Report, quoting the Li Kwan-ha report, p. 336 and the Pelly Report, p. 364.

2 Transcript of the Commission of Inquiry in Hong Kong University, Part III, pp. 3,644–3,646. Fulton denied that he had ever done such a thing.

3 *Hong Kong Standard* & *South China Morning Post*, 19.3.81.

4 Commission of Inquiry Report, p. 237 and Pelly Report, p. 389.

5 Transcript of the Commission of Inquiry in Hong Kong University, Part V, p. 6,914.

6 *Hong Kong Standard* & *South China Morning Post*, 20.3.81.

7 Transcript of the Commission of Inquiry in Hong Kong University, Part V, pp. 6,816–6,817.

8 Evidence of Detective Inspector Tin, *Hong Kong Standard* & *South China Morning Post*, 13.2.81.

9 Commission of Inquiry Report, p. 76.

10 *Hong Kong Standard* & *South China Morning Post*, 10.2.81.

11 Commission of Inquiry Report, p. 76.

12 *Hong Kong Standard* & *South China Morning Post*, 13.2.81.

13 *Hong Kong Standard* & *South China Morning Post*, 14.2.81.

14 Transcript of the Commission of Inquiry in Hong Kong University, Part V, p. 7,573.

15 Inspector Norman MacKillop stated to the Inquiry that when he joined the SIU on 14 September, MacLennan's name was top of the SIU's list even though they knew of three other homosexual inspectors – *Hong Kong Standard* & *South China Morning Post*, 17.2.81.

16 Commission of Inquiry Report, p. 245.

17 Chief Inspector Norman "Norrie" M. MacKillop. He did not respond to a request for an interview.

18 Commission of Inquiry Report, pp. 75 & 238, and Pelly Report, p. 384.

19 Commission of Inquiry Report, p. 245.

20 Commission of Inquiry Report, p. 236. Haldanes, sadly, were to treat Fulton as something of a joke.

21 Commission of Inquiry Report, pp. 75 & 238, and Pelly Report, pp. 384, 388.

22 Commission of Inquiry Report, p. 78.

23 Governor's manuscript note asking the AG whether there was truth in Fulton's allegation, in memorandum AG to Governor, ?1.2.80, in the Bridgewater Collection.

24 Commission of Inquiry Report, pp. 75, 238 & 240, and Pelly Report, p. 384.

25 Quinn interviews with Chief Superintendent C.A. John Sheppard, 19.6.80 and 26.6.870.

26 *Hong Kong Standard* & *South China Morning Post*, 13.2.81.

27 Commission of Inquiry Report, p. 77.

28 Information Interviewee I, 22.1.15.

29 Colin Donald Campbell Logan, civil servant (born 1938). *Private Eye Business News*, 18.6.81; *Hong Kong Standard* & *South China Morning Post*, 6.11.80.

30 The evidence about the Lee Garden Hotel is, however, suspicious. It was strange

that MacLennan would have taken a prostitute to a hotel known to be frequented by government servants. We have only the SIU's word for it that the register was checked. The management of the hotel was also known to be corrupt and affiliated with the Chinese Communist Party's United Front operations in Hong Kong.

31 Commission of Inquiry Report, p. 77.

32 *Hong Kong Standard* & *South China Morning Post*, 11.2.81; 13.2.81.

33 Commission of Inquiry Report, p. 77.

34 Commission of Inquiry Report, p. 77; *Hong Kong Standard*, 20.11.80.

35 *Hong Kong Standard* & *South China Morning Post*, 20.12.80.

36 Commission of Inquiry Report, p. 82; *Hong Kong Standard* & *South China Morning Post*, 13.2.81.

37 *Hong Kong Standard* & *South China Morning Post*, 26.2.81.

38 *Hong Kong Standard* & *South China Morning Post*, 28.2.81.

39 Transcript of the Commission of Inquiry in Hong Kong University, Part V, pp. 6,950–7,090; *Hong Kong Standard* & *South China Morning Post*, 4.3.81 and 13.3.81.

40 *Hong Kong Standard*, 8.11.80.

41 Commission of Inquiry Report, p. 225.

42 Commission of Inquiry Report, pp. 82, 225; *Hong Kong Standard* & *South China Morning Post*, 12.3.81.

43 Commission of Inquiry Report, p. 83.

44 *Hong Kong Standard* & *South China Morning Post*, 29.11.80.

45 *Hong Kong Standard* & *South China Morning Post*, 12.11.80, 13.11.80, 14.11.80, 15.11.80.

46 *Hong Kong Standard* & *South China Morning Post*, 28.2.81.

47 *Hong Kong Standard* & *South China Morning Post*, 13.2.81.

48 Commission of Inquiry Report, p. 212; *South China Morning Post*, 9.12.80.

49 *Hong Kong Standard* & *South China Morning Post*, 13.2.81.

50 *South China Morning Post*, 9.12.80.

51 Commission of Inquiry Report, p. 79; *Hong Kong Standard* & *South China Morning Post*, 13.3.81. Moor later claimed that he had been unaware of the Yuen Long incident when he approved the creation of the court file, but this could not have been so given its contents and his earlier involvement in the pursuit of John MacLennan. He had, for instance, been told on 10 October of Fulton's allegation that he had been ordered to set up MacLennan — Commission of Inquiry Report,

p. 78; *Hong Kong Standard* & *South China Morning Post*, 1.5.81.

52 *Hong Kong Standard* & *South China Morning Post*, 2.12.80; 20.11.79; Commission of Inquiry Report, p. 83.

53 Commission of Inquiry Report, pp. 79–80.

54 Commission of Inquiry Report, p. 80; *Hong Kong Standard* & *South China Morning Post*, 27.3.81.

55 Commission of Inquiry Report, p. 225; *Hong Kong Standard* & *South China Morning Post*, 11.2.81.

56 Interview with Danny Wong, 14.5.15.

57 Commission of Inquiry Report, p. 80; *Hong Kong Standard* & *South China Morning Post*, 29.1.81.

58 Commission of Inquiry Report, pp. 80–81, Li Kwan-ha Report p. 337, and Pelly Report, p. 364.

59 John Beveridge opening statement to the Commission of Inquiry in the Bridgewater Collection; Commission of Inquiry Report, Li Kwan-ha Report, p. 338, Pelly Report, p. 365.

60 Commission of Inquiry Report, pp. 82, 96, and Li Kwan-ha Report, p. 338.

13 Stumbling Blocks

1 Letter Elsie Elliott to Norman St. John Stevas, 23.8.79, and Letter Howard Lindsay to Elsie Elliott covering Martin Potter's letter, 27.8.79, Elsie Tu (Elliott) Papers in Hong Kong Baptist University Library, MSS 13 11.7 Cases of Homosexual Charges 1975–1981.

2 Letter Howard Lindsay to Attorney General, 30.8.79, Elsie Tu (Elliott) Papers in Hong Kong Baptist University Library, MSS 13 11.7 Cases of Homosexual Charges 1975–1981.

3 Commission of Inquiry Report, p. 89; telegram British Ambassador Bangkok to the Governor, 30.8.79, Elsie Tu (Elliott) Papers in Hong Kong Baptist University Library, MSS 13 11.7 Cases of Homosexual Charges 1975–1981.

4 Letter Attorney General to P.T. Moor, 31.8.79, in the Bridgewater Collection.

5 Interview with Justice Kemal Bokhary, 18.3.15.

6 Information from Interviewee D, 11.8.15. Others do not believe Moor was homosexual: email "Cambus" to the author, 30.6.16.

7 *Hong Kong Standard* & *South China Morning Post*, 1.5.81.

8 Commission of Inquiry Report, p. 89.

9 Commission of Inquiry Report, p. 89. It is not clear to what other inquiry the Governor was referring.

10 Draft telegram Attorney General to Ambassador in Bangkok, 5.9.79, Elsie Tu (Elliott) Papers in Hong Kong Baptist University Library, MSS 13 11.7 Cases of Homosexual Charges 1975–1981.

11 Howard Lindsay's letter to the Coroner, 23.1.80, Commission of Inquiry Report, pp.349–354; Transcript of the Commission of Inquiry in Hong Kong University, Part II, pp. 2,257–2,259; Commission of Inquiry Report, p. 160; interview with Justice Beeson, 11.6.15.

12 Statement of Clare-Marie Beeson for the Attorney General, 1.2.80, in the Bridgewater Collection; interview with Justice Beeson, 11.6.15.

13 Commission of Inquiry Report, p. 240; *Hong Kong Standard*, 18.6.80.

14 Commission of Inquiry Report, pp. 75, 238, 239, 244, and Pelly Report, pp. 384–385; Transcript of the Commission of Inquiry in Hong Kong University, Part III, p. 3,612.

15 Commission of Inquiry Report, pp. 89–90 and Howard Lindsay's letter to the Coroner, 23.1.80, p. 353; Transcript of the Commission of Inquiry in Hong Kong University, Part II, pp. 2,286–2,294, 2,342–2.345; *South China Morning Post*, 30.6.80; Howard Lindsay letter to Attorney General, 24.11.79, Elsie Tu (Elliott) Papers in Hong Kong Baptist University Library, MSS 13 Correspondence and Press Statements 1979–1981 13 1.

16 Commission of Inquiry Report, p. 13, 90, and Howard Lindsay letter to Coroner of 23.1.80, p. 354.

17 Elsie Elliott note of her meeting with the Attorney General, 20.12.79, Elsie Tu (Elliott) Papers in Hong Kong Baptist University Library, MSS 13 11.7 Cases of Homosexual Charges 1975–1981.

18 Commission of Inquiry Report, pp. 90–91.

19 Elsie Elliott, *The MacLennan Affair*, p. 5.

20 Commission of Inquiry, p. 193.

21 Commission of Inquiry, p. 91; Transcript of the Commission of Inquiry in Hong Kong University, Part VII, p. 11,941.

22 The AG made it clear in his testimony that he regarded what had been done by the SIU before September, when he believed Moor had taken over supervision from Clancy and had brought Quinn under control, as irrelevant to the prosecution:

"I now know wrongly, in the back of my mind I had the thought that no doubt this allegation related to the period prior to Mr Moor taking control at the beginning of September"; Commission of Inquiry, p. 91; Transcript of the Commission of Inquiry in Hong Kong University, Part VII, pp. 11,566–11,567.

14 Suicide

1 The last time Bobby Po had sex with MacLennan was on 10.11.79 — Commission of Inquiry Report, p. 83.

2 Commission of Inquiry Report, pp. 83, 95.

3 John Conway, "Conway Report", p. 26.

4 Commission of Inquiry Report, p. 80; *Hong Kong Standard* & *South China Morning Post*, 15.12.79, 4.11.80.

5 Commission of Inquiry Report, p. 83; *Hong Kong Standard* & *South China Morning Pos*t, 4.11.80. The case of blackmail against the three prostitutes collapsed when brought to court in May 1980. It is noteworthy that all the cases brought against procurers or prostitutes who were police informers somehow failed to secure a conviction or brought minimal penalties.

6 After his court appearance, Colin Logan wrote a cringing letter of thanks to the Commissioner of Police for the way the SIU had handled his case. CDC Logan letter to Roy Henry, 15.12.79, Elsie Tu (Elliott) Papers in the Hong Kong Baptist University Library, MSS.13 Death of John MacLennan. Documents 1980 13.3: "All of the officers handling my case, and especially Messrs. Brooks, Quinn and McKillop [*sic*], have carried out their duties meticulously but always in a considerate and tactful way [...] Hong Kong has a Police Force with the very highest standards of professionalism and yet also with a human face. I will always be grateful to them and you, Sir, have good reason to be proud."

7 Aileen Bridgewater, *Talk of Hong Kong*, p. 284.

8 He was checked for some minor driving infringement when driving without his driving licence in October and asked to produce it at Ho Man Tin police station — Certificate dated 30.10.79 in the Bridgewater Collection.

9 Commission of Inquiry Report, p. 95 and Pelly Report, p. 367.

10 Commission of Inquiry Report, p. 95; letter John MacLennan to his family, 2 January 1980, Bridgewater Collection; *South China Morning Post*, 13.3.80.

11 Commission of Inquiry Report, Pelly Report, p. 383

12 Commission of Inquiry Report, Pelly Report, p. 366. Information from Interviewee I, 22.1.15.

13 Letter John MacLennan to his family, 2.1.80, Bridgewater Collection; also in

Commission of Inquiry Report, pp. 276–278.

14 Transcript of interview Aileen Bridgewater and "Slasher" George, 23.8.80, in the Bridgewater Collection.

15 Commission of Inquiry Report, p. 96, and Pelly Report, p. 366.

16 Andrew Hodge memorandum to the Governor, ? July 1980, Para. 15 (2), page 7, in the Bridgewater Collection; Commission of Inquiry Report, p. 95, and Pelly Report, p. 367; *Hong Kong Standard*, 5.3.80.

17 Interview with Iain Grant, 4.6.15; Aileen Bridgewater Diary, 8.8.80, in the Bridgewater Collection.

18 Commission of Inquiry Report, p. 95, and Pelly Report, pp. 367–368.

19 *Hong Kong Standard*, 14.6.80.

20 Commission of Inquiry Report, Pelly Report, p. 367.

21 Commission of Inquiry Report, pp. 95–96, and Pelly Report, p. 368; *Hong Kong Standard*, 5.3.80.

22 Interview with Iain Grant, 4.6.15.

23 Commission of Inquiry Report, p. 97, and Pelly Report, p. 367.

24 Interview with Iain Grant, 4.6.15. Superintendent Marcus "Marc" N.W. Pelly, a rugby player and one of the founders of the Kowloon Rugby Football Club — *KRFC Club News*, 7 January 2011. It is unconfirmed but believed that Pelly has died.

25 Commission of Inquiry Report, pp. 96–97, Li Kwan-ha Report, p. 338 and Pelly Report, pp. 367, 376.

26 Commission of Inquiry Report, p. 99. On the day of his death, John MacLennan's bank account held only HK$65.15.

27 Commission of Inquiry Report, p. 97, Li Kwan-ha Report, p. 339 and Pelly Report, pp. 370, 376.

28 Commission of Inquiry Report, pp. 82, 98, and Pelly Report, pp. 365, 371.

29 Commission of Inquiry Report, pp. 97, 255, and Pelly Report, pp. 370.

30 Interview with Iain Grant, 4.6.15.

31 *South China Morning Post*, 13.1.90.

32 Transcript of interview Aileen Bridgewater and "Slasher" George, 23.8.80, in the Bridgewater Collection.

33 Commission of Inquiry Report, p. 99, and Pelly Report, p. 372.

34 John MacLennan's Warrant Card was never found, so either both Station Sergeant Li and P.C. Lee at the armoury had not bothered to ask him to show it,

or he threw it away as he made his way back to his flat.

35 Commission of Inquiry Report, pp. 99–100, and Pelly Report, p. 372.

36 Commission of Inquiry Report, p. 319.

37 A copy of the withdrawal page of the register is at Commission of Inquiry Report, p. 121.

38 Commission of Inquiry Report, p. 100, and Pelly Report, p. 372; *Hong Kong Standard*, 11.3.80.

39 A copy of this is in the Commission of Inquiry Report, p. 121.

40 *South China Morning Post*, 11.3.80.

41 Commission of Inquiry Report, p. 100, and Pelly Report, p. 373.

42 Commission of Inquiry Report, p.106, and Pelly Report, pp. 373, 378–379.

43 Commission of Inquiry Report, Pelly Report, p. 374.

44 Interview with Iain Grant, 4.6.15.

45 Commission of Inquiry Report, p. 101, and Pelly Report, p. 365.

46 Commission of Inquiry Report, p. 101, Li Kwan-ha Report, p. 340, and Pelly Report, pp. 374–376; *South China Morning Post*, 11.3.80.

47 Commission of Inquiry Report, p. 101, and Pelly Report, pp. 374, 376; John Conway, "Conway Report", p. 29.

15 Investigation

1 There were actually five bullet wounds, but the fifth, to the abdomen, was concealed by clothing and had been fired under it, leaving no entrance hole on the jersey or shirt. The fifth wound was found by the pathologists.

2 Commission of Inquiry Report, p. 106, Li Kwan-ha Report, p. 34, and Pelly Report, p. 378.

3 Commission of Inquiry Report, p. 106.

4 Commission of Inquiry Report, pp. 100 & 275.

5 Commission of Inquiry Report, p. 106, and Pelly Report, p. 381.

6 Commission of Inquiry Report, p. 106, and Pelly Report, pp. 378–379. Senior Assistant Commissioner David Toby "Toby" Emmet, MBE, QPM, CPM, at the time of MacLennan's death OC CID (Kowloon). Superintendent George David Brooke, CPM.

7 *South China Morning Post* & *Hong Kong Standard*, 9.4.81.

8 Commission of Inquiry Report, p. 106.

9 Commission of Inquiry Report, p. 106, Li Kwan-ha Report, p. 34, and Pelly

Report, p. 378.

10 Dr Wong, the police pathologist, said that either Trotman or Quinn brought the suicide note into the bedroom, counter to their evidence that they had left it on the table — *South China Morning Post & Hong Kong Standard*, 10.4.81.

11 Photographs in the Bridgewater Collection.

12 Quinn: "Everybody was emotionally upset"; Transcript of the Commission of Inquiry in Hong Kong University, Part V, p. 6,987.

13 Moor passed this instruction through Assistant Commissioner Jack Johnston, who had earlier been DCI and who took over the appointment of District Commander Kowloon from Li Kwan-ha on the day that MacLennan died; *South China Morning Post & Hong Kong Standard*, 24.3.81.

14 Commission of Inquiry Report, Li Kwan-ha Report, p. 119.

15 Commission of Inquiry Report, p. 106, Li Kwan-ha Report, p. 341, and Pelly Report, p. 378.

16 Commission of Inquiry Report, pp. 105–106, Li Kwan-ha Report, p. 34, and Pelly Report, p. 378; *South China Morning Post & Hong Kong Standard*, 10.4.81.

17 Commission of Inquiry Report, p. 106, and Pelly Report, pp. 378–379, 381.

18 Commission of Inquiry Report, pp. 102–104, and Pelly Report, pp. 377–378; *South China Morning Post & Hong Kong Standard*, 12.8.80. Lau was working for Trotman and took photos as instructed by him.

19 Commission of Inquiry Report, pp. 137–141.

20 Dr Wong was the attending pathologist, Dr Yip accompanied him despite the fact that it was his day off.

21 Commission of Inquiry Report, p. 105, and Pelly Report, p. 375.

22 Commission of Inquiry Report, pp. 100, 285, where the post-mortem report is accredited to Dr Wong, although he did not himself affix his name or sign it.

23 The post-mortem report at Commission of Inquiry Report, p. 285, is less specific, and states only: "gunshot wounds of chest with injuries to chest and aorta".

24 Copy no. 194403 of death certificate no. 1049 KPR issued on 19.9.80 by Chan Yuk-shing, Registrar, in the Bridgewater Collection.

25 John Conway, "Conway Report", pp. 14–16.

26 John Conway, *To Speak for the Dead*, p. 26.

27 Aileen Bridgewater interview with "Slasher" George, 23.8.80.

28 Letter (31) CP/Wel/K/MacLennan/B from K.L. Yuen, Force Welfare Officer to Mrs MacLennan, 26.5.80, stating that John MacLennan had left a will, that Yuen held his passport, but regretting that there was no trace of MacLennan's watch, pocket

book or gold cuff links. He sent photographs of the funeral — in the Bridgewater Collection; letter (41) CP/Wel/K/MacLennan from K.L. Yuen to Mrs Katherine MacLennan, 25.6.80 — both in the Bridgewater Collection. The list of property in no. 8 Cell compiled by Inspector Peters is in the Bridgewater Collection and at Commission of Inquiry Report, pp. 248–252. The list of property taken by Pelly for the Inquiry is at Commission of Inquiry Report, pp. 253.

29 Commission of Inquiry Report, pp. 131–132.

30 Statements by those involved prior to the death reached a figure of eight or nine each by the end of the Inquiry, taken by: the SIU; Marc Pelly; Li Kwan-ha; the Coroner's Officer; the CAPO inquiry into Fulton's complaint; the Carratu team and the legal team of the inquiry. Some, like Quinn, gave two or even three statements to each interrogator. No statements exist of anyone involved in the follow up to the death.

31 John Conway, "Conway Report", pp. 20–22.

16 Outcry

1 Undated manuscript note in the Bridgewater Collection.

2 Two police officers were convicted and fifteen acquitted of corruption in the trial of the Mong Kok police syndicate on 24.7.78 — FCO 40/1047 Hong Kong Annual Review 1978.

3 Elsie Elliott letter to the Governor, 29.1.80, in Elsie Elliott (Tu) Papers in the Hong Kong Baptist University Library, MSS 13 Manuscripts 1978–1987 12 4.

4 Attorney General Memorandum to the Governor, 1.2.80, in the Bridgewater Collection.

5 Aileen Bridgewater Diary, 15.1.80, in the Bridgewater Collection.

6 John Conway, "Conway Report", p. 5.

7 Manuscript transcript of interview by Aileen Bridgewater with Mr and Mrs MacLennan, 31.8.83, in the Bridgewater Collection.

8 Commission of Inquiry Report, p. 107; *Hong Kong Standard*, 14.6.80.

9 Manuscript transcript of interview by Aileen Bridgewater with Mr and Mrs MacLennan, 31.8.83, in the Bridgewater Collection.

10 Manuscript notes from Aileen Bridgewater interview with Mr and Mrs MacLennan, 31.8.83, in the Bridgewater Collection.

11 Manuscript notes from Aileen Bridgewater interview with Mr and Mrs MacLennan, 31.8.83, in the Bridgewater Collection.

12 Commission of Inquiry Report, p. 107; John Conway, "Conway Report", p. 5; manuscript transcript of interview by Aileen Bridgewater with Mr and Mrs

MacLennan, 31.8.83, in the Bridgewater Collection.

13 Lidster telexed to the Commissioner of Police at 11.25 a.m. on 16.1.80 saying parents had given permission for an autopsy and wanted a cremation with the ashes to be sent to them in United Kingdom. The funeral service was to include Psalm 23 and the hymn "Eternal Father Strong to Save". No family would be attending. Commission of Inquiry Report, pp. 107; a copy of Lidster's telex of 16.1.80 is at p. 145 and the Coroner's Authorization of Cremation C-138/80 dated 17.1.80 in the name of John Richard MacLennan is at p.146.

14 Letter from Roy Henry to Mrs MacLennan, 16.1.80, in the Bridgewater Collection.

15 Letter from Martin Rowlands to Mrs MacLennan dated 31 January 1980, in the Bridgewater Collection.

16 *South China Morning Post*, 8.3.80, 11.3.80.

17 Commission of Inquiry Report, Pelly Report, p. 380; Report of Professor A. Keith Mant, Department of Forensic Medicine, Guy's Hospital, Commission of Inquiry Report, p. 302.

18 Police photographer PC 5827 — Commission of Inquiry Report, Li Kwan-ha Report, p. 341.

19 Autopsy Report KPM.184/80 Commission of Inquiry Report, pp. 285 et ff., and Pelly Report, p. 379.

20 Report of Professor A. Keith Mant, Department of Forensic Medicine, Guy's Hospital, Commission of Inquiry Report, p. 303.

21 *Hong Kong Standard*, 14.3.80.

22 Commission of Inquiry Report, p. 240.

23 Commission of Inquiry Report, p. 241. MacKillop's account was not fully accepted by Justice Yang who disbelieved that Fulton had apologized, but an apology would not have been out of character.

24 Commission of Inquiry Report, pp. 159, 181; Letter Elsie Elliott to Attorney General, 19.1.80, in Elsie Elliott (Tu) Papers in the Hong Kong Baptist University Library, MSS 13 Correspondence and Press Statements 1979–1981 13 1.

25 Commission of Inquiry Report, pp. 11, 159, 180, and Pelly Report, p. 382; *Sun*, 19.1.80.

26 Commission of Inquiry Report, p. 107.

27 Interview with Elsie Tu, 29.1.11; *Hong Kong Standard*, 9.7.80. One of the pallbearers was Inspector Lloyd Conway, son of John Conway; Aileen Bridgewater Diary, 1.7.80. The Reverend Anderson foolishly wrote to the press during the year in opposition to what he believed were Elsie Elliott's attacks on the police.

His congregation told him to stop writing to the press or leave — *South China Morning Post*, 1.9.80.

28 *Sun*, 23.1.80.

29 Commission of Inquiry Report, pp. 159 & 349 et ff., and Pelly Report, p. 385 Transcript of the Commission of Inquiry in Hong Kong University, Part VII, p. 11,585; *South China Morning Post*, 30.6.80; Letter Howard Lindsay to the Coroner, 23.1.80, in Elsie Elliott (Tu) Papers in the Hong Kong Baptist University Library, MSS 13 Correspondence and Press Statements 1979–1981 13 1.

30 Commission of Inquiry Report, Pelly Report, p. 382.

31 Commission of Inquiry Report, pp. 159, 167.

32 Letter A.G. to Elsie Elliott, 25.1.80, Elsie Elliott (Tu) Papers in the Hong Kong Baptist University Library, MSS 13 Correspondence and Press Statements 1979–1981 13 1.

33 Clemence had been promoted to Chief Superintendent by the time this occurred.

34 Commission of Inquiry Report, p. 169.

35 Commission of Inquiry Report, p. 170, and full text as part of AG's press release, pp. 405–406.

36 Commission of Inquiry Report, p. 180. Letter Elsie Elliott to the AG, 24.1.80, in the Bridgewater Collection.

37 Letter from Elsie Elliott to Police HQ Edinburgh, 24.1.80, Elsie Elliott (Tu) Papers in the Hong Kong Baptist University Library, MSS 13 11.7 Cases of Homosexual Charges 1975–1981 and MSS 13 Manuscripts 1978–1987 12 4. Their reply is also in the same file. She then contacted the Central Scotland Police at Stirling, who replied on 4.2.80 that MacLennan had served in the Stirling and Clackmannanshire Police from 3.10.69 to 3.10.73 and that nothing was known to his detriment during his service — MSS 13 11.7 Cases of Homosexual Charges 1975–1981.

38 Commission of Inquiry Report, Pelly Report, p. 383.

39 Letter from Michael King to Elsie Elliott, 31.1.80, in the Elsie Elliott (Tu) Papers in the Hong Kong Baptist University Library, MSS 13 Manuscripts 1978–1987 12 4.

40 Commission of Inquiry Report, p.180. Letter Elsie Elliott to the Governor, 29.1.80, in the Elsie Elliott (Tu) Papers in the Hong Kong Baptist University Library, MSS 13 Manuscripts 1978–1987 12 4.

41 Memorandum AG to Governor, ?1.2.80, in the Bridgewater Collection.

42 Commission of Inquiry Report, p.169, with a copy of the Governor's letter to Elsie Elliott p. 397.

43 Memorandum AG to the Governor, 5.2.80, Commission of Inquiry Report, p. 170.

44 Letter Howard Lindsay to the Coroner, 25.1.80, in the Elsie Elliott (Tu) Papers in the Hong Kong Baptist University Library, MSS 13 11.7 Cases of Homosexual Charges 1975–1981.

45 Commission of Inquiry Report, p. 202; *Hong Kong Standard*, 9.7.80.

46 FCO 40/1057 Visit by Governor of Hong Kong to United Kingdom; FCO 40/1156 Visit by Governor of Hong Kong to United Kingdom.

47 *Sun*, 26.1.80.

48 Invoice, Hong Kong Funeral Home, 20.1.80; invoice Donald Cameron & Son, Dingwall, to Mr J MacLennan, March 1980, in the Bridgewater Collection; Registry Certificate no. 137, Ross and Cromarty District Council, Fodderty Cemetery, Mr J. MacLennan, 8.2.80; manuscript transcript of interview by Aileen Bridgewater with Mr and Mrs MacLennan, 31.8.83; all in the Bridgewater Collection.

49 Photograph in the Bridgewater Collection.

17 Inquest

1 Aileen Bridgewater (1934–2014). Arrived Hong Kong 1973. Founder of Helping Hand, Kidney Patients' Trust Fund and Spare a New Toy Appeal (SANTA).

2 Interview Aileen and Ken Bridgewater, 15.5.13.

3 Aileen Bridgewater Diary, 24.1.80; transcript of the Commercial Radio Aileen Bridgewater interview with Elsie Elliott, 24.1.80; Aileen Bridgewater statement to the Commission, 18.2.80 — all in the Bridgewater Collection; Interview Aileen and Ken Bridgewater, 15.5.13; Commission of Inquiry Report, pp.179–180.

4 Letter N.J.V. Watt, Commissioner for Television and Entertainment Licensing, 29.1.80, to the AG covering transcript of Ian Whitely's interview on TVB of 22.1.80, in Elsie Tu (Elliott) Papers in Hong Kong Baptist University Library, MSS 13 Death of John MacLennan. Documents 1980 13.3.

5 Telegram Elsie Elliott to the MacLennan family, 11.2.80, in Elsie Tu (Elliott) Papers in Hong Kong Baptist University Library, MSS 13 Manuscripts 1978—1987 12 4; Commission of Inquiry Report, p. 160.

6 Sir John William Hansen, KNZM (born 1945), between 1979 and 1988, magistrate, coroner, district court judge, family court judge then High Court Master in Hong Kong. Master of the New Zealand High Court, 1988. Judge of the High Court, 1995; retired in 2008. Justice of the Court of Appeal of the Solomon Islands 2009; Justice of the Court of Appeals of Samoa 2009.

7 John Conway, "Conway Report", p. 21.

8 Commission of Inquiry Report, Pelly Report, pp. 382–390.

9 Commission of Inquiry Report, Pelly Report, p. 366.

10 Commission of Inquiry Report, Pelly Report, pp. 390–391.

11 The Coroner's Officer was an official whose function was to assist to the Coroner in investigating matters connected with a death, who could be a police officer in routine cases, a lawyer where things were more complicated.

12 Elsie Elliott, "The MacLennan Affair", pp. 9–10. Commission of Inquiry Report, p. 106.

13 Commission of Inquiry Report, pp. 12, 166, 202. Downey became a judge in 1981; *Hong Kong Standard*, 9.7.80.

14 Commission of Inquiry Report, p. 164.

15 Transcript of the Inquest, Coroner's opening address to the jury, in Elsie Tu (Elliott) Papers in Hong Kong Baptist University Library, MSS 13 Death of John MacLennan. Inquest & Inquiry: Statements, Reports, Correspondence and Papers, 1980–1996 13.6.

16 David John Leonard, who became a judge in 1981, and at time of writing was still a Justice of the Brunei Court of Appeal.

17 Governor's file note, 2.3.80, in Elsie Tu (Elliott) Papers in Hong Kong Baptist University Library, MSS 13 Documents 1978–1981 13 2.

18 Aileen Bridgewater Diary, 3.3.80–5.3.80, in the Bridgewater Collection.

19 Andrew Scott Hodge (died 2001), Crown Counsel in 1975, Senior Crown Counsel, later Director of Public Prosecutions. He appeared in the High Court of South Australia without a leader at the age of 28. He left Australia in 1975 and returned to Western Australia in 1985. President of the Australian Criminal Lawyers' Association in 1991 and 1992. Commemorated in the Hodge Award, an annual award recognizing the contribution made by a young criminal lawyer to the practice of criminal law in Western Australia.

20 Commission of Inquiry Report, pp. 164, 166; *Hong Kong Standard*, 4.3.80.

21 Commission of Inquiry Report, pp. 109–110; *Hong Kong Standard* & *South China Morning Post*, 8.3.80.

22 *Private Eye*, 25.4.80; manuscript note in the Aileen Bridgewater Collection.

23 Commission of Inquiry Report, p. 167.

24 Commission of Inquiry Report, pp. 12, 202; *Hong Kong Standard*, 13.3.80; Aileen Bridgewater Diary, 12.3.80, in the Bridgewater Collection.

25 Elsie Tu (Elliott) Papers in Hong Kong Baptist University Library, MSS 13 Death of John MacLennan. Documents 1980 13.3; pp. 7–10 only in the Bridgewater Collection.

26 Commission of Inquiry Report, pp. 344–346.

18 Campaign

1 Aileen Bridgewater Diary, 15.3.80 and 18.3.80, in the Bridgewater collection.

2 Commission of Inquiry Report, p. 203; *Hong Kong Standard* & *South China Morning Post*, 14.3.80.

3 Duncan Campbell, *New Statesman*, 23.3.80; Commission of Inquiry Report, pp. 12, 204.

4 "Letter from Hong Kong",*Private Eye*, 25.4.80.

5 "Inquest Panel was not Convinced", *Newsweek*, 31.3.80; Commission of Inquiry Report, p. 204.

6 Telex from London Office of the RHKP to Commissioner, 9.4.80, in Elsie Tu (Elliott) Papers in Hong Kong Baptist University Library, MSS 13 Death of John MacLennan. Documents 1980 13.3.

7 *South China Morning Post*, 30.4.80.

8 Commission of Inquiry Report, pp. 179, 181; Elsie Tu (Elliott) Papers in Hong Kong Baptist University Library, MSS 13 Manuscripts 1978-1987 12 4.

9 Letter Governor to Elsie Elliott, 21.3.80, in Elsie Tu (Elliott) Papers in Hong Kong Baptist University Library, MSS 13 Correspondence and Press Statements 1979–1981 13 1.

10 The two British MPs wrote to the FCO on 8.5.80; *Hong Kong Standard*, 9.7.80; *South China Morning Post*, 9.5.80; Commission of Inquiry Report, p. 204.

11 HKRS70-8- 1869 Homosexuality 1980–1983.

12 Aileen Bridgewater Diary, 20.3.80, in the Bridgewater Collection.

13 Interview with Elsie Tu, 29.6.11.

14 Manuscript transcript of Aileen Bridgewater interview with Elsie Elliott, 23.8.80, in the Bridgewater Collection; Aileen Bridgewater Diary, 25.4.80 and 26.4.80, in the Bridgewater Collection.

15 AG memorandum to Crown Counsel S.N. Westbrook, 23.3.80, in Elsie Tu (Elliott) Papers in Hong Kong Baptist University Library, MSS 13 Correspondence and Press Statements 1979–1981 13 1.

16 Brief for the AG by S.N. Westbrook, 26.3.80; Moor as Acting Commissioner of Police met the AG on 28.3.80 and on 2.4.80 wrote to him; all in Elsie Tu (Elliott) Papers in Hong Kong Baptist University Library, MSS 13 Death of John MacLennan. Documents 1980 13.3.

17 Brief by Acting AG, G.P. Nazareth, to the Commissioner of Police, 23.4.80, in Elsie

Tu (Elliott) Papers in Hong Kong Baptist University Library, MSS 13 Death of John MacLennan. Documents 1980 13.3.

18 This was on 22.5.80; Commission of Inquiry Report, pp. 12, 172, 204; South China Morning Post, 23.5.80.

19 Commission of Inquiry Report, pp. 170, 398, 399; memorandum from Governor to A.G., 22.4.80, in the Bridgewater Collection.

20 *Hong Kong Standard*, 9.7.80.

21 *Private Eye*, 23.5.80; FCO 40/1351 Hong Kong Laws on Homosexuality.

22 *New Statesman*, 12.5.80; *Gay News*, 15.5.80.

23 *South China Morning Post*, 16.5.80; *Hong Kong Standard*, 17.5.80; Commission of Inquiry Report, p. 205.

24 Aileen Bridgewater Diary, 23.5.80, in the Bridgewater Collection. Aileen attended and at the press conference was the subject of a concerted effort by Astin and the police solicitor to persuade her that suicide by five bullets with a low powered police revolver was possible. She was told by Astin that he thought the police had panicked at the scene of death, and so failed to conduct a proper investigation.

25 Press release by the Government Secretariat Press Office, 23.5.90, in the Bridgewater Collection.

26 Aileen Bridgewater Diary, 24.5.80, in the Bridgewater Collection; Elsie's response was "never!"

27 *South China Morning Post*, 24.5.80; Aileen Bridgewater, "Notes on the Short Story and Other Inquiry Matters" in the Bridgewater Collection.

28 Aileen Bridgewater Diary, 24.5.80; manuscript notes of transcript of Aileen Bridgewater interview with Elsie Elliott, 24.5.80; both in the Bridgewater Collection.

29 *Sun*, 24.5.80.

30 *South China Morning Post*, 28.5.80; *Hong Kong Standard*, 31.5.80.

31 Commission of Inquiry Report, pp. 12–13, 205–206; *South China Morning Post*, 1.6.80.

32 On 2.6.80 — Commission of Inquiry Report, p. 13.

33 Commission of Inquiry Report, pp. 173, 206.

34 *South China Morning Post*, 2.6.80. Dr. Denny Huang Mong-hwa (1920–2007), doctor and politician. Member of the Urban Council of Hong Kong, 1967–1986; Hong Kong member to the Chinese People's Political Consultative Conference, 1986–1998.

35 *Kung Sheung Daily News*. 22.3.80.

36 *Star*, 4.6.80.

37 *Hong Kong Standard*, 4.6.80.

38 *Star*, 6.6.80; *South China Morning Post*, *Star* & *Hong Kong Standard*, 14.4.81. He tried to demonstrate this at the flat to Justice Yang and Conrad Seagroatt during the Inquiry, but got stuck half way in.

39 Manuscript notes of events on 6.6.80 in the Bridgewater Collection.

40 Commission of Inquiry Report, p. 173.

41 *Hong Kong Standard*, 6.6.80 and 9.7.80.

42 Aileen Bridgewater Diary, 6.6.80, in the Bridgewater Collection; *Hong Kong Standard*, 8.6.80; Commission of Inquiry Report, pp. 13, 206.

43 Aileen Bridgewater Diary, 7.6.80, in the Bridgewater Collection. Interview Aileen and Ken Bridgewater, 15.5.13.

44 *Hansard*, 10.6.80.

45 *Hong Kong Standard*, 14.6.80 & 9.7.80; Commission of Inquiry Report, p. 206.

46 Commission of Inquiry Report, pp. 13, 174, 206, 402-404; *Hong Kong Standard*, 18.6.80.

47 The AG's press statement of 19.6.80 is printed in full at Commission of Inquiry Report, pp. 40–-408.

48 Commission of Inquiry Report, p. 408.

49 Commission of Inquiry Report, p. 175 and full text at p. 405; *Hong Kong Standard*, 20.6.80; Aileen Bridgewater Diary, 19.6.80, in the Bridgewater Collection.

50 Commission of Inquiry Report, pp. 176, 206.

51 *Star*, 20.6.80; Commission of Inquiry Report, p. 13.

52 *South China Morning Post*, 20.6.80; Commission of Inquiry Report, p. 207; the full text of Elsie Elliott's press release is in HKRS570-8-3383 Police — Case of John MacLennan.

53 Commission of Inquiry Report, pp. 13, 175, 207; *South China Morning Post*, 30.6.80.

54 Commission of Inquiry Report, p. 207.

55 HKRS545-1-176-2 Public Order and Security 1971–1983.

56 *Hong Kong Standard*, 9.7.80.

57 Stephen Ashley Burns, Assistant Solicitor, Johnson Stokes & Master.

58 Commission of Inquiry Report, pp. 13, 177–178.

59 *Hong Kong Standard* & *South China Morning Post*, 3.7.80.

60 *Hong Kong Standard*, 9.7.80; *South China Morning Post*, 5.7.80. Commission of Inquiry Report, pp. 13, 208.

61 HKRS570-8-3384 Police — Case of John MacLennan.

62 *Hong Kong Standard*, *South China Morning Post*, *Sun*, 5.7.80.

63 R.D. Clift minute to Peter Blaker and Blaker to Governor telex, 4.7.80, FCO Freedom of Information Act papers in the Bridgewater Collection.

64 Telex Governor to Peter Blaker, 6.7.80, FCO Freedom of Information Act papers in the Bridgewater Collection.

65 *Hong Kong Standard*, 6.7.80 and Kevin Sinclair's interview with Roy Henry, *South China Morning Post*, 6.7.80.

66 *Hong Kong Standard*, 9.7.80.

67 *Hong Kong Standard*, 11.7.80; AG's Statement to the Legislative Council — HKRS570-8-3383 Police — Case of John MacLennan.

19 Commission of Inquiry

1 FCO 40/1263 Hong Kong Annual Review for 1980; the Governor would be on leave until 10 August.

2 Statement at HKRS570-8-3383 Police — Case of John MacLennan; *South China Morning Post*, 12.7.80.

3 *Hong Kong Standard*, 12.7.80.

4 Commission of Inquiry Report, p. 208. The Chinese press had noted Tony Pannell's statement of 1.6.80 contradicting the AG.

5 FCO 40/1156 Visit by Governor of Hong Kong to United Kingdom, 14.7.80; *South China Morning Post*, 3.8.80.

6 Aileen Bridgewater Diary, 11.6.80, in the Bridgewater Collection.

7 Interview with Aileen and Ken Bridgewater, 13.5.11.

8 Aileen Bridgewater Diary, 7.7.80, in the Bridgewater Collection. Miller returned to New Zealand in 1980 and is an accident compensation advocate there.

9 *Hong Kong Standard*, 10.7.80; Commission of Inquiry Report, p. 208; FCO 40/1263 Hong Kong Annual Review for 1980.

10 *Star*, 10.7.80; Lord Fenner Brockway wrote to Lord Trefgarne, the FCO Minister in the Lords, on 9.8.80; Lord Trefgarne provided written answers on 17.8.80 and 8.9.80 — *Hansard*; in Elsie Tu (Elliott) Papers in Hong Kong Baptist University Library, MSS 13 Manuscripts 1978–1987 12 4. Lord Fenner Brockway asked Lord Trefgarne a verbal question on the same subject on 20.8.80 — HKRS570-8-

3383A Police — Case of John MacLennan.

11 Commission of Inquiry Report, p. 11.

12 The Honourable Dato Seri Paduka Sir Ti-Liang Yang, GBM, JP, LLD, DLITT (born Shanghai 1929). Called to the bar in Gray's Inn in 1954. Magistrate, Hong Kong in 1956. Senior Magistrate in 1963. Acting District Judge, 1964–1968. Acting Puisne Judge in 1971. Conducted Riot Compensation Boards, 1966–1967 and the Kotewall Court Rainstorm Disaster Inquiry in 1972. High Court Judge in 1975. Presided in the Godber case in 1975, the Happy Valley horse doping case in 1975 and the Leung Wing-san inquiry in 1976 — Star, 11.7.80; South China Morning Post, 12.7.80. Justice of Appeal in 1981. Vice President Court of Appeal in 1987. Chief Justice in 1988. Candidate for Hong Kong's first Chief Executive in 1996. Member of the Executive Council, 1997–2002.

13 FCO 40/931 Appointment of Commissioner Against Corruption In Hong Kong, 3.5.78.

14 The Sub-committee's remit had only been agreed on 5.7.80: "Should the present laws governing homosexual conduct in Hong Kong be changed and, if so, in what way." The Sub-committee consisted of: Justice T.L. Yang, Chairman; the Attorney General; Dr Ambrose King, New Asia College; Selina Chow, film producer; Robert Ribeiro, Barrister; Dr. George Ou Tai-wei, Psychiatrist; Mr Lam Wah-hui, teacher; Mr T.C. Bridgeman, Swire; Andrew Hodge, Secretary — HKRS70-8- 1869 Homosexuality 1980–1983.

15 Interview with Sir Ti-Liang Yang, 5.9.16.

16 *South China Morning Post*, 14.7.80. Norman Chan Tak-lam, SBS, JP (born 1954). Hong Kong Civil Service in 1976. Deputy Director of Monetary Management at the Exchange Fund of Hong Kong in 1991. Executive Director then Deputy Chief Executive of the Hong Kong Monetary Authority in 1993; Regional Vice-Chairman of the Standard Chartered Bank in 2005; Director of the Office of the Chief Executive of the Hong Kong Special Administrative Region in 2007; Chief Executive of the Hong Kong Monetary Authority in 2009. He declined to be interviewed for this book.

17 *Hong Kong Standard*, 17.7.80.

18 Alan E. Harrison, Solicitor, Legal Aid Department; Commission of Inquiry Report, p. 16.

19 *South China Morning Post*, 20.7.80; Commission of Inquiry Report, p. 15. Justice Michael Hugh Neligan. Recorder in 1987. Judge criticized in a case where he gave a man who had abused three boys the sentence of only 12 months.

20 Interviews with Murray Burton, 9.2.15 and 19.9.16.

21 Justice Anthony (Tony) Francis Neoh, SC, QC, JP (born 1947). Administrative Officer Hong Kong Government; called to the Hong Kong Bar in 1979; Deputy High Court Judge in 1992; Chairman of the Technical Committee of the International Organization of Securities Commissions, 1996–1998; Senior Adviser to the Board of the Bank of China (Hong Kong) in 2006; Hong Kong Securities and Investment Institute Honorary Fellow in 2008; Board member of China Life; Director of Forbes in 2010; Chief Adviser and member of the International Consultation Committee of the China Securities Regulatory Commission. He did not respond to a request for an interview.

22 R. Murray Burton, Solicitor, Zimmern & Co. Interview with Murray Burton, 9.2.15.

23 Justice Conrad Seagroatt, QC, member of the Criminal Injuries Compensation Board; Deputy High Court Judge, Hong Kong.

24 Interview Justice Seagroatt, 29.5.15.

25 *South China Morning Post*, 24. & 25.7.80.

26 *South China Morning Post* and *Hong Kong Standard*, 24.7.80; *South China Morning Post*, 25.7.80 & 29.7.80; Aileen Bridgewater Diary, 26.7.80, in the Bridgewater Collection.

27 *Star*, 30.7.80.

28 Letter Hamish Gray MP to Elsie Elliott, 5.8.80, in reply to her letter of 27.7.80, in the Elsie Tu (Elliott) Papers in Hong Kong Baptist University Library, MSS 13 Manuscripts 1978–1987 12 4; Dennis Canavan, MP, asked Douglas Hurd, Minister of State FCO on 4.8.80 whether the Government would consult the Governor about an independent inquiry and legal aid for expert witnesses — HKRS570-8-3383A Police — Case of John MacLennan.

29 John Albert Conway (1917–?); Civilian clerk in Inverness HQ of Northern Constabulary, living at Conon Bridge. Uniformed and CID policeman for 35 years. Served for a time in the Northern Ireland Forensic Science Laboratory. Had been several times to Hong Kong for the Northern Constabulary on fraud cases connected with triads — John Conway, *To Speak for the Dead*, p. 9.

30 *The Law List*, 1972, p. 94; 1973, p. 97.

31 Aileen Bridgewater Diary, 28.7.80, in the Bridgewater Collection.

32 Aileen Bridgewater Diary, 3.8.80, in the Bridgewater Collection.

33 Interview Aileen and Ken Bridgewater, 15.5.13.

34 Aileen Bridgewater Diary, 4.8.80, in the Bridgewater Collection.

35 Interview with Justice Conrad Seagroatt, 29.5.15.

36 Interview with Murray Burton, 9.2.15.

37 Aileen Bridgewater Diary, 11.8.80, in the Bridgewater Collection.

38 Letter Elsie Elliott to Justice Yang, 9.8.80, in Elsie Tu (Elliott) Papers in Hong Kong Baptist University Library, MSS 13 Correspondence and Press Statements 1979–1981 13 1.

39 *South China Morning Post* and *Hong Kong Standard*, 12.8.80.

40 Interview with Sir Ti-Liang Yang, 5.9.16.

41 Commission of Inquiry Report, pp. 17, 222.

42 Interview with Murray Burton, 9.2.15.

43 Commission of Inquiry Report, pp. 293 et ff.

44 *Star*, *South China Morning Post* & *Hong Kong Standard*, 21.8.80.

45 Commission of Inquiry Report, pp. 135, 151, 152; John Conway, "Conway Report", pp. 18–19.

46 *South China Morning Post* & *Hong Kong Standard*, 13.8.80.

47 Commission of Inquiry Report, pp. 17, 222.

48 Transcript of the Commission of Inquiry, Testimony of Chief Inspector Quinn, Hong Kong University Library, Pt. I, p. Q5.

49 Transcript of the Commission of Inquiry, Testimony of Chief Inspector Quinn, Hong Kong University Library, Pt. I, p. Q28.

50 *Star, South China Morning Post* & *Hong Kong Standard*, 15.8.80.

51 Email Justice Seagroatt to the author, 3.7.15.

52 Interview with Justice Seagroatt, 29.5.15.

53 *Star, South China Morning Post* & *Hong Kong Standard*, 16.8.80; *South China Morning Post* & *Hong Kong Standar*d, 17.8.80.

54 Aileen Bridgewater Diary, 19.8.80–20.8.80, in the Bridgewater Collection.

55 Interview with Justice Conrad Seagroatt, 29.5.15; interview with Sir Ti-Liang Yang, 5.9.16.

56 Interview with Barrie Barlow, 31.1.15; Sir Ti-Liang Yang recalled that Neligan's chambers sent someone out to Hong Kong to escort him home, and that he had to be helped off the plane at London Heathrow Airport on his arrival.

57 Interviews with Murray Burton, 9.2.15 and 19.9.16; interview with Justice Conrad Seagroatt, 29.5.15. Murray Burton recalled that in the days prior to this, Neligan, with whom he worked closely, had begun to appear more and more distressed.

58 Appendix 4 to a paper by the Crown Solicitor for the Governor, 25.3.81, FCO 40/1351 Hong Kong Laws on Homosexuality.

59 *Star*, *South China Morning Post* & *Hong Kong Standard*, 11.9.80.

60 Annex D to a paper by the Crown Solicitor for the Governor, 25.3.81, FCO 40/1351 Hong Kong Laws on Homosexuality.

61 Appendix 4 to a paper by the Crown Solicitor for the Governor, 25.3.81, FCO 40/1351 Hong Kong Laws on Homosexuality.

62 Commission of Inquiry Report, p. 17. John Caldwell Beveridge, QC (born 1937). Called to the Bar, Inner Temple in 1963; Freeman City of London in 1965; Liveryman Worshipful Company of Goldsmiths; Conservative member Westminster City Council, 1968–1972; Recorder of the Crown Court (Western Circuit), 1975–1996; Junior Master Westmeath Foxhounds, 1976–1979; QC in 1979; Bencher, Inner Temple in 1985; Commander Star of Honour (Ethiopia) in 1992; Chairman of the Bar Council; Trustee, Dogs Trust in 1998; Vice-President Manchester Dogs Home, 1999–2013; Chairman St. James's Conservation Trust, in 1999, then Patron. He did not respond to requests for an interview for this book.

63 Interview with Sir Ti-Liang yang, 5.9.16.

20 The Carratu Investigation

1 Aileen Bridgewater, *Talk of Hong Kong*, pp. 281–289 and Diary, 22.8.80 & 23.8.80, in the Bridgewater Collection.

2 Manuscript transcript of Aileen Bridgewater interview with "Slasher" George, 22.8.80, in the Bridgewater Collection.

3 Aileen Bridgewater Diary, 23.8.80, in the Bridgewater Collection.

4 Baggy shirts, often of Hawaiian pattern, were worn by plain clothes Hong Kong police officers to cover revolvers carried in a holster hanging from the belt — information from a retired police officer.

5 Manuscript transcript of Aileen Bridgewater interview with "Slasher" George, 26.8.80, in the Bridgewater Collection; Aileen Bridgewater, *Talk of Hong Kong*, pp. 282–283.

6 At their second interview on 26.8.80, George said that he had been met by these at Kai Tak airport, which contradicted his earlier account and seemed unlikely. His stories were in places confused, and Aileen was herself not sure what to make of him.

7 Manuscript transcript of Aileen Bridgewater interview with "Slasher" George 22.8.80, in the Bridgewater Collection.

8 Manuscript transcript of Aileen Bridgewater interview with "Slasher" George 22.8.80, in the Bridgewater Collection.

9 Aileen Bridgewater Diary, 25.8.80, in the Bridgewater Collection. George had been

trying to reach Aileen for over a day, but she was staying at the Royal Hong Kong Golf Club in Fanling for the weekend.

10 Aileen Bridgewater Diary, 25.8.80 & 26.8.80, in the Bridgewater Collection.

11 Aileen Bridgewater Diary, 25.8.80, in the Bridgewater Collection.

12 Aileen Bridgewater, *Talk of Hong Kong*, p. 288; Manuscript transcript of Aileen Bridgewater interview with "Slasher" George, 26.8.80 and Aileen Bridgewater Diary, 27.8.80, both in the Bridgewater Collection.

13 Aileen Bridgewater Diary, 30.8.80, in the Bridgewater Collection; interview with Aileen and Ken Bridgewater, 15.5.13.

14 John Conway, "Conway Report", p. 22.

15 Commission of Inquiry Report, p. 17; *Hong Kong Standard*, 11.9.80.

16 Interview with Sir Ti-Liang Yang, 5.9.16.

17 *Star*, *South China Morning Post* & *Hong Kong Standard*, 11.9.80.

18 Vincent N. Carratu, FIPI, Managing Director then Chairman of the Carratu Group of Companies. Retired from the Metropolitan Police in 1963. He did not respond to requests for an interview for this book.

19 Commission of Inquiry Report, pp. 18, 212; *South China Morning Post*, 17.9.80.

20 Aileen Bridgewater was told that half of Gurka's company was owned by Carratu and that it had been alleged that he was known for dirty tricks and planting counterfeit money on suspects — Aileen Bridgewater Diary, 6.10.80, in the Bridgewater Collection.

21 Commission of Inquiry Report, pp. 18, 222; *South China Morning Post*, 12.10.80; *Hong Kong Standard*, 30.10.80.

22 Interviews with Justice Conrad Seagroatt, 29.5.15, and Justice Kemal Bokhary. 18.3.15.

23 *South China Morning Post*, 18 & 19.9.80; *Star*, 19.9.80.

24 *South China Morning Post*, 24.9.80.

25 Aileen Bridgewater Diary, 18.9.80, in the Bridgewater Collection.

26 Aileen Bridgewater Diary, 2.10.80, in the Bridgewater Collection.

27 Commission of Inquiry Report, p. 22.

28 Commission of Inquiry Report, p. 19.

29 Interview with Sir Ti-Liang Yang, 5.9.16.

30 *South China Morning Post*, 13.1.90; Vincent Carratu email to Ken Bridgewater, 11.12.13.

31 Interview Aileen and Ken Bridgewater, 15.5.13.

32 Interview Aileen and Ken Bridgewater, 15.5.13.

33 Aileen Bridgewater Diary, 29.9.80, in the Bridgewater Collection.

34 Aileen Bridgewater, *Talk of Hong Kong*, p. 290; Aileen Bridgewater Diary 2.10.80–5.10.80. Interview with Murray Burton, 19.9.16.

35 Interview with Murray Burton, 9.2.15.

36 *South China Morning Post & Hong Kong Standard*, 3.10.80; *Star, South China Morning Post & Hong Kong Standard*, 4.10.80, 7.10.80 & 17.10.80.

37 *Star & South China Morning Post*, 1.11.80; *South China Morning Post*, 2.11.80.

38 *South China Morning Post & Hong Kong Standard*, 16.5.81.

39 *South China Morning Post*, 14.7.81.

40 At the auction of McLean's effects, which started on 29.11.80, Aileen Bridgewater acquired a box of old tapes and later found that they were not blanks but records of McLean's telephone conversations, including of some of his criminal dealings. She played excerpts from some of these on air and they were promptly seized by the police — *South China Morning Post*, 9.12.80 & *Star*, 10.12.80.

41 *South China Morning Post*, 17.10.80.

42 *South China Morning Post*, 23.11.80.

43 Commission of Inquiry Report, pp. 20, 212.

44 Commission of Inquiry Report, pp. 20, 213.

45 *South China Morning Post*, 17.10.80; *South China Morning Post & Hong Kong Standard*, 16.10.80 & 30.10.80.

46 *South China Morning Post*, 14.10.80 & 19.10.80; *Far Eastern Economic Review* 17.10.80. Sinclair was not fully correct; Carratu's team had managed to interview four of the prostitutes giving evidence against MacLennan.

47 Commission of Inquiry Report, p. 222; *Hong Kong Standard*, 30.10.80.

21 Opening Moves

1 Opening Address by John Beveridge, 29.10.80, p. 25, in the Bridgewater Collection. He was following the Salmon Rules.

2 Commission of Inquiry Report, p. 16.

3 Commission of Inquiry Report, p. 15. Audrey Eu Yuet-mee, LLB, LLM, SC, JP (born 1953); called to the Hong Kong Bar in 1978; QC in 1993; Chairlady of the Hong Kong Bar Association, 2000–2012; member of the Legislative Council in 2005; founder of the Civic Party. She did not respond to a request for an interview.

4 Opening Address by John Beveridge, 29.10.80, p. 20, in the Bridgewater Collection.

5 Commission of Inquiry Report, pp. 222–224.

6 Commission of Inquiry Report, pp. 219–221, 225–226.

7 *Who's Who*, 1980, p. 211; Law List, Barristers, 1980, p. 210.

8 Interview with Justice Conrad Seagroatt, 29.5.15.

9 Interview with Murray Burton, 9.2.15.

10 Aileen Bridgewater Diary, 15.1.81, in the Bridgewater Collection.

11 Interview with Barrie Barlow, 31.1.15.

12 Interview with Barrie Barlow, 31.1.15.

13 Interview with Justice Kemal Bokhary, 18.3.15

14 *Hong Kong Standard*, 21.11.80.

15 Interview with Barrie Barlow, 31.1.15.

16 Transcript of the Commission of Inquiry in Hong Kong University, Part III, p. 4,095.

17 Interview with Justice Conrad Seagroatt, 29.5.15.

18 At the end of Aileen Bridgewater's testimony on 10.4.81, Hodge's final remark "Congratulations Mrs Bridgewater on getting off so lightly" was drowned on the PA system by Beveridge calling "No, no, no, no, no" — Aileen Bridgewater Diary, 10.4.81, in the Bridgewater Collection.

19 Justice Kemal Bokhary, *Recollections*, p. 477.

20 Aileen Bridgewater Diary, 13.5.81, in the Bridgewater Collection.

21 Reeder had left the week before; *South China Morning Post* & *Hong Kong Standard*, 11.11.80.

22 Letter Vince Carratu to Elsie Elliott, 25.11.80, in the Elsie Tu (Elliott) Papers in Hong Kong Baptist University Library, MSS 13 Correspondence and Press Statements 1979–1981 13 1.

23 *South China Morning Post* & *Hong Kong Standard*, 10.2.81.

24 Aileen Bridgewater Diary, 22.2.81, in the Bridgewater Collection.

25 Aileen Bridgewater Diary, 1.3.81, in the Bridgewater Collection.

26 Letter Vince Carratu to Elsie Elliott, 15.6.80, in the Bridgewater Collection.

27 Aileen Bridgewater Diary, 22.2.81, in the Bridgewater Collection.

28 Interview Aileen and Ken Bridgewater, 15.5.13.

29 Aileen Bridgewater Diary, 6.10.80, in the Bridgewater Collection.

30 Transcript of the Commission of Inquiry, pp. 125–141, in FCO papers released

under the Freedom of Information Act, in the Bridgewater Collection, attached to minute from Paul Fifoot, Legal Adviser FCO, to Footman, 15.7.88.

31 Commission of Inquiry Report, pp. 20, 222; *Star*, *South China Morning Post* & *Hong Kong Standard*, 31.10.80.

32 *Hong Kong Standard*, 22.10.80.

33 Commission of Inquiry Report, pp. 21, 216; *Star*, 8.1.81; *Hong Kong Standard*, 9.1.81; interview Murray Burton, 9.2.15.

34 Commission of Inquiry Report, pp. 216–217.

35 MacLehose telex to Ford, 15.1.80, FCO 40/1351 Hong Kong Laws on Homosexuality.

22 The SIU Case Collapses

1 The test was carried out on 28.4.81, Commission of Inquiry Report, p. 100.

2 *South China Morning Post* & *Hong Kong Standard*, 29.4.81; Commission of Inquiry Report, pp. 254, et ff.

3 *South China Morning Post* & *Hong Kong Standard*, 30.4.81; Commission of Inquiry Report, pp. 301, et ff.

4 Press release, 2.5.81, HKRS570-8-3382 Police — Case of John MacLennan; the test was on 3.5.81.

5 Commission of Inquiry Report, pp. 332, et ff; *South China Morning Post* & *Hong Kong Standard*, 5.5.81.

6 *Star, South China Morning Post* & *Hong Kong Standard*, 31.10.80 & 1.11.80; *South China Morning Post* & *Hong Kong Standard*, 4.11.80, 6.11.80 & 7.11.80; *South China Morning Post*, 5.11.80; *Hong Kong Standard*, 8.11.80.

7 *South China Morning Post* & *Hong Kong Standard*, 11.11.80.

8 *South China Morning Post* & *Hong Kong Standard*, 12.11.80, 13.11.80, 14.11.80.

9 *Hong Kong Standard*, 20.11.80; *South China Morning Post* & *Hong Kong Standard*, 21.11.80.

10 *South China Morning Post* & *Hong Kong Standard*, 22.11.80, 28.11.80 & 29.11.80.

11 *South China Morning Post* & *Hong Kong Standard*, 2.12.80 & 3.12.80; *South China Morning Post*, 5.12.80.

12 *South China Morning Post* & *Hong Kong Standard*, 9.12.80.

13 Commission of Inquiry Report, p. 225.

14 *South China Morning Post* & *Hong Kong Standard*, 15.1.81.

15 *South China Morning Post* & *Hong Kong Standard*, 15.1.81.

16 *South China Morning Post*, 4.3.80; HKRS70-8-1873 Homosexuality 1980–1983.

17 *South China Morning Post* & *Hong Kong Standard*, 28.1.81.

18 The Li Kwan-ha Report is at Commission of Inquiry Report, pp. 336–346, and the Pelly Report at pp. 355–391.

19 Commission of Inquiry Report, Li Kwan-ha Report, p. 342.

20 *South China Morning Post* & *Hong Kong Standard*, 25.3.81 & 26.3.81.

21 *South China Morning Post* & *Hong Kong Standard*, 1.4.81 & 2.4.81.

22 *South China Morning Post* & *Hong Kong Standard*, 9.4.81.

23 *South China Morning Post* & *Hong Kong Standard*, 11.4.81.

24 Commission of Inquiry Report, p. 256.

25 *South China Morning Post* & *Hong Kong Standard*, 14.4.81 & 15.4.81.

23 Discrediting the Police

1 *South China Morning Post* & *Hong Kong Standard*, 10.2.81; *South China Morning Post*, 11.2.81.

2 *South China Morning Post* & *Hong Kong Standard*, 11.2.81, 12.2.81, 13.2.81, 14.2.81.

3 *South China Morning Post* & *Hong Kong Standard*, 17.2.81, 18.2.81, 19.2.81, 20.2.81.

4 *South China Morning Post* & *Hong Kong Standard*, 17.2.81, 18.2.81, 19.2.81, 20.2.81, 24.2.81; *Hong Kong Standard*, 26.2.81; *Star*, *South China Morning Post* & *Hong Kong Standard*, 21.2.81.

5 Interview with Barrie Barlow, 31.1.15.

6 Interview with Iain Grant, 4.6.15.

7 *South China Morning Post* & *Hong Kong Standard*, 26.2.81, 27.2.81.

8 Transcript of the Commission of Inquiry in Hong Kong University, Part V, p. 7,076.

9 *South China Morning Post* & *Hong Kong Standard*, 4.3.81, 6.3.81, 7.3.81; *Star, South China Morning Post* & *Hong Kong Standard*, 10.3.81, 11.3.81. Transcript of the Commission of Inquiry in Hong Kong University, Part V, pp. 6,755–6,756, 6,832, 6,870, 7,268, 7,428, 7,584–7,586, 7,609, 7,618.

10 Transcript of the Commission of Inquiry in Hong Kong University, Part V, pp. 7,548–7,564.

11 Interview Justice Kemal Bokhary, 18.3.15.

12 Transcript of the Commission of Inquiry in Hong Kong University, Part V, p. 6,988.

13 *South China Morning Post* & *Hong Kong Standard*, 13.3.81, 14.3.81, 18.3.81; *Star, South China Morning Post* & *Hong Kong Standard*, 17.3.81.

14 *South China Morning Post* & *Hong Kong Standard*, 19.12.80.

15 *South China Morning Post* & *Hong Kong Standard*, 24.3.81.

16 *South China Morning Post* & *Hong Kong Standard*, 19.3.81, 20.3.81, 21.3.81.

17 *South China Morning Post* & *Hong Kong Standard*, 27.3.81, 28.3.81, 31.3.81, 1.4.81.

18 *South China Morning Post* & *Hong Kong Standard*, 1.5.81, 2.5.81.

19 Roy Henry's statement of 1.5.81 is in the Elsie Tu (Elliott) Papers in Hong Kong Baptist University Library, MSS 13 Death of John MacLennan. Inquest & Inquiry: Statements, Reports, Correspondence and Papers, 1978–1979 13.5.

20 FCO brief for Lord Carrington, 26.9.80, FCO papers released under the Freedom of Information Act in the Bridgewater Collection.

21 *Star*, 8.4.81.

22 Transcript of the Commission of Inquiry in Hong Kong University, Part VI, pp. 11,370–11,371.

23 There is no documentary record of this. Interview Murray Burton 9.2.15.

24 Interview Peter Crush, 18–19.3.15.

25 Transcript of the Commission of Inquiry in Hong Kong University, Part VI, p. 11,394.

26 *South China Morning Post* & *Hong Kong Standard*, 12.5.81, 13.5.81; Aileen Bridgewater Diary, 12.5.81, in the Bridgewater Collection.

27 Transcript of the Commission of Inquiry in Hong Kong University, Part VI, pp. 11,400–11,401.

28 Transcript of the Commission of Inquiry in Hong Kong University, Part VI, pp. 11,492–11,493.

29 Transcript of the Commission of Inquiry in Hong Kong University, Part VI, pp. 11,509.

30 Transcript of the Commission of Inquiry in Hong Kong University, Part VI, pp. 11,514–11,517.

24 Hostile Witnesses

1 *South China Morning Post* & *Hong Kong Standard*, 11.12.80; *South China*

Morning Post & *Star*, 12.12.80; *South China Morning Post, Hong Kong Standard, Sun* & *Star*, 10.12.80.

2 Transcript of the Commission of Inquiry in Hong Kong University, Part II, pp. 2,317, 2,419–2,420, 2,423, 2,429.

3 Transcript of the Commission of Inquiry in Hong Kong University, Part II, pp. 2,368–2,390.

4 *South China Morning Post* & *Hong Kong Standard*, 29.1.81.

5 Transcript of the Commission of Inquiry in Hong Kong University, Part II, pp. 3,606 et ff.

6 Transcript of the Commission of Inquiry in Hong Kong University, Part II, p. 3,771.

7 Transcript of the Commission of Inquiry in Hong Kong University, Part II, pp. 3,634–3,635.

8 Transcript of the Commission of Inquiry in Hong Kong University, Part II, pp. 3,908–3,915.

9 Transcript of the Commission of Inquiry in Hong Kong University, Part II, p. 3,853.

10 Aileen Bridgewater Diary, 22.1.81, 23.1.81, in the Bridgewater Collection; *Star*, 16.1.80; *Star, South China Morning Post* & *Hong Kong Standard*, 17.1.81; *South China Morning Post* & *Hong Kong Standard*, 20.1.81, 21.1.81, 22.1.81, 23.1.81, 27.1.81.

11 Transcript of the Commission of Inquiry in Hong Kong University, Part II, p. 4,464–4,467.

12 Aileen Bridgewater Diary, 10.2.81, in the Bridgewater Collection.

13 Elsie Elliott letter to John Richard Duffy — Elsie Tu (Elliott) papers in the Hong Kong Baptist University Library, "The Death of Inspector MacLennan", 20.4.81.

14 Aileen Bridgewater Diary, 8.5.81, in the Bridgewater Collection.8.5.81; *Star*, 8.5.81; *South China Morning Post* & *Hong Kong Standard*, 9.5.81.

15 *South China Morning Post*, 6.6.80.

16 Letter Elsie Elliott to Howard Lindsay, 19.4.81, in the Elsie Tu (Elliott) Papers in the Hong Kong Baptist University Library, MSS 13 11.7 Cases of Homosexual Charges 1975-1981.

17 *South China Morning Post* & *Hong Kong Standard*, 20.12.80.

18 Transcript of the Commission of Inquiry in Hong Kong University, Part II, p. 2,999.

19 *South China Morning Post* & *Hong Kong Standard*, 6.1.81; Transcript of the Commission of Inquiry in Hong Kong University, Part II, pp. 3,043–3,097.

20 Letter Elsie Elliott to Howard Lindsay, 19.4.81, in the Elsie Tu (Elliott) Papers in the Hong Kong Baptist University Library, MSS 13 11.7 Cases of Homosexual Charges 1975–1981.

21 Elsie Elliott letter to Joe Duffy, 18.5.81; Commission of Inquiry, p. 396.

22 Elsie Elliott letter to Judge Duffy, 3.3.87, in the Elsie Tu (Elliott) Papers in the Hong Kong Baptist University Library, MSS 13 Manuscripts 1978–1987 12 4.

23 Elsie Elliott letter to Judge Duffy, 6.3.96, in the Elsie Tu (Elliott) Papers in the Hong Kong Baptist University Library, MSS.13 Death of John MacLennan. Inquest & Inquiry: Statements, Reports, Correspondence and Papers, 1980–1996 13.6

24 Judge Duffy letter to Elsie Elliott, 14.3.87, in the Elsie Tu (Elliott) Papers in the Hong Kong Baptist University Library, MSS 13 Manuscripts 1978–1987 12 4.

25 Intervention

1 Aileen Bridgewater Diary, 7.5.81, in the Bridgewater Collection.

2 11.9.80, 26.9.80, FCO 40/1160 Visit By Secretary of State for Foreign Affairs to Hong Kong.

3 11.12.80, FCO 40/1264 H.M.G.'s Responsibilities for Internal Matters In Hong Kong.

4 *Hong Kong Standard*, 16.1.81, 28.1.81.

5 Chief Secretary memorandum for the Executive Council, 25.3.81, in FCO 40/1351 Hong Kong Laws on Homosexuality.

6 Minute by Crown Solicitor, F.M.T. Jones, to the Governor, post 26.2.81, FCO papers released through the Freedom of Information Act, in the Bridgewater Collection.

7 Minute Morrice to R.D. Clift, 23.12.80, FCO papers released through the Freedom of Information Act, in the Bridgewater Collection.

8 Telex Lord Carrington to Governor, 101630 Feb. 80, informing him that he had met the AG on 9.1.80. Minute 12.1.80 by R.D. Clift to Donald, DUS; minute R.D. Clift to Peter Blaker, 16.2.81; FCO papers released through the Freedom of Information Act, in the Bridgewater Collection.

9 Donald handwritten memo to Sir Edward Youde, 9.2.81, FCO papers released through the Freedom of Information Act, in the Bridgewater Collection.

10 AG telex to Governor, 2.1.81, in FCO 40/1351 Hong Kong Laws on Homosexuality.

11 The Salmon principles stated that:

(1) Before any person becomes involved in an inquiry, the Tribunal must be satisfied that there are circumstances which affect him and which the Tribunal proposes to investigate.

(2) Before any person who is involved in an inquiry is called as a witness, he should be informed of any allegations which are made against him and the

substance of the evidence in support of them (the Salmon letters).

(3) (a) He should be given an adequate opportunity of preparing his case and of being assisted by his legal advisers.

(b) His legal expenses should normally be met out of public funds.

(4) He should have the opportunity of being examined by his own solicitor or counsel and of stating his case in public at the inquiry.

(5) Any material witness he wishes called at the inquiry should, if reasonably practicable, be heard.

(6) He should have the opportunity of testing by cross-examination conducted by his own solicitor or counsel any evidence which may affect him.

12 Commission of Inquiry Report, p. 16; on 7.1.81.

13 Transcript of the Commission of Inquiry in Hong Kong University, Part II, pp. 3,039–3,040. Beveridge had made it clear in his opening address on 24 October that the Commission was following the Salmon rules, which Barlow would have known. The reason for his effrontery was political.

14 Interview Justice Conrad Seagroatt, 29.3.15.

15 *South China Morning Post*, 15.1.81; Transcript of the Commission of Inquiry in Hong Kong University, Part II, pp. 3,504 et ff.

16 Telex Governor to R.D. Clift, 13.2.81, FCO papers released through the Freedom of Information Act, in the Bridgewater Collection.

17 Minute R.D. Clift to Peter Blaker, 16.2.81, FCO papers released through the Freedom of Information Act, in the Bridgewater Collection.

18 Telex Lord Carrington to Governor, 16.2.81, FCO papers released through the Freedom of Information Act, in the Bridgewater Collection.

19 Letter Zimmern & Co, Solicitors for the Commission, to AG, 18.2.81 (listing six points which would affect him, including giving immunity to the two prostitutes who had testified against Howard Lindsay); FCO papers released through the Freedom of Information Act, in the Bridgewater Collection.

20 Governor letter to R.D. Clift, 28.2.81, FCO papers released through the Freedom of Information Act, in the Bridgewater Collection.

21 Governor minute to AG, 26.2.81, FCO papers released through the Freedom of Information Act, in the Bridgewater Collection.

22 Letter Justice Yang to the Chief Secretary, 4.3.81, in FCO 40/1351 Hong Kong Laws on Homosexuality.

23 Interview with Barrie Barlow, 31.1.15.

24 F.T.M. Jones, Crown Counsel, Acting Crown Solicitor, later Acting Attorney

General.

25 Minute AG to Governor, 6.3.81, FCO papers released through the Freedom of Information Act, in the Bridgewater Collection.

26 Brief by F.M.T. Jones, undated, FCO papers released through the Freedom of Information Act, in the Bridgewater Collection.

27 Interview with Barrie Barlow, 31.1.15.

28 Record of the Governor's Meeting with Minister Peter Blaker, 10.3.81, in FCO 40/1351 Hong Kong Laws on Homosexuality.

29 Minute by P. Morrice to Mr Clift, 13 March 1981, in FCO papers forwarded under a Freedom of Information Request.

30 Decision of the Hong Kong Executive Council 25.3.15, in FCO 40/1351 Hong Kong Laws on Homosexuality.

31 FCO 40/1276 Visit by Secretary of State for Foreign Affairs to Hong Kong and the Far East, telexes, 13 April 1981.

32 Rt. Hon. Sir Andrew Peter Leggatt QC, PC (born 1930); Recorder 1974–1982; Bencher Inner Temple 1976; a member of the Top Salaries Review Body from 1979–1982; Chairman of the Bar 1981–1982; High Court Judge 1982; Lord Justice of Appeal 1990–1997; Chief Surveillance Commissioner 1998–2006; Chairman of independent review of tribunals 2000–2001. Sir Andrew was unable to recollect any detail about the case; email Sir Andrew Leggatt to the author 25.9.16.

33 Telex Governor to FCO, 15.4.81, in FCO 40/1351 Hong Kong Laws on Homosexuality.

34 Interview with Sir Ti-Liang Yang, 5 September 2016.

35 On 29.4.81; Commission of Inquiry Report, p. 16.

26 Endgame

1 *Hong Kong Standard* & *South China Morning Post*, 16.1.81.

2 Aileen Bridgewater Diary, 13.5.81, in the Bridgewater Collection.

3 Aileen Bridgewater Diary, 15.5.81, in the Bridgewater Collection.

4 Transcript of the Commission of Inquiry in Hong Kong University, Part VII, pp. 11,585–11,931.

5 Aileen Bridgewater Diary, 15.5.81, in the Bridgewater Collection.

6 Interview with Justice Conrad Seagroatt, 29.5.15.

7 Transcript of the Commission of Inquiry in Hong Kong University, Part VII, pp.

12,027–12,030.

8 *Hong Kong Standard* & *South China Morning Post*, 21.5.81; *Hong Kong Standard*, 22.5.81.

9 *Hong Kong Standard* & *South China Morning Post*, 2.6.81. Sir Robert Andrew Morritt CVO (born 1938), later Chancellor of the High Court of England and Wales.

10 Interview with Sir Ti-Liang Yang, 5.9.16; *Hong Kong Standard* & *South China Morning Post*, 3.6.81.

11 *Hong Kong Standard* & *South China Morning Post*, 29.5.81.

12 *Hong Kong Standard* & *South China Morning Post*, 29.5.81.

13 *Hong Kong Standard* & *South China Morning Post*, 30.5.81.

14 *Hong Kong Standard* & *South China Morning Post*, 2.6.81.

15 *Hong Kong Standard* & *South China Morning Post*, 30.5.81.

16 *Hong Kong Standard* & *South China Morning Post*, 28.5.81.

17 Transcript of the Commission of Inquiry in Hong Kong University, Part VII, pp. 12,405–12,448.

18 Transcript of the Commission of Inquiry in Hong Kong University, Part VII, pp. 12,405–12,448.

19 *Hong Kong Standard* & *South China Morning Post*, 3.6.81.

27 The Commission Report

1 Interview with Murray Burton, 9.2.81.

2 *Hong Kong Standard* & *South China Morning Post*, 2.8.81. The single copy of the draft report was nearly destroyed by a fire in the Government Secretariat, where it had been stored in a locked cabinet, but in the event the draft was unscathed; interview with Sir Ti-Liang Yang, 5.9.16.

3 Memorandum covering the Report to the Executive Council, 22.8.81, in FCO 40/1351 Hong Kong Laws on Homosexuality; *South China Morning Post*, 29.9.81; *Hong Kong Standard* & *South China Morning Post*, 30.9.81.

4 Commission of Inquiry Summary, p. 16, paragraph 110.

5 Commission of Inquiry Report, pp. 113–114.

6 Commission of Inquiry Report, pp. 117, 119, 161.

7 Commission of Inquiry Report, p. 85; Commission of Inquiry Summary, pp. 7–8.

8 Commission of Inquiry Report, p. 92.

9 Commission of Inquiry Report, pp. 75, 242–243.

10 Commission of Inquiry Report, p. 116

11 Commission of Inquiry Report, pp. 86–88.

12 Commission of Inquiry Report, p. 88.

13 Commission of Inquiry Report, p. 92.

14 Commission of Inquiry Report, pp. 47, 71.

15 Commission of Inquiry Report, pp. 49, 51.

16 Commission of Inquiry Report, pp. 73, 79.

17 Commission of Inquiry Report, p. 74.

18 Commission of Inquiry Report, pp. 165–179.

19 Commission of Inquiry Report, p. 92.

20 Commission of Inquiry Report, p. 174.

21 Commission of Inquiry Report, p. 176.

22 Commission of Inquiry Report, pp. 177–179.

23 Commission of Inquiry Report, pp. 179–183.

24 Commission of Inquiry Report, pp. 179–183.

28 Justice T.L. Yang

1 Brief by F.M.T. Jones for the Governor, undated, FCO papers released under the Freedom of Information Act, in the Bridgewater Collection and in part, 25.3.81, FCO 40/1351 Hong Kong Laws on Homosexuality.

2 Post visit note McQuade, 14–28.10.81, FCO 40/1279 Visit by FCO officials to Hong Kong.

29 Aftermath

1 Note on a meeting between Nicholas Ridley, Minister of State at the FCO, and HE the Governor of Hong Kong, 25.8.81, – FCO 40/1281 Visit to the United Kingdom by the Governor of Hong Kong.

2 Note by Clift of the Hong Kong Desk to Ridley, Lord Privy Seal, 28.9.81, FCO 40/1351 Hong Kong Laws on Homosexuality.

3 Minute A. R. Rushford to Mr. Williamson, Hong Kong & General Desk, 28.8.81, FCO papers released under the Freedom of Information Act, in the Bridgewater Collection.

4 *South China Morning Post*, 29.9.81; *South China Morning Post* & *Hong Kong Standard*, 30.9.81.

5 Letter Governor to Hong Kong & General Department, 17.9.81, FCO papers released under the Freedom of Information Act, in the Bridgewater Collection.

6 Letter H. Steel of AG's department letter to A.R. Rushford, CMG, 20.10.81; memorandum A.R. Rushford, Deputy Legal Adviser, to R.D. Clift, 22.10.81; letter R.D. Clift, Hong Kong & General Department, to Governor, 23.10.81, FCO papers released under the Freedom of Information Act, in the Bridgewater Collection.

7 *South China Morning Post*, 2.10.81.

8 The release of 29.9.81 is at HKRS570-8-3382 Police — Case of John MacLennan.

9 *South China Morning Post*, 11.11.81.

10 17.12.81 R.D. Clift Hong Kong & General Department, FCO reply to a question by Robin Cook MP. Thirteen police officers were named in the report. Three had been referred to the Complaints Against the Police Office; the Commissioner of Police was considering administrative action against three officers. FCO 40/1351 Hong Kong Laws on Homosexuality

11 *South China Morning Post*, 1.10.81.

12 MacLehose telex to FCO, 29.9.81, FCO 40/1351 Hong Kong Laws On Homosexuality.

13 Elsie Elliott, "The MacLennan Affair", undated but 10.81, in Hong Kong University, Hong Kong Baptist University Library, and the Bridgewater Collection.

14 Elsie Elliott, "The MacLennan Affair", p. 14, undated but 10.81, in Hong Kong University, Hong Kong Baptist University Library, and the Bridgewater Collection.

15 Letter Elsie Elliott to the AG, 3.6.81, in Elsie Tu (Elliott) Papers in Hong Kong Baptist University Library, MSS 13 Correspondence and Press Statements 1979–1981 13 1.

16 Letter Elsie Elliott to Justice Yang, 2.10.81, Elsie Tu (Elliott) Papers in Hong Kong Baptist University Library, MSS 13 Death of John MacLennan. Inquest & Inquiry: Statements, Reports, Correspondence and Papers, 1980–1996 13.6.

17 Letter Max Lucas for the AG to Elsie Elliott, 3.11.82: "all matters were dealt with". "No real point in canvassing the whole matter again", Elsie Tu (Elliott) Papers in Hong Kong Baptist University Library, MSS 13 Manuscripts 1978–1987 12 4.

18 Letter Elsie Elliott to AG, 27.10.82, Elsie Tu (Elliott) Papers in Hong Kong Baptist University Library, MSS 13 Manuscripts 1978–1987 12 4.

19 Letter Elsie Elliott to AG, 10.11.82, Elsie Tu (Elliott) Papers in Hong Kong Baptist University Library, MSS 13 Manuscripts 1978–1987 12 4.

20 *South China Morning Post* & *Hong Kong Standard*, 6.10.81.

21 Aileen Bridgewater manuscript note of a conversation with Vincent Carratu, ?8.83, in the Bridgewater collection.

22 Henry Lethbridge, "Pandora's Box: The Inspector MacLennan Enigma", *Hong Kong Law Journal*, vol. 12, no. 1, pp. 4–30.

23 *Hong Kong Standard*, 6.2.82.

24 Interview Elsie Tu, 29.6.11.

25 *Star*, 8.1.81; HKRS70-8-1873 Homosexuality 1980–1983.

26 Copy in the Bridgewater Collection.

27 Letter Elsie Elliott to Martin Rowlands, 29.1.82, Elsie Tu (Elliott) Papers in Hong Kong Baptist University Library, MSS 13 Manuscripts 1978–1987 12 4.

28 *South China Morning Post* & *Hong Kong Standard*, 1.2.81.

29 *Guardian*, 27.2.82; HKRS531-1-4 Editorial and Articles of Police Interest 1980–1982.

30 *South China Morning Post*, 1.2.83; interview Jim Kushner, 5.8.15; email Peter Moss to the author, 20.5.11; information from an anonymous friend of Peter Winder, 8.10.15; interview with Stuart Wolfendale, 20.9.16.

31 The release for the report's issue is at HKRS70-8-1869 Homosexuality 1980–1983; *South China Morning Post*, 8.6.83.

32 The Law Reform Commission of Hong Kong, "Report on Laws Governing Homosexual Conduct", p. A1.

33 20.6.83, HKRS70-8-1869 Homosexuality 1980–1983.

34 White Paper, "Homosexual Offences: Should the Law Be Changed?" (Hong Kong: Government Printer, 1988).

35 Edward Douglas-Scott-Montagu, 3rd Baron Montagu of Beaulieu, was convicted in 1954 of sex on his own property with a male RAF serviceman; he was imprisoned for twelve months.

36 The Law Reform Commission of Hong Kong, "Report on Laws Governing Homosexual Conduct", pp. 20–21, 23.

37 Press release, 14.1.82, HKRS70-8-1871 Homosexuality 1980–1983.

38 *Hong Kong Standard*, 11.10.85.

39 *Hong Kong Standard*, 11.6.82.

40 Email "Cambus" to the author, 30 June 2016.

41 Interview with Stuart Wolfendale, 20.9.16.

42 The police were still doing this in the late nineties, although they no longer asked details of employers.

43 Interview Jim Kushner, 5.8.15.

44 Interview with Graham Elsom, 27.7.15.

45 *Hong Kong Standard*, 13.2.82; HKRS70-8-1873 Homosexuality 1980–1983.

46 *Gay News*, 8.7.81. The Law Reform Commission of Hong Kong, "Report on Laws Governing Homosexual Conduct", p. 104 and Annexure 12, p. A121, give detail of a submission Neil Duncan and Mr T.L. Tsim of the Movement for Homosexual Law Reform gave to the sub-committee, which included a proposition for reform that they had submitted to the Government in 1979.

47 *Star*, 4.6.82. The Waltzing Matilda survived, and when it moved location in 1989, became the New Wally Matt Lounge, which today, after several more moves, is still the "Wally Matt".

48 Interview with Danny Wong, 14.5.15.

49 The Festival has been running ever since.

50 *South China Morning Post*, 18.1.89, 22.9.96.

51 Interview Aileen & Ken Bridgewater, 15.5.13.

52 Wikipedia has multiple references for the North Wales child abuse scandal at https://en.wikipedia.org/wiki/North_Wales_child_abuse_scandal.

53 Wikipedia has multiple references for the Kincora Boys' Home scandal at https://en.wikipedia.org/wiki/Kincora_Boys%27_Home.

54 Wikipedia has multiple references for the Elm Guest House scandal at https://en.wikipedia.org/wiki/Elm_Guest_House_child_abuse_scandal.

55 His obituary in *The Times* of 1.6.00 is glowing.

56 Letter Elsie Elliott to the Governor, 5.10.80, in Elsie Tu (Elliott) Papers in Hong Kong Baptist University Library, MSS 13 11.7 Cases Of Homosexual Charges 1975–1981.

57 Letter Elsie Elliot to Gordon Huthard, 4.10.81, in Elsie Tu (Elliott) Papers in Hong Kong Baptist University Library, MSS 13 Death of John MacLennan. Inquest & Inquiry: Statements, Reports, Correspondence and Papers, 1980–1996 13.6.

58 Andrew & Elsie Tu, *Shouting at the Mountain*, p. 173.

59 The AG was unclear in public on his attitude to this issue. His press release of 18.3.80, after the Inquest, included comment that changing the law on homosexuality must "be approached in a very balanced way because account would have to be taken not only of purely legal considerations but also of social attitudes and consequences", HKRS70-8-1869 Homosexuality 1980–1983. His press release of 25.5.80 said that he agreed that the law on homosexuality be reviewed by the Law Reform Commission and at the Commission of Inquiry gave his view that the law in the United Kingdom on homosexuality was more

appropriately framed than in Hong Kong. *South China Morning Post* & *Hong Kong Standard*, 13.5.81.

60 Aileen Bridgewater Diary, 23.6.81, in the Bridgewater Collection.

61 Minute by Clift of a meeting with the AG, 2.6.71, — FCO 40/1273 Visits to the United Kingdom by Officials from Hong Kong.

62 *South China Morning Post*, 11.6.83.

63 Companion of the Order of St Michael and St George.

64 Commander of the Most Excellent Order of the British Empire.

65 Interview with Justice Conrad Seagroatt, 29.5.15.

66 *South China Morning Post*, 22.7.81.

67 Interview with an anonymous source, 21.1.15.

68 HKRS70-8-1873 Homosexuality 1980–1983, 19.5.81.

69 Interview with Justice Kemal Bokhary, 18.3.15; Barrie Barlow, 31.1.15.

70 *South China Morning Post*, 14.4.85 & 12.5.98.

71 *South China Morning Post*, 22.6.83, 16.8.83, 17.8.83.

72 *South China Morning Post*, 11.7.93.

73 *South China Morning Post*, 5.10.81, 10.9.87.

74 *South China Morning Post*, 3.4.82.

75 *South China Morning Post* & *Hong Kong Standard*, 11.4.81.

76 Power of Attorney given to John Conway by Katherine MacLennan, 3.12.81, in the Bridgewater Collection.

77 Letter Aileen Bridgewater to Hampton, Winter & Glynn, 19.3.83, in the Bridgewater Collection.

78 *South China Morning Post*, 25.2.83; *South China Morning Post* & *Hong Kong Standard*, 21.3.83; letter John Conway to the Governor, 16.3.83, in the Bridgewater Collection.

79 Letter J.A. Harrison to the Director, Councils & Administration Branch, Hong Kong Government, 16.3.83; letter Aileen Bridgewater to Hampton, Winter & Glynn, 19.3.83, in the Bridgewater Collection.

80 *Hong Kong Standard*, 17.11.82.

81 Letter John Conway to Sir Edward Youde, 1.3.83, in the Bridgewater Collection.

82 *Hong Kong Standard*, 4.11.85.

83 *Hong Kong Standard*, 11.12.87. The correspondence is: letters John Conway to Sir Geoffrey Howe, Foreign Secretary, 27.11.87, and to Margaret Thatcher, Prime

Minister, 30.11.87, enclosing his "Conway Report", and minute Paul Fifoot, Legal Adviser FCO to Footman, Hong Kong & General Desk, 15.7.88: "The latter [the Conway Report] does not call for any serious response [being full of] assertion, it is completely devoid of evidence and reads very like a trailer for a TV soap opera."

84 *Hong Kong Standard*, 9.6.88; John Conway, *To Speak for the Dead* (Nuneaton: John Conway, 1994), Chapter 2, pp. 9, et ff.

85 *South China Morning Post*, 22.12.85. Aileen Bridgewater, *Talk of Hong Kong* (Hong Kong: Phoenix Books, 1985), Chapter 23, pp. 280, et ff.

86 Manuscript interview notes, Aileen Bridgewater with Mr and Mrs MacLennan, 31.8.83, in the Bridgewater Collection.

87 Interview Ken & Aileen Bridgewater, 15.5.13.

88 *South China Morning Post*, 16.2.81, 18.2.81; *Hong Kong Standard*, 17.2.81.

89 Aileen Bridgewater Diary, 27.6.81, in the Bridgewater Collection.

90 Elsie Tu, Chapter 33, "The MacLennan Case", *An Autobiography*, (Hong Kong: Longman, 1988).

91 Andrew and Elsie Tu, *Shouting at the Mountain: A Hong Kong Story of Love and Commitment* (Hong Kong: Chameleon, 2004), p. 201 "Justice and Injustice".

92 Ken Bridgewater, *Open Verdict* (Singapore: Trafford, 2013).

93 John Conway, "Conway Report", p. 24.

94 Manuscript interview notes, Aileen Bridgewater with Mr and Mrs MacLennan, 31.8.83, in the Bridgewater Collection.

Bibliography

THE NATIONAL ARCHIVES, KEW

Allegations of Corruption against the Police in Hong Kong, 1981, FCO 40/1354.

Allegations of Corruption and Bribery in Hong Kong,1977, FCO 40/827.

Allegations of Corruption and Bribery in Hong Kong, 1977, FCO 40/828.

Allegations of Corruption and Bribery in Hong Kong, 1980, FCO 40/1209.

Appointment of a Commissioner against Corruption in Hong Kong, 1978, FCO 40/931.

Appointment of Attorney General and Solicitor General in Hong Kong, 1978, FCO 40/854.

Appointment of Attorney General and Solicitor General in Hong Kong, 1978, FCO 40/855.

Appointment of Chief Justice Hong Kong, 1973, FCO 40/441.

Appointment of Governor of Hong Kong, 1978, FCO 40/929.

Appointments of Senior Officials in Hong Kong, 1980, FCO 40/1259.

Baron MacLehose of Beoch, LCO 57/562.

Corruption Case Proposals by Hong Kong for Dismissal under Colonial Regulation 55; Police Officers, 1978, FCO 40/869.

Dependent Territories Senior Appointments Board, 1978, FCO 40/873.

Dependent Territories Senior Appointments Board, 1979, FCO 40/1035.

Disturbances by Police in Hong Kong,1977, FCO 40/836.

Disturbances by Police in Hong Kong,1977, FCO 40/837.

Extradition Case: Peter Fitzroy Godber, Former Chief Superintendent in the Hong Kong Police; Application of "Double Criminality Rule"; UK relations with Hong Kong, 1973–1974, HO 306/143 .

Guidelines for the Governor of Hong Kong, 1971, FCO 40/329.

Handling of Parliamentary Business on Hong Kong, 1981, FCO 40/1260.

Handling of Parliamentary Business on Hong Kong, 1981, FCO 40/1261.

Her Majesty's Government's Responsibility for Internal Affairs in Hong Kong, 1981, FCO 40/1264.

Hong Kong Annual Review, 1977, CO1071/183.

Hong Kong Annual Review, 1978, FCO 40/1047.

Hong Kong Annual Review, 1980, FCO 40/1263.

Hong Kong Review, 1978, CO 1071/184.

Hong Kong Review, 1979, CO 1071/185.

Hong Kong Review, 1981, CO 1071/187.

Hong Kong Review,1980, CO 1071/186.

Legislation on Homosexuality in Hong Kong: including report of the Commission of Inquiry into the Inspector MacLennan case (HKK 380/1), 1981, FCO 40/1351.

Local Intelligence Committee Assessment of Political Situation in Hong Kong,1977, FCO 40/757.

Local Intelligence Committee Assessment of Political Situation in Hong Kong, 1978, FCO 40/940.

Local Intelligence Committee Assessment of Political Situation in Hong Kong, 1981, FCO 40/1298.

Policy on Salaries for Civil Servants in Hong Kong, 1978, FCO 40/1029.

Policy on Salaries for Civil Servants in Hong Kong, 1978, FCO 40/1030.

Policy on Salaries for Civil Servants in Hong Kong, 1979, FCO 40/1127.

Presence of Warsaw Pact Countries in Hong Kong, 1978, FCO 40/949.

Progress Reports on Security Branch of Government of Hong Kong, 1977, FCO 40/846.

Quarterly Progress reports from Hong Kong, 1978, FCO 40/944.

Quarterly Reports on Hong Kong, 1981, FCO 40/1265.

Quarterly Reports on Hong Kong, 1981, FCO 40/1266.

Relations between Hong Kong and the Soviet Union, 1980, FCO 40/1153.

Reports on Leading Personalities in Hong Kong, 1980, FCO 40/1258.

RHKP Annual Review, 1977, FCO 40/1026.

Secondment of Deputy Commissioner of Police in Hong Kong, 1977, FCO 40/835.

Visit of Lord Carrington, Secretary of State for Foreign and Commonwealth Affairs, to Hong Kong, 1979, FCO 40/1053.

Visit of Lord Carrington, Secretary of State for Foreign and Commonwealth Affairs, to Hong Kong, 1979, FCO 40/1054.

Visit of Lord Carrington, Secretary of State for Foreign and Commonwealth Affairs, to Hong Kong in September, postponed, 1980, FCO 40/1160.

Visit of Lord Carrington, Secretary of State for Foreign and Commonwealth Affairs, to Hong Kong in September, postponed, 1980, FCO 21/1815.

Visit of Lord Carrington, Secretary of State for Foreign and Commonwealth Affairs, to Hong Kong in September, postponed, 1980, FCO 21/1849.

Visit of Lord Carrington, Secretary of State for Foreign and Commonwealth Affairs, to Hong Kong in March to April, 1981, FCO 40/1274.

Visit of Lord Carrington, Secretary of State for Foreign and Commonwealth Affairs, to Hong Kong in March to April, 1981, FCO 40/1275.

Visit of Lord Carrington, Secretary of State for Foreign and Commonwealth Affairs, to Hong Kong in March to April, 1981, FCO 40/1276.

Visit of Lord Goronwy Roberts, Minister of State for Foreign and Commonwealth Affairs, to Hong Kong, 1978, FCO40/955.

Visit of Norman Fowler, Minister of Transport, to Hong Kong, in April, 1980,

FCO 40/1155.

Visit of John Nott, Secretary of State for Trade, and Cecil Parkinson, Minister of State for Trade, to Hong Kong, 1980, FCO 40/1157.

Visit of Police Advisers to Hong Kong, 1978, FCO 40/1021.

Visit of Sir Murray MacLehose Governor of Hong Kong to the United Kingdom, 1978, FCO 40/954.

Visit of Sir Murray MacLehose Governor of Hong Kong to the United Kingdom, 1979 and January 1980, FCO 40/1057.

Visit of Sir Murray MacLehose Governor of Hong Kong to the United Kingdom, 1980, FCO 40/1156.

Visit of Sir Murray MacLehose Governor of Hong Kong to the United Kingdom, 1981, FCO 40/1281.

Visits of Foreign and Commonwealth Officials to Hong Kong, 1978, FCO 40/1055.

Visits of Foreign and Commonwealth Officials to Hong Kong, 1978, FCO 40/1056.

Visits of Foreign and Commonwealth Officials to Hong Kong, 1980, FCO 40/1159.

Visits of Foreign and Commonwealth Officials to Hong Kong, 1981, FCO 40/1279.

Visits of Officials from Hong Kong to the United Kingdom, 1981, FCO 40/1273.

HONG KONG PUBLIC RECORD OFFICE

Case of John MacLennan, Police, HKRS570-8-3382.

Case of John MacLennan, Police, HKRS570-8-3383.

Case of John MacLennan, Police, HKRS570-8-3383A.

Case of John MacLennan, Police, HKRS570-8-3384.

Case of John MacLennan, Police, HKRS570-8-3385.

Editorials and Articles of Police Interest 1980–1982, HKRS531-1-4.

Editorials and Articles of Police Interest 1983–1984, HKRS531-1-5.

Editorials and Articles of Police Interest 1983–1984, HKRS531-1-6.

Homosexuality (Social Implications, Legislation, Crimes Connected With) 1979–1984, HKSR 545-1-14-1.

Homosexuality 1976–1979, HKRS 70-9-548.

Homosexuality 1976–1979, HKRS70-8-1870.

Homosexuality 1980–1983, HKRS70-8-1869.

Homosexuality 1980–1983, HKRS70-8-1871.

Homosexuality 1980–1983, HKRS70-8-1873.

Prostitution, HKRS70-8-3639.

Public Order and Security 1971–1983, HKRS545-1-176-2.

Triad Societies 1979–1984 (Including Hong Kong Triad Societies Operating in the United Kingdom), HKRS545-1-229-2.

GOVERNMENT PUBLICATIONS

Commission of Inquiry, *Report of the Commission of Inquiry into Inspector MacLennan's Case 1981* (Hong Kong: Government Printer, 1981).

Commission of Inquiry, *A Summary of the Report of the Commission of Inquiry into Inspector MacLennan's Case 1981* (Hong Kong: Government Printer, 1981).

Hansard, 10 June 1980.

Hong Kong Government, *Homosexual Offences: Should the Law Be Changed?* (Hong Kong: Government Printer, 1988).

Law Reform Commission of Hong Kong, The, *Report on Laws Governing Homosexual Conduct* (Topic 2) (Hong Kong: Government Printer, 1983).

PAPERS

AILEEN AND KEN BRIDGEWATER COLLECTION

Anonymous and undated, "Britain's Triad Secret Service".

Beveridge, John, QC, "Opening Address by Leading Counsel to the Commission", 29.10.80.

Bridgewater, Aileen, Diary, 14.1.80– 6.10.80 (photocopy).

Bridgewater, Aileen, Diary 1.1.81– 31.12.81.

Bridgewater, Aileen, miscellaneous papers:

Aileen Bridgewater's involvement in the MacLennan Case, typescript, undated.

"Anomalies", manuscript, undated.

Blake, Simon. "The Inspector Who Knew Too Much", read on Commercial Radio by Aileen Bridgewater, 7.6.8.

Bridgewater, Aileen. "Neligan and Me" manuscript, undated.

Bridgewater, Aileen to Home Office Pathology Department, 17.6.80.

Bridgewater, Aileen to Nicholas Carroll, Sunday Times, 7.7.80

Bridgewater, Aileen to Schweizerische Graphologische Gesellschaft, 6.7.80.

Bridgewater, Aileen to the City Coroner, New York, 17.6.80.

Bridgewater, Aileen to the Inquiry, statement, 28.10.80.

Carney, W.J., Home Office to Aileen Bridgewater, 30.6.80.

Carroll, Nicholas, *Sunday Times*, to Aileen Bridgewater, 16.7.80.

Chan, Norman T.L. to Aileen Bridgewater, 23.10.80.

Chronology 1974–1980, manuscript, undated.

Chronology, manuscript, 10.7.80 –5.8.80.

"Discrepancies", manuscript, undated.

Deputy Chief Constable,Central Scotland Police, to Aileen Bridgewater, 6.6.80.

Dr Haldimann Edgar to Aileen Bridgewater, 19.7.80.

Interview notes with Elsie Elliott after the Inquest, manuscript, ?.3.80.

Interview notes with Elsie Elliott, manuscript, 24.1.80.

Interview notes with Elsie Elliott, manuscript, 23.3.80.

Interview notes with Howard Lindsay, manuscript, undated.

Interview notes with Mr and Mrs MacLennan (missing p.2), manuscript, 31.8.83.

Interview notes with Mr and Mrs MacLennan, manuscript, 1.9.83

Interview notes with "Slasher" George (Sam), San Po Kong, manuscript, 23.8.80.

Interview notes with "Slasher" George (Sam), USRC, manuscript, 25.8.80.

Interview with Elsie Elliott, manuscript, 24.5.80.

Note on testimony of Elsie Elliott to the Inquiry, manuscript, 1981.

Note re: fingerprints, manuscript, undated.

Notes, "Best of Aileen", manuscript, 27.7.80.

Notes by Aileen Bridgewater after the Inquest, manuscript, ?.3.80.

Notes on aspects of the MacLennan case, manuscript, undated.

Notes on call-in comments re MacLennan case, manuscript, 2.5.80.

Notes on chronology post mortem, manuscript, undated.

Notes on John Conway, manuscript, 12.11.80.

Notes taken by Aileen Bridgewater at the Inquest, manuscript, ?.3.80.

Quotations from the MacLennan case, typescript, undated.

Session of hypnosis, manuscript, undated.

"Some Outstanding Questions of Public Concern over the Death of Inspector John MacLennan", typescript, undated.

Statement of Claire-Marie Beeson, 1.2.80.

Talk "Can't Win", manuscript, undated.

Two sets of papers released under Freedom of Information Act request by the FCO, one correspondence with Hong Kong on the MacLennan case, 1980–1981; the second papers relating to John Conway's "The Conway Report", 1988.

Typewritten notes on Attorney General's press conference of 23.5.80, undated.

Conway, John, "The Case of Inspector John MacLennan (deceased)", paper sent to "His Excellency the Governor of Hong Kong", 1 March 1983.

Conway, John, "The Conway Report", October 1987.

Conway, John, miscellaneous papers:

Crime Information Form by ex-police officer Iqbal Khan, undated.

Law lists 1972, p.94, 1973, p.95, Handwriting Experts.

Letter from ex-police officer Iqbal Khan 17.9.80.

Sketch Plan of Flat 410B, HMT Service Flats, 15.1.80.

Statement to the Commission of Inquiry, 25.10.80.

Triad chain of command in Hong Kong Police, diagram, undated.

Dawson, Deputy Commissioner CJR, "The Police and the Public: A Change of Attitude", extracts from a speech on 20 November 1973.

Elliott, Elsie, "The MacLennan Affair", 1981 (also in Hong Kong University Library, Special Collection Hong Kong Pamphlet, 354.2052 E4).

Elliott, Elsie, miscellaneous papers:

Attorney General to P.T. Moor, minute, 31.8.79.

Attorney General to Roy Henry, "Operation Rockcorry", 31.8.79 (pp.1–2 only).

Attorney General to the Governor, minute, 1.2.80.

Carratu, Vincent N. to Elsie Elliott, 15.6.81.

Elliott, Elsie giving an account of her actions in 1980, typescript, undated (pre 7.80),

Elliott, Elsie to Attorney General, 24.1.80.

Elliott, Elsie to Governor, 28.11.78.

Elliott, Elsie to Professor Usher, 24.6.80.

Elliott, Elsie to Professor Usher, 2.10.80.

Elsie Elliott to the Inquiry, statement, 1981.

Governor to Attorney General, minute, 22.4.80.

Henry, Roy to the Governor, "Operation Rockcorry", 20.8.79.

List of Homosexuals, ?.10.78.

Notes on homosexual arrests by SIU, typescript, ? 1980.

Professor Usher to Elsie Elliott, 12.9.80.

Rowlands, Martin, "Employment of Homosexuals in the Civil Service", Secretariat Confidential Circular No. 106/82, 5.1.82.

Law List, 1980, p.210, Barristers, showing John Beveridge.

MacLennan family miscellaneous papers:

Bridgewater, Aileen to Mrs MacLennan, 19.3.83.

Cameron Donald & Son, Invoice for John MacLennan, deceased, ?.3.80.

Harrison, A.E., Legal Aid department, to Mr and Mrs MacLennan, 10.11.80.

Henry, Roy to Mrs MacLennan, 16.1.80.

Hodge, A.S. to Roy Henry, minute, 17.3.80 (pp. 7–10 only).

Hong Kong Funeral Home Debit Note, 20.1.80.

Mrs MacLennan to Aileen Bridgewater, 29.3.83.

Ross and Cromarty District Council Registry Certificate for Fodderty Cemetery, 8.2.80.

Rowlands, Martin to Mrs MacLennan, 31.1.80.

"Statutory Declaration" by Mr and Mrs MacLennan regarding the name of John MacLennan, 5.12.80.

MacLennan, Inspector John, estate:

Acknowledgement of John Conway's letter to the Governor of 1.3.83, 5.3.83.

"Breakdown List of Property of I.P.J. MacLennan (Property received from Mr M.M.W. Pelly, SP), undated.

Bridgewater, Aileen's show script, 31.9.81.

Bridgewater, Aileen to Hampton, Winter & Glynn, 4.2.83.

Bridgewater, Aileen to Hampton, Winter & Glynn, 14.3.83.

Bridgewater, Aileen to Hampton, Winter & Glynn, 19.3.83.

Bridgewater, Aileen to Hampton, Winter & Glynn, undated (?11.4.83).

Bridgewater, Aileen to Justice, London, 29.4.83.

Bridgewater, Aileen to the President of the Law Society, undated.

Conway, John to Aileen Bridgewater, 10.12.82.

Conway, John to Governor, 16.3.83.

Extract from Committee minutes on losses of property in police custody, 1982.

Hampton, Winter & Glynn to John Conway, 29.12.82.

Hampton, Winter & Glynn to Aileen Bridgewater, 11.2.83.

Hampton, Winter & Glynn to Aileen Bridgewater, 2.3.83.

Hampton, Winter & Glynn to Aileen Bridgewater, 17.3.83.

Hampton, Winter & Glynn to Aileen Bridgewater, 8.4.83.

Hampton, Winter & Glynn to Aileen Bridgewater, 13.4.83.

Harrison, J.A. to Aileen Bridgewater, 16.3.83.

Harrison, J.A. to Aileen Bridgewater, 18.3.83.

"Inspector John MacLennan— Missing Effects", undated.

"List of Exhibits", ?.9.81.

"List of Personal Effects of the Late Inspector John MacLennan Held by the Commission of Inquiry as at 2.7.81".

Mrs MacLennan to Hampton, Winter & Glynn, 20.9.81.

Mrs MacLennan to Hampton, Winter & Glynn, 30.9.81.

Murdoch MacPhail & Co to Hampton, Winter & Glynn, 7.1.83.

Power of Attorney signed by Katherine MacLennan, 3.12.82.

Property list signed by P. Peters, 28.1.80.

"Property of J. MacLennan Stored in Kowloon City Station" (No. 8 Cell), undated.

Re: Katherine MacLennan's Power of Attorney, signed by John Conway, minute, 10.12.82.

Receipt from Aileen Bridgewater to Hampton, Winter & Glynn for Estate of Late Inspector John MacLennan, Deceased, ?. 83.

Two receipts from Woo, Kwan Lee, solicitors.

Yuen, K.L. to Mrs Katherine MacLennan, with property list, 25.6.80.

Yuen, K.L. to Mrs MacLennan, minute, 26.5.80.

MacLennan, Inspector John, miscellaneous papers:

Bank statements for John MacLennan's Bank of Scotland account, 1973 –1978.

Bank statements for John MacLennan's Chartered Bank account, 1973–1981.

Birth certificate of John MacLennan, 7.10.50.

Burns, Inspector Christopher to Brigadier Silvan, 20.9.76.

Burns, Inspector Christopher to John MacLennan, Metropolitan Police College, telegram, ?.77.

Certificate of proof of production of driving licence by John MacLennan, 30.10.79.

Death certificate of John Richard MacLennan, 19.9.80.

Death certificate of John Richard MacLennan corrected to John MacLennan, 15.12.80.

Diary for John MacLennan, 1978.

Exhibit label 1980.

Expatriate Inspectors' Association membership card for John MacLennan, 20.3.78.

Hong Kong driving licence for John MacLennan, 9.3.76.

Hong Kong driving licence for John MacLennan, 18.8.78.

International Police Association, Hong Kong section, membership card for John MacLennan, 1.8.74.

John MacLennan's address book for Scotland, undated.

John MacLennan's vaccination certificates, undated.

MacLennan, John to the MacLennan family, 2.1.80.

St. John Ambulance training certificate for John MacLennan, ?.9.77.

The Theft Act 1968, Chief Constable Frank A. Brown, undated.

Training School notebook, undated .

Who's Who, p. 211, showing John Beveridge, 1980.

HONG KONG UNIVERSITY

Commission of Inquiry into Inspector MacLennan's Case, "Papers of Inspector MacLennan's Inquiry" [Commission Transcript], donated by DME Evans, Hong Kong University Library, MSS 345.2052 H7 M1.

ELSIE TU (ELLIOTT) PAPERS

Tu, Elsie, Papers in Hong Kong Baptist University Library, "The Death of Inspector MacLennan", MSS. 13.

Cases of Homosexual Charges 1975–1981, MSS 13 11.7.

Clippings 1980, MSS 13 12.2.

Clippings 1981–1989, MSS 13 12.3.

Correspondence and Press Statements 1979–1981, MSS 13 13.1.

Death of John MacLennan. Documents, MSS.13 13.3.

Death of John MacLennan. Inquest & Inquiry: Statements, Reports, Correspondence and Papers, 1978–1979, MSS.13 13.5.

Death of John MacLennan. Inquest & Inquiry: Statements, Reports, Correspondence and Papers, 1980–1996, MSS.13 13.6.

Death of John MacLennan. Inquest and Notes, MSS.13 13.4.

Death of John MacLennan. Report of the Commission of Inquiry, MSS.13 14.1.

Documents 1978–1981, MSS 13 13.2.

Manuscripts 1978–1987, MSS 13 12.4.

Press Clippings 1979–1980, MSS 13 12.1.

BOOKS

Akers-Jones, Sir David, *Feeling the Stones* (Hong Kong: Hong Kong University Press, 2004).

Bokhary, Kemal, *Recollections*, (Hong Kong: Sweet & Maxwell, 2013).

Booth, Martin, *Opium: A History* (New York: St. Martin's Griffin, 1996).

Booth, Martin, *The Triads: The Chinese Criminal Fraternity* (London: Harper Collins, 1990).

Bowring, Philip, & Cottrell, Robert, *The Carrian File* (Hong Kong: *Far Eastern Economic Review*, 1984).

Bresler, Fenton, *The Trail of the Triads: An Investigation into International Crime* (London: Weidenfeld & Nicolson, 1980).

Bridgewater, Aileen, *Talk of Hong Kong* (Hong Kong: Phoenix Books, 1st edition 1985, 2nd edition 1988).

Bridgewater, Ken, *Open Verdict* (Singapore: Trafford, 2013).

Cartland, Rachel, *Paper Tigress: A Life in the Hong Kong Government* (Hong Kong: Blacksmith Books, 2014).

Collett, Nigel, *Firelight of a Different Colour: The Life and Times of Leslie Cheung Kwok-wing* (Hong Kong: Signal 8, 2014).

Conway, John, *To Speak for the Dead* (Nuneaton: John Conway, 1994).

Elliott, Elsie, *Crusade for Justice: an Autobiography* (Hong Kong: Heinemann Asia, 1981).

Elliott, Elsie, *The Avarice, Bureaucracy and Corruption of Hong Kong* (Hong Kong: Friends Commercial Printing Factory, 1971).

Emmett, Chris, *Hong Kong Police Man* (Hong Kong: Earnshaw Books, 2014).

Lethbridge, H.R., *Hard Graft in Hong Kong: Scandal, Corruption, the I.C.A.C.* (Oxford: Oxford University Press, 1985).

Mann, Peter, *Sheriff of Wanchai: How an Englishman Helped Govern Hong Kong in Its Last Decades as a British Colony* (Hong Kong; Blacksmith Books, 2016)

Morgan, W.P., *Triad Societies in Hong Kong* (Hong Kong: Government Press, 1960).

Roberts, Denys, Another Disaster: *Hong Kong Sketches* (London: Radcliffe Press, 2006).

Sandbrook, Dominic, *Seasons in the Sun: The Battle for Britain*, 1974-1979 (London: Penguin, 2013).

Sinclair, Kevin, *Asia's Finest: An Illustrated Account of the Royal Hong Kong Police* (Hong Kong: Unicorn, 1983).

Sinclair, Kevin and Ng Kwok-cheung, Nelson, *Asia's Finest Marches On: Policing Hong Kong into the 21st Century* (Hong Kong: Kevin Sinclair, 1997).

Tu, Andrew & Elsie, *Shouting at the Mountain: A Hong Kong Story of Love and Commitment* (Hong Kong: Chameleon Press, 2004).

Tu, Elsie, *An Autobiography* (Hong Kong: Longman, 1988).

Welsh, Frank, *A History of Hong Kong* (London: Harper Collins, 1997).

Whitehead, Kate, *Hong Kong Murders* (Oxford: Oxford University Press, 2001).

Wong, Danny, *Drops in Nan's Ocean* (New York: Vanta, 2006).

Wong, Danny, *Waltzing Matilda Memoirs* (Milton Keynes: Author House, 2010).

ARTICLES

Broadhurst, Roderic and Lee King Wa, "The Transformation of Triad 'Dark Societies' in Hong Kong: The Impact of Law Enforcement and Political

Change", *Security Challenges*, vol. 5, no. 4 (summer 2009), pp. 1–38.

Lethbridge, Henry, "Pandora's Box: The Inspector MacLennan Enigma", *Hong Kong Law Journal*, vol. 12, no. 1, pp. 4– 30.

JOURNALS

"The MacLennan Inquiry", editorial, *Hong Kong Law Journal*, vol. 12, no. 1, 1982, pp. 1–3.

Hong Kong Standard

New Statesman, The

Oriental Daily

Private Eye

Security Challenges, "The Transformation of Triad 'Dark Societies' in Hong Kong: The Impact of Law Enforcement, Socio-Economic and Political Change", by Roderic Broadhurst and Lee King Wa, vol. 5, no. 4 (summer 2009), pp. 1–38.

South China Morning Post

Star, The

Sun, The

PAPERS, THESES ETC.

Conway, John Albert, "Conway Report", Nuneaton, Warwickshire, 10.87.

Conway, John Albert, "Conway Report to the Governor", Sailors' and Soldiers' Home, 22, Hennessy Road, Hong Kong, 1.3.83.

Tse Kin Kuen, "An Evaluation of Anti-Corruption Policy in Hong Kong since 1945", dissertation for the degree of M. Soc. Sc. (Public Administration), Hong Kong University, 1985.

Tu, Elsie, "The MacLennan Affair", 1981 (in the Bridgewater Collection; also in Hong Kong University Library, 354.2052 E3 1307847; and in the Hong Kong Public Record Office, HKRS570-8-3382 Police — Case of John MacLennan).

DRAMA

Allcock, Agnes, *Behind the Curtain*, Trueheart Theatre, London, 28.4.13 & 26.5.13.

INTERVIEWS

Interviews were conducted in a variety of locations in Hong Kong, as well as by Skype and email with interviewees located at a distance. Interviewees were asked whether they would allow their names, direct quotations from what they had said or the information they had given to be used in the book, and told that they had the right to amend or delete any information that they did not wish to see published. All interviews were typed and submitted for comment and amendment before a final copy was agreed upon with the interviewee. Copies of interviews which interviewees had agreed to be on the record were placed in the Bridgewater Collection.

The following were interviewed and agreed that their name should be given:

Mr Barrie Barlow, SC, interviewed in his Chambers, 31.1.15, corrected by emails, 13 and 15.2.15.

Justice Clare-Marie Beeson, interviewed in the Foreign and Correspondents' Club, 11.6.15, amended by post, 8.9.15.

Justice Syed Kemal Shah Bokhary, GBM, JP, QC answers by email 16.3.15, interviewed at his home in Stanley, 18.3.15, amended by email, 20.3.15 and supplemented, 7.9.15.

Mrs Aileen Bridgewater, interviewed at her home in Hang Ha Po, 15.5.13.

Mr Kenneth Bridgewater, interviewed at his home in Hang Ha Po, 15.5.13 and emails, 26.1.14 and 20.3.14.

Mr Murray Burton, interviewed at the Foreign and Correspondents' Club, 9.2.15 and at the Hong Kong Golf Club, Deep Water Bay, 19.9.16.

Inspector Peter Crush, interviewed at Il Bel Paese Restaurant, Discovery Bay, 18.3.15, corrected by two emails, 19.3.15 and 18.2.16.

Mr Graham Elsom, interviewed at the Foreign Correspondents' Club, 27.7.15, amended by email, 28.7.15.

Mr Geoffrey Emerson, email of 26.3.15, interviewed at the Foreign Correspondents' Club, 23.4.15.

Chief Inspector Iain Grant, interviewed by Skype 4.6.15, amended by email, 6.6.15.

Assistant Commissioner Peter Hunt, PDSM, email, 5.2.12, interviewed at the Foreign Correspondents' Club, 15.1.15, amended by email

17.1.15.

Sir Andrew P. Leggatt, QC, PC, emails, 24.9.16, 25.9.16.

Mr Peter Moss, interviewed at the home of Aileen and Ken Bridgewater in Hang Ha Po, 18.5.11, emails 19.5.11, 20.5.11, 22.5.11, 18.3.15, 28.7.15, 9.8.15.

Justice Conrad Seagroatt, letter 9.3.15, interviewed in Judges Chambers, 29.4.15, amended by email, 2.7.15, email 3.7.15, letter 4.7.16.

Mrs Elsie Tu, interviewed at the home of Aileen and Ken Bridgewater in Hang Ha Po, 21 and 29.6.11.

Chief Superintendent Stephen Harvey Verralls, interviewed at the Foreign Correspondents' Club, 21.1.15 and at Club 97, Lan Kwai Fong, 11.2.15, emails 12.2.15, 24.7.15, 16.9.15, 24.11.15.

Mr Stuart Wolfendale, interviewed at the Foreign Correspondents' Club, 20.9.16.

Mr Danny Wong, interviewed at the Oriental Club, London, 14.5.15.

Chief Justice Sir T.L. Yang, interviewed at the Red Cross Headquarters, West Kowloon, 5.9.16, amended by email 11.9.16.

The following anonymous interviewees agreed that information that they had given could be used:

Cambus — a retired police officer, interviewed by email, 26.6.16, 28.6.16, 30.6.16, 3.7.16, amended by email 5.7.16.

Interviewee A — a retired police officer, interviewed at the Hong Kong Jockey Club, Happy Valley, 5.2.15, and email 16.2.15.

Interviewee B — a retired businessman, interviewed in Wanchai, 5.8.15.

Interviewee C — a businessman, interviewed in his office in Kowloon Bay, 25.3.15, amended by email, 26.3.15, email, 31.3.15.

Interviewee D — a retired police officer, interviewed on Lamma Island 11.8.15.

Interviewee E — a retired police officer, interviewed in Wai Tau Tsuen, 7.16.

Interviewee F — a retired police officer, interviewed in Ned Kelly's Bar, Tsim Sha Tsui 6.15, and at Wai Tau Tsuen, 27.7.15.

Interviewee G — a retired banker, interviewed at the Hong Kong Club,

13.4.16.

Interviewee H — a solicitor, interviewed at the Foreign Correspondents' Club, 21.1.15.

Interviewee I — a retired civil servant, interviewed at the Foreign Correspondents' Club, 22.1.15.

Interviewee J — a retired police officer, in the Foreign Correspondents' Club, 21.1.15.

Interviewee K — a retired police officer, in the Helena May club, 14.9.12.

The following refused to be interviewed :

Mr Norman Chan Tak-lam, GBS, JP.

Superintendent Jack Trotman.

The following did not respond to a request for an interview:

Mr Nigel A.C. Aiken, QC, SC.

Mr Ernest Raymond Astin.

Mr John Caldwell Beveridge, QC.

Inspector Christopher Burns.

Justice Henry Stanislaus Daniell.

Justice Joseph Michael Duffy.

Assistant Commissioner Peter George Else, PMSM.

Ms Audrey Eu Yuet-mee, SC, JP.

Senior Inspector Michael Fulton.

Mr John Calvert Griffiths, CMG, SC, QC.

Commissioner of Police Mr Li Kwan-ha, CBE, QPM, CPM.

Inspector Craig Loughrin.

Justice Neil MacDougall.

Chief Inspector Norman MacKillop.

Mr Anthony Francis Neoh, SC, JP.

Justice Patrick Michael Rattigan.

Index

C

D

E

F

G

H

I

M

N

O

P

Q

S

U

V

W

Y

Z